américo castro

and the Meaning of Spanish Civilization

américo castro

and the
Meaning of Spanish Civilization

Edited by
José Rubia Barcia
with the assistance of
Selma Margaretten

UNIVERSITY OF CALIFORNIA PRESS
Berkeley • Los Angeles • London

University of California Press
Berkeley and Los Angeles, California

University of California Press, Ltd.
London, England

Printed in the United States of America

CONTENTS

PORTRAITS OF AMÉRICO CASTRO

To accompany *Américo Castro and the Meaning of Spanish Civilization,* edited by José Rubia Barcia (Berkeley, Los Angeles, London: University of California Press, 1976).

1907

1931

1969 or 1970

PREFACE

This book is not intended to be, in spite of appearances and coincidences, what the Germans call a *Festschrift* and the French *Mélanges* or, at least, not in any ordinary way. Both words imply a kind of literary cocktail to be served at an imaginary banquet in honor of a great man of letters. This is what Américo Castro undoubtedly was but in a very controversial, exciting, and vital manner. Most of the contributors to this book had the privilege of knowing him personally, some as long-time friends and admirers, some as former students, some as followers and disciples. Each already has proven his capacity to confront others' ideas objectively with something of the passion and critical judgment that Américo Castro himself so deeply appreciated and felt.

Our purpose is to offer the English-speaking world a systematic organization of Américo Castro's thought and theories. In presenting these chronologically from the Middle Ages to Modern Times, we have taken into consideration their impact, originality, and lasting contribution to a better understanding of the past history and future events of the Spanish-speaking world. It is not an exercise in dehumanized culture, especially if one remembers that the New World, called America from Canada to Argentina, is mainly divided into a conglomeration of peoples who speak Iberian languages or English. The interchange of knowledge about the deep currents that inform, unify, and differentiate either of these two halves, can and must serve not only a cultural but also a practical goal. And there is no more urgent goal today than the achievement of comprehension and tolerance among men, especially among close neighbors.

Six of the essays included here were offered originally as lectures in a symposium at the University of California, Los Angeles, on May 10, 1973. The remainder were solicited later and were written especially for this book, with three exceptions:

The Meaning of Spanish Civilization by Américo Castro himself; *The Evolution of Castro's Theories* by Guillermo Araya Goubet; *Literature and Historical Insight* by Stephen Gilman.

The Meaning of Spanish Civilization signals the first outward expression of Américo Castro's new attitude in defense of what he considered the "peculiar" and very significant value of the Iberian Peninsula's contributions to Western civilization. It has not been reprinted since 1940, when Castro delivered it as a lecture at Princeton University. It constitutes a true prologue, in an intuitive way, to almost everything that Américo Castro tried to expose, develop, and justify in a series of books still unwritten at that time. The only justification for its appearance here as a second prologue is the decision to include immediately following it as a third prologue, Guillermo Araya Goubet's essay, which presents a panoramic view of the ultimate results of Américo Castro's thinking and serves to familiarize the reader with some of Castro's original insights and very personal and special vocabulary.

Guillermo Araya Goubet's *The Evolution of Castro's Theories* is a shorter version of his long essay "Evolución del Pensamiento Histórico de Américo Castro" (1968) and is included here with the author's consent. Araya was unable at the time of our request to prepare a shorter version himself. He was then a political prisoner in his native Chile and had not yet been able to leave his country to go into exile. I remember hearing Américo Castro express in the highest terms his appreciation for Araya's work. Since I wholeheartedly agree with Don Américo on this point, I not only wanted to add here an expression of my own personal and intellectual esteem for Professor Araya Goubet but also my gratitude for his confidence and generosity in allowing me to adapt his original study so that it could be included in this book.

Literature and Historical Insight by Stephen Gilman was first published in Spanish, with the title "Américo Castro, Historiador y Crítico del *Libro de Buen Amor*" (*Insula,* xxix, no. 314-315, 1973, p. 6). Although it was not conceived originally for this book, its content, its tone, and its conclusions provide an ideal culminating piece for the entire volume. I am grateful to Professor Gilman for permission to use his illuminating article in this way.

Special thanks are due to Luis and Carmen Castro for authorizing us to reprint their father's lecture *The Meaning of Spanish Civilization* and for placing at our disposal the photographs that appear here; to Professor Paul C. Smith for the translation into English of Professor Araya's essay and for reading several others' essays and making valuable suggestions; to Leslie Deutsch and Professor Carroll B. Johnson for the first and painstaking versions of most of the essays written in Spanish by Professor González-López, Rodríguez-Puértolas, Antony van Beysterveldt, Rodríguez-Cepeda, Rubén Benítez, Franco Meregalli, Marcos Morínigo, and José Luis Aranguren; to Professor Enrique Rodríguez-Cepeda for preliminary work on the Index and help in verifying several quotations and notes; and to Selma Margaretten, who so intelligently and generously assisted me in every aspect of the preparation of the manuscript. Ms. Margaretten had previously worked under the supervision of Américo Castro himself on the reworking, translation, and revision of the manuscript materials that were to become *The Spaniards*. Her deep knowledge of and her acquaintance and familiarity with every aspect of Castro's work, as well as her mastery of English and Spanish, made her contribution invaluable.

Finally I am deeply grateful to the Del Amo Foundation for its generous help towards the successful completion of this project, and to Mr. Robert Y. Zachary of the University Press at Los Angeles for his great understanding and patience.

Los Angeles, California   J. R. B.
15 March 1976

CONTRIBUTORS

JOSÉ LUIS L. ARANGUREN, former Professor of Ethics at the University of Madrid, is now Professor at the University of California at Santa Barbara. His publications include many books and essays on ethics, Catholicism and Protestantism, social and political sciences, history, and literary criticism. Some of his works have been translated into English.

GUILLERMO ARAYA GOUBET, former Dean and former Professor of Philology at the Universidad Austral (Chile), has been Visiting Professor for the last three years at the University of Bordeaux (France). He has written extensively on Américo Castro. He also wrote a book on Ortega y Gasset and is the author of many other publications.

RUBÉN BENÍTEZ, Professor at the University of California, Los Angeles, has published books on Bécquer and other nineteenth-century authors, as well as numerous essays, critical editions, and articles on Spain and Spanish American novelists and poets. He is also a creative writer.

ANTHONY A. VAN BEYSTERVELDT, Visiting Professor at York University, Toronto, Canada, in 1968-69, is presently Professor of Spanish Literature in the Department of Romance Languages of Bowling Green State University, Ohio. His works include studies on Spanish courtly love and Golden Age Theater.

STEPHEN GILMAN, Professor at Harvard University, wrote his dissertation on the *Quijote apócrifo* under the direction of Américo Castro. He has published studies on *Poema del Cid, La Celestina,* the novels of Galdós, etc. He is co-editor of a forthcoming anthology of Américo Castro's essays in English to be titled *An Idea of History.* Guggenheim Fellow, 1950-51.

EMILIO GONZÁLEZ-LÓPEZ, Emeritus Professor and former Chairman at Hunter College, New York, Executive Officer of the Ph.D. Program in Spanish, New York City University, is a Member of the Royal Galician Academy. He is the author of numerous books on the history of Galicia, Spanish civilization, Spanish literature, and individual writers such as Pardo Bazán, Valle Inclán, etc.

CARROLL B. JOHNSON, Professor and Chairman of the Spanish and Portuguese Department at the University of California, Los Angeles, has written studies on the comedia, prose of the Golden Age, etc. He is also the author of a book on Guzmán de Alfarache soon to be published.

FRANCO MEREGALLI, Professor at the University of Venice, Italy, was previously at Oviedo, Milán, Madrid, Göttingen. He has published books, essays, and articles on Castilian chronicles, Cervantes, Calderón, writers of the twentieth century, Spanish-Italian literary inter-influences, etc.

JAMES T. MONROE, Associate Professor of Arabic and Comparative Literature at the University of California, Berkeley, is the author of works on the Muwashshaḥaṭ and other types of Arabic poetry, a book on Islam and the Arabs in Spanish Scholarship (1969), and a recent bilingual Hispano-Arabic Poetry: A Student Anthology (1974).

MARCOS A. MORÍNIGO, Emeritus Professor at the University of Illinois, was previously at Buenos Aires and Tucumán (Argentina), Caracas (Venezuela), and the University of Southern California. He was written works on philology, Guarani language, the presence of America in the theater of Lope de Vega, Hispano-Americanism, etc.

ENRIQUE RODRÍGUEZ-CEPEDA, Associate Professor at the University of California, Los Angeles, has published works on the theater of the Golden Age and the eighteenth century (Vélez de Guevara, Moratín), and also on Zorrilla, Gabriel y Galán, Unamuno.

JULIO RODRÍGUEZ-PUÉRTOLAS, Professor at the University of California, Los Angeles, is a specialist on Medieval Literature (*Fray Iñigo de Mendoza, Poesía de protesta en la Edad Media castellana . . .*). His works also include studies on the Golden Age and on Modern times. He is co-editor of a forthcoming Américo Castro's *Obras Completas*. National Award for the Humanities Fellow, 1976-77.

JOSÉ RUBIA BARCIA, Professor at the University of California, Los Angeles, is former Chairman of the Department of Spanish and Portuguese (1963-69). His publications include several books and numerous essays and articles, mainly on the Modern period (Valle Inclán, Unamuno, Lorca, etc.). He is also a creative writer of narrative prose and poetry as well as for the theater. Guggenheim Fellow, 1962.

JOSEPH H. SILVERMAN, Professor of Spanish Literature and Provost of Adlai E. Stevenson College, University of California, Santa Cruz, has published studies on Golden Age drama, the picaresque novel, Cervantes, Sephardic balladry, Judeo-Christian literature and life, and Valle Inclán.

ABBREVIATIONS OF CASTRO'S WORKS

AVH   *Aspectos del vivir hispánico: Espiritualismo, mesianismo, actitud personal en los siglos XIV a XVI.* Santiago de Chile: Cruz del Sur, 1949, 168 pp. Enlarged edition with many cuts and additions of "Lo hispánico y el erasmismo" (1940, 1942). 2d ed. revised with many cuts and additions. Madrid: Alianza, 1970, 167 pp.

CCE   *Cervantes y los casticismos españoles.* Madrid-Barcelona: Alfaguara, 1966, 364 pp. Includes revised introduction to 1966 edition of *La Realidad histórica de España.* 2d ed. Edited by Paulino Garagorri with additions and corrections from Castro's papers. Madrid: Alianza-Alfaguara, 1974.

CCL   *"La Celestina" como contienda literaria (casta y casticismos).* Madrid: Revista de Occidente, 1965.

CVQ   "Como veo ahora el Quijote." Preliminary study to M. Cervantes Saavedra. *El ingenioso hidalgo don Quijote de la Mancha,* Part I. Madrid: Ed. Magisterio Español, 1971, pp. 9–102.

DEN   *Dos ensayos: Descripción, narración, historiografía y Discrepancias y mal entender.* México: Ed. Porrúa, 1956, 74 pp. First essay is new version of preliminary observations to *La Spagna nella sua Realtà Storica.* Florence: Sansoni, 1955.

ECD   *De la edad conflictiva. El drama de la Honra en España y en su Literatura.* Madrid: Taurus, 1961, 221 pp. 2d ed., very augmented and corrected, 1963, 279 pp. 3d ed., very revised, 1967. 4th ed., 1972.

ECS   *Los españoles: cómo llegaron a serlo.* Madrid: Taurus, 1965, 297 pp. Revised and amplified edition of *Origen, ser y existir de los españoles* (1959). Revised and published together with *"Español," palabra extranjera: razones y motivos* (1970) under the title *Sobre el nombre y el quién de los españoles.* See *SNQ.*

ENC   *De la España que aún no conocía.* México: Finisterre, 1972. 3 vols. Vol. 1, 278 pp.; vol. 2, 304 pp.; vol. 3, 276 pp.

EPE   *"Español,"* palabra extranjera: razones y motivos. Madrid: Taurus, 1970, 113 pp. Reprinted in *Sobre el nombre y el quién de los españoles,* 1973. See *ECS.*

ESH   *España en su historia. Cristianos, moros y judíos.* Buenos Aires: Losada, 1948, 709 pp. See *The Structure of Spanish History,* English translation with revisions and modifications by Edmund L. King. Princeton: Princeton University Press, 1954, 689 pp.

ETC   "Erasmo en tiempo de Cervantes," *Revista de Filología Española,* XVIII (1931), 329-389, 441. Reprinted in *Semblanzas y estudios* (1956), pp. 145-188, and in *Hacia Cervantes* (1957 and 1960).

HCer   *Hacia Cervantes.* Madrid: Taurus, 1957. 2d ed., very revised. Madrid: Taurus, 1960, 390 pp. 3d ed., considerably revised, 1967.

IPP   *Iberoamérica. Su presente y su pasado.* New York: The
or   Dryden Press, 1941, 267 pp. 2d ed., revised and
IHC   augmented, 1946, 304 pp. 3d ed., revised with the assistance of Raymond S. Willis, and published as *Iberoamérica: Su historia y su cultura.* New York: Henry Holt and Company, 1954 (reprinted 1963, 1964), vii + 248 + lxxi pp. 4th ed., with a new prologue in Spanish by the author and revised by "Jorge Campos" (a pseudonym), New York, London, Toronto: Holt, Rinehart and Winston, 1971, viii + 248 + lxxi pp.

LEL   *Lengua, enseñanza y literatura (esbozos).* Madrid: Victoriano Suárez, 1924, 335 pp.

LHE   "Lo hispánico y el erasmismo," *Revista de Filología Hispánica* (Buenos Aires), II (1940), 1-34 (Part 1); IV (1942), 1-66 (Parts 2 & 3). Separate printing with "Los prólogos del Quijote," Buenos Aires: Instituto de Filología, 1942, 126 pp. Revised and included in *Aspectos del vivir hispánico,* 1949, 1970.

OSE   *Origen, ser y existir de los españoles.* Madrid: Taurus, 1959, 175 pp. Revised and augmented, with title *Los españoles: cómo llegaron a serlo,* 1966.

PCer *El pensamiento de Cervantes*. Madrid: Hernando, 1925, 406 pp. (Junta para Ampliación de Estudios. Centro de Estudios Históricos. *RFE*. Anejo VI). Revised edition, augmented, with notes by the author and Julio Rodríguez-Puértolas. Madrid-Barcelona: Ed. Noguer, 1972, 410 pp.

PLR *La peculiaridad lingüística rioplatense y su sentido histórico*. Buenos Aires: Losada, 1941, 159 pp. 2d ed., very revised, Madrid: Taurus, 1961, 150 pp.

RHE *La realidad histórica de España*. México: Ed. Porrúa, 1954, 684 pp. New version of *España en su historia*, 1948. Both the *Realidad* and *España* are included in the English translation, *The Structure of Spanish History*, 1954. Revised edition, 1962, 479 pp. Limited edition of 100 copies with new prologue, 1965. The 1962 edition appeared with the addition of the new prologue again in 1966 (pagination of the prologue is 3-41, the same as the text). To avoid confusion (!) I have used the 1962 text (*RHE* 1962) and where specific reference is made to the prologue, I have used used the 1966 text (*RHE* 1966). The prologue was also reprinted with revisions as "Más sobre el pasado de los españoles," in *Cervantes y los casticismos españoles* (1967), pp. 185-253. All later editions of *RHE* (1962) contain the 1965 prologue and text without modifications: 1967, 1971, 1973, 1975. English trans. *The Spaniards: An Introduction to their History* with revisions and additions, 1971; see *SIH*.

SAN *Santiago de España*. Buenos Aires: Emecé, 1958, 152 pp.

SEE *Semblanzas y estudios españoles*. Homenaje a Américo Castro de sus ex-alumnos de Princeton University. Princeton, N.J.: Insula, 1956, 440 pp. Bibliography by Albert Brent and Robert Kirsner; selection of texts and notes, preliminary notes by Juan Marichal. Contains selections later published in *Hacia Cervantes*, 1957.

SIH *The Spaniards. An Introduction to their History*, trans. Willard F. King and Selma L. Margaretten. Berkeley,

Los Angeles, and London: The University of California Press, 1971, 628 pp. Contains material from *The Structure of Spanish History* and *La realidad histórica de España*, 1962 and 1966 eds., with additions of preface, chapters i, xii, and xiv and addendum and appendix.

SNQ   *Sobre el nombre y el quién de los españoles*. Madrid: Taurus, 1973, 406 pp. Contains *Español: palabra extranjera* (1970) and *Los españoles: cómo llegaron a serlo* (1965) with new material and prologue by Rafael Lapesa.

SSH   *The Structure of Spanish History*, trans. Edmund L. King. Princeton: Princeton University Press, 1954, 689 pp. Based on *España en su historia*, revised and augmented. Later included in part in *The Spaniards*, 1971.

STE   *Santa Teresa y otros ensayos*. Madrid: Historia Nueva, 1929, 278 pp. New edition with cuts and additions published as *Teresa la santa y otros ensayos*. Madrid: Alfaguara, 1972, 321 pp.

VLV   *Vida de Lope de Vega (1562–1635),* in collaboration with Hugo A. Rennert. Madrid: Sucesores de Hernando, 1919, 562 pp. 2d ed., with additions by A. Castro and F. Lázaro Carreter, Salamanca: Anaya, 584 pp.

Less frequently cited works by Américo Castro for which no abbreviations are given:

La enseñanza del español en España, Madrid: Victoriano Suárez, 1922, 109 pp.

Les grands romantiques espagnols. Introduction, translation, and notes by Américo Castro. Paris: La Renaissance du Livre, 1922, 176 pp. (Les Cent Chefs-d'oeuvre Étrangers, no. 72)

Cervantès. Paris: Les Editions Rieder, 1931, 80 pp. (Maîtres des Littératures, XI.)

Españoles al margen. Madrid: Ed. Júcar, 1973, 193 pp. with prologue by Pedro Carrero Eras. It contains the following selection: "El pueblo español" (Previously published in *Esa gente de España,* 7 ensayos de Américo Castro, Raúl Morodo, Sergio Vilar, et al., Costa-Amic, editor; Mexico, 1965), reprinted in *ENC,* III, 11-31; "Algunos aspectos del siglo XVIII (Introducción metódica)," previously published in *LEL,* pp. 291-333; "Jovellanos," previously published in "El Sol" (Madrid, July 21, 1933), reprinted in *SEE,* pp. 405-411, and in *ENC,* II, 203-210; "Francisco Giner," previously published in "La Nación" (Buenos Aires, June 6, 1937), reprinted in *SEE,* pp. 413-419, and in *ENC,* II, pp. 213-220; "Manuel B. Cossío," previously published in "Revista de Pedagogía" (Oct. 1935), reprinted in *SEE,* pp. 421-435, and in *ENC,* II, pp. 223-241; "Esbozos pedagógicos (La organización de las Facultades de Letras)," previously published in "El Sol" (Madrid, Summer 1920), reprinted in *LEL;* "De grata recordación (Juan Valera y Alberto Jiménez)," previously published in "Cuadernos" (Paris, No. 22, January, 1957), reprinted in *ENC,* II, pp. 245-264; "Homenaje a una sombra ilustre (Una residencia de estudiantes)," previously published in "Residencia" (México, December, 1963), reprinted in *ENC,* II, pp. 267-272; "Minorías y mayorías," previously published in "El Nacional" (Caracas, February 5, 1953).

Wherever possible I have included references to the two English translations alongside the Spanish, but not in parenthesis because in many cases it is not a direct translation: *ESH = SSH; RHE* (1954, 1962, 1966) = *SIH.*

Part I
Prologues

1

WHAT'S IN A NAME: AMÉRICO CASTRO (Y QUESADA)
José Rubia Barcia

"Man is only the sum of his acts
or functions."
Ortega y Gasset, *Ideas sobre la
novela* (1925).

When a child is born in the Spanish-speaking world he automatically receives the gift of a set of at least three names: a given name, a first surname, and a second surname. The same thing can happen to a child born in the English-speaking world, but with some meaningful differences.

For the Spanish-born child, the choice of a given name, or of several given names, is generally limited to Christian names taken from the list of saints in the Catholic Church. The parents usually give the child their own given name, or that of his grandparents or godparents, or the name or names of the patron saints of the day the child is born. Since the saints of the Catholic Church have come from very diversified backgrounds, their names are also of very diversified origins, with meanings frequently unknown to the bearers. For instance, names of Teutonic origin are Alfonso, which means "noble by birth," and Matilde, which means "heroine"; of Greek origin are Eugenio, meaning "noble, well-born," and Elena, meaning "light"; of Latin origin, Adriano, meaning "black," and Ursula, meaning 'little she-bear"; of Hebrew origin, Daniel, meaning "divine judge," and Isabel, which means "worshiper of God." Each of these names has belonged, at some time, to a person who attained Catholic sainthood, and his namesake is thus assured protective patronage in heaven during his lifetime and, in turn, the namesake celebrates his saint's day every year.

The implicit and original meaning of these names is not always unknown to or overlooked by their bearers. In many cases, especially in literary works, names become symbolic of the nature of the characters, thus reverting to their probable original usage. It is well-known that in primitive societies the name embodied the essence of personality, and was sometimes avoided or concealed to safeguard the inner soul. In modern Spanish literature Unamuno went farther than most in consciously accepting the magic power of the name, not only as a literary device in his creative work, but also in respect to his own person. His complete name was Miguel de Unamuno y Jugo. And he knew that Miguel, in Hebrew, meant "Who is like God?"[1] and that Jugo, his second surname seldom used by him to sign his work, meant "juice" or "essence." To these he would add still another family surname, Larraza, dividing it into "la" and "raza," to read "jugo de la raza" or "essence of the Spanish people." Naturally, it cannot be definitely known if Unamuno became what he finally was because of the magic power of his name, or by chance, or through conscious effort and work, or as the result of a combination of all these factors. But what is clear is that the end effect was the establishment of a perfect harmony between his name, his life, and his work.

The first surname or middle name and the second surname or last name of a person of Spanish origin have in common the fact that both are parental family names. In the case of Unamuno, for example, the first surname, Unamuno, was also the first surname of his father, grandfather, and all his paternal ancestors; while Jugo was the first surname of his mother and his mother's father, grandfather, and all her paternal ancestors. A child inherits, therefore, the first surname of his father and the first surname of his mother, in that order, and he, in turn, will transmit to his own children only his first surname. A Spanish woman keeps her complete name all her life, whether she is married or single, but she transmits to her children her first surname as their second surname, thus keeping it alive, but only for one generation. This relatively respectful recognition of a woman's own identity may be more ephemeral than in the case of the man, yet it is greater than that allowed in other cultures.

The traditional origin of Spanish given names, disregarding

their patronymic or matronymic sources, offers very few peculiarities and, in general, follows the pattern established in almost every other culture through the ages. The most common formula is, perhaps, the implicit or explicit "son of" with the first name of the father. In Castile, the prevailing fashion was to add the suffixes -az, -ez, -iz, -oz, and -uz, which carried precisely that meaning, to the Christian name of the father. Even today there is a great abundance of names ending in -ez, like Hernández, Martínez, Rodríguez, Sánchez, Pérez, and López which originally meant son of Hernando, Martín, Rodrigo, Sancho, Pero or Pedro, and Lope.

Most human beings, male and female, go through life more or less satisfied with their given and inherited names and without creating a problem of adequacy between the accepted meanings of those names and their individual actions. But there are others who want, so to speak, to "make a name for themselves," either by justifying the name or by changing it to another more meaningful one. The process may be entirely conscious, but it also may be the result of chance, destiny, or the workings of those mysterious forces that preside over human life and that, in many cases, have very little to do with reason. This is especially true of the Spaniard, who is so skeptical of rationality. After all, it was the Spanish painter, Goya, who was the first to say, at the end of the eighteenth century, that "the dream of reason produces monsters,"[2] in a prophecy completely realized in our own time in the most technically advanced countries. And another Spaniard, the philosopher Ortega y Gasset, after saying that reason "is only a small island floating on the sea of primary vitality,"[3] had to invent a new category of human reason and call it "razón vital," or vital reason, to keep human sanity in check.

On the other hand, every artist in the past reached the same conclusion through his intuitive powers, convinced that things could not exist without a name, that the name creates the object, that it creates reality itself, and that one justifies the other and cannot exist without the other in a continuous process of correlation. Thus, artists and philosophers once more walk hand in hand.

It would be a great mistake to attribute to sheer frivolity the

decision of an American writer, born Samuel Langhorne
Clemens, to change his inherited name to Mark Twain, or for
an Englishman like Eric Blair to change his to George Orwell;
or for a woman like Mme. Dudevant to change not only her
name but also seemingly her sex and nationality and become
George Sand. Among other celebrated French writers who have
also changed their names, a few may be recalled: Marie Henri
Beyle became Stendhal; François Marie Arouet, Voltaire; and
Jacques Anatole Thibault, Anatole France. Among Spaniards
there are also several well-known cases: Cecilia Böhl de Faber,
who, like Mme. Dudevant in France, also changed her name
and ostensibly her sex to become Fernán Caballero; José
Martínez Ruiz, fleeing perhaps from the commonness of his
three inherited names, would first try Cándido, then Ahrimán,
and finally adopt Azorín. Similarly, Ramón José Simón Valle
Peña would become, in the most striking and eloquent example,
the famous Don Ramón María del Valle Inclán y Montenegro.

Somehow, and once more without any rational explanation,
one is able to see how the created names fit the created work
perfectly, and how they are far superior to the given and
inherited ones. But we have already seen that it is also possible
to be born with a potentially meaningful name to be filled out,
as in the case of Unamuno, with a no less meaningful life and
work.

This is probably true of the man whom we honor in this book.
He was known by his students and younger friends as Don
Américo; by his close friends and peers as simply Américo or
Castro; by his readers as Américo Castro; at birth he was
registered as Américo Castro Quesada. In the title of this essay
I have placed the name Quesada, inherited from his mother,
in parentheses because he did not use it to sign his written work
in the last forty years of his life. Consequently, very few persons
remember or know that it was, in fact, Don Américo's second
surname. But we shall come back to this later.

The given name Américo is not, to my knowledge, a Christian
name, that is to say, no man with that name ever became a saint
in the Catholic Church. In fact, I do not know of any other
Spaniard who was given the name Américo as a first name,
although it is not unusual in Brazil. It is the Spanish masculine
form of América, the name given to the New World by the

German geographer Martin Waldseemüller in his *Cosmographiae Introductio,* published in 1507. It is derived from the Latin form of the Italian name Amerigo, belonging to Amerigo Vespucci, a Florentine sailor, merchant, and adventurer who was appointed "piloto mayor" or chief pilot of Spain in 1508, after receiving Spanish naturalization papers in 1505. The discovery of the continental New World or Mundus Novus was falsely attributed to Amerigo Vespucci by Waldseemüller. Symptomatically enough, it seems that the part of continental America first seen by Amerigo Vespucci was what was to become Brazil. And it was in Brazil, in the little town of Cantagalo, state of Rio de Janeiro, that Américo Castro was born in 1885 of Spanish parents.

I never asked Don Américo why his parents were in Brazil at that time, or how they came to choose the name they gave him, and he never volunteered the information himself in all the years of our close association and friendship. Perhaps it was better this way. We know for certain that he was born in Brazil, that after the Spanish Civil War he claimed Brazilian citizenship in order to be able to move about since Spanish Republican passports were no longer valid, that he changed his Brazilian nationality to that of the United States in 1942 or 1943, and that he did not become a Spanish citizen again when he decided to go back to Madrid in his last years.

Don Américo's family returned to Spain from Brazil when he was only five years old. He attended the University of Granada, graduating in 1904, and one year later he left for France to teach and also to continue his studies at the Sorbonne for the next three years. Upon his return to Spain he came into contact with the great Hispanist, Don Ramón Menéndez Pidal, and through him, with the famous Institución Libre de Enseñanza, first under the direction of its founder, Don Francisco Giner de los Ríos, and afterwards, headed by his successor, Don Manuel B. Cossío.

The non-Catholic nature of his given name, Américo, seems to be entirely fitting in the non-Catholic Institución. It was a kind of a posteriori adaptation to the ideals of Francisco Giner, since Don Américo had never attended his classes.

The Spain of that time was slowly coming out of its almost total immersion in the Catholic faith of the previous four hundred years. For the first time in modern Spanish history some Spaniards were going to be educated in their own country, in a completely laical manner, respectful of every religion but free of legal or moral obligation to follow any religion in particular, and especially the official Roman Catholicism. Francisco Giner de los Ríos was the spearhead of the new movement and in time became the man responsible for the appearance of a new elite of Spaniards who, in turn, began to make their weight felt in every sphere of Spanish life, not only in Spain itself, but also in Spanish America and non-Spanish-speaking countries as well. The movement included as its goals: a critical appraisal of the past and present, the destruction of old myths, the updating of Spanish history and life, and the acquisition of a sense of possible moral and intellectual equality, if not superiority, in relation to the most industrially advanced European nations.

I met Don Américo for the first time, and only for a few minutes, in 1935 at the Centro de Estudios Históricos in Madrid, which was an offshoot of the old Institución. By that time he was already a prominent national figure. Since the founding of the Centro in 1910 by Ramón Menéndez Pidal, he had been in charge of the Department of Lexicography. In 1915 he became professor of History of the Spanish Language at the University of Madrid, the most important university in the country. From 1917 on he wrote for the newspapers, mainly on literary and educational problems. In particular, he wrote for *El Sol,* the most pretigious newspaper in Madrid and for *La Nación* of Buenos Aires, the most prestigious newspaper in Spanish America—one foot on each side of the Atlantic! Shortly afterward he would be physically present in the New World for the second time.

This second contact with America took place in 1923 in Buenos Aires on the occasion of the founding of the Instituto de Filología Hispánica. This institution was to be left in the hands of another young Spaniard by the name of Amado Alonso, who would, in time, become an outstanding scholar and teacher in his own right, and largely responsible for the training of a school of very notable Argentinian scholars. That trip to Buenos Aires also took Don Américo to Chile, a country of great philological tradition, where he gave several courses and lectures.

From Chile he came to the United States in 1924 as a visiting professor at Columbia University, where another young Spaniard by the name of Federico de Onís was already distinguishing himself as the counterpart of Amado Alonso in the Northern Hemisphere. Federico de Onís created the Casa Hispánica at Columbia, founded the *Revista Hispánica Moderna,* and was responsible for the emergence of a group of distinguished North American Hispanists. The year 1924 also saw Don Américo in nearby Mexico for the first time, perhaps through the intervention of his close friend, the outstanding Mexican scholar and writer, Alfonso Reyes, whom he had met in Spain where Reyes had lived for years. Mexico proved to be fascinating for Don Américo, who would repeat his visit to the old New Spain many times. This first visit to Mexico extended to Cuba and Puerto Rico. In these three countries, as he had done before in Buenos Aires and Chile, he gave some courses in their respective universities and also some public lectures that proved to be a great success. After returning to Madrid he was invited by the University of Berlin as "Gastprofessor" for the academic year 1930–1931.

Don Américo was still in Germany when the traditional Spanish monarchy fell by popular vote and through an exemplary democratic process. A very civilized and peaceful republic was born which, at the time, seemed to incarnate the dreams of the late Francisco Giner and enjoyed the support of all his followers. Don Américo was immediately appointed Spanish ambassador to Germany at a time when Germany was beginning to feel the first birth pains of Naziism as an echo of a similar, though prior, process in Italy. After the First World War all Europe had been involved in a deep economic and moral depression with growing signs of dogmatic intransigence and a tendency toward rule by force. Spain seemed to be going in the opposite direction. The discrepancy made hard times almost inevitable. Don Américo renounced his diplomatic post and decided to go back to Madrid and to other endeavors more to his liking: among them, the creation of a Department of American Studies in the Centro de Estudios Históricos, which published a scholarly review entitled *Tierra Firme.* A similar institution and journal had existed in Germany for many years, but not in Spain. Don Américo once again felt the attraction of America and once more he left Spain for Buenos Aires in 1936, never suspecting that this time he would stay in this part of the world for the next thirty years.

What happened in Spain between 1936 and 1939 forever marked the life of every Spaniard who was an adult or reached adulthood in those years. The facts are too well-known to be repeated here. As a lasting consequence, more than half a million Spaniards left the country, among them, the best of the Spanish intelligentsia. The country itself was left in ruins and, shamefully, in the hands of a despicable tyranny.

The savage Spanish (so-called Civil) War inevitably also marked the life of Américo Castro. Up to 1936 he was a Spaniard very much interested in America. From that year on he was going to be an American very much interested in Spain. This new situation allowed him to look at Spanish life and culture from afar, with a serene new perspective that gave him the insight and the vision possible only when one is deprived of distracting details and blinding pseudo-patriotism. His first name, Américo, was now fulfilling the prophecy implied in its meaning.

He had found a most convenient platform from which to stand up and look at the world, in the enviable intellectual climate of the universities of the United States, based on the peaceful coexistence of the most diversified ideas, the availability of excellent libraries, the lack of extreme economic pressures, and all kinds of facilities for proceeding at one's own pace. Don Américo taught and worked first at the University of Wisconsin (1937-1939) and afterwards at Texas (1939-1940), Princeton (1940-1953), Houston (1955), and California (La Jolla, 1964-1968).

It was at Princeton, in 1943, that I met Don Américo for the second time in my life. The riptide of the Spanish conflict had carried me to the shores of Cuba in 1939. Don Américo had heard of my lectures on Hispano-Arabic culture at the University of Havana. The recently acquired interest of Don Américo in that culture was the determining factor for the invitation he extended to me to come to the United States to teach, not Arabic, but Spanish, in the ASTP (army specialized training program) program. I accepted, and, at the end of the summer of 1943, I found myself at the railroad whistlestop in Princeton, stepping down from a strange train, in a strange country, with a man I hardly recognized waiting for me. Don Américo's appearance seemed to have changed in harmony with deeper and less visible changes in concepts, opinions, and personality. I remembered him from our first encounter in Madrid and from subsequent photographs in newspapers and magazines as a tall, imposing, almost athletic man, with a hard and penetrating look in his eyes, and a well-kept moustache and beard. The man I now met had a clean-shaven face, was slightly bent over, not tall by American standards, casually dressed, with eyes that were warm and cordial, and a voice that was soft and kindly. This second encounter of ours marked the beginning of a long and profound friendship that grew during a year of daily contact at Princeton. One thing impressed me especially in those days: in one of our frequent walks together, I heard him say that one ought not to publish anything before the age of fifty. Very poor advice for an aspiring young scholar, but strongly felt by him because of the great metamorphosis he was undergoing. The only thing common to the old and the new Don Américo was the same passionate temper in defending or attacking his own or others' ideas.

By this time Don Américo had already expressed in articles, essays, prologues, lectures, and books, his thoughts on philological problems, the Spanish Classical theater, the picaresque novel, the art of Cervantes, the teaching of Spanish, St. Theresa de Jesus, and many other topics. Among other volumes, the following works had appeared in book form: *La enseñanza del español en España* (1922), *Conferencias dadas en el salón de honor de la Universidad* (de Chile) (1924); *Lengua, enseñanza y literatura* (1924), and the most successful of them all up to that time, *El pensamiento de Cervantes* (1925). This was the first book of Don Américo's to be internationally reviewed, acclaimed, and translated into other languages. Paradoxically, the ideas expressed in this book were also the first to be disavowed by the new Don Américo. Other books followed: *Santa Teresa y otros ensayos* (1929), *Iberoamérica. Su presente y su pasado* (1941), *La peculiaridad lingüística rioplatense* (1941).

These last two books were not published in Spain but in the Americas, showing Don Américo's new tendency to confront American problems directly, at the same level as Spanish Peninsular problems.

In the same spirit and a few months before, Don Américo had proved a decisive factor in the organization of the first congress of Iberoamericanists. Don Américo now preferred the terms *Iberoamérica* and *Iberoamericanismo* in place of the more common *Latin America* and its derivations when referring to the cultures of the Spanish- and Portuguese-speaking peoples. Language was becoming, for him, the decisive sign for the differentiation of cultures. It was at the University of California at Los Angeles that the first Ibero-Americanist congress took place, and it was at that congress that the decision was made to publish the first journal to appear in this country, and for that matter, in any country, dedicated entirely to Ibero-American literature. This was due, to a great extent, to the vision and initiative of Don Américo, who was the first to see the Spanish-speaking world as a single cultural unit, and the Portuguese-speaking world as another unit, each closely related to the other. His attention, however, was concentrated on the Spanish-speaking world, which he considered to be as significant and valuable for universal culture and civilization as any other human aggregates of different language with internationally recognized prestige.

In this sense, his lecture "The Meaning of Spanish Civilization," given at Princeton in 1940, proved to be the turning point in his thinking. The value of this lecture is such that it has been reprinted as a second prologue to this volume. On that occasion he began the elaboration of a new concept of history which he was to apply to Spanish history and, consequently, to Spanish life in general and to Spanish literary creation in particular. It would take the next twenty-five years of his life and half a dozen books to perfect and justify his theories and, at the same time, to fulfill the inherited meaning of his full name, Américo Castro Quesada.

Until approximately 1938, halfway through the war in Spain and after two uninterrupted years in America, only his given name, Américo, seems to have been totally justified by his life and work, with a strong possibility that it became a determining reason for his Americanist vocation. Nevertheless, it is also my not-too-rational contention that the other two surnames of Don Américo cast their shadows and even perhaps their spell over the rest of Don Américo's accomplishments.

As has been mentioned before, the second surname of Don Américo—in the Spanish tradition, his mother's first surname— was Quesada. Perhaps it would not be amiss to recall that in Spanish the word for "the fatherland" is "la Patria," a grammatically feminine noun, and therefore a case could be made for an identification of one's mother with one's country. Something of this sort is meant by Spanish-American politicians when they refer to Spain as "la madre patria." I have also mentioned that Don Américo did not use his mother's first surname in the last forty years of his life, as if he were not satisfied with it. But it so happens that this name, Quesada, is also one of several that did not satisfy the prototype of the Spanish hero, the immortal Don Quixote de la Mancha. When Cervantes begins his novel, he presents his future knight-errant as an old man living in a little village with a given name Alonso and a first surname at the beginning of the book which is not quite clear, oscillating among several possibilities: Quijada, Quesada, Quejana, or Quijano. Quesada is a strong choice since, in contrast to the others, it already existed in Cervantes' time as a fairly common surname.[4] In fact, a theory has been advanced to the effect that the figure of Don Quixote was modeled after an actual Quesada, born, like Don Américo's parents, in the Moorish city of Granada. Yet the name is also tied, like Don Américo, to the New World. I am obviously referring to Gonzalo Jiménez de Quesada, who died close to or past eighty after an amazing life dreaming the impossible dream of El Dorado, while at the same time immersed in hard reality. He was the founder of Santa Fé de Bogotá, the capital of present-day Colombia, named Santa Fé as a tribute to the Santa Fé in his native province of Granada (Spain), headquarters of the Catholic sovereigns before the conquest of that city, and Bogotá as a tribute to the indigenous world he had encountered. It is also significant that the most important people to carry the name Quesada were Argentinians, Peruvians, Costa Ricans, and Cubans but, with the exception of Don Américo, very few, if any, well-known Spaniards. The name Quesada, in Cervantes' masterpiece, was one of the hidden seeds that would mature into Don Quixote, in the same way that the name Quesada, as the second and seldom used surname of Don Américo would mature into his quixotic nature.

No theme is more important or constant throughout the entire life of Don Américo than the life and art of Cervantes, whose character and meaning were to have a tremendous and ever-changing fascination for him. He showed this interest as far back as 1917 when he published an early article commenting on the appearance of the critical edition of *El Ingenioso hidalgo Don Quijote de la Mancha* by Rodríguez Marín. A few weeks before his death he sent me a copy of what was probably his last essay entitled "Como veo ahora el Quijote" ("How I Now See the *Quixote*"). In the fifty-four years between these two works he published more than twenty essays, prologues, and articles on the subject, in addition to the famous book *El pensamiento de Cervantes*. In spite of the great success of this book and its being out of print for many years, Don Américo would not authorize a new edition until he was convinced that his readers were familiar with the change in his approach and thought that resulted in total disagreement with the conclusions reached in that book.[5] The title *El pensamiento de Cervantes,* emphasizing as it does Cervantes' thinking, is an indication of a starting point in the life of Don Américo similar to that of Don Quixote when he was still Alonso Quesada, a fairly reasonable man. Predominantly reasonable also were those schooled in the principles of the Institución Libre de Enseñanza, great admirers of pre-Nazi Germany, which represented for them the almost perfect model of reason applied to everyday life. Germany was also the natural birthplace of history as an abstract science. But a few years later most of Germany went up in flames and almost disappeared from the face of the earth in a holocaust provoked by the extreme irrationality of abstract rationality. Once again men felt the need for a complete change. The undivided human being would have to become the agent and the subject of history, with all his limitations, dreams, and conquests rationalized a posteriori instead of a priori.

In an essentially quixotic manner, Don Américo would declare, after the appearance of his *España en su historia* (1948) in reply to the lack of comprehension by the German-born and German-educated Leo Spitzer, that "truth without a *where,* a *how,* and a *toward* does not interest [him] any longer."[6] And he would add:

> It is understandable that the intention to write the history of a nation almost as if it were a confession or a biography, without following strict "scientific" criteria, will be found disconcerting. Technical historians would have considered this to be a piece of literary frivolity. On the other hand, for philosophers committed to the idea of life (anguished reason in Kierkegaard; historical reason in Dilthey; vital reason in Ortega y Gasset), it would be only natural that they could not become interested in empirical historical knowledge.[7]

From here on, Don Américo would never look back, feeling that he was in tune with the most advanced philosophical trends and therefore justified in his attitudes. His occasionally apparent arbitrariness, his passion, and his polemics were like Don Quixote's, always at the service of deeply felt convictions and higher ideals. New beliefs were to replace old beliefs and become new facts, but always functional and well-articulated facts, with an inner capacity to excite and stimulate. New truths would have the virtue of destroying old truths and providing a more convincing background for future enterprises.

It seems to me that all this completely justifies removing the parentheses I have placed around the hidden surname Quesada, in order to bring to light the newly acquired meaning that Don Américo's modesty would not have allowed while he was alive.

In the middle of his set of names, and in a clearly privileged position, we now find the parental surname Castro.

I remember hearing Don Américo say, on more than one occasion, that his ancestors came from Galicia, up in the northwest part of the Iberian Peninsula, and that they went from there to Andalusia after the expulsion of the last remnants of the Moorish population. Among his relatives, he would add, was a bishop of Granada named Castro. Undoubtedly Castro is a very old Spanish word, used as a family name from time immemorial. It is of Latin origin and is derived from *castrum,* meaning "fortified hill" or something similar. As a toponymical denomination, it is very common in the Spanish region of Galicia where there are more than fifty places with that name. Among the most famous Galicians with this name there is the tragic and moving figure of Inés de Castro,[8] forever present in the Portuguese soul, and Rosalía de Castro,[9] the finest poetess Spain ever produced. But the truth is that Don Américo did not start thinking about Galicia until he was confronted with the need to reinterpret the myth of the Apostle Santiago, by other names: Sant Iago, Santi Yagüe, Shant Jaqub, Sancti Jacobus, St. Jacques, and St. James. And that would not happen until late in his life. Ironically, it would also take him many years to pay his first visit to the shrine of St. James in Santiago de Compostela, not having been there during his life in Spain before the Civil War. When he finally did visit the town of Santiago de Compostela in the summer of 1958,[10] he was deeply moved upon contemplating the imposing marvel of its cathedral and the Obradoiro plaza, with its granite face and narrow veins, and its sleepy and misty old age. It must have been for him like the discovery of a long-lost mother.

Traditional history has recorded few facts and legends regarding the Apostle Santiago. Santiago el Mayor or St. James the Elder was one of the twelve apostles, and it was said that he went to Spain to preach the doctrine of Christ, but returned to the Holy Land where he was decapitated by order of Herod Agrippa in the year 44 A.D. The legend has it that two of his followers put his body in a small boat, which floated perfectly in spite of being made of stone, and rowed with it from one end of the Mediterranean sea to the other, crossed through the present Strait of Gibraltar, and went up the entire coast of Portugal to reach Galicia. They stopped at a place called Padrón, placed the body of the Apostle in an oxcart, and drove him to the center of a grove where they buried him.

It is not said how long the trip took, or in what state the body reached its destination, or the reason for selecting such a remote place for the burial. Old chronicles mention that centuries later, when most of the Iberian Peninsula was of the Islamic faith, a bright star appeared over a Galician field, giving rise to the name Compostela, *Campus stellae,* or the field of the star.

People gathered under the star and, digging there, uncovered the sepulcher of Santiago, who promised to help them fight the infidels. At the time the Christians were a minority in the Peninsula and needed all the help they could get to survive as such. The Apostle Santiago, riding a white horse and handling a sharp sword effectively, made his first appearance in the service of Christian soldiers at the battle of Clavijo in 822, during the reign of Alfonso II. People of the Islamic faith had first entered the Peninsula in 711, more than one hundred years before the battle of Clavijo. They converted most of the indigenous population of the Peninsula and with their help were able to create the most advanced culture of the time. Their impact, contribution, and importance were to prevail for almost eight centuries, from 711 to 1492, the year the Moorish kingdom of Granada was conquered and destroyed by the so-called Catholic Sovereigns, Isabella and Ferdinand, and the year America was discovered.

These eight centuries of intense and varied life in the Iberian Peninsula are usually thrown together in conventional Spanish histories under the denomination of the "War of the Reconquest." Ortega y Gasset was the first to call our attention to the absurdity of the concept when he said: "I do not understand how a thing that lasted for eight hundred years could be called a Reconquest."[11] To understand better the absurdity of the concept, let us apply the same way of thinking to American reality for a moment and pretend that the descendants, but only the pure descendants, of the American Indians with their customs and religions have an exclusive right to the American land. Counting from the date of the discovery, 1492, let eight hundred years pass until we reach the year 2292, when every American of non-Indian ancestry would be considered a foreigner and thrown out of the country. It was high time for someone to take a good look and try to understand what really happened in the Iberian Peninsula during those eight hundred years.

Don Américo applied his great knowledge and tremendous capacity and enthusiasm to this task and offered us his interpretation, with meaningful implications for any type of national history and for Spanish life today, in a series of essays and books. It began with the aforementioned lecture, *The Meaning of Spanish Civilization* (1940) and was continued in the following major works: *España en su historia: Cristianos, moros y judíos* (1948); *La realidad histórica de España* (1954); *Santiago de España* (1958); *Origen, ser y existir de los españoles* (1959); *De la edad conflictiva* (1961); and again *La realidad histórica de España* (1962) that kept the same title as the 1954 edition, although the content was radically revised and its organization changed. This last work, with several additional chapters, was the basis for the latest English version, published by the University of California Press with the title *The Spaniards. An Introduction to Their History* (1972).

Notice that the book *Santiago de España* appears almost in the middle or halfway through the series of titles. Notice also that, for Don Américo, Santiago is not of Galicia, but of Spain and, although he deletes, adds, and revises some chapters in the successive editions of *España en su historia,* he always includes, with slight modifications, the same chapters on Santiago as the central and main key for the understanding of Spanish history.

The basic assumption of Don Américo's theory is that the figure of Santiago was created by the imagination of the Christian minority as a counterpart to the figure of the prophet Mohammed serving the Islamic majority.[12] The shrine of Santiago became a Christian Mecca for the thousands of pilgrims who would pour into Spain every year for centuries. Belief creates a kind of reality far superior to what our senses can offer, and once established as a fact, it will function as such if it responds to deep-felt needs. For Don Quixote, the windmills are real giants to prove his valor, and Dulcinea, a real beauty to prove his love.

Muslims and Christians alike needed supernatural help. The author of the *Poem of the Cid* understood to what future historians would be blind when he wrote:

The Moors shout: Mohammed! And the Christians: Santiago!
(Los moros llaman: Mafomat! e los cristianos: Santi Yagüe!

The Christians with their backs to Christian Europe would end up using their own brand of intransigence and dogmatism to disrupt the peaceful coexistence of the Christians with the other peoples in Spain of the Muslim and Jewish faiths. However, this coexistence of three faiths for almost eight hundred years could not help but leave a profound mark on the victors and on what was going to become the first modern nation in Europe, unified politically, economically, and religiously. Santiago would continue to be the spiritual leader in the American crusade, by another name, the American conquest by Spain. Because Santiago would also cross the Atlantic and appear in battles against the peoples of other faiths who inhabited this hemisphere. He came with Columbus, disembarked, and with his shining sword in hand, he began to ride his white horse along the entire length of the continent. There are testimonies that he was seen thirteen times between 1518 and 1892. In Peru alone, as late as 1805, there were 138 knights of the Order of Santiago. There are also eight cities named Santiago in America. Finally, he became the patron saint of Chile. In the words of Don Américo, the end result was that: "The victorious race Semitically blended the notions of religion and state to create a culture made of faith, virility, and beauty that extended from California and Texas to the faraway distances of Bolivia and Chile."[13]

That culture is a Spanish culture, and Spanish is mainly a philological concept for Don Américo, in accordance with his own preference and background. Therefore, for him, the inhabitants of the Iberian Peninsula up to the Arabic invasion were not Spaniards; on the other hand, all those who are born within the Spanish language, who contribute to it, and who use it are Spanish, regardless of their racial or cultural history. In the Iberian Peninsula, the descendants of Celts, Iberians, Phoenicians, Romans, Visigoths, Arabs, Jews, etc., will be Spanish once they speak Spanish. And in America the descendants of Mayans, Aztecs, Toltecs, Incas, Chibchas, etc., or in modern times the descendants of Italians, Lithuanians, Greeks, Lebanese, etc., will also be Spanish Americans when they, too, speak Spanish.[14] Don Américo felt at home wherever Spanish was spoken, whether it was in Buenos Aires, Mexico, or Madrid.

Before finishing I would like to add one last irrational touch: In the last week of July, 1972, I received first a telegram and later a letter from a former student of mine in Spain giving me the sad news and some details of Don Américo's death. He was swimming in the Mediterranean Sea, in the little Catalonian resort town of Lloret de Mar, when he suddenly lost consciousness and died. He was eighty-seven years old and had worked until the very last day of his life. A perfect death to culminate a perfect life! And it was also symbolically a perfect day. Don Américo died on July 25, which is a national holiday in Spain. The festivity of the patron saint of the country falls on that day, and the patron saint of Spain is Santiago de Galicia, or Santiago de España.

NOTES

1. In a footnote to Sonnet XXIX in his book *De Fuerteventura a París*, he explicitly says: "Miguel is a Hebrew name meaning 'Who is like God?' " (see Miguel de Unamuno, *Obras completas* [Madrid: Afrodisio Aguado, 1959–1964], XIV, 505). The same meaning is attached to the name in the four-line poem, "Etimologías" (*Obras*, XV, 329).

2. See *The Complete Etchings of Goya. With a Foreword by Aldous Huxley*. (New York: Crown, 1943), p. 43.

3. See José Ortega y Gasset, *El tema de nuestro tiempo* (12th ed.; Madrid: Espasa-Calpe, 1968), p. 55. (First published in 1923.)

4. The last name Quesada has a toponymic origin. The famous historian, Gonzalo Argote de Molina, in his book *Nobleza de Andalucía* (ed. Manuel Muñoz y Garnica; Jaén: López Vizcaíno, 1866), says that the first one to use it was Pero Díaz de Toledo, governor of the Christian frontier fort of Cazorla in the old Moorish kingdom of Jaén. He had earned the right to keep it as a family name after conquering the renowned town of Quesada from the Moors of Granada (p. 353). The same name was also used to designate the nearby castle that guarded the mountain pass of Puerto Auxin in the Sierra de Cazorla, also known as the Sierra de Quesada. Both the town and the castle of Quesada changed hands many times. The king of Granada, Mohammed Mir, took the castle for the last time in 1369 (p. 61).

In an article by Joaquín Vallvé Bermejo ("La división territorial en la España musulmana. La cora de Jaén," *Al-Andalus*, XXXIV, 1, 1969, pp. 64–65) he writes: "Quesada (Qayšāṭa or Qayŷaṭa) is mentioned for the first time in the XIIth. century in historical sources as well as in Arabic biographical repertories." Al-Ḥimyarī (Al-Rawd al Miꞔtar, p. 165, no. 155) describes it as a castle that looks like a city and which is at a distance of twelve miles from the town of Jódar. The Arabic names given by Al-Ḥimyarī do not seem to have any specific meaning and they sound like transcriptions of orally transmitted words or faulty readings from different manuscripts.

Confronted up to now by a lack of solid evidence regarding the etymology of the last name "Quesada," and conscious of the unscientific nature of my hypothesis I would like, nevertheless, to suggest the possibility of some kind of connection, if not with "Quesada" itself, at least with "Quijada"—which happens to be an alternative in the ambiguity game of Cervantes for "Quesada" and for "Quijote"—and the Arabic name in its plural form qihād (= lomos de camello). If one looks at the castle of Quesada, from a distance, the similarity with a camel's silhouette is apparent and if not the camel itself, at least three "humps" in a row that could bring to mind the image of a camel. There is nearby a town with the name Peal del Becerro following a parallel trait of description. And perhaps one can also add some significance to the fact that the poet Antonio Machado, after a visit to the sanctuary of Tiscar, at the foot of the castle, wrote a poem describing the castle up above. From that poem come these lines: "En la sierra de Quesada / Hay un águila gigante / Verdosa, negra y dorada / Siempre las alas abiertas / Es de piedra y no se cansa." The poem by Machado is to this day engraved in a rock close to a fountain existing at the sanctuary of the Virgin of Tiscar. The comparison of the castle to a gigantic eagle follows the animal image of the silhouette of the camel.

5. *PCer* (1972).

6. "Respuesta a Leo Spitzer," *Nueva Revista de Filología Hispánica,* Año III, no. 2 (1949), p. 150; reprinted in *ENC,* III, 251.

7. "El enfoque histórico y la no hispanidad de los visigodos," *Nueva Revista de Filología Hispánica,* Año III, no. 3 (1949), p. 234.

8. Inés de Castro (c. 1310-1355), a Galician noblewoman who was murdered by King Afonso IV of Portugal for political reasons after she had married his son, Dom Pedro. Her remains were later placed in a magnificent mausoleum at Alcobaça. Many writers have told her story, among them, Camõens in *Os Lusíadas.*

9. Rosalía Castro or Rosalía de Castro (1837-1885). Author of the following books of poetry: *Cantares gallegos* (1863), *Follas novas* (1880), and *En las orillas del Sar* (1884), English trans. *Beside the River Sar* (1937). She also wrote two novels: *La hija del mar* (1859) and *El caballero de las botas azules* (1867).

10. Domingo García-Sabell, "La amistad con don Américo Castro," 314, 315 *Insula* (1973), 3. For Don Américo's own account of his first visit see "En Santiago de Compostela," in *ENC,* I, 245-253.

11. José Ortega y Gasset, *España invertebrada* in *Obras completas* (5th ed.; Madrid: Revista de Occidente, 1957), III, p. 118. (First published in 1921.)

12. In *Galicia feudal* (2 vols., Vigo: Galaxia, 1969), which I only very recently had an opportunity to read, Victoria Armesto mentions that the English writer, Richard Ford, was probably the first to advance the theory that Santiago is the counterpart of Mohammed. As a preliminary to discussing Américo Castro's ideas on that theory, she says: "Richard Ford was one of the first, if not the first, to introduce the theory that Santiago de Compostela originated as an answer to Cordoba . . . Richard Ford was a rich young man, a cultural dilettante, who visited Seville in 1830 and remained in Spain for three years. As a result of his "Spanish experience" he wrote (between 1840 and 1845) the book *Handbook for Travellers in Spain,* which is considered a classic book in England . . . In a first edition—which Ford withdrew from circulation for fear that Spaniards would consider it too "offensive"— he explains the Jacobbean cult as a fruit of Muslims' roots.

"To make a tomb a center of pilgrimage is—in Ford's opinion—an oriental idea; thus, after guessing the emotional impact that a holy city could have over its clientele, both Spanish Christians and Moors decided to create a Peninsular

Jerusalem and a Peninsular Mecca. The Moors pointed to Cordoba as the city that kept Mohammed's bones, and the Christians founded also their mountainous capital with a buried prophet" (vol. I, pp. 113-114). Américo Castro does not mention Richard Ford, and for that matter neither does anyone else, to my knowledge, with the exception of Victoria Armesto. I have read lately the rare first edition of Mr. Ford's book and was very much impressed not only with his sensitivity and intuition but also with his extraordinary erudition. I am sure that Américo Castro would have been very happy if he had known and read Ford's book, which, paradoxically enough, confirmed all his ideas before they were written and even added new insights to them. It makes better sense, for instance to first consider Santiago as anti-Cordoba—following Ford— without invalidating the anti-Mecca idea shared by both Castro and Ford. The most impelling reasons are Cordoba's proximity and the fact, underlined by Ford, that another name for Cordoba was *Ceca* or *Zeca* (derived from the old Egyptian Sēkos or house of purification). Ford adds: "In sanctity it ranked as the third of mosques, equal to the Alaksa of Jerusalem, and second only to the Caaba of Mecca . . . A pilgrimage to this *Ceca* was held to be equivalent in the Spanish Moslem to that of Mecca, where he could not go; hence *andar de Mecca en Ceca*, [*sic*] became a proverb for wandering, and is used by Sancho Panza, when soured by blanked tossings." (*A Hand-book for Travellers in Spain and Readers at Home* [London: John Murray, 1845], Part I, p. 299). With pragmatic logic Ford expounds further on the case for Santiago and among other things he says: "Mahomet appeared on the Orontes to overthrow Count Roger, as Santiago, mounted on his war-horse interfered at Clavijo in 846 [*sic*] to crush the Moslem. There was no mention of Santiago, or his visit to Spain, or his patronage, in the time of the Goths (S^n· Isidoro, 'Or.,' vii. 9), and simply because there being no Moors then to be expelled, he was not wanted." (Ibid., Part II, p. 662).

13. *CCL*, pp. 90-91.

14. "His collective dimension [that of the American Negro] is 'Anglo-Saxon,' by virtue of his language, culture, and the *Horizon* of his intimate way of life" (*ECD* [1961], p. 106). "A descendant of Italians or Lithuanians in Argentina or in North America ultimately ends up, in certain important cases, by behaving like Spanish- or English-speaking people in areas which are sometimes completely unknown to him. For this reason we speak of a Hispanic world or an Anglo-Saxon world, whose reality is maintained as an integral whole, no matter how much antipathy some Hispano-Americans feel for Spaniards and vice versa" (p. 109).

2

THE MEANING OF
SPANISH CIVILIZATION
Américo Castro

The essential end of the sciences of nature is to bring rational clarity and unity to what is apparently confused and variable. But historical science, or the science of human culture, aspires to a special kind of clarity based on the perception of the meaning of human accomplishments, ordering them according to the perspective of their values. A human fact can never be reduced to the conceptual plan of a definition that attempts to include its whole content, as is the case with mathematical or physical definitions. An historical fact always signifies something, that is, it acknowledges an end or value which transcends it. One cannot define a Gothic cathedral as he would define a material object, because it is only possible to perceive its esthetic, religious, and social values. I recall this only to make it clear that Spanish civilization, that great aggregate of history, cannot be made up of a mere enumeration of facts, but rather, consists in the exposition of its meaning and values, in order that the tones of that civilization which developed in the Western world may be made audible.

An intention of a historical construct is never objective, that is, it can provide nothing similar to what we call the axiomatic or logically demonstrable in rational sciences. The evidence that historical judgment provides will depend on how we integrate

This lecture, delivered on December 11, 1940, as the inaugural address for the Emory L. Ford Chair of Spanish, was written with listeners rather than readers in mind. Some adjustments have been made to make it more readable, without changing any of its ideas. It was printed and distributed free by the Jennie Wetherbee Baker Memorial Fund of Princeton University, with an Introduction by Harold W. Dodds, President. *Editor's Note.*

our own lives within the historical life we are trying to understand; because history is not explained, it is understood. But this does not mean that historical science consists in relativism or psychological arbitrariness; it means that the understanding of history presupposes a vital projection of the historian within the historical fact. Thus, a person cannot understand the historical fact of America if he is not in sympathy with the American historical fact. A person, for example, who does not understand vitally what an American means when he says "democracy," "cooperation," and "every man has to be given a chance" cannot know the true meaning of American history, which will then become for him a series of phantasmal events. But if the historian's vital perception is in tune with the facts before him, then American history emerges as a clear picture in which the historian's own life is expressed in one way or another.

The result of what has just been said is that the history of Spanish culture cannot be undertaken from a point of view vitally foreign to it, because then we would be talking about something that does not exist and we would fail to perceive the essence of its values. If we think that every civilization should have its inspiration in the rationalistic attitude of the eighteenth century, in the development of the technics of physics, and in the pursuit of an ordered and general happiness, then the answer would be that Spanish civilization was never interested in such ends, and that what it has accomplished and is accomplishing today is based on other purposes and preferences. Modern man has been living in an order which has seemed to him the height of perfection, a stage in the journey of ideas and normal experiences towards that utopian realm called "infinite progress." Consequently, for Western man, the problem of existence has derived not so much from his venturing into the realm of the uncertain as from his being situated within unchangeable cultural boundaries. (Incidentally, I shall recall something important related to American Hispanism: it is quite notable that the great movement of curiosity for things Spanish should reach its height with Ticknor and Prescott precisely at the time of American expansion toward the West in a great moment of effort and adventure.)

Let us say at once that the Spanish soul is always uncovering something of primal humanity which is forever struggling with elementary problems of human geology. It is very natural, then, that in rigidly structured societies, in which each individual considers as solved all primary problems related to the ultimate intimacy of conscience, the Spanish way of life should produce impressions which are disconcerting, sometimes annoying and impertinent, and often original and charmingly surprising. I have devoted the best part of my time to the study of this problem for many years.

Because of the peculiar nature of Spanish reality, for centuries the most important aspects of that civilization have given rise to interminable controversies within and without Spain. For that reason, at times the Spaniards themselves have not succeeded in approaching their own problems in their true light, especially in attempting to see them from a conceptual or logical point of view, or in pragmatic form, concentrating on material wealth, warlike might, or technical efficiency. We are not going to enter into any controversy here, nor are we going to analyze again the well-known historical reasons which have caused the history of Spanish civilization to be attacked so often on religious or political grounds. We shall limit ourselves to recalling that the way in which Spanish life has been realized in history is different from what we observe in the other great peoples of the West. Hence, its originality and the constant attraction it exercises, even on those who note its absence of wealth, material power, or industrial technology. All of this ought to be useful to us in seeking out some essential characteristics of the Spanish way of life, because a people express themselves in their creations and in their omissions, in their replies and in their silences, when they are confronted by the ultimate problems of life and death.

In order to understand Spanish life one must forget for a moment the idea that material success and prosperity are necessary in order to be able to define a culture in essence. Spanish life has never known what in America is called prosperity, nor has it experienced any period in which all social and economic forces have functioned normally, as in the France of Louis XIV, in nineteenth-century England, etc. At the climax of its imperial moment, the Spanish state went bankrupt several times. The emperor Charles V had to delay his return to Spain several months, after his dramatic abdication in 1554, because he lacked funds to pay the people of his household; for the same reason it was necessary for him to postpone the funeral of his mother, Joan the Mad. In the seventeenth century King Philip IV, monarch of two worlds, once had difficulty getting the meals of the day prepared in the royal palace. Spain, rich in all types of art, has never invented, in truth, a single comfortable piece of furniture. The upholstered chair, the chaise-longue, and the sofa are not Spanish inventions. Even in moments of greatest political and military splendor, when prodigious forms of civilization were flourishing, everyday life was always difficult and problematic for Spaniards. Keeping these things in mind, we find that we shall have to search for the meaning of Spanish civilization and its high values independently of the idea of material happiness, which seeks to forge for itself a pleasant life through technical applications and inventions that smooth off the roughness of natural circumstances. Spanish civilization shows scanty output in material production. Her contributions are not easy to gauge. They would not take up much room in the pavilions of world's fairs.

Today, more than at any other moment in world history, we can contemplate such a state of things with serenity, because today it is pertinent to ask whether this so-called "progress," which is based on a pure intellectualism and a craving for epicurean joys, may not be, after all, more productive of horrors than benefits.

In several important areas of thought and ethics more than one idea of culture and life, unquestioned thirty years ago, has now reached a crisis. Whenever this has happened in Western culture, Spanish civilization has begun to show its reserves, permanent and intact, not affected seriously by the oscillations between progress and human grief and misery. In these ominous times we are beginning to see that face to face with tangible and apparently irrepressible weapons, the arms of the spirit, with their imponderable character, can be as effective or more effective than material weapons. Armaments, lines of defense, are of little use to those lacking inner defense. To bring out the essential man, wholly and in strong relief, was and is the main concern of Spanish civilization.

Western culture has lived for almost three centuries under the star of clear, distinct ideas, thinking that whatever escapes reason and concept either does not exist or is not worthy of note, or is comparable to obscure forms of being. This was a great virtue, and nothing that has been gained through such a method should be lost. Today, however, we cannot help but smile on remembering that the nineteenth century tried to make science a religion and believed that progress was the result of a social mechanism that, once set in motion, was never going to stop—the myth of infinite progress. In that atmosphere of applied science, technology, and well-being Spanish values suffered a great depreciation. The principal Spanish theme has always been man as a naked and absolute reality, and very secondarily, the products with which man tries to replace the consciousness of his existence. To a Spaniard, his fellow human beings are more interesting for what they really are than for the social function they represent or for what they produce. If a man who is known to be stupid as a man publishes a very voluminous book, to a Spaniard, he is just as stupid as he was before. The same is true if he is immensely rich or occupies a high position. That ability and habit of taking moral x-rays has implied great misfortunes for the Spaniard in his practical life, and has made it quite difficult for him to organize his social life, which must rest on objective products, whether or not their authors are worthy or unworthy of esteem. If, however, a Spaniardd does not discover a deep, authentic, and vital relationship between what a person is and what he does, then neither the person nor his work interests him. It is difficult to convince the average Spaniard that a man who is lacking in mental energy or expressive originality in his relations with other people may be worth something for other reasons. It is common to hear things like this: "That gentleman may be very learned, but as a man, he is a blockhead." As I said before, having such a nature has cost Spaniards a fabulous price as a human group and as individuals. But one must become resigned to the fact that it is so, in the same way that one must accept the fact that Americans avoid encounters with their intimate problems and those of others, and consider talking about them a form of barbarism. Our understanding and esteem of a given culture is in direct ratio to our acceptance of its inner necessity.

At the present time the Spanish way of life needs less than ever before to offer excuses for being the way it is. Today Western civilization is passing through a crisis from which we do not know how it is going to survive. And it would be a naive error to believe that the problem affects only Europe and not the lands on this side of the ocean. Illusory faith in reason has collapsed. Reason has ceased to be a guide. Its place has been taken by brutal action, working through dark forms of collective will that disintegrate and annihilate the individual. If we could hear the millenary voice of the Spanish genius, it would say something like this: "Search for the man behind the slogan."

The dehumanization of man, in which he becomes the servant of the things he creates and forgets that he was once their master, is truly a great peril. Quevedo, the great seventeenth-century Baroque figure, gravely reminded Spain that "as poor men, we conquered the riches of others; as rich men, these same riches are conquering us." This writer, on commenting upon the seventeenth-century custom of decorating the tombs of men who never went to war with war trophies, says: "The stone has what the buried man did not have. Arms which used to be for defense are now mere ornaments."

The same concern for man himself led Don Quixote to condemn firearms and the man who invented them: "I am convinced that he is in hell receiving the reward of his diabolical invention, by which he made it easy for a base and cowardly hand to take the life of a gallant gentleman."

It has been the custom to classify this as ardent Romanticism, although the spectacle of our declining civilization may, perhaps, cause some to think otherwise. At every moment today we find ourselves at an impasse as regards forms of government, economics, science, and education. Half a century ago universal happiness always seemed to be around the corner. This belief is vanishing nowadays. Shortly after the Renaissance another dream, the Golden Age, also vanished. How much light the study of the Spanish Counter-Reformation would throw on our historical moment!

But in order to bring more clarity to this analysis, I am going to make some harmless remarks on the various stages of technological development.

I. In the beginning man lived on what the earth, like a mother chary of her nourishment, gave to him spontaneously.

II. Man detaches himself from nature and forces her to increase her production. Technical instruments which extended human activity were used for this purpose. This is the period of what I shall call "humanized technique." Man tills the soil with an implement that is more effective than his bare hand, but is still an extension of it.

III. Technique is dehumanized because the technical instrument now operates without the direct collaboration of man and is converted into something autonomous. Little by little man perceives that he is being ruled by the machine that was once his slave or collaborator. Technological machines are thus becoming a second nature, a creation that is imposing itself inexorably on human beings. When we traveled on foot or on horseback along a road opened by the hand of man, we felt ourselves to be masters of our course; traveling on a train or in an automobile we feel ourselves carried along by a world that dominates us, a force that may condition our acts and destinies.

In this third stage of technique, man lets himself be dragged along by circumstances as inevitable as Nature herself which operate like a second nature and will not let him escape. Paradoxically, this brings about a return to primitivism, to the times when man's life was regulated by the material nature that surrounded him, that is, when man was least human. This man today, adjective of the machine and vitally disintegrated, is in the right state of maturity to fall victim to some external force, as has already happened to many peoples. Any gesture of authentic manliness, of free life, is something extravagant, worthy only of ridicule and rejection.

The Spaniard, however, has resisted as much as he could the passing from humanized to dehumanized technique. Some thirty years ago Unamuno, that compendium and symbol of Spanish character, uttered the famous exclamation: "Inventions, let others do the inventing!" In other words: "We don't want to know anything about the inventions of foreigners."

Long centuries of experience and anguish have accustomed the Spaniard to dialogues with his bare ego, with an ego which is not that of Descartes, of the "cogito, ergo sum," in which the dazzling clarity of reason leaves in shadow whatever is not clear and distinct—the troubled zone of the humanly extrarational. The Spanish ego is that of Calderón, in *Life Is a Dream*, in which the prince, Segismundo, on returning from his ephemeral reign at court and hearing that it was all a fallacious dream, exclaims:

> A woman I did love.
> And methinks this at least must have been true,
> For now I see that everything is ended,
> And only this remains.

The Spanish ego is the ego of Cervantes, an ego that prolongs the will to existence in the most opposite directions, because it is felt that any exclusivistic or partial attitude leads to never-ending labyrinths. Or again, this Spanish ego is the ego of Francisco Giner, the most inspiring educator Spain ever had. Giner wanted for Spain a present which at the same time was Spain's traditional past and her splendid future. Or again, it is the ego of Goya, who exalted painting to such heights and in whose works beauty and horror coexist as supreme deities in a dubious contiguity of paradise and inferno. Or again, it is the ego of Lope de Vega, in whose life love and duty in ceaseless struggle created the unfathomable humanity of his personality and his art. And the list could be prolonged with the names and works of the most genuine representatives of the Spanish genius from the Middle Ages to the present.

It has been said time and again that placid impressions and gentle smiles rarely occur in the entire course of Spanish historical life. Light and gay tones are dominated by gravity and meditativeness. Likewise, critics have pointed out the ever recurrent presence of didactic and sententious style in Spanish literature. What is the reason for all this? It is simply the fact that the Spaniard cannot isolate himself within an abstraction. He has to maintain his will in constant unification with both personal conduct and rational analysis. Nebrija and Luis Vives, the two great humanists of the Spanish Renaissance, did not succeed in abstracting themselves from their religious emotion when they set upon their classical studies. In the realm of concepts the Spaniard feels himself more isolated than Robinson Crusoe on his island. This is the reason why science, abstract philosophy, and techniques are rare and, on the other hand, the moral direction is always present. For his happiness and his misfortune the Spaniard has always depended on his integral ego, which contains both his security and his oscillation as well. The world does not exist for him, nor does it serve him in any way, if it is not integrated in the consciousness of his existence. For that reason the Spaniard has scarcely been interested in philosophy, except when it has been able to escape pure rationalism. This is the explanation for the fact that Krausism found such a strange acceptance in nineteenth-century Spanish thought, an incomprehensible fact for those not familiar with the intimacy of the Spanish soul. Krause (1781–1832) was a second-rate philosopher who had very little influence in Germany. His work became known around 1840 to Julián Sanz del Río, a Castilian who would have been a great mystic in the sixteenth century. From about the middle of the last century Krausist philosophy found a reception in Spain that must have surprised the Germans themselves. Why such a trace in the best atmosphere of Spain? Krause, lifted by the wave of Romanticism, is a pantheist. For him, man's conscience is both the seat of natural infinity and spiritual infinity. The knowledge of finite things is only possible through a rational union with the infinite. Philosophy thus loses its abstract function and leads toward morality and education, and in that way it comes to occupy the center of life. Almost everything worthwhile achieved by Spain in culture and education in the nineteenth and twentieth centuries has its indirect origin in that Romantic influence on the Spanish genius, represented then by one of the greatest figures in modern education—Giner de los Ríos, a Krausist.

Krause's metaphysics rests on "panentheism," a term coined by him to express his idea that the world is not God, but that God is the entity in whom contrary elements find their unity. The soul of man, capable of contemplating the absolute, is pervaded by a profound religious and spiritual sense. The highest forms of Spanish sensibility in the nineteenth century responded to that idea, in a manner comparable to the way in which the best of Spain in the sixteenth century was charmed by the spiritualism of Erasmus, for whom the true temple was not the visible, but that which lies in the deepest intimacy of a pure soul.

Turning to a more recent epoch, it is no less noteworthy that so-called existential philosophy should have found a favorable soil in Spain, a singular fact if one bears in mind the scant affection of Spaniards for philosophical meditation. The Dane Sören Kierkegaard (1813–1855) left a deep impression on the work of Miguel de Unamuno, who learned Danish in order to read him. The reason is similar to the one mentioned in regard to Krause. For Kierkegaard, ultimate truth of being has its origin in the irreducible tension between the world and God, between reality and the idea, between time and eternity, between faith and knowledge. Within that irreducible tension Kierkegaard situated the problem of existence. The sense of being lies in the inner, subjective life, which is, in turn, the foundation of the true and the ethical. According to Kierkegaard, belonging to any herd corrupts and despiritualizes man's nature. One must think "existentially," living for the absolute, without being a member of anything.

Here, then, is the ideal framework into which fits much of the thought and sensibility of Unamuno, that Spaniard par excellence, for whom the tragic struggle between the conscience of the finite individual and the limitless beyond constitutes life and artistic creation. Never, perhaps, has the anguish of wanting to rise above the human, without ceasing to be human, been expressed so beautifully.

But Unamuno is above all an artist whose doctrine is not easily separated from his emotion; he is as much of a poet in prose as he is in verse. On the other hand, if we desire a rigorous expression of existential philosophy, we must go to the work of José Ortega y Gasset. This man began his philosophic career as a neo-Kantian, a trend which, like any purely intellectualist tendency, was bound to be fruitless on Spanish soil. Fortunately Ortega y Gasset discovered more ample horizons in the phenomenology of Husserl, in the historical vitalism of Dilthey, in Auguste Comte (insofar as the latter supersedes his own positivism), in Bergson, etc. Ortega's culture is of the broadest scope, not only as knowledge but also as unlimited vital curiosity. He is a great teacher, a writer of rare beauty, and at the same time a man of the world. Polymorphism is a characteristic trait of certain aspects of Spanish civilization, and Cervantes had already said of himself: "And he confines and restricts himself to the narrow limits of the narrative, though he has the ability, capacity, and brains enough to deal with the whole universe . . ."

Ortega's ideas flourished in the same historical climate that produced figures of the stature of Max Scheler and Martin Heidegger in Germany. Ortega, however, as befitting his Spanish nature, is, at the same time, both a thinker and an artist, and in his writings he has touched on the four cardinal points of human interest. But I am not going to analyze Ortega's philosophy at this point, because it would be inopportune.[21] I shall, however, refer to some of his Spanish traits, as reflections of that culture of which he forms an inseparable part. All of the aforementioned non-Spanish thinkers, including those who possess the greatest expressive sensibility and art, write in an objective and impersonal way. This is true, for example, of Bergson and Scheler. Ortega, on the other hand, sometimes philosophizes while bearing the burden of his empirical ego; accordingly, he embodies in his thought what he feels about himself, including what he believes others are going to think or are thinking about his writings. Hence his constant concern for making sure of his originality, the priority of his ideas, for showing that he has prophesied this or that happening, for announcing the publication of works which are sometimes mere projects, wrapped in a seductive title. At the same time, this great thinker takes part as a great actor in the philosophical spectacle of which he is the author. This sort of thing could only take place in Spain. The Iberian mind can never "take off" from the vital base on which it is grounded. We should recall that Velázquez, in his masterpiece, *Las Meninas,* included himself painting the picture, along with the spectators, in this case, the king and queen of Spain.

To live, to think, to create artistically, to become for the Spaniard, is the staging and the integral representation of his very existence. Hence, the essential importance that gesture and attitude assume for the Spaniard, as I have brought out else-where.[2] But in spite of what Spain has received from the outside, the essential part of her history always comes from within herself. The position of Spanish civilization in respect to foreign influence is the same as that of an original work with respect to its sources, particularly those sources that served merely to stimulate or inspire. Erasmism and Stoicism in the sixteenth and seventeenth centuries, and existentialism in the twentieth, sometimes produced consequences as far removed from their origins as a chemical compound can be from the elements that enter into its composition. Cervantes would not have written as he did without the influence of Erasmus and neo-Stoicism, but one has to submit Cervantes to a detailed analysis to discover such influences. On another plane, Giner de los Ríos vitally transformed Krausism into something that Krause would not have recognized. And the same thing could be said of Unamuno, Ortega, Picasso, Falla, and present-day Spanish poetry which has scaled unsuspected heights. For three thousand years gains from other cultures have emerged from the crucible of Spain transformed into something different.

It is now noteworthy that the Hispano-Arabs created in southern Spain a culture superior to that of the lands from which they came. Philosophy, science, art, all kinds of interest-ing life found cultivation and preeminence among them. As we know, Romance was spoken along with Arabic until the twelfth century in southern Spain.

The Hispano-Arabs introduced Greek philosophy and other essential branches of knowledge into the Western world. This contact was established through the school of translators of Toledo in which Arabic works were translated into Latin. The archdeacon of Segovia, Domingo Gundisalvo (known by his Latin name, Dominicus Gundisalus), who lived in the first half of the twelfth century and was, accordingly, a contemporary of the author of the *Poema del Cid*, was an outstanding figure in that group. Domingo Gundisalvo not only translated Arabic philosophers into Latin, but he also wrote original treatises. It is odd that in his book on immortality, influenced doubtless by the thinking of Ibn Gabirol, the archdeacon of Segovia would say that "souls recognize their origin of issue in the source of life, and that nothing can come between them and the

fountain of life nor divide the waters that flow from it." Around
the year 1140 the *Poema de Mío Cid* was written; it is different
from European epic poems and already contains the seed of
what one day will be the European novel, because in the *Poema
del Cid* the epic myth dissolves into a picture of everyday life.
The Cid of the poem is the hero who carries out marvelous feats
and is, at the same time, the owner of some mills which he
exploits like any bourgeois tradesman. (Suppose that in the
French *Chanson de Roland* someone told the hero he had better
stop killing Moors and go to Bordeaux to attend to his wine-
press.) Here is the seed of integral realism in Cervantes,
including Don Quixote as well as Sancho. The novelistic genre
has indeed been one of Spain's great creations. Beginning with
the Oriental tales, the genius of Castile cultivated novelistic
forms throughout the centuries. *The Celestina* and *Lazarillo
de Tormes* represent prior stages in the development of the
genre before the *Quixote*. With Cervantes the novel reaches its
height of perfection and is harvested by universal literature.

From other points of view, the theater and religious literature
left deep traces outside of Spain. In the seventeenth century,
excluding England, European literature seemed disoriented and
lifeless. It was difficult to find the relationship between the
neoclassical forms of the Renaissance and the ultimate intimacy
of the human soul. Then the Spanish theater, founded by Lope
de Vega, showed France how a stage character could live in a
world that transcended him, going beyond the limits of Italian
Renaissance comedy or popular farce. Following the vital road
opened by Spain, the genius of Corneille created the tragedy
and the comedy of the seventeenth century. Regarding *Le
Menteur*, Corneille says something that we can now understand
much better: "When I decided to go from the heroic to the
naive, I found that I did not dare descend from so high a plane
without availing myself of a guide, and I let myself be led by
the famous Lope de Vega." Corneille learned in Spain that to
live is to reason and to feel, to be heroic and comic, that life is,
in short, an integral whole, and that great art is possible only
on that basis. Looking at the problem in this way, one can
understand the meaning of Spanish influence during the seventeenth century.

But there is something more. The discovery of the intimate

panorama of the soul itself owes more than is generally believed to Spanish mysticism and asceticism, whose works were translated many times. Some day we shall have to incorporate in the history of literature, as a chapter in the record of the human spirit, the influence of Luis de Granada, Theresa de Jesús, and St. John of the Cross on Europe.

Better known than what I have just spoken of is Spanish influence on the creation of human archtypes such as the heroic knight and the courtier, who take their models from the Spanish Amadis de Gaula and Gracián. The distinct trail of Gracián can be traced from La Rochefoucauld to Schopenhauer and Nietzsche.

Toward the end of the eighteenth century Europe exhausts her store of rationalistic motives. Then Spain again comes to the rescue with her humanism intact and injects new life with her Romancero, theater, and art, and also with the striking heroic lesson of her struggle against Napoleon from 1808 to 1814. Authorities on European Romanticism know about this. What happened then is quite significant. It shows that the best part of Spanish civilization has nothing to do with her political greatness or wretchedness. Strong or weak, rich or in misery, Spain is always the same. At the beginning of the nineteenth century the bare soul of Spain appears in the greatest genius of modern painting: Goya. In reality he had no masters; he imitated no one. Goya's art, a creation ex-nihilo, of incalculable dimension, seems to span chasms of technique.

At the present time, when suffering and misery make Spain one great open wound, there is another leading figure of contemporary art: Pablo Picasso. According to the Art Institute of Chicago, all the roads of present-day art converge on Picasso and all hopes radiate from him.

Parallel to Picasso we have García Lorca, whose poetry has become so popular in America and will grow in popularity everyday. His poetry springs from the fountain of Andalusian popular songs, and from their melody comes the musical wonder of Manuel de Falla, who, like Lorca, is Andalusian. The latter's poetry owes its primary elements to the Andalusian milieu in which the poet perceives what no one had expressed before him. The Andalusian soul lives in longing for a world beyond, another world that the art of García Lorca peoples with marvels. Lorca is not a surrealist who exposes the deep, incoherent play of the subconscious. His art consists in extending his life in harmony with the great world beyond of every being, and he brings us into this world of wonder, full of delightful perturbation. Realistic poetry, then, but a realism only possible within the framework of Spanish existentialism.

I cannot come to the end of my lecture without speaking of the Spanish extension in this hemisphere where Spain expended the best part of herself in a creative effort for more than three centuries. Mexico, Peru, Colombia, and the Antilles were not colonies, but were, rather, expansions of the national territory that were enriched with rare artistic and ideal generosity.

I believe that my interpretation of Spanish history could be corroborated by the Spanish colonization of the New World. The juridical difficulties which the Spanish kings had to cope with from the beginning of the conquest cannot be explained if we think that the Spanish settlements merely aimed at the utilitarian exploitation of the new lands. By virtue of what title to property were the Spaniards in America? This was the main concern for the Spanish court, besieged by theologians and jurists anxious to have the king conduct that magnificent enterprise legally. Only in Spain could such a problem be raised which had been solved without wincing by other countries for whom force and title to occupation were one and the same.

After endless arguing Spain's leaders agreed upon the idea that the Spaniards were acting in behalf of the pope for the purpose of Christianizing the Indians. These people should not be enslaved nor ill-treated, as sons of God and Spanish subjects. If laws were occasionally violated that meant nothing, for nowhere were laws absolutely enforced. After all, Indians survived (with the exception of the Antilles) from New Mexico to Punta Arenas. But now, facts are less interesting for me than their significance. What I want to bring out is that Spain, as a whole, transferred herself to America. The cathedral of Santo Domingo is like any other Gothic cathedral built at that time in Spain, when the Gothic style was still alive. Afterwards we have Renaissance, Baroque, or Neoclassical monuments spread out over Mexico and many other Spanish countries until the end of

Spanish rule. In this way we can follow the evolution of European art in Spanish America from the sixteenth until the end of the eighteenth century.

And this is not all. The fact that the new Spanish countries were an enlargement of Spain brought as a consequence the fact that the Spaniards and natives intermarried and so produced a new race. We have already seen that for the Spaniard, man and his milieu form a vital unity. In the same way that Spaniards and natives were fused together, Spanish art and native art were combined according to the most original patterns. In Mexico and in other Spanish American countries there are numerous monuments representing this tendency toward harmony. During the Middle Ages in Spain herself a similar fusion was brought about between Christian and Muslim art, the so-called Mudéjar architecture. As a result of this tendency toward vital union, great care was taken to preserve in written form the oral tradition of Mexican history. Father Sahagún and others achieved this gigantic task. The Spaniards, however, destroyed the teocalis, because in them the Mexicans performed their ritualistic human sacrifices. They tore open their victims, then extracted their hearts, and by observing the palpitations on a stone, predicted the future. Some historians still say that the Spaniards destroyed Mexican civilization. But the Mexicans did not know the wheel nor the domestic use of light until the arrival of the Conquistadors.

Spain exploited the gold and silver mines because precious metals were needed for the furtherance of religious, moral, and vital ideals. Thus temples and palaces arose as the tangible expression of a spiritual purpose. They embodied the Spanish sense of life, always conceived in its wholeness in a deeper way than any intellectual construction. In this light we must understand the building of those 365 churches in Cholula, Mexico, as many as the days of the year!

Most of the American gold was spent by the Spaniards on such undertakings as churches, palaces, schools, hospitals, and printing presses. But this is not all. During the sixteenth century many believed that the Indians were authentic survivals of the primitive perfection of the Golden Age, even though they were the innocent victims of their false priests. Consequently, the bishop of Michoacán, Vasco de Quiroga, deemed it advisable to put into practice among the Indians the Utopia of Thomas More, shortly after this book was published. Thus the most utopian humanism became reality sustained by the power of an incredible will. Dream, illusion, ideal? Today less than ever can we adopt a disdainful attitude toward such superhuman conceptions.[3]

The human soul is expressed through the different cultures. Each one of them signifies an attitude toward divine problems, natural problems, and those of one's own conscience. Germanic culture, after centuries of rather crude existence, aspired to bring the world into a metaphysical and scientific totality, in which the German assumed the role of spectator. French culture tried to bring clarity to man's relations with himself and with his world. The Frenchman has devoted his best efforts to forging the expressive instrument of the French language through which he clarifies the entire confusion of human life. Since the seventeenth century French civilization has used thought to discipline life. Hence, for a Frenchman not to be intelligent is the worst condition for a human being.

But if Germany is "Wissenschaft" and France is "clarté," what is Spain? The fact that we do not have a ready formula is very significant. The reason is that, for a Spaniard, living is always an open problem, and not a solution to be confined in a slogan. To live or to die are for him equivalent points of departure which today, less than ever, cannot be considered an impertinence. Today it seems certain that only those countries able to face death will be able to survive. The best part of Spanish civilization is to be found in its religious, moral, and artistic achievements. Science and technique were activities in the service of human wholeness. According to a Spanish saying, one must do things "with all one's soul." A drama of Unamuno's bears the title, "Nothing Less than a Whole Man." I believe that any contact with Spanish civilization will pave the way for a new and fruitful humanism.

NOTES

1. I am going to give, however, a sample of his philosophical style: "Physico-mathematical reason, whether in its crude form of naturalism or in its beatific form of spiritualism, was in no condition to confront human problems. By its

very makeup it could do nothing more than search for man's nature. And, naturally, it did not find it. For man has no nature. Man is not his body, which is a thing, nor his soul, psyche, conscience, or spirit, which is also a thing. Man is not a thing. Man is a drama. His life is a pure and universal happening which happens to each one of us and in which each one in his turn is nothing but a happening. All things, be they what they may, are now mere interpretations which he exercises himself in giving to whatever he comes upon. He does not come upon things; he poses or supposes them. What he does come upon are pure difficulties and pure facilities for existing. Existence itself is not presented to him ready-made, as it is to the stone; rather, shall we say . . . in coming up against the fact of his existence, an existence happening to him, all he comes up against, all that happens to him is the realization that he has no choice but to do something in order not to cease existing. This shows that the mode of being of life, even as a simple existing, is not a being already. Man is not *a being already,* since the only thing that is given to us and that *is* when there is human life is the having to make it, each one for himself. Life is a gerundive, not a participle; a *faciendum,* not a *factum.* Life is a task. Life, in fact, sets plenty of tasks for us. When the doctor—surprised at Fontenelle's having reached the age of a hundred in full health—asked him what he felt, the centenarian replied: 'Rien, rien du tout . . . seulement une certaine difficulté d'être.' We ought to generalize and say that life always, and not only at a hundred, consists in *difficulté d'être.* Its mode of being is formally a being difficult, a being which consists in problematic toil. Compared to the sufficient being of the substance or thing, life is an indigent being, an entity which possesses, properly speaking, only needs. The star, on the other hand, continues forever along the line of its orbit, asleep like a child in its cradle" (*Philosophy and History: Essays presented to Ernst Cassirer,* ed. Raymond Kribansky and H.J. Paton [Oxford: The Clarendon Press, 1936], p. 302-303).

2. *LHE,* 1940, Part 1, pp. 9-11.

3. See Otis H. Green and Irving H. Leonard, "On the Mexican Booktrade in 1600: A Chapter in Cultural History," *Hispanic Review,* IX-1 (January 1941), pp. 1-40. "Books reflecting the best culture of the period were shipped to Mexico,—from Copernicus to Erasmus, from Greek authors to important philosophers of the Renaissance." At the end of their unusually interesting study Professors Green and Leonard say: "The implications of the foregoing facts are for the most part obvious. The liberalizing tendencies of the sixteenth century were not so effectively crushed as has been frequently asserted. . . . We have no right to condemn, in sweeping terms, the Spanish colonial regime as 'tres siglos de teocracia, oscurantismo y barbarie' " (pp. 13-14).

3

THE EVOLUTION OF CASTRO'S THEORIES
Guillermo Araya Goubet

When the most prolific and tenacious of the detractors of
Américo Castro's historical thought formulates the plan for
his own work, he refers to Don Américo in the following words:
"Because Castro has been the most subtle and audacious, the
most ingenious and original, and the most recent of those who
have examined the horizons of Spain's past, his theses are going
to be the ones most discussed in these pages."[1] If we exclude
the adjective "audacious" which can be interpreted in an
ambiguous way, there is in this sentence an unmistakable
recognition of the value of Don Américo's work and a declaration
of its absolute contemporaneity, a feature that enhances the
attraction that any intellectual effort holds for the reader. In the
abstract, this alone would more than justify the decision of
anyone interested in this subject to undertake the study of
Castro's work.

Examining his work from an historical point of view in the
broadest sense of that term, that is to say, including under the
word "history" any concern for the Peninsula's past (its
language, literature, thought, religious or cultural life), we
find that his writing falls into two stages. In the first stage
Castro worked with inherited points of view and ideas common

For a more complete treatment of the theme of this chapter by the same
author see: "Evolución del pensamiento histórico de Américo Castro," *Estudios
Filológicos,* no. 3 (Valdivia, Chile: Instituto de Filología de la Universidad
Austral, 1967), pp. 7-66; *Evolución del pensamiento histórico de Américo
Castro* (Madrid: Taurus, 1969); "Idea de la historia de Américo Castro,"
Estudios Filológicos, no. 7 (1971), pp. 7-35; "Evolución y proyecciones del
pensamiento de Américo Castro," in *Estudios sobre la obra de Américo Castro,*
ed. Pedro Laín Entralgo (Madrid: Taurus, 1971), pp. 41-66. Hereafter cited as
Estudios. Editor's note.

to Hispanists of his own and earlier times. Such ideas and points of view—according to Castro's own reflections on the matter—were characterized by a positive feature and by a negative one, which by necessity was inherent in the first. On the one hand, the same patterns and concepts were applied to the culture and history of Spain as to other European countries. But on the other hand, simultaneously, and almost inevitably, the historian became pessimistic and bitter on realizing that phenomena handled in this way revealed in their Hispanic manifestation a clearly deficient aspect when compared to the same phenomena in non-Hispanic Europe: "My Hispanic work aspires to be constructive and inspiring in a different form from the way I conceived it some forty years ago. At that time I tried to bring to light what there had been in Spain of Europeanism (Erasmus, 'Renaissance' thought, eighteenth-century Enlightenment) without previously plunging to the depths of collective feeling."[2]

The second stage of Américo Castro's writing begins when his traditional way of examining Spanish history reaches a critical point. With increasing clarity he attempts to understand Spain as a special historical phenomenon to which the historical categories that yield good results in explaining the past of other European countries are not applicable, or lead to misunderstandings and misinterpretations of Spain's history. He admits that if he had persisted further in his attempts at retrospective Europeanism, he would never have found out "which had been the agents and which the determining circumstances in the history of the present inhabitants of the Iberian Peninsula."[3] On deciding to explain Spain as an historical peculiarity within Europe, he also eliminated any attempt to assimilate or reduce Spanish values to equivalent or comparable events by basing them on a single scale of values, applicable to historical happenings both inside and outside the Iberian Peninsula. This position forces the historian not to juggle or shift around, for motives of patriotic nationalism, the true nature of Spain's past, no matter what face it shows, and even when at first it appears negative and difficult to accept.

Thus, Castro's work appears to be divided into two distinct stages, according to his evaluation of their merits, based, in turn, on the fundamental principle from which each one derives.

Even though there are works of exceptional value such as *El pensamiento de Cervantes* (1925) in the first stage, for him the second stage is more important and original, and the one that is normally taken into account when this author's name is mentioned. This second phase of his production is also the one that has caused the greatest impact within the ranks of Hispanism and provoked the greatest amount of hostile criticism as well.

Within Américo Castro's spiritual biography we must single out 1938 as the year when his Europeanizing view of Spain reaches a crisis. The beginning of the second phase was stirred up by the question of what role Islam had played in the history of Spain. Only after having written his essays on "Lo hispánico y el erasmismo" (1940, 1942) did he begin to understand the function of the Islamic element in Spanish history:

> Until not many years ago my opinions on this matter [the role of Islam in Spanish history] were the same as everyone else's. When in 1938 I wrote an essay on certain problems of the fifteenth and sixteenth centuries, I noticed how difficult it was to introduce the Islamic element into the historical picture, or to leave it out, and I ended up by improperly avoiding the question. At that time I didn't know how to approach the problem because the secular way of examining history and the authority of certain great historians still weighed heavily on me. . . . Only after having written my essays on *Lo hispánico y el erasmismo* as an aspect of "vital situations," did I clearly begin to see the meaning of Islam for history. The Christian Middle Ages then appeared to me as a struggle of Christian groups to subsist against a world that during the second half of that period continued to be superior to them in every way, except in boldness, bravery, and epic expression.[4]

The work in which Don Américo first expounded in detail his non-Europeanist view of Spain appeared in 1948 as *España en su historia,* in other words, ten years after he first realized how inadequate his historical perspective of Spain had been up to that time. Moreover, the book clearly conveys to the reader the great enthusiasm with which it was written. The author seems astonished and perplexed as he enters a fascinating and unknown world, but one which, nonetheless, had been there within his reach all the time. The first edition of his *Peculiaridad lingüística* (1941) also belongs to his second stage, though it is a less significant example than his 1948 book. *España en su historia* appeared as *La realidad histórica de España* in 1954. In spite of the change in title and modifications of earlier works, it still preserves, in essence, the characteristics of the first study. Only after the appearance of this 1954 edition, which is a thoroughly revised version of *España en su historia,* does Castro begin the revision and definitive maturation of his doctrine which culminates in the 1962 edition of *La realidad histórica de España.* Despite certain precise qualifications we shall make in due course, we believe that this date closes the last stage of his intellectual production.

Castro had already foreseen in his 1948 book the possibility of further development in his thought: "If possible, we should like to deal with how Spain continued living, but only by denying its living experience in the sixteenth and seventeenth centuries (*vivir desviviéndose*), when Hispanic possibilities became universal."[5] The work anticipated here is doubtless *De la edad conflictiva* (1961). But what came after the relatively minor revision of 1954 is not only a development of what he had previously thought out and clarified, but also a new level of depth in addition to some corrections and new ideas. In short, it was an authentic evolution in his historical thought. Obviously, the impetus for this evolution comes in part from the rather adverse criticism of his 1948–1954 work. But the stimulus also comes, in a very special way—as we shall see later—from a kind of inner impulse characteristic of Don Américo himself.

There are several pieces of evidence provided by the author himself which lead me to close the period of evolution regarding the main innovations in his historical thought with his second stage in 1962, even though he published other books after this date. In the 1960 prologue to the second edition of his *Peculiaridad lingüística rioplatense,* he already begins to make judgments to this effect:

> I have not sought to bother nor to reproach Spaniards or Argentinians—that is to say, myself—in the series of books and studies begun in 1940 with the *Peculiaridad lingüística* and culminating in *Origen, ser y existir de los españoles* and *Santiago de España,* passing through *La realidad histórica de España,* which in 1961 [it actually appeared in 1962] will appear with quite a few changes. In these twenty years my ways of seeing things have only been corroborated, thanks to the points of view which have been successively dominating in height the preceding ones.[6]

Note that Américo Castro refers to a greater "height" that his points of view had been attaining. This subsequent greater "height" is the result of the evolution of his ideas. The "culmination" that Castro believed he had achieved in *Origen, ser y existir de los españoles* turned out not to be entirely so, for this book was revised and also changed its title. In 1965 it became *Los españoles: cómo llegaron a serlo,* which was, in turn, incorporated into *Sobre el nombre y el quién de los españoles* (1973) with a new prologue.

In the 1961 prologue to the second edition of his *De la edad conflictiva* he states: "It is becoming more and more evident that the 'human structure' of the inhabitants of the Iberian Peninsula is not the one which has been assigned to them in books for at least seven hundred years. The reasons for such an anomalous situation are made clear for the first time—beyond any shadow of a doubt—in this volume." The final word has an asterisk referring to the following footnote: "Subsequent to this book a revised edition of *La realidad histórica de España* has appeared in which these ideas are developed further."[7]

Though the concepts of historical dwelling place (*morada histórica*) and living or functional context (*vividura*) already appear in the 1954 edition of *La realidad histórica de España,* only two years later Castro will write his essay on historical theory published as *Dos ensayos.* Constant meditation on historical theory and methods, in addition to the enormous number of subjects that he had to keep studying in order to test the efficacy of his points of view and answer criticism directed against them, convinced the author that no matter how much he revised and expanded his original work of 1948-1954, his cumulative work up to that point demanded a more clear-cut and definitive decision. He therefore decided to divide his major work into *parts.* The first part would contain the essentials of his historical concept of Spain, and the other aspects that were not a necessary part of this section would be left for another volume, no matter how important they might be from other points of view. This explains what Castro says in the prologue to the 1962 edition of *La realidad histórica de España*:

> Although this volume constitutes an entirety of ideas intended to establish a basis for any future essay on the history of the Spaniards,—and in this sense it is a completely independent

work—the author considers it only a "first part." Its continuation will lay greater importance on the social and cultural situation of Spanish Christians, Moors, and Jews, and on the forms of civilization born of the harmony and tearing apart of those castes, and from the ties and conflicts with Europe. It is to this harmony and tearing apart of castes that the slice of human reality known as the Spanish people owes its originality, its great achievements, and its problems.[8]

The preparation of a second part of the book is confirmed twice in the same work, and he reiterates this same intention in his 1965 prologue: "The first edition of this work came out in 1962, and it went out of print before I was able to finish the second part, in which I complete and expand upon what I expounded in the first part."[9] Observe that the author speaks of the first edition of this work referring to the one of 1962, thus revealing in a very clear way that for him it is a different book from the 1948 and 1954 works. Finally, in *The Spaniards* (1971), one of his last works, he speaks of having provided the "framework" for Spain's vital dwelling place and that someday he hopes to "furnish" that dwelling; in conclusion, he offers an outline for that possible history.[10]

A rough comparison of the 1962 book with the 1948 and 1954 versions will easily show that all the chapters on literary subjects have been removed from the later work. All the subjects that properly outline Spain's fundamental historical framework, according to the author's own view, appear in the 1962 book. There is a more classical and clearly ordered treatment of subjects, and his complete and calm control of a now totally mastered field is apparent. Basically, the major intuitions are the same as those in the 1948 book, but they are ordered and controlled from a "height" that clearly reflects a summit reached after a long evolution. Likewise, if we compare the 1966 edition of *La realidad histórica* with the 1962 version, we find that the 1966 book coincides line for line with the 1962 one, except for the inclusion of a long and important prologue written in 1965. This means that the author seems to be fully satisfied with what he has accomplished up to that year.

Castro confirms everything we have said until now directly by assigning to the year 1960 the definitive achievement of the highest level of his doctrine. The pertinent lines are "But when

Ortega was writing his work [*La idea del principio en Leibniz* 1947)], who had even the slightest idea of what the inner structure of Spanish life was really like in those years? We had just begun to pull away the veil around it, but total clarity did not come about until around 1960."[11] We are now at the threshold of *De la edad conflictiva* and the 1962 edition of *La realidad histórica*. The famous prologue to the 1966 edition of *La realidad histórica* is dated June 1965; in February of that year he had written the introduction to *Los españoles: cómo llegaron a serlo,* which is the revised edition of *Origen, ser y existir de los españoles* (1959). In it he points out:

> This now very revised book was ready to be printed in 1958 in circumstances quite different from the present ones. My points of view were not properly reconciled then; even though I felt certain about what the main problem of the Spanish past was, I still had to clarify, beyond a shadow of doubt, the way in which to present my theories. That objective was achieved in *De la edad conflictiva* and in *La realidad histórica de España* (1962).[12]

There is no doubt that with the 1962 edition of *La realidad histórica* Américo Castro achieves the fulfillment of the evolution of his thought as shown by everything we have said so far. But this should not be interpreted in a pedestrian way. His work as a writer continued after that year, always undertaking subjects concerned with Spanish history. In other words, quantitatively, his research continued, but after 1962 his works are based on what had already been published in a definitive and mature way. It is the productiveness of his doctrine already worked out completely in the 1962 edition of his basic work that enabled him to cultivate other fields, and not simply the evolutionary revision of what was written up to that point, as occurs when we compare the 1962–1966 editions with the 1948–1954 ones.

The appearance of his books after 1962 is explained in part by his desire to disseminate his ideas. As we shall see later, historical research, for Castro, is not an activity that is pertinent only in a special field of knowledge. History achieves its full meaning only when it creates an adequate awareness of the past in a community that recognizes that past as its very own. This is why he would say that "making the truth known is as important as having discovered it."[13] This is why it is necessary

to make it "easily accessible to everyone" (*bolsillable*),[14] or to
defend it as occurred with every inch of land won in the border
wars between Christians and Moors in Spain.

> The way in which I am carrying out this task of rectifying the
> history of Spain as it is now accepted is similar, in a certain way,
> to a border war, in which vanguard and rearguard actions
> alternate; the obstacles appear simultaneously in several places.
> There are those who attempt to invade the already conquered
> terrain, and then the enemy must be driven out. If I do not do it,
> no historian will come to help me.[15]

Evidence of the astonishing process of twenty-four years
(1938-1962) of intellectual activity that was needed to achieve
a satisfactory formulation of his doctrine of Spain's fundamental
historical autochthony is found within Américo Castro's writings
in the change of title undergone by several of his books. This
change had already affected to a certain extent the collection of
articles originally called *Lo hispánico y el erasmismo* (1942),
which appeared in book form in 1949 with the title *Aspectos
del vivir hispánico*. *España en su historia* (1948) became *La
realidad histórica de España* (1954); the English version was
entitled *The Structure of Spanish History* (1954). *Origen, ser y
existir de los españoles* (1959) appeared six years later as *Los
españoles: cómo llegaron a serlo*. The first edition of *Iberoamérica, su historia y su cultura* (1954) was originally published
as *Iberoamérica, su presente y su pasado* (1941). In some cases
he explains why he has proceeded in this way. In *La realidad
histórica*, for example, he says that "a greater interest in the
problem of what is the authentic reality of history" has obliged
him to revise the title of the work.[16] The original title *Origen,
ser y existir de los españoles* seemed to him "excessive and
unclear"; as a result he had to choose a new title "more fitting
of its main subject."[17] And when there is no change of title in
a book—a change always signifying a thorough revision of
everything expounded in the first edition—there are, nonetheless,
modifications or major innovations. The prime example of this,
described earlier, is the 1962 edition of *La realidad histórica*
when compared with the 1954 work. This is why the word
"renewed" or "revised" normally appears in all editions subsequent to the first one of any of his books.

The basic modifications included in the 1962 edition of *La realidad histórica* appear in chapters i and viii, and parts of chapters iii, iv, v, vi, and vii. Chapter i ("Statement of the Problem: in Search of a Non-Fabulous Reality") is intended to dismiss certain ways of historical interpretation, and chapter viii ("In search of a Better Social Order: Yearnings and Realities") describes the characteristics of Spanish anarchism and the Hispanic economy *a lo divino*. Chapter iii examines in even finer detail the problem of castes in Spanish history; chapter iv analyzes the concept of "vital dwelling place" (*morada vital*) and his concept of life as a center of historical happening. Chapter v contains new arguments on the non-Spanishness of the Romans and Visigoths. Background and explanations on the Moriscos are added in chapter vi, and vii attempts to explain the concept of the innate worth of a person based on his faith and proposes that it is desirable to be masters of history rather than its slaves. These modifications and innovations aim to establish a basis for every piece of historical research concerning events that transpired in the Peninsula.

What then are the most important differences among the three versions of this book? The first two are very close to each other. Both visibly preserve the concerns of the historian of literature and language that so strongly influenced Don Américo to write this book. This accounts for the predominance of literary and linguistic themes. In the final edition he has completely developed his conviction that cultural manifestations sprout up from a particular life that explains them, and that this life has to be categorized by history, a discipline with its own foundations. This categorization of life by history must precede the study of its different aspects, which, as its contents, can be treated individually. This is why the 1962 edition is the result of a journey toward the roots and the foundation of what had been treated individually in the two earlier editions.

What most clearly characterizes the 1962 text is its intention of formulating an overall historical vision of Spain and not simply its literature, language, or art, etc. This is done in a negative way by excluding all those subjects (language, literature, Catalonia, for example) which had been treated in the two earlier editions or which departed from the book's main purpose. These subjects would make up the second volume of the book promised in 1962. All of this justifies, in the 1966 edition, the author's calling the 1962 edition the "first edition" of this book. And the major differences between it and the 1948 and 1954 versions fully justify his doing so.

The negative criticism of the first two editions of his work contributed to Américo Castro's making an even greater effort to forge an authentic historical vision of Spain, one that would satisfy him and help him in his usual studies on language and literature:

> The disagreements and storms of incomprehension stirred up by earlier books of mine were useful to me [Remember that for him this 1962 edition is a "different book" from those of 1948 and 1954], thanks to them I realized that mental languages are sometimes as hermetic as the sounds of an unknown language. Once the depth of the errors in force had been plumbed, I extended my foundations to the region of the most elementary common sense, in order to syllabify my historical expression as slowly and distinctly as possible.[18]

It was when Américo Castro found himself in disagreement with the Europeanizing view of Spain that he began the long process of seeking out a satisfactory way to make the history of his people understandable in his own eyes. Spain resisted revealing her meaning to the historiographical categories that were useful for understanding the other European Romanic and Germanic peoples. One of the pillars of his doctrine is his insistence on discovering the autochthony of Spain's past and on not expressing this past with a nomenclature that is alien to it. And within the realm of what is Spanish, he is particularly interested in detecting the basic foundation rather than the leafy variety of its manifestations:

> My problem is especially that of the roots of what is Spanish and not its frondage. The subject of this and other works of mine is not politics, religion, economics, or Catalanism, oppressive centralism, technique, etc. Those who kindly suggest (and there are quite a few) that I write a systematic and well-structured work, do not realize that . . . my interest lies precisely in what is Spanish about the economy (for example), and not in the economy of the Spaniards.[19]

The peculiar historical autochthony of Spain also rests on the peculiar way in which what we can properly call the way of life of the Spaniards came about. Neither this people nor any other have been in existence forever, yet there is a specific moment in the past when the Spaniards begin to exist as a collective historical agent. The "livingtogetherness" (*convivencia*) of three distinct castes of believers after the coming of the Muslims to the Peninsula in 711 structured a very special way of life that was produced only in Spain. Religious tolerance—Islamic in inspiration—permitted the harmonious coexistence of Christians, Moors, and Jews until the end of the fifteenth century. The dominance of the Christian caste over the others led to the exclusion, subjugation, and expulsion of the other two, starting in 1492. Ultimately, the history of the Peninsular people can be summed up in the results generated by this "livingtogetherness" of the earlier centuries and by its breaking apart beginning in the fifteenth century:

> Let me anticipate a little of what I shall later develop: Peninsular life was reconstituted after the Muslim occupation in accordance with a system of castes based on one's being Christian, Moorish, or Jewish. After the disappearance of Moors and Jews from the social scene, respect for the pure lineage (*lo castizo*) of people—in other words, for their "Old Christian" ancestry—continued to be very intense. Awareness of the value per se of the caste now free from Jewish and Muslim contamination was strengthened and magnified thanks to imperial victories far from Peninsular soil. But within the mother country—once the coexistence of the three castes which had made possible the Christian hegemony was broken up and forgotten, once the collaboration of the Moors and Jews was suppressed—the Old Christians, deprived of common tasks, were paralyzed. The "honor" of being a Spaniard, the ideal of becoming fully one's self, of possessing "being," finally came to fill up the whole range of existence itself.
>
> This is, in brief, the marvel and the drama that I propose to make manifest, comprehensible, and worthy of esteem in the course of this book.[20]

And in 1965 he reiterates the same thing:

> Without the earlier intertwining of the three castes (Moors, Christians, Jews) and their purism, tension, and tearing apart between 1492 and 1609, neither *La Celestina* nor *Don Quixote*

would exist, nor would the Empire have been structured in that form, nor would it have been economically unproductive. Nor would the Spaniards have developed their religious, philosophical, and scientific culture as they did in the first half of the sixteenth century, nor fallen into the ignorance and intellectual collapse of the eighteenth century—a serious mortgage still not entirely paid off. I trust that in time such elementary truths will occupy the place of the legends and twisted truths now in effect.[21]

Just as Américo Castro's historical interpretation of Spain is born in reply to the fact that existing histories of Spain at that time left him unsatisfied, so, too, his theoretical historiographical work comes forth as a response to and rejection of the basic premises that served as the foundations for those works on the history of Spain.

Castro expressly rejects the simplistic statements of causality that seek to establish in the factors of race, geography, economy, and in the indelible psychology of human groups, the particular historical bias presented by a people's past.[22] As for what he refers to as the "living by denying the reality of one's existence" (*vivir desviviéndose*) of certain thinkers and historians who would like to extirpate from Spain's past certain centuries judged "guilty," Castro tries to explain the persistence of some of these premises as a "Spanish" way of understanding history. He says that "Spanish historiography, with its determination to include a past that does not belong to it [from Tubal to our time] and to exclude the most characteristic elements of its reality, [Moors and Jews] is an inherent part of the very process of Spanish life."[23] In a short sentence he also declares himself, without naming him, opposed to Toynbee's explanation of historical events, agreeing on this with Ortega, because he considers it to be somewhat simple: "This situation [living-togetherness—struggle of nine centuries between Christians and Moors] does not fit into the somewhat simple scheme of "challenge" and "response," nor is it resolvable . . . into climatic or economic circumstances that are always dependent on how man handles them."[24]

Nor does he agree with Unamuno's slipping off into his *intrahistoria*. He believes that Don Miguel's idea reflects instead an anguished life situation caused by the smallness of what was important in his time rather than a satisfactory category to distinguish what is properly historical from what is not. The "intrahistoria" may constitute at most the plain from which the tall peaks of what is truly historical may rise, but they are not a substitute for it:

> Unamuno was ignorant of the fact, or claimed to be, that the rustic life buried in its immediate present, lacked historical volume, either internal or external; it was temporally flat. It is evident that without a terrain on which to affirm himself, the architect could not erect towers and castles visible from a distance, from a distance in time. But to mix up the horizontal dimension with the vertical was a simple fallacy. Those who do things that are "historifiable" doubtless require traditional plains of humanity upon which to affirm themselves and expand—faithful people to believe, farmers to work, people to understand and suffer the new truths, etc. But the inhabitants of the world of "intrahistoria" and its well-worn customs and usages, cannot and should not come out into the light of any history; by themselves, as an absolute, they would serve as a subject for men-ants, myopic to life. . . . Born and raised among insignificant things, Unamuno, the same as other Spaniards who were not resigned to living at the level of vulgarity, withdrew to the fortress of his "intrahistoria." What he constructed *upon* this idea—dream and illusion—survives in enduring essays, novels, and poetry. The idea itself, as an historiographical instrument, is ineffective.[25]

In editions of his major work prior to 1962 there are no references to Unamuno's concept of "intrahistoria." The fact that he does take a position in this regard in that year is explained by the fact that in *Dos ensayos* (1956) he had already made his well-known tripart distinction between what is "Describable" (*describible*), "narratable" (*narrable*), and "historifiable" (*historiable*). This small book is an integral part of the body of his doctrine, which culminates in 1962, and therefore its contents must be handled as if it were just that in order to know what concept of history Américo Castro favors as a replacement for the points of view he has rejected.

History is based on a fundamental reality that precedes any analysis and exists prior to any investigation. This basic reality is life itself, and on it is based what Américo Castro calls historical life: "a functional activity whose reason for existence consists precisely in its immanent continuous tending toward a future from a present that includes its past."[26] Philosophers are the ones who investigate this basic object; it is enough for the historian to take it as his point of departure. Historiography must distinguish the subject agent, the structure, and the values of this historical life on the one hand, and, on the other, point out the different levels of perspective that make it up: the "describable," the "narratable," and the "historifiable," granting its attention willingly to that dimension of the past in the historical life that it is considering:

> The principal moments of it [the game of historiography] are to introduce the subject of the historical movement, in connection with its circumstances, expressing the values through which it acquires historical dimension. The conjunction of these three demands (subject agent, structure, value) permits the construction of a form of history in which life maintains its dynamic mobility; it also permits the ordering of past life according to different levels of perspective, as merely describable or narratable, or as a legitimate historiographical subject.[27]

Let us take up each of these concepts in turn.

The historical subject agent always appears in its collective guise; it is a human group. This group is united by its consciousness of "selfhood" (*ipseidad*), in other words, it is united because it knows, collectively and individually, that it is a continuation of what it was and an anticipation of what it desires to be. Its past becomes one with its present so as to determine its future. Normally its ethnic name sums up and symbolizes its consciousness of "selfhood." Within the historical autochthony of Spain there occurs the event, unparalleled in the Western World, that before it was *Spanish*—Aebischer has shown that this word is a Provençalism[28]—the ethnic marker of the Peninsular people's consciousness of "selfhood" was the term "Christian" created through the "livingtogetherness" of castes described earlier.[29] In another work he calls this consciousness of "selfhood" the ethnic "we":

> The history of those who are today called Spanish or English began to exist when certain peoples began to distinguish themselves as "we English" or "we Spaniards." And it will cease to be when the "we" of those who inhabit Great Britain or the Iberian Peninsula

give themselves another label. The moment in which we situate that "we" as a closed reality would be like the vortex of a triangle whose base would represent the happenings and events that are dependent on and inseparable from that "we." In the case of Rome, her history would extend *ab urbe condita* up to the time when the name *Romani* became fragmented into several others.[30]

Two questions are immediately raised as to the subject agent: When did that particular historical agent begin to exist and when did it cease to exist? Since 1954 Castro has called the particular structure of an historical agent its "dwelling place of life" (*morada vital* or *morada de la vida*). This term does not appear in *España en su historia,* but for all practical purposes, the concept is already in the book as well as in the others that concern us. The "dwelling place of life" is the entirety of dynamic "invariants" of a particular historical agent. It is the parabola drawn by everything encompassed by the consciousness of "selfhood" or the ethnic "we." It makes up what is particular to one people as opposed to another. The deeds and works generated by the historical agent find their true meaning within the particular mode of being from which they have arisen. This awareness of feeling themselves inserted in a particular dwelling place of life is called the "living context" (*vividura*).[31] Don Américo has also distinguished between the conceptual and the "experiential" (*lo vivencial*). Thus, for example, *gana,* "urge to do something" expresses the "experiential" aspect of *voluntad,* just as *honra* expresses that of *honor.* The "living context" would be the experiential aspect of the "dwelling place of life."

This "inwardness" is not a static and finished reality, analogous to a function or, as I shall point out later, to an "invariant." But "inwardness" is an ambiguous term. It may designate the *fact of living* circumscribed by a horizon made up of certain internal and external possibilities and obstacles, and in this case I shall call it the "dwelling place of life" (*morada de la vida*); or it may designate *the mode according to which* men live within this dwelling place or demonstrate awareness of existing within it, and then I shall call it "living context" or "living functioning" (*vividura*). The *vividura,* which may also be called the "functional structure," is the conscious awareness, the conscious aspect of the unrevealed operation of the vital dwelling place.[32]

The Inquisition that existed for three hundred forty years in Spain is not an institution that can be analyzed in a vacuum as if it were a physical body. Why it existed and what characteristics it had are to be understood only within the way of living and being—in short, of the "dwelling place of life"—of the Spaniards. It was, for example, impossible to establish the Inquisition in Naples, even though this kingdom belonged to Spain at the time of that religious institution's greatest activity. The place occupied by religion as a whole in Spain compared to France or England can only be explained by the diversity of the "dwelling places of life" in which religion is inserted in each case. The "dwelling place of life" is a concept which emerges as a necessity based upon the diversity of historical life.[33]

A change in dwelling occurs because of an historical "cataclysm." It is necessary to lose the consciousness of "selfhood," to speak another language, not to understand the previous one, and to orient oneself towards another form of collective life. When this occurs, one "dwelling place of life" has disappeared and the way is prepared for the appearance of another. A "dwelling place of life" will be retained by a people as long as its capacity not to let itself surrender to another people lasts, or as long as it sustains its existential impetus.[34] Its values constitute the highest creation that, in its diverse orders, the historical agent and its corresponding "dwelling place" can achieve. And their particular nature demands that they be "capable of living together" (convivibles) and that the historian capture them "experientially" for them to exist in their full power. Only this level of excellence of existence is properly "historifiable," the genuine subject of history.[35]

In a lower category than the "historifiable" exists what Américo Castro calls the "narratable" (lo narrable), and which covers everything that is "important" and is also at the service of human life. Narratable life encompasses everything that is called progress and civilization. The express form of these vital manifestations is the chronicle.[36]

The "describable" forms the lower stratum of collective life. This concept includes forms of life peculiar to primitive peoples in which the repetition or reiteration of their actions is the only thing that makes them endure, and not their exemplary or radiant quality as is true of historifiable or narrable values.[37] The conceptual distinction between these three categories of happening obviously does not prevent their being superimposed on the different historical agents.

History, for Castro, is thus constituted by the demands of selectivity and by a necessity for the "living together" of those values that make up its goal. This need cannot be dispensed with and it emphasizes the importance of the historian as a concrete person. Only by means of the historian's awareness, "from his experience of the life of others," is it possible to fathom the valuable past of any people. Without the historian to act as "medium" the most select achievements of the "dwelling places of life" are beyond our understanding:

> Historical writing demands that the historian enter into other peoples' awareness through his own awareness, in other words, to make use of his experience of the living of other persons. This brings to focus the problem of whether history is a science or a literary form. One must set sail in the ship of life with full awareness of what one is doing and where he is.[38]

A truly historifiable creation is able to free itself from those merely chronicable events that accompany its appearance. It has a profound effect on the human conscience and thoroughly obliges a person's experience to follow the same direction in which its valuable quality manifests itself. As Castro explains:

> In order to last as a value with possibilities for coexistence (convivible) it [that creativity which is properly historifiable] need not continue to be attached to its original circumstances, nor to be at the service of a partial or momentary need; its purpose affects the entire conscience of human life. And even though that conscience is not impartial, the interest that it satisfies is a different one. The person who truly knows how to use Plato or Galileo, the idea or image of a great historical age, or something like that, does not emerge from that experience in the same way as someone who uses a vehicle for moving from one place to another, no matter how progressive he may be. The historical experience, if it really happens at all, does not leave the life of the historian in parenthesis.[39]

By properly understanding the selectivity that characterizes history and the importance of the historian in historiographic endeavors, according to current theories, many ambiguities and misunderstandings of Don Américo's thought can be avoided.

Together with the biographical factor of Américo Castro's having shifted from philology to history—the first being a discipline in which the world of meaning is omnipresent—the rejection of traditional documentary positivism that characterizes the "professional" historians, must also have affected his criteria of selectivity for determining what is historical. Perhaps the importance attached to the exaggerated esteem for the documentary towards the end of the nineteenth century was also a factor. This documentalism was apparent specifically in the type of leveling, antievaluative scholarship and in the oblivion in which the supposed theoreticians of research were left:

> Specialists are reluctant to analyze and reflect on the hypotheses on which their very specialization is based. And this is said "sine ira et studio" because the same thing happened to me over a period of many years. When we were young we were required to have a knowledge of purely instrumental techniques, without any awareness of what the reality of the object over which we practiced that technique was like. Apply it to the manuscripts and to whether the battle was fought on an upward or downward slope, in August or March . . . But as far as wondering about the meaning and human value of those who were speaking, writing or thinking, that was neither scientific nor serious. One day a distinguished Indo-Europeanist said to me, when I asked about the relationship between language and the speaker: "ça c'est de la philosophie."[40]

How long have the Spaniards been in existence? When was the "dwelling place of life" we call Spain constituted? Castro's reply to these questions since 1948 has been invariable. From 1948 until 1965 (*Los españoles: cómo llegaron a serlo*), he strengthened his initial opinion by adding new facts and premises. From his point of view it is possible to speak of "Spaniards" only after 711, the year of the Islamic invasion of the Peninsula. The dwelling place of life was constituted precisely because of this self-awareness of "we Christians," which came into being among the Romano-Visigothic peoples in the north of that territory. This occurred when they themselves felt stirred by the arrival of that powerful invading people, which put to the test its will either to make itself felt in history or disappear:

When subsequently Spaniards are spoken of, we will have to understand by that term a kind of people who in the north of Hispania, in the eighth and ninth centuries, began by endowing their condition as Christian believers with a *sociopolitical dimension* and thus called themselves "Christians," a new event that was without parallel in the life of the Western world. This happened as a consequence of the form of life that men as powerful as the Romans in their Imperial age projected upon them, and whose ethnic name was also religious, "Mohammedans" or "Muslims."[41]

The cataclysm of the Arab invasion produced a violent break with the previous tradition of the Peninsular peoples and began to forge the birth of a new historical agent. The Romance tongues—and Castilian in particular—also began to acquire their peculiar characteristics about the same time as the occurrence of this enormous new event. If the Spanish historical agent, and the dwelling place of life that is particular to it, began to be constituted in the eighth century, the historifiable aspect of this people cannot go back beyond that period. Does this mean, then, that neither Isidore of Hispalis, nor Trajan, nor the "Dama de Elche," nor Argantonius constitutes part of Spain's historical past? The answer is definitely negative. We would not know exactly which "ethnic we" to attribute to the sculptors of that "most Spanish" lady of Elche, but we certainly could attribute Isidore to the Visigothic ethnic "we," Trajan to the *romani,* and Argantonius to a perhaps imperfectly realized Turdetanian "dwelling place of life."

Castro's dating of the beginnings of Spanish history in such a determined way has brought him a heavy cloud of criticism, because his position is a revolutionary one in this regard, when compared to the traditional stance taken by other historians. In one way or another, almost all the historians who studied Spain had interpreted everything that happened within the Peninsula as being Spanish. From the time of Father Mariana's *Historia de España* (1601), it was already customary to consider that "Tubal, son of Japhet, was the first man to come to Spain"—understanding by Spain a name that was suitable for embracing in its bosom Viriatus, Rodrigo Díaz de Vivar, Martial, and Quevedo. Jiménez de Rada in the thirteenth century, Florián de Ocampo in the sixteenth century and de las

Cajigas, Ramos Oliveira, Pericot, and Criado del Val in our own time have asserted the existence of a geological "Spaniard" born together with Peninsular geography. Such a phenomenon would have been possible because the "original" Spaniards would have transmitted biologically determined psychological characteristics to all the peoples who have been coming to the Peninsula since time immemorial:

> If all this were true, [omitted from *Realidad* (1962): (the eternal existence of the Spaniard)] those who today are called Spaniards would possess a uniform and static reality, repeated over thousands of years, with a magical ability to assimilate—while never losing its own forms of life—Ligurians, Iberians, Celts, Phoenicians, Carthagenians, Romans, Visigoths, Berbers, Arabs [added in *Spaniards* (1971): "and Jews."; omitted in *Realidad* (1961): "The sustained continuity of the original inhabitants, of the aborigenes, was established, according to popular belief, by biological propagation and by some accompanying 'psychological characteristics.' "] Alone among the peoples of the West, the Spaniard would belong to a kind of man untouched by time and circumstances, with an unchanging essence and psychic structure, unaffected by the necessity of facing himself, other men, and the world of which he is a part.[42]

But isn't Seneca "Spanish"? Aren't the Spaniards characterized by "Senecanism," their own brand of Stoicism? Seneca is an author who wrote in Latin and found himself inserted within the customs in force among the writers of the Roman Empire. If Seneca had been Spanish, Virgil would have been Italian. But Seneca does not appear in any history of Spanish literature nor is Virgil or Cicero found in any history of Italian literature. Moreover, nothing is farther from the truth than characterizing the Spaniards as any kind of Stoics. A people stamped with the invariant of "personal absolutism" is far removed from deserving the attribute of "apathetic" as characterizing its dwelling place. The same holds true for the "Spanishness" of other Latin-Roman writers such as Lucan and Martial, also born in Hispania; they are not "Spaniards," or proto-Spaniards either, by any stretch of imagination.[43]

In no way whatsoever should the qualifier "Spaniards" be given to the Visigoths. They are not Spaniards for the same reason the Franks are not French and the Longobards are not Italians. Spanish toponymy clearly reflects the separation between Romans and Goths in the Peninsula; for this reason the toponyms *Godo, Gudillos, Godinhos,* etc., abound opposite *Romanos, Romainhos,* etc. Castro shrewdly observes that among the Visigoths there was a clear distinction between Church and State—something that has been impossible throughout all the truly Spanish history, in which, in the Semitic way, both realities are identified as one. This situation made it possible for Isidore (afterwards the Saint) and other Catholic prelates not to feel inhibited because of their position from collaborating with the *Arian* king Leovigildo in bringing about the assassination of his son, the *Catholic* prince Hermenegildo; such a situation is impossible within the authentically Spanish dwelling place of life. It was not until 1586," one thousand years after what the Visigoths considered a vituperable rebellion, and the later Spaniards glorious martyrdom," that Hermenegildo was canonized, at the personal request of Philip II.[44]

In short, if we consider the "Spanishness" of the Iberians, Romans, Goths, etc., it follows that the French and Italians have also *always* existed. Thus, any pretension of considering as Spanish every people who have set foot in the Peninsula is patently absurd. Statements like those of Justinus are useless in defending the existence of the "eternal Spaniard." Concerning the Hispano-Romans Justinus says: "Corpora hominum ad inediam laboremque, animi ad mortem parati. Dura omnibus et adstricta parcimonia. Bellum quam otium malunt; si extraneus deest domi hostem quaerunt" (XLIV, I, i, 2). And Castro comments: "The psychobiological generalizations prevent us from getting at the functional peculiarity that we are pursuing, and besides, it would not be difficult to find other peoples, ancient or modern, equally long-suffering and abstemious."[45]

All the ethnic elements previous to the forging of the Spaniard, beginning with the eighth century, act only as a condition of what is Spanish, but which, in itself, is not yet Spanish.[46] Don Américo illustrates the relationship between the conditioned and the condition by saying:

> A principle that has guided me as I planned my historiographical tasks is that the conditioning elements of any human phenomenon must not be confused with what is conditioned by them. The books

of chivalry and the ballads (*Romancero*) made possible the *Quixote*, but the innovatively critical vision that Cervantes projects on them owes nothing at all to them.[47]

By joining his vision of Spain's historical autochthony to the historiographical hypotheses that serve as suitable instruments for his exegesis, Américo Castro also believed it necessary to replace the Europeanist terminology used to divide Spanish history into periods with a terminology that better reflects the peculiar autochthonous character of the background of the Spanish historical reality. There is already an isolated effort in this direction in *España en su historia*. There he states that one can speak of a single-age (*uniévica*) Spain because the Spanish dwelling place of life has always been immersed in its vital integralism and its religious orthodoxy without ever coming out of them.

In *De la edad conflictiva* he develops his point of view further. There he asserts that instead of the Spanish Middle Ages it is more appropriate to refer to those centuries by dividing them into three periods: (1) the age of the three castes living in harmony (until the end of the fourteenth century); (2) the age of the breaking-up of that harmony (until the seventeenth century); (3) the age of the absolute predominance of the Christian caste (from the seventeenth century until the present).[48]

Finally, he states in *Los españoles: cómo llegaron a serlo*, that instead of Counter Reformation, in Spain it would be more proper to speak of a "Counter Jewry" (*Contrajudería*) because this was the bias that religious intolerance, coming from the dominant Christian caste, took here.[49]

How can one find a clear and distinct criterion to judge the legitimacy of Américo Castro's historical thought? It could be that, no matter how brilliant and seductive his interpretation of Spain seems to us, his entire intellectual effort is no more than a theorization that is out of harmony with the real past of the Spanish people. I believe I have found the criterion that guarantees the truth of his doctrine in the fruitful results that characterize it. In one way or another, truth is always something abstract that has value beyond any concrete phenomenon. For this very reason true knowledge rests on certain basic premises that are productive, that serve to explain different phenomena always, of course, within the same sphere of reality in the light of those premises for which they were initially formulated.

How can the productive character of his doctrine be proved? On the one hand, there is the application that Américo Castro himself has made of his points of view to different aspects of Spain's past. As for history in a narrow sense, the exegesis that he makes of eighteenth-century Spain in the introduction to the 1966 edition of *La realidad histórica de España* and his synthesis of the history of the New World in his *Iberoamérica* are magnificent examples of the productivity of his thought.[50] As for literature, history in a broad sense, his books *De la edad conflictiva* and *"La Celestina" como contienda literaria* crown the foundations so firmly constructed in *La realidad histórica de España*. Eighteenth-century Spain, enlightened and rationalistic at the level of the reigning foreign dynasty, was only imported; it was a new style of furniture for the Spanish people who never gave up their own dwelling place of life, anchored firmly in their faith. But the rationalistic importations never thrived.

Ever since the expulsion of the Jews and the establishment of the Inquisition in Spain, every effort to make rational activity and the relevance of thought take root in Spain, at the edge of and without conflict with faith, has had the same fate. It always clashes with a strong, institutionalized reaction that defends the rights of "eternal Spain" (Spain based on the only true religion). And whether his name be Sanz del Río or Ortega, there are always men who insist on importing what is found in Europe and not at home. The expulsion of the Jews, the caste concerned with thought and science—the Christian caste asserted itself through its bellicose conduct— cut off forever the continuity of cognitive rational activity in Spain:

With better judgment than at other times, Unamuno says: "Sr. [Don Gumersindo de] Azcárate was profoundly right in believing that our culture in the sixteenth century must have been *interrupted*; otherwise we would not have forgotten it." Yet Unamuno believed that the past had not died, because "what is forgotten does not die but descends into the quiet sea of the soul, into its eternal part." In this case the phrase is graceful but inaccurate. What became of the thought of Vives, the humanism of Nebrija, Valdés, and Francisco Sánchez de las Brozas, the science of Pedro Núñez? "Culture" had to be imported in the twentieth century, and in risky, always precarious circumstances. Even the novelistic technique of Cervantes was reborn prodigiously in Galdós by way of the strong influence of Cervantes in other European literature.[51]

The history of Iberoamerica is explained, in its stages of colonization and independent life of the present-day nations, by the same ideas that explain the Peninsular past. The fantastic will, dazzled into conquering worlds in the imagination of the conquerors, extracted from the books of chivalry before their eyes had seen them, a will blinded also by the intoxication of the certainty that true faith produces, dazzled also by a faith that had triumphed secularly over the other two against whom it had fought—all this explains why in less than fifty years the conqueror's boot tread the soil of the Caribbean Islands, Mexico, California, and lands as far away as the incredibly distant kingdom of Chile. Anarchy, *caudillismo,* personalism, the social weight of religion—these are all factors of the present-day Iberoamerican nations which go back to a dwelling place of life that was structured in the Peninsula and carried from there to the New World.

The Age of Conflict is, for Castro, the period when racial purity of blood came to be the maximum criterion for judging the level of a person's social esteem—and not infrequently, whether or not a person would be exterminated. The literary theme of "honor" (*honra*) that pervades the theater and literature of the sixteenth and seventeenth centuries is the reflection, artistically reworked, of this profound and tragic conflict which ended the "livingtogetherness" of three castes. *La Celestina* reflected the Judeo-Spanish anguish of the time and was probably intended to destroy and reverse the traditional history structures.[52]

On the other hand, the productiveness of Américo Castro's thought is also revealed by the fact that at the present time it is almost impossible, in absolute terms, to approach almost any point of Spanish history and culture without stating one's position in regard to Castro's doctrine. The impact of his work is thus equivalent to an intellectual revolution within the scope of Spanish history and philology. One must either yield to his doctrine or have very good reasons for not doing so. But it is impossible to remain impartial; one always has to take a stand in this regard. And the path of interpretation that the scholar will have to follow will be determined according to the decision he makes regarding Castro's theories.

The acceptance of Américo Castro's points of view demands the restating of many problems that have been considered resolved until now. Within the areas of Spanish philology, literary history, and interpretation many points of view would have to be totally renewed and reconsidered. I strongly believe that, little by little, the literary research that recognizes its initial impulse as originating in Américo Castro's works will grow appreciably in coming years.

NOTES

1. Claudio Sánchez-Albornoz. *España, un enigma histórico* (Buenos Aires: Sudamericana, 1956), I, 18–19.

2. *RHE* (1962), p. xiv.

3. *RHE* (1962), p. xv; *SIH*, pp. 2–3.

4. *ESH*, pp. 47–48: *SSH*, p. 82. See also *AVH* (1949), (1970).

5. *ESH*, p. 635.

6. *PLR* (1961), p. 16.

7. *ECD* (1963), p. 23.

8. *RHE* (1962), p. xxviii.

9. *RHE* (1962), pp. 213, 351; *RHE* (1966), p. 3.

10. *SIH*, p. 584.

11. *RHE* (1966), p. 35.

12. *OSE*, p. 12.

13. *ECS*, p. 7.

14. *CCL*, p. 12.

15. *ECS*, pp. 136–137.

16. *RHE* (1954), p. 7.

17. *ECS*, p. 7.

18. *RHE* (1962), p. xxix.

19. *RHE* (1966), p. 7.

20. *SIH*, p. 49; *RHE* (1962), p. 29.

21. *RHE* (1966), p. 4.

22. *SIH*, pp. 24–29; *RHE* (1962), pp. 4–9.

23. *SIH*, p. 24; *RHE* (1962), p. 4.

24. *SAN*, p. 56.

✓ 25. *RHE* (1962), p. xix.

26. *SIH*, p. 106; *RHE* (1962), p. 116.

27. *DEN*, p. 11.

28. Paul Aebischer, "El étnico 'español': un provenzalismo en castellano," in *Estudios de Toponimia y Lexicografía Románicas* (Barcelona: CSIC, 1948), pp. 13-48. See also Rodríguez-Puértolas, p. 120 in this volume.

29. *RHE* (1962), p. 126; *SIH*, pp. 117-118. See also *RHE* (1962), pp. 108-109; *SIH*, p. 96-98.

30. *ECS*, pp. 68-69.

31. *ECS*, p. 63.

32. *SIH*, p. 98; *RHE* (1962), pp. 109-110. For a discussion of "experiential" (*vivencial*) see *SIH*, p. 296, n. 44; *RHE* (1962), pp. 273-274.

33. See *DEN*, p. 15.

34. *SIH*, p. 104; *RHE* (1962), p. 115. See also *SIH*, p. 189; *RHE* (1962), p. 156.

35. *DEN*, pp. 22, 25-26.

36. *DEN*, pp. 23-24.

37. *DEN*, p. 23.

38. *DEN*, p. 34.

39. *DEN*, p. 26.

40. *ECS*, p. 247.

41. *RHE* (1962), p. xx.

42. *SIH*, p. 24; *RHE* (1962), p. 4.

43. *SIH*, p. 177; *RHE* (1962), pp. 146-147. See also *DEN*, pp. 55 ff., for an analysis of the Spaniards' non-Senecanism, and Rodríguez-Puértolas, p. 115 in this volume.

44. See *SIH*, pp. 185-186; *RHE* (1962), pp. 153-154.

45. "They are made to suffer privations and travails; their spirit defies death; they are all of extreme frugality; they prefer war to peace, and if they have no enemy outside their country, they seek one inside it." *SIH*, p. 33, *RHE* (1962), p. 13.

46. *SIH*, p. 32; *RHE* (1962), p. 13.

47. *ECS*, p. 199.

48. *ECD* (1963), p. 41.

49. *ECS*, p. 33. For a fuller treatment of the role of the Jews and *conversos* in this volume see the chapters by J. Silverman and C. Johnson.

50. See also the chapter by M. Moríñingo in this volume.

51. *SIH*, p. 93; *RHE* (1962), pp. 65-66. See also the chapter here by R. Benítez on Cervantes and Galdós.

52. *CCL*, p. 156.

Part II
On the Formation of
Spain's Vital Structure

4

THE HISPANIC-ARABIC WORLD
James T. Monroe

Mention of the Arabs and their role in the formation of Spanish culture has for many centuries elicited a widely varying response among Spanish scholars, ranging from outright hostility on the one hand, to gullible and uncritical acceptance of the most extravagant hypotheses concerning Arab 'influences" on the other. The topic, furthermore, shows no signs at present of losing its capacity for arousing nationalistic passions. It is within this context of debate and controversy, often more personal and acrimonious than calmly reflective, that the ideas of Américo Castro about medieval Spain and the Arab role in its formation need to be placed. To begin with, a rapid review of the thoughts of some major Spanish scholars on the subject of the Arabs in Spain is necessary.[1]

It can be stated without much exaggeration that ever since 1492 Arabic studies in Spain have been largely in the hands of people who were politically dissatisfied with the main currents and trends of Spanish history. For example, the earliest Arabists were Moriscos who strove against great odds to salvage their secretly practiced religion, Islam, from annihilation, and their Eastern way of life from disappearance. These men did not succeed in their task, and during the seventeenth century Arabic studies practically vanished from Peninsular soil, at the very moment when they were beginning to flourish in the rest of Europe. In the eighteenth century Arabism found an enlightened protector in Charles III, and one of these Arabists, José Antonio Conde, became an *afrancesado* and was forced to

---

This essay is the result of work presented in two lectures; one at the Conference in Memory of Américo Castro held at UNCA on May 19, 1973, and the other at a meeting of the Society for Spanish and Portuguese historical Studies, held at at UCSD during March 22-24, 1974. *Editor's note.*

flee to France to save his life. His successor, Pascual de Gayangos, was a liberal and lived among liberal Spanish exiles in London during the early part of the nineteenth century. He was prevented from publishing in Spain because his ideas ran counter to the official version of Spanish history espoused by the Establishment intellectuals of his time. In the second half of the century it was the turn of the Krausist group, as well as of other progressive Spaniards of a liberal stamp, in particular Francisco Codera, to continue the study of Arabic. At the same time, pure-blooded Christian Spain began to marshal its forces for a traditional counter-offensive.

The call to battle was sounded by Francisco Javier Simonet, a bigot intellectually, and a Carlist politically, who tried to show that every achievement of note made by the Andalusian Muslims had been the result not of Eastern cultural importations, but of the fact that the Andalusians had been ethnically Spaniards and, therefore, he implied, racially superior to mere Orientals. Caught within a nationalistic cul-de-sac, future Arabists in Spain were able to stress not so much the Islamic and Eastern origin and nature of al-Andalus on the cultural level, but rather its Spanish roots, based largely on racial arguments. This attitude constituted an insidious undercurrent to the otherwise brilliant works of Julián Ribera and Miguel Asín Palacios.

In recent times, this tendency has to some extent informed the view of the past adopted by the Romance scholar Ramón Menéndez Pidal. In his view Spain represents an unbroken cultural continuity whose origins can be traced back as far as the ancient Celtiberian past. For a period in their history the Spaniards of the south were brought within the Islamic sphere of influence, though not thereby losing their Spanish identity, for they succeeded in Hispanizing Islam. They adopted the outward ways of Arab life, but remained Spaniards at heart.

The historian Claudio Sánchez-Albornoz, while he held essentially the same views, abandoned the restrained prose of his mentor, and in a somewhat strident tone he claimed that the Arab invasion was a national disaster from which Spain has never been able to recover, and the cause of all its present shortcomings. The Arab invasion, he tells us, inhibited development along Western lines (he admits by implication the thesis of Arab "influences"), and is the direct cause of Spain's failure to modernize. Given the limitations imposed upon these two authors by the fact that they were not professional Arabists and, therefore, had to rely on secondary sources, it must be admitted that they represent two intellectually honest attitudes insofar as they attempt to come to grips with a problem that was really marginal to their main interests in the Romance field. It should be mentioned, however, that the almost paranoic and decidedly anti-Semitic arguments put forward by Sánchez-Albornoz tend to make the reader suspicious of his conclusions.

In contrast, the claims made by Ignacio Olagüe in a recent book entitled *Les arabes n'ont jamais envahi l'Espagne*[2] are a travesty of honest scholarship. His method may best be described as an application to historiography of the techniques used in science fiction. This author rewrites history using only those sources that suit his thesis, in order to show that the very notion that the Arabs ever invaded and conquered Spain is a mere calumny concocted by an international conspiracy of Spain-haters to detract from his country's honor and prestige. Need it be added that Olagüe is a Falangist historian in the pay of those insidious forces that have controlled Spain since the last Civil War?

It can be seen from the above outline that the theme of the Arabs in Spain is far too often treated nationalistically and even as a political football rather than as a subject of serious scholarly research. From this point of view, the theme is broad enough to accommodate everyone according to his own individual tastes.

In this context, the ideas of Américo Castro about the Arabs are a positive continuation of the liberal and progressive current that predominated in the pre-Simonet era, insofar as they attempt to study the major achievements of Peninsular Islam as a prolongation of Eastern culture, studied in their own circumstances, without regrets, and evaluated according to their impact on Christian Spain.

It would be well to begin with Américo Castro's basic and revolutionary postulate according to which the Celtiberians, Romans, and Visigoths who occupied the Peninsula were not Spaniards any more than the Gauls were Frenchmen or the Anglo-Saxons, Englishmen. This postulate, which seems acceptable to most non-Peninsular European and American historians, places the rise of Spain as an individual nation at a far later date than that acceptable to most Spanish historians. It also has an important corollary. If Spanishness was something that grew and developed as a result of the Islamic conquest of Hispania, then it follows that Spanish historians need not regret the fact that their nation was "dishonored" by the Arab conquest, since those Peninsular peoples conquered by the Arabs were not yet Spaniards. There was, for Castro, a break in cultural continuity to be attributed to the deep impact of Islamic ways of life on the Christian population of what is today northern Spain, and out of this impact Spanishness developed. At the same time the peoples in the south of Hispania, the majority of whom eventually entered the Islamic community, had originally not been Spaniards either. In converting to the newly introduced religion, and contributing significantly to the development of an Islamic culture in the Arabic language, they saw no conflict with their Spanish cultural heritage, since this heritage had never been Spanish in the first place. At the same time it should not be thought that when the Arabs conquered Hispania their Islamic culture was fully formed and in its Classical stage. On the contrary, it was still flexible, in a state of formation, and willing to adopt native elements and influences. The latter, however, were Visigothic or late Roman, not Spanish. This observation is amply supported by the evidence of Arabic documents, which show in many ways that the culture that developed in al-Andalus followed many of the basic trends also encountered in other nations conquered by the Arabs. Thus, while the historian of Spain need no longer mourn over the subjugation of his biological ancestors, the historian of al-Andalus is faced with the task of studying Andalusian culture from within its Islamic context rather than appealing to an imaginary Spanish heritage.

The above remarks explain, furthermore, why the greatest historians of al-Andalus in modern times have been the Spaniard Conde,[3] who wrote before Simonet's nationalistic ideas diverted the course of Andalusian historiography in Spain from its proper channels; the non-Spaniards Dozy[4] and Lévi-Provençal[5] who were not affected by the Spanish nationalism that came to prevail in the second half of the nineteenth century; and the Spaniard Ambrosio Huici Miranda,[6] a liberal who was forcibly removed from his position in Spanish academia after the recent Civil War, and has subsequently conducted his research in isolation from the Spanish centers of learning.

From Américo Castro's point of view the term "Spanish Muslims" becomes an absurdity and can serve no useful purpose as an historical concept. This is not to deny, of course, that there were important Romance elements incorporated into Andalusian culture, but only to stress that they were Romance rather than Spanish, and that despite their importance on the level of folklore, they were not as dominant as the Islamic and Eastern forces that shaped and molded the high culture of the Andalusian state. Thus, for example, the strophic and, as it now seems clear,[7] originally accentual-syllabic *muwashshaḥs* and zajals invented in al-Andalus owe their source of origin to Romance folk poetry in meter and form, but not in content, since the themes used and the sentiments expressed in this kind of poetry fall predominantly within the sphere of Arabic literary and rhetorical conventions. While there is no serious reason to deny this Romance influence, it is quite obvious that strophic Andalusian poetry, the main bulk of which has been lost because it was of secondary interest to the native Arab compilers of the great Andalusian anthologies, never rose in their view above the status of a minor genre in no way equal in literary prestige to the Arabic poetry composed in the classical meters of the East.

The major merit of Castro is that he raised the study of this problem of cultural interaction above the more or less sterile positivistic level of influence studies. By applying philosophical concepts to history; by creating new concepts such as that of the "dwelling place of life,"[8] he was able to explain certain features of Spanish culture that had been only dimly discerned before him. It is the mark of a great mind that it not only sees a problem where none has been recognized previously, but that it then proceeds to invent the intellectual instruments with which to handle the problem it has defined. Where before Islamic influences on Spain had been poorly and rather naively perceived and defined, we learn, through the concept of the dwelling place of life that a people, namely, the Muslims who conquered al-Andalus, imposed upon that country, as upon other regions of the Islamic world, their own dwelling place of life within which religion, as a binding political and social, not to mention cultural force, occupies a central position. So central was this position indeed, that religious cohesion in what we refer to as the Islamic world, was to become the one connecting link joining disparate regions, once the fragile political structure of the caliphate collapsed. The Islamic community in fact, by learning how to develop a cultural life of its own under the aegis of religion, outgrew the need for a political unity and has been able to survive into the twentieth century in a state of total political fragmentation as surprising as is its remarkable cultural uniformity. Islam became, in a sense, a Roman Empire with no Rome and no emperor to rule it; a Papacy without a pope.[9]

In al-Andalus alone, this strong religious unity provides the explanation for the astonishing tenacity with which a people were able to continue being Islamic despite four periods during which central authority collapsed. What held together the *reyes de taifas* was not the fact that they were Arabs, Berbers, Sclavonians, or native Andalusians of Romano-Visigothic origin, but the fact that they were all Muslims, and that when danger threatened from without, they were persuaded to appeal to Islam as a rallying point against the Reconquest. Within such a dwelling place of life it is futile for the historian to seek to explain events by appealing to concepts of racial heritage. Allah, not inherited genetic affinities, came to be the main motive force behind Andalusian history.

Likewise, through the concept of the dwelling place of life Castro explains to us that historically the peoples of Christian Spain began to use their own religion in new and unsuspected ways in response to the challenge posed by Islam. When we use the term "Christian kingdoms" to designate those political entities that arose in the north of the Peninsula after the Islamic conquest, we should note that the application of a religious epithet "Christians" to designate a people ethnically is an indication of a lack of political self-awareness among those people. The usage has no precedents in Europe outside Spain. The different peoples of the northern area of the Peninsula in the early Middle Ages had no single term by which to call themselves other than that of the religion they shared in common. They called themselves collectively Christians, as the peoples of the south called themselves Muslims. It is curious to note in passing that in the Arabic chronicles too, the only common term used to designate the northern enemies was *Naṣārā* (Christians). Otherwise the people of the individual kingdoms were called *Jalāliqa* (Galicians), *Rūm* (Leonese and Castilians), *Bashkuns* (Basques and Navarrese), *Ifranj* (Aragonese and Catalonians). Castro also reminds us that while the Muslims went on pilgrimages to Mecca, the Christians developed their own anti-Mecca, namely Santiago de Compostela, and the fact that both these shrines fulfilled a cultural function that was felt to be parallel is shown by Ibn Darrāj al-Qasṭallī, a court poet under al-Manṣur, in a poem in which he congratulates his patron for having destroyed the city of Santiago (the event occurred in 387/997), and then urges him to proceed to the conquest of Mecca and the holy places of Islam from the Fāṭimids and Abbāsids:

> Your victory has covered the earth with universal light, just like the sun when it spreads daylight over the earth.

> From now on devote yourself to pilgrimage with Muslims, now that you have destroyed the Christians' shrine of pilgrimage,

> For [the Fāṭimids of] Egypt and Kairouan have expanded [their frontiers], while the eyes of al-Hijaz strain in expectation [of your arrival].[10]

Thus the importance of Américo Castro's historical thought lies in that it illustrates not how influences operate on a superficial level, but how on a deeper level the impact of a much feared and yet admired enemy can bring about developments along new lines. New ways of life that change old habits and modes of behavior can be learned from an emeny out of the sheer need and will to survive. Furthermore, the changes wrought upon Christian Spain by the Islamic presence had a positive and creative effect, for in Castro's words, "the tendency to conquer in order to spread Christianity was preceded in time by the conquest to spread Islam."[11] To put it differently, the Spanish Empire, with all its extraordinary achievements, would not have been possible as we know it, had not the Spanish people learned how to be religious imperialists from their Muslim enemies. And so, in reading Castro's works we come to the inevitable conclusion that medieval, as well as many aspects of modern Spain, cannot be understood properly if they are separated from the Islamic elements and context that formed so integral a part of them.

While it thus seems that the challenge of Islam on Iberian soil produced the Christian response Américo Castro has discussed at length in his works, it is no less true that this Christian response had profound and dislocating effects on Andalusian Islam, effects that in many ways altered its structure and made its history diverge in some respects from that in the Middle East. But here we are faced with many difficulties. A complete history of al-Andalus from 711 to 1492 has not yet been written from a modern, critical point of view. The periods best known to us are those of the Caliphate of Cordova, the age of the Almoravids, and that of the Almohads, thanks to the recent works of É. Lévi-Provençal,[12] J. Bosch Vilá,[13] and A. Huici Miranda[14] respectively. The *taifa* period and that of the kingdom of Granada are known only in part, through scattered and often outdated articles. But even the three comprehensive histories of particular ages now at our disposal are external histories. Their authors have succeeded admirably in collating the information contained in the major extant Arabic chronicles. The internal, or cultural history remains to be written, and voluminous works in Arabic on literature, philosophy, religion, mysticism, and law have hardly been tapped by historians. Today such a state of affairs can and should be remedied, because we are now in possession of a large number of published texts pertaining to these disciplines. It would seem reasonable that to the bare bones of history provided by the names, dates, and sequence of events contained in the chronicles should be added the flesh consisting of the history of ideas, aspirations, and cultural values recorded in many other scattered works. In what follows an attempt will be made to outline how such a task may be approached, tentative though the conclusions reached may be, and to show how such an endeavor can begin to reveal to us the inner pulse of al-Andalus.

Castro has shown that religion was the basic element cementing the structure of Islamic society, yet this preponderant role of religion as a cohesive force developed over a long period of time. As a twentieth-century Westerner, one cannot fail to be struck when one notes that the Mediterranean world of late antiquity lacked the notion of ethnic and religious solidarity that eventually came to characterize many areas and periods of European civilization. The Hellenistic and Roman Empires were agglomerations of many different ethnic and religious groups that were allowed to maintain their own distinctive cultural traits and religions under surprisingly tolerant political establishments, and when repressions did occur, they were normally carried out for political reasons. Along with the official worship of Roman emperors, for example, the cults of Isis, Mithra, and many other divinities were granted ample freedom. In Hispania, and as late as the Visigothic period, religion and race were not issues over which people felt it appropriate to lay down their lives, as the peaceful coexistence of a Romance and Catholic population with Visigothic and Arian rulers seems to show. Recent investigations have further demonstrated that the Christian clergy in Hispania often found itself siding with and protecting Jews persecuted by the Visigothic monarchs.[15]

When the Arabs entered the Mediterranean scene, they thus encountered a varied array of peoples accustomed to living in social harmony despite their religious and cultural differences. When they were invited to interfere in Hispanic affairs, they found themselves after a short time to be the masters of a land basically ruled by Roman law and institutions, although it had suffered from the general decline of urban life affecting the western regions of the former Roman Empire. Hispania had consequently reverted to an agrarian way of life and was controlled largely by local warlords and holders of great country estates. Themselves organized along tribal lines, the Arabs brought with them their old rivalries, but as they married into the native aristocracy they found themselves involved in local feuds for many years after the conquest.

In the East, the Umayyad state had based its power on the support of the Arab tribes to the exclusion of the conquered non-Arab peoples, but the perpetual rivalries between the tribes finally succeeded in undermining Umayyad authority. In contrast, the Abbasid regime had the foresight to appeal to the neo-Muslim elements of society from the moment it launched its revolution in Khorasān, and when the latter was won, it included them in the new government. The Andalusian Umayyads seem to have learned a lesson from the failure of their forefathers in the East. They began to adopt Abbasid policies, and as early as the reign of ʿAbd ar-Raḥmān II (206/822–238/852), local converts to Islam were given a share in the responsibilities of government, so that gradually the predominance of Arab over Muwallad came to be a thing of the past. This state of affairs was paralleled by the rebirth of city life. Toward the end of the ninth century of the Christian era, and under the emirate of ʿAbdullāh (275/888–300/912), certain events occurred which tend to confirm the accuracy of this observation. For one thing, the hegemony of Cordova over the provinces of al-Andalus reached its nadir, and the capital came to be under constant attack from the provincial warlords. The Romantic historian Dozy viewed this series of rebellions as a national war between Spaniards and Arabs, and saw the divisions as being drawn along ethnic lines, but a closer look at sources not known to him shows that such a conclusion is unfounded. First of all, who were these Spaniards and Arabs who crossed swords on the battlefield? The leaders of Seville were championed by the powerful Banū Ḥajjāj family, who considered themselves to be pure-blooded Arabs within the Arab patrilineal system, but who, as Ibn al-Qūtiyya informs us,[16] were in fact descendants of a marriage between Sarah, granddaughter of the Visigothic king Witiza, and a Muslim gentleman from the East. They thus derived their Arab affiliation from their paternal ancestor, but their landed wealth and aristocratic prestige came from the Visigothic royal line through the maternal side of the family.

In the mountains of Ronda, Ibn Ḥafṣūn, the descendant of a native Peninsular warlord who had converted to Islam, was classified as a Muwallad merely because it was the male side of the family that was native. He, like his Sevillian rivals, struggled at times against the central power of Cordova, and at times against his neighbors. In Granada, an Arab confederacy struggled bitterly both against Cordova and against Ibn Ḥafṣūn. Its spokesman, the poet Saʿīd ibn Jūdī, who headed a revolt against ʿAbdullāh on one occasion declared: "Tell ʿAbdullāh to flee, for the rebel has appeared in the canebrakes. Leave our kingdom, O sons of Marwān, for royal authority rightfully belongs to the sons of the Arabs."[17]

On the surface of things it appears absurd to refer to the Umayyads, of all Muslim dynasties, as though they were not Arabs, but when we read between the lines, we get a distinct impression that the Arab tribes of Granada no longer considered the Umayyads of Cordova to be favoring their ethnic interests. The Granadines therefore viewed the Umayyads as traitors to the cause of Arabism, no doubt because the latter had come to lean too heavily on Muwallad support for Arab comfort. The point to be derived from the above observations, is that what Dozy presented as a national struggle between Arabs and Muwallads was in reality a struggle between the central interest of urban Cordova and the local interests of agrarian warlords. Two ways of life, namely the urban and the agrarian had reached a point of conflict that was settled in favor of urbanism by ʿAbd ar-Raḥmān III in the early part of the tenth century. At his court the poet and prose writer Ibn ʿAbd Rabbihi, a descendant of a Muwallad, composed a vast encyclopedia of the Islamic humanities and sciences entitled *Kitāb al-ʿIqd al-farīd* ("The Book of the Unique Necklace").[18] Hardly anything of native provenance is mentioned in this work. Instead, it arranges and expounds the fields of knowledge that had already been canonized in the East, and with which an educated Muslim was expected to be familiar. Its purpose was, therefore, to promote the cultural Islamization of the peoples of al-Andalus regardless of their ethnic background for, on a cultural level, all Muslims could aspire to respect and equality.

In his book the author includes a section in which he discusses the Eastern movement known as the Shuʿūbiyya.[19] The latter had been a literary polemic initiated in the East during the ninth century by the culturally Persianized secretaries of state chanceries, who had argued that they and the non-Arab Muslims were superior in culture to the Muslims of Arab origin. Behind the more obvious racial appeal in the debate over the relative merits of Arabs versus non-Arabs there lay, however, a far more serious question, namely, whether Islamic civilization was to remain a narrowly provincial culture dominated exclusively by Arab ways of life and religious ideals, or whether it could be broadened in scope to include the sciences and philosophy of the ancient world still being kept alive by neo-Muslims of Greek and Persian origin. The question was ultimately resolved in favor of the latter, and Islam ceased under Abbasid rule to be an Arab monopoly, and entered a golden age as its horizons were extended to encompass the cultures of the conquered peoples of the empire.

One of the interesting things about Ibn ᶜAbd Rabbihi's treatment of the Shuᶜūbī debate in al-Andalus is that he was reviewing it after the matter had already been settled in the East. Furthermore, he is not original, in that he merely transcribes passages quoted from Eastern partisans of either side without ever mentioning the specific situation in al-Andalus or allowing his own views to obtrude. Instead he acts as an objective reporter, and throughout the discussion he seems to be implying that the issue at stake between Arabs and non-Arabs can only be resolved through a spirit of mutual cooperation, and that Islam is flexible enough to accommodate both factions. As a Muwallad servant of an Arab dynasty, the author is adopting an eclectic point of view that was in harmony with the generally supraracial policies of the Cordovan regime.

But at the same time that the intellectual leaders of al-Andalus were attempting to harmonize dissident groups by Arabizing them culturally in the broader Islamic sense developed in the East, they were also open to native influences. This is symbolized by the appearance about this time of the *muwashshaḥ* form of poetry, invented according to extant sources, by Muqqadam ibn Muᶜafā al-Qabrī, and first cultivated after him by his contemporary Ibn ᶜAbd Rabbihi. The *muwashshaḥ,* as we know it today, broke with the quantitative prosody of classical Arabic poetry by adopting the stress-syllabic meters of Romance folk poetry, from which it also borrowed strophic rhyme schemes not found in the monorhymed *caṣīda.* Its colloquial *kharja* often preserved fragments of traditional Romance women's songs. Thus in Andalusian literature as in the East, the concept of Arabism came to be broadened to include non-Arabic elements. Gradually, the older ethnic concept of Arabism came to be superceded and replaced by the newer ideal of Islamism, which allowed for the incorporation of foreign cultural elements. In an epic-style *urjūzà* narrating the campaigns of ʿAbd ar-Raḥmān III against local warlords as well as against the northern Christians, and composed by Ibn ʿAbd Rabbihi,[20] we find that a new polarity is proposed, namely one between those loyal to the Caliph and those disloyal to him. The disloyal groups, be they Arab or non-Arab, Muslim or Christian, are treated with severity, whereas the loyal subjects and vassals of the Caliph are rewarded generously for their support regardless of their ethnic or religious affiliation. It is instructive to note that when the Christian queen, Toda of Navarre, appeared in Cordova to affirm her submission to her Muslim sovereign, the poem stresses that she was warmly received and well treated, like any loyal Muslim vassal would have been.[21] The impression is unavoidable that at this stage in Andalusian history matters of state were still considered to take precedence over feelings of ethnic or religious solidarity, as had traditionally been the case in late antiquity.

Toward the end of the tenth century, under the rule of al-Manṣūr, we encounter the distinguished figure of the court poet Ibn Darrāj al-Qasṭallī cited above. Ibn Darrāj descended from an old Berber family whose ancestors had crossed the straits during the Arab conquest. And yet, despite being a Berber ethnically, he could aspire to occupy a privileged position at court because of his loyalty to al-Manṣūr, an ethnic Arab. Our Berber poet outlived the caliphate, and after its collapse, he toured the various *taifa* courts in search of financial security. Using the same panegyrical terms he had formerly applied to the Arab al-Manṣūr, he now sang the praises of Muwallad leaders of native ancestry, often including in his poems references to their illustrious Visigothic or Roman lineage. He even traveled for a brief period to the Berber lands of North Africa, but soon returned to al-Andalus in disgust, after having observed the lower cultural level of his ethnic brethren beyond the straits. In other words, as a sophisticated Andalusian poet, he felt that his cultural ties to Andalusian society were stronger than his ethnic ties to Berberism.[22]

Similarly, in the *taifa* kingdom of Denia, established by the Sclavonian and, therefore, neo-Muslim general Mujāhid, a court secretary of Basque origin named Ibn García took up the pen to compose a famous Shuʿūbī diatribe against the Arabs.[23] Appearing as it did, in the eleventh century, long after Shuʿūbism had become a dead issue, this work is somewhat puzzling. What in fact was its purpose? Was Ibn García whipping a dead horse? It has been suggested that Ibn García's treatise against the Arabs should be understood against the background of the westward wanderings of the Hilālī bedouins.[24] After the Fāṭimids had moved the seat of their capital from Tunisia to Egypt in the second half of the tenth century, they lost control of the Maghrib to the Berber Zīrid dynasty. In revenge, the Fatimids unleashed against the west hordes of Arab bedouins of the Banū Hilāl tribe, who proceeded to sack and plunder, and to reduce the flourishing urban life of North Africa to the state of ruin deplored by Ibn Khaldūn as late as the fourteenth century. Not enough attention has been paid by historians of al-Andalus to the second wave of Arabization that reached the shores of the Peninsula, but there are indications in available documents, particularly in the *Dhakhīra* of Ibn Bassām, that some groupings of Hilālī bedouins were immigrating to the eastern seaports, much to the horror of cultured Andalusians, and that they were being settled on the land by the princes of the Levantine seaboard. There are thus strong reasons to suspect that in attacking the Arabs as a race, Ibn García was merely using traditional themes taken from earlier Shuʿūbī literature to censure not so much the old Arab invaders of the Peninsula, who had by now been assimilated into a new urban society, but rather that second wave of Hilālī Arabs who must have appeared to him as uncouth barbarians. If this interpretation of the facts is accurate, Ibn García's reaction against the Arabs would prove to be similar in nature to that of Ibn Darrāj against the Berbers of North Africa. His work would be, not racially anti-Arab, but culturally anti-bedouin.

Up to this point things had gone well for the Muslims of al-Andalus, but with the momentum gained by the Christian Reconquest from the eleventh century on, the traditional Islamic attitude of religious tolerance was to be modified drastically. It should also be noted that on the Christian side, the war had up to now been waged on grounds that were not primarily religious, but rather political. With the increasing influence of the Order of Cluny in northern Spain, however, a new ideal aiming at cultural and religious standardization began to develop. It was destined eventually to destroy the ancient Mediterranean tradition of religious tolerance on Iberian soil. When a certain "monk of France," possibly Hugh of Cluny himself, sent a letter to Muqtadir ibn Hūd of Saragossa advising him to accept Christianity, a new attitude toward Muslims was beginning to take shape.[25] The sack of Barbastro by a combined army of papal, Norman, and Spanish forces, and the fall of Toledo profoundly impressed the rank and file of al-Andalus who had to pay for any losses in territory with ever more burdensome taxation. They became painfully aware of the relative helplessness of their own princes to stem the Christian advance, and acceding to pressures from below, the *taifa* leaders were forced to appeal to the Almoravids in an attempt to halt the enemy. The Almoravids ruled with the unanimous support of the Mālikī jurists, themselves often members of the lower classes, and spokesmen for a strong populist movement that placed severe limitations on the authority of the rulers. Gradually tolerance in religious matters, along with independence of thought, were sacrificed on the altar of expediency. At the same time that the great *zajal* poet Ibn Quzmān was introducing to Arabic literature the language of the common man along with themes derived from the marketplace,[26] the classical poet Ibn Khafāja was describing the orchards of Valencia, thereby finding escape from a burdensome reality by cultivating his own poetic garden. In one poem he speaks of science and philosophy in the following terms:

> Adopt the faith of one occupied with God's works, and of one who implores God; of one who endures sorrow, and avoid the secrets of science.

> Do not concern yourself with lengthy tomes or enquire into them, for you will gain nothing but sorrow and worry.

> When spears clash against each other, [strive to] be the lower end of the spear, for often is the upper end of a Yazanī spear broken.[27]

Out of dire necessity, the philosophers of al-Andalus, not to speak of its rulers, adopted Ibn Khafāja's advice to maintain a low profile. Ibn Bājja taught that the philosopher could never hope to influence society in a positive way, and that all he could aspire to was self-improvement.[28] Ibn Ṭufayl[29] and Ibn Rushd[30] added to this idea the doctrine that one version of truth was to be taught to the ignorant masses, another to the ignorant jurists, and yet a third was to be imparted in secret to the enlightened philosophers. A little knowledge was felt to be a dangerous thing because it could only lead to undermining the faith of the common people. Under the Almoravids, and later under the Almohads, the diatribe of Ibn García against the Arabs was interpreted as a potentially dangerous source of division within the Islamic community, and a number of jurists took up the pen to refute him *post mortem* with arguments that were primarily religious, not racial or ethnic in their approach.[31] At all costs, unity had to be preserved within the Islamic community and Arab culture was now redefined narrowly in religious terms. While non-Muslims were persecuted and expelled from Andalusian soil, the Romance elements in the *muwashshaḥa* were disguised or eliminated. The colloquial *kharja* disappeared, and the stress-syllabic Romance meter was often replaced by the classical quantitative meters of Arabic. By the time we reach the kingdom of Granada, where there were no Mozarabs, and where Romance was no longer spoken, Peninsular Islam had become a fossil of its former self, though it continued to produce literary and artistic works of rare beauty.

In a broad sense, the history of al-Andalus thus reveals a line of development. At first tribal and ethnic ties played a major role in an essentially agrarian society, but with the gradual spread of urbanization under the aegis of Islam, cultural broadmindedness and religious tolerance were favored. Ethnic friction was successfully kept at a minimum as long as the fortunes of the nation were on the rise and its leaders could count on popular support. It sometimes happens in history, that during periods of hardship and oppression the ruling aristocracies tend to become more universal in their outlook while the masses turn inward and approach fanaticism. Ibn Rushd tells us that in private he was able to discuss Greek philosophy freely with the enlightened Almohad emir Abū Yaʿqūb Yūsuf, who encouraged him to write his commentaries of Aristotle's works,[32] but the same Ibn Rushd was later stoned by the rabble and expelled from the mosque of Cordova when his views became known publicly. To maintain appearances, the emir was even forced to banish him from court for a decent interval. The mystic Ibn al-ʿArabī preached love and tolerance for all God's creatures, including the infidel,[33] and in one of his poems declared:

> My heart has taken on every shape; it has become a pasture for gazelles and a convent for Christian monks;
>
> And a temple for idols, and a pilgrim's Kaʿba, and the tables of a Torah, and the pages of a Koran.
>
> I believe in the religion of love; wherever love's camels turn, there love is my religion and my faith.[34]

Ibn al-ʿArabī soon realized, however, that Sunnī Andalus was not receptive to his teachings, and so he travelled to the East where he revolutionized the thought of Ṣūfism, leaving his true intellectual heritage in Persia.[35] Similarly, the mystic Shushtarī, who in his colloquial *zajals* sang to the common people of divine love, in one poem expressed his total alienation from society by declaring:

> A little sheik from the land of Meknès sings in the middle of the marketplaces:
> "What have I to do with men, and what have men to do with me? . . ."[36]

After emigrating to the East, Shushtarī died and was buried in Damietta. The Christian threat from without thus favored the development in al-Andalus of a strict orthodoxy unparalleled in the East, as I. Goldziher already noted years ago,[37] and this led to intellectual stagnation.

The comparison with the East leads to a final point. When Arab rule came to an end in Baghdad with the collapse of the Abbasids, Persian and Turkish dynasties continued to rule in the name of Islam. As the example of the Ottoman Empire shows, these non-Arab dynasties were acceptable both to Arabs and non-Arabs alike, because both the rulers and the ruled were fellow Muslims. In contrast, al-Andalus found itself inextricably caught in a web of its own Islamic weaving as the concept of ethnic identity gave way to one of religious identity, and finally the concept of religious identity came to be understood at its narrowest. When the Christian conquerors appeared on the scene, al-Andalus was unable to accept them as legitimate rulers because they were not Muslims. This feeling is clearly expressed in an oft-quoted statement attributed to Muꞌtamid of Seville, according to which that sovereign preferred to be a camel driver in Africa rather than a swineherd in Castile. After all had been lost, in the kingdom of Granada, an anonymous Morisco composed a poem to the Ottoman Sultan Bāyazīd II soon after the first revolt of Las Alpujarras.[38] In it he makes it very clear that the conversion imposed upon the inhabitants of Granada by Cardinal Cisneros was accepted involuntarily and under threat of death. He further appeals to the Sultan, in the name of Islam, to come to the rescue of his unfortunate Andalusian correligionaries. In this last gasp of Arabic poetry on Iberian soil one can sense that Islam had become the main cohesive force binding the Moriscos culturally, after their leaders had failed them politically.

The history of al-Andalus thus reveals a remarkable success in overcoming ethnic differences, followed later by the creation of a united front with which to resist to the end and at all costs the inroads of a new and intransigent form of Christianity that broke with the ancient tradition of Mediterranean religious and ethnic tolerance Islam had presided over and perpetuated for a time. It is ironic to think that in resisting Christian intransigence the Andalusian Muslims were themselves forced into a position of intransigence that eventually sapped their vitality and destroyed them.

Américo Castro has shown that the challenge of Islam on Iberian soil produced the Christian response of the Reconquest. At the same time, it should not be overlooked that in its earlier and more successful period, when Western Christendom was in disarray, Islam perpetuated the ancient Mediterranean system of tolerance throughout the lands it controlled. It was only after the tenth century, when Christendom began to organize itself on a crusader basis, that intolerance began to characterize Andalusian history.

It is the opinion of the present author, that the study in depth of medieval Spain from this point of view would open up new and unsuspected perspectives for the historian. It is to the credit of Américo Castro that he was the first to lay the theoretical foundations for such a line of investigation. This in turn invites one to reflect on the future of medieval Spanish studies in this post-Castro era that now looms before us.

Américo Castro has provided us with new tools and brilliant insights with which to come to a more accurate understanding of that cultural entity we call Spain. But if medieval Spain was the result of a cultural interaction between Christians and Muslims (not to mention Jews), as Don Américo has taught us, then one becomes disturbed to see the inadequate way in which this subject is handled in our major universities today. As they are presently structured, no department of Romance Languages or of Near Eastern Studies in this country is really a suitable place to study, if one wishes to learn about Spain as Castro envisioned it. Because Romance departments do not normally include Arabic or Hebrew studies in their curricula, they fall into the error of perpetuating a pure-blooded, outmoded, and one-sided account of the total picture. Similarly, Near Eastern departments do not offer any provisions for the study of Latin and the Peninsular Romance languages while, when it comes to Andalusian culture, they hardly treat it adequately, being more concerned with the heartlands of Islam. And so, this richly rewarding interdisciplinary field falls between two stools. It stands as an irony that Great Britain, whose Hispanists have on the whole not looked upon Américo Castro's ideas with any-thing approaching enthusiasm, already offers a combined doctor-ate in Arabic and Spanish in several of its major universities. Can the United States, where Don Américo taught for so long and to whose culture he contributed so much, afford to lag behind, honoring a great man in words only, while our teachers continue to repeat in the classroom ideas they no longer fully believe, simply because it is too hard a task to change established modes of imparting instruction to their students?

NOTES

1. The ensuing review is a brief summary of conclusions arrived at by the author in a more detailed study entitled *Islam and the Arabs in Spanish Scholarship (Sixteenth Century to the Present)* (Leiden, 1970).

2. (Bordeaux: Flammarion, 1969).

3. Antonio Conde, *Historia de la dominación de los árabes en España* (Paris: Baudry, 1840). New ed., Barcelona, 1844. English translation by Mrs. Jonathan Foster, *History of the Dominion of the Arabs in Spain,* 3 vols. (London: C. Bell, 1854. Reprinted, 1909-1913).

4. Reinhardt P. Dozy, *Histoire des musulmans d'Espagne jusqu'á la conquête de l'Andalusie par les Almoravides, 711-1110* (Leiden, 1861). English translation by Francis Griffen Stokes, *Spanish Islam: A History of the Moslems in Spain* (New York, 1913). A revised edition of the French original by E. Lévi-Provençal was later published in 3 vols. (Leiden, 1932).

5. E. Lévi-Provençal, *Histoire de L'Espagne musulmane. I: De la conquéte a la chute du Califat de Cordoue (710-1031 J.C.)* (La Caire, Imp. de l'Institute français, 1944). Spanish translation by E. García Gómez, *Historia de España musulmana hasta la caída del califato de Córdoba (711-1031 de J.C.).* Included as vol. 4 in *Historia de España,* edited by R. Menéndez Pidal (Madrid: Espasa-Calpe, 1950); edited as vol. 5 in the 1957 edition. See also the French 2d revised edition of E. Lévi-Provençal, *Histoire de l'Espagne musulmane,* 3 vols. (Paris, 1950-1953).

6. Ambrosio Huici Miranda, *Historia política del imperio almohade,* 2 vols. (Tetuán: Marroquí, 1956-57).

7. Thanks chiefly to the research of E. García Gómez. See especially, *Las jarchas romances de la serie árabe en su marco* (Madrid, 1965); *Todo Ben Guzmán,* 3 vols. (Madrid, 1972).

8. Defined in *SIH* (1971) pp. 97-104.

9. Gustave Edmund von Grunebaum, *Classical Islam: A History (600-1258).* Translated from the German by K. Watson (London: Allen & Unwin, 1970).

10. Ibn Darrāj al-Qasṭallī, *Dīwān,* ed. Maḥmūd ʿAlī Makkī (Damascus, 1961), poem no. 128, 11.37-39, p. 463.

11. *RHE* (1962), pp. XXVI-XXVII.

12. Lévi-Provençal, op. cit.; see n. 6.

13. Jacinto Bosch Vilá, *Historia de Marruecos: Los almorávides* (Tetuán: Marroquí, 1956).

14. Huici Miranda, op. cit.; see n. 7.

15. See E.A. Thompson, *The Goths in Spain* (Oxford, 1969).

16. Ibn al-Qūtiyya, *Ta'rīkh iftitāḥ al-Andalus,* edited by ʿAbdullāh Anīs at-Tabbāʿ (Beirut, 1957), p. 32.

17. Ibn Ḥayyān, *Kitāb al-Muqtabis,* edited by M. Melchor Antuña (Paris: P. Geuthner, 1937), III, 30 (Textes arabes relatifs à l'histoire de l'occident musulman, 3).

18. Ibn ʿAbd Rabbihi, *Kitāb al-ʿIqd al-farīd,* edited by Aḥmad Amīn, 7 vols. (Cairo, 1962).

19. Ibid., vol. 3, pp. 403-412.

20. J. T. Monroe, translation and commentary, "The Historical Urjūza of Ibn ʿAbd Rabbihi: A Tenth-Century Hispano-Arabic Epic Poem," *Journal of the American Oriental Society*, XCI (1971), 67-95.

21. Ibid., 11. 432-435, p. 94.

22. See J. T. Monroe, *Risālat at-Tawābiʿ wa-z-zawābiʿ (The Treatise of Familiar Spirits and Demons) by Abū ʿĀmir ibn Shuhaid al-Ashjaʿī, Al-Andalusī*. Berkeley, Los Angeles, London: University of California Publications, Near Eastern Studies, 1971) vol. 15, pp. 1-14.

23. J.T. Monroe, translation, *The Shuʿūbiyya in al-Andalus: The Risāla of Ibn García and Five Refutations* (Berkeley, Los Angeles, London: University of California Publications, Near Eastern Studies, 1969) vol. 13.

24. See especially the review of *The Shuʿūbiyya* by M. Brett, *Bulletin of the School of Oriental and African Studies of the University of London*, XXXIV (1971), p. 408.

25. See D.M. Dunlop, "A Christian Mission to Muslim Spain in the Eleventh Century," *Al-Andalus*, XVII (1952), 259-310; Allan Cutler, "Who was the 'Monk of France' and When did he write?," *Al-Andalus*, XXVIII (1963), pp. 249-269.

26. See E. García Gómez, *Todo Ben Guzmán*.

27. Ibn Khafāja, *Dīwān*, edited by Karam al-Bustānī (Beirut, 1961), 11. 1-3, p. 267.

28. See *Tadbīr al-Mutawaḥḥid: El. régimen del solitario*, edited and translated into Spanish by M. Asín Palacios (Madrid and Granada, 1946).

29. Ibn Ṭufayl, *Ḥayy ibn Yaqẓan: El filósofo autodidacto*, translated into Spanish by F. Pons Boïgues (2d ed.; Madrid, 1954).

30. See George Fadlo Hourani, *Averroes 1126-1198: On the Harmony of Religions and Philosophy*, E.J.W. Gibb Memorial Series (London: Luzac 1961), vol. 21. A translation, with introduction and notes of Ibn Rushd's *Kitāb faṣl almaqāl*.

31. Translated by J.T. Monroe, op. cit.; see n. 24.

32. Hourani, op. cit.; see n. 31.

33. Reynold Alleyne Nicholson, *Studies in Islamic Mysticism* (Cambridge: The University Press, 1921), pp. 149-161.

34. Ibn al-ʿArabī, *The Tarjumān al-Ashwāq*, a collection of mystical odes by Muhyiʿddín ibn al ʾArabī, edited and translated by R.A. Nicholson (London: Royal Asiatic Society, 1911), pp. 66-70.

35. Henry Corbin, *Creative Imagination in the Ṣūfism of Ibn ʿArabī*, translated from the French by R. Manheim, Bollingen Series, vol. XCI (Princeton: Princeton University Press, 1969).

36. Shushtarī, *Dīwān*, edited by ʿAlī Sāmī an-Nashshār (Alexandria, 1960), pp. 272-275. The poem is studied by L. Massignon, "Investigaciones sobre Šuštarī: Poeta andaluz, enterrado en Damieta," *Al-Andalus*, XIV (1949), 29-57.

English translation in J.T. Monroe, *Hispano-Arabic Poetry: A Student Anthology* (Berkeley, Los Angeles, London: University of California Press, 1974), p. 308.

37. In a lecture delivered before the Hungarian Academy of Sciences in 1876, and published in Budapest in Hungarian by that Academy in 1877. I have only been able to see the Spanish translation made by F.M. Pareja, "Los árabes españoles y el islam," *Actas del primer congreso de estudios árabes e islámicos: Córdoba 1962* (Madrid, 1964), pp. 3–77.

38. J.T. Monroe, translation and commentary, "A Curious Morisco Appeal to the Ottoman Empire," *Al-Andalus,* XXXI (1966), pp. 281–303.

5

THE MYTH OF SAINT JAMES AND ITS FUNCTIONAL REALITY
Emilio González-López

The historical thought of Américo Castro regarding the Iberian Peninsula has a special significance and one of its most illuminating confirmations is found in the particular case of Galicia. Castro reevaluates the role played by Galicia in the creation of the myth of St. James the Apostle and his shrine at Santiago de Compostela, as well as in the subsequent formation of the Hispano-Christian ideal. It was this ideal that gave vigor to the Reconquest of Spanish territory from the Muslims through the last part of the Middle Ages and kindled the enthusiasm that helped to shape the spirit and culture of the Spanish nation.

Américo Castro devoted two key chapters in the original and successive versions of *España en su historia* (1948) to this very theme: "The Origins of the Christian Reaction: Santiago of Galicia" and "Santiago, An International Attraction." He also dedicated a separate book, *Santiago de España* (1958), to the same subject.

Castro's ideas project new light on the value of the Jacobean myth itself in relation to its own origins and to the legend of the Apostle St. James, who is said to have brought Christianity to Spain. He offers us, besides, a new view of the role that Christian Spain, and especially Galicia, played in the creation of the myth that transformed the Apostle St. James into Santiago of Spain.

One of the aspects of Castro's broad, complex, and fruitful interpretation of Spanish history—the beginnings of the nation and the importance of the myth of Santiago in that emergence—was implied intuitively years before in the brilliant work, *Historia de la Iglesia de Santiago de Compostela*, written by the Galician historian Antonio López Ferreiro, a canon of Compostela.[1] This work is an authentic history of Galicia, which, for him, began with the discovery of the grave of St. James the Apostle in Compostela in the early years of the ninth century during the reign of Alfonso II, the Chaste, of Asturias. López Ferreiro anticipates Castro in not paying any particular attention to what happened in Galicia before that time.

Castro's work, on the other hand, signifies a complete break with the conventional theories of both professional historians and those Spanish essayists who concentrated on history from the closing years of the last century through the first four decades of this one. One of the basic assumptions of the old interpretation of Spanish history as defended by nineteenth-century positivists was the decisive role played by Spanish geography, and especially the Castilian plateau, in the formation of the Hispanic character and the development of the history of the Spanish people.

The impact of geography as one of the determining factors of history was adopted by the Hispanic symbolists, those members of the Generation of 1898 who were constantly searching for the eternal essences in the Spanish character. This view was held by the two great essayists of the Generation of 1898, Miguel de Unamuno, in his *En torno al casticismo,*[2] and Angel Ganivet, in his *Idearium español.*[3] Unamuno stresses the special condition of the land, especially on the plateau, whereas Ganivet emphasizes the shape of the Iberian Peninsula. According to these interpretations, the decisive geographical factor had doubtless been operating on the inhabitants of that region since the beginning of their prehistory, not to mention their history. Connected with this idea was the *ethnos,* or group of peoples who had developed on that land as an inseparable part of it and eventually became a *solera* (an aged wine used to strengthen new vintage) that helped to shape all the invaders of that territory.

Ramón Menéndez Pidal, on the other hand, tries to eliminate the geographical factor in the formation of the character of the Spanish people and the Spanish nation because he considered it more of a dead weight than a positive factor.[4] But the absence of the geographical factor in his theory was more apparent than real because it is, in fact, covertly present in accord with the symbolist or neo-Romantic philosophy that saw in Spain certain eternal, unchanging traits going back to pre-Roman or perhaps even to prehistoric times.

José Ortega y Gasset, the great thinker who devoted many essays to getting to the heart of the nature and value of Spanish culture, tried to ignore the geographical factor and the *ethnos* that dates back to remote times when history becomes myth in his work *España invertebrada*.[5] Ortega sought the interpretation of Spanish history in more recent events such as the Germanic invasions that put an end to the Roman Empire and opened a new historical era in Europe. Although his interpretation took into account both political institutions and cultural forms in looking for reasons and excuses to explain Spain's cultural vulnerability instead of her strong points, it failed to answer the real and most important question: What was the origin of the Hispanic world that had not been affected by the Germanic invasions to the same extent as other Western European countries? It is this Hispanic world, so untouched by the Germanic invasions, that Ortega considers the *solera* of the Spanish *ethnos,* and it is in this opinion that Ortega's separation from the traditional doctrine of a mythical *ethnos* is seen to be more apparent than real. *España invertebrada* did not go beyond mere hypothesis and, therefore, was not an in-depth examination of Spain's intense living experience, of the reality of her vital historical process.

Américo Castro's interpretation of Spanish history not only does not rely at all on the geographical factor, but it also ignores that *ethnos* associated with it. Nor does Castro feel any attraction for the historical hypotheses such as the one formulated by Ortega, which has its raison d'être in a desire to explain the progress of political and cultural institutions among the peoples of Western Europe rather than in any desire to delve deeply into Spain's own historical process. It is, of course, precisely in that process, in the midst of its sometimes tumultuous current, that Castro places himself in order to capture the crucial moment when the collective soul of the Spanish people becomes transformed into a Hispanic spiritual unity. He wants to seize that moment when a people acquires a collective awareness of being Spanish, and he finds it in the centuries when Christian Spain was being forged into a unity of life and culture in the struggle against the Moors. In the process, Castro studied the effects of the symbiotic relationship between the Christian, Arabic, and Judaic cultures. The main concern is, of course, the series of influences absorbed by the Christian world from each of the other two, for they boasted the superior culture. In fact, evidence of their profound influence was found not only in the conquered territories but it also extended toward the Christian kingdoms. In addition to these investigations, Castro uncovered the extraordinary role played by the myth of Santiago and his shrine at Compostela in the formation of the Hispano-Christian ideal of Reconquest against the Moors, in the communication between Christian Spain and the rest of Europe, and in the development of a Christian culture in northern Spain.

The myth of St. James the Apostle—by the term "myth" we mean a symbol of creative vitality functioning in the spirit of a people and in the formation of their culture—was the guiding light for the Christians in northern Spain and their primary source of encouragement in times of uncertainty and confusion. It is not necessary to delve in scholarly fashion into the authenticity of the evangelization of St. James in Spain or to study the transfer of his remains to the Iberian Peninsula and his burial at Compostela in order to appreciate the importance and historical value of this myth. What is important is the collective belief in the myth, and even more than the belief itself, the fact that it was the myth of St. James of Compostela which, year after year, brought thousands of pilgrims from all over Europe to his shrine. It was also the reason for the existence and survival of the Spanish Christian world against its powerful adversary whose borders stretched from the north of Spain to India and who was not only more cultured but also better prepared militarily and politically.

Seen in this light, the myth takes on the aspect of a catalyst in the history of Spain, of Christian Spain, and of Galicia in particular, where the grave and shrine of the Apostle are located, and to which the myth gives appearance and existence:

> The history of the Spaniards would not, in truth, have taken the
> course it did without the belief that there reposes in Galicia the

body of one of Christ's disciples and companions, beheaded in Palestine and carried to Spain by miraculous means; thus he returned to the land formerly Christianized by him, according to a tradition about which there would be no point in arguing, a tradition that had existed since before the arrival of the Arabs. Faith in the physical presence of the Apostle gave spiritual support to those who fought against the Moors; the extraordinary veneration in which he was held led to the erection of marvelous buildings both in Santiago and along the routes of the pilgrims, and it had cultural consequences both inside and outside Spain. The Order of Cluny and others of no less importance were established in the north of the Peninsula, attracted by the success of the pilgrimages; millions of people moved along the *via francigena,* or the French Highway, and those people kept up the connection between the Christian Spanish kingdoms and the rest of Europe. Art, literature, institutions, customs, and forms of linguistic expression interacted with religious belief in that prodigious historical event, which took place in the northwestern corner of Spain, the *finis terrae* of Christian Europe, where the outlines of the countryside are blurred by mists in which the land itself appears to be suspended.[6]

One of the most valuable contributions of Américo Castro's interpretation of the St. James Apostle myth is the importance he gave to the shrine at Compostela as a Christian Mecca not only for the Christians in northern Spain who were fighting the Moors, but also for all Western Europe and even for the Mozarabs or Christians living in the lands occupied by the Arabs in Spain:

> Similar miracles had occurred elsewhere occasionally, but without taking on transcendental importance; on the other hand, the peculiar circumstances in the northwest of the Peninsular transformed this miraculous appearance into an indispensable aid, consonant with forms of belief oblivious to the boundaries between heaven and earth, between miracle and the reality of experience. Indeed, with the belief in Santiago there appears a most original type of existence, something that I shall call integral "theobiosis," without an exact parallel in Christian Europe though probably akin to ways of life in Muslim and Jewish states where the notions of state and religion are confused. The cult of Santiago was not a simple manifestation of piety eventually useful in the struggle against the Moor. The truth is, on the contrary, that the belief emerged out of the humble plane of folklore and assumed immeasurable dimensions as an answer to what was happening on the Muslim side: a type of war sustained and won by religious

faith was to be opposed (not rationally, of course) by another
fighting faith, grandly spectacular, strong enough in turn to sustain
the Christian and carry him to victory.[7]

The Jacobean myth served to nationalize completely the figure
of Santiago in two ways: first, in Castile he became the leader
of the Christian armies fighting against the Muslim hordes,
symbolized by Santiago the Slayer-of-Moors. This equestrian
version of Santiago came to the aid of the Christian troops in a
vision during the battle of Clavijo. His very presence led to the
offering to Santiago, which was a tribute paid to the Church in
Compostela first by the kings of Asturias, and then by those of
León and Castile, and later by the kings of Spain, and even by
the towns in territories gradually recaptured from the Moors.
The second form of nationalization was the Galician one, in the
symbol of the saintly pilgrim whose presence was felt not only
in the shrine at Compostela but also on the Jacobean roads
leading to the Apostle's grave that crossed all France and much
of the Iberian Peninsula. The many hospitals, lodgings, and
small shrines scattered along these roads in the name of the
Apostle served, of course, to make his presence even more real
and immediate. St. James the Apostle was thus transformed into
the Santiago of Spain, as Castro says, "Hence, the reason for
calling Santiago of Spain the Santiago of my concerns. His
power to produce effective results functioned in real life for the
Spaniards, who, in turn, fulfilled themselves as believers in
Santiago."[8]

Santiago is the national saint of Spain; he was a creation of
Christian Spain in a way that was not to be repeated with any
other saint. This is why Ferdinand II, king of León and Galicia,
raised Santiago to the level of a national patron of Spain at the
time when these two kingdoms were separated from Castile. It
is also why there has always been strong resistance to the idea of
a second patron. Francisco de Quevedo, a knight of the Order
of Santiago, expressed this resistance in a particularly angry way
when he rebuffed the attempt by the Carmelites to make St.
Theresa of Avila the co-patron of Spain. He first defended the
exclusive patronage of Spain in his *Memorial por el patronato
de Santiago*, 1627, which he directed to the Council of Castile

and which resulted in his exile to his domains in La Mancha. The following year Quevedo wrote *Su espada por Santiago* (*His Sword for Santiago*) and addressed it to the Count-Duke of Olivares. These two treatises represent the most genuine expression of national sentiment concerning the Apostle Santiago and his value as a source of courage to the Spanish people in the face of threats from the Moors and other enemies later on.

In *Santiago de España*, Américo Castro emphasizes the vast difference separating Santiago from any other saint in the Spanish mind. He is something like a fresh breath of life in the Hispano-Christian world in the areas of politics, war, literature, and religion, particularly the Church of Compostela:

> Now I am particularly concerned with Santiago of Spain, so different, both vitally and politically, from all the other white-robed, equestrian, and martial figures of Christian Europe. Santiago spurred the bishops of Compostela on to new heights of apostolic dignity. The kings of León called themselves "emperors" in return, without any legitimate justification to explain this imperial rank, since they deliberately ignored the existence of an apostolic see within their very kingdom. Santiago rose like a cry of supportive hope in opposition to the enemy's Mohammed. The belief in Santiago maintained its tension in epic poetry, in the *Crónicas*, in Berceo, in the *Poema de Fernán González*, and the *Poema de Alfonso Onceno*.[9]

Castro writes that even if the Santiago of Galicia was a fusion of the two Jameses in the Gospels, St. James the Moorslayer had certain characteristics entirely foreign to everything that is said about either James in the Gospels, the Acts of the Apostles, the ecclesiastical history of Eusebius of Caesarea, and other hagiographical sources:

> The Santiago in whom the ninth-century Spaniards believed is one who later is mentioned in the *Crónica General* of Alfonso the Learned in the narration of the miraculous apparition of the Apostle at the battle of Clavijo (822 [*sic*]), in terms corresponding to what was expected by the people, accustomed by tradition to imagine Santiago, and before that the Dioscuri, as descending from above mounted on a white horse to favor his protégés.[10]

The author opposes those civil and ecclesiastical factions who, in coldly erudite fashion, go about in search of historical accuracy regarding the burial of Santiago in Compostela. For him, the value of this shrine lies after all not so much in the death or remains of the Apostle, as in his having given life to the most fruitful of Christian Spain's politico-religious beliefs:

> The error of these learned ecclesiastics consisted in trying to demonstrate what was rationally undemonstrable. Beliefs are established in the vacuum left by another belief, and they take root and gain strength by virtue of well-defined necessities and circumstances that exist independently of all demonstration. Vital phenomena (despair, hopefulness, the acceptance or rejection by the credulous or the skeptical person of the beliefs prevailing around him) cannot be treated as physical objects. Let us consider how absurd it would be to try to demonstrate "scientifically" that the body of an Apostle was brought from Haifa to Galicia in A.D.44, in the custody of angels, and that some eight hundred years later it gave signs of its presence. History, that is to say, the life of a people which is perceptible in its connected sequence of values, is not a sequence of "events," isolatable by means of logical abstractions. The important thing in the present instance is the intensity of the belief in Santiago and its immeasurable consequences; for it is conceivable that a marvelous occurrence might be "authentic" in the way in which the aforementioned ecclesiastics demand, and at the same time insignificant and sterile as an event connected with human actions and the creation of human values.[11]

Don Américo's words are an equally valid answer to those who challenge the Apostle Santiago's burial place as Compostela; they serve to reply to the scrupulous Catholics such as two of Spain's most famous historians, the Jesuits, Father Juan de Mariana,[12] a sixteenth-century Castilian, and Father Juan Francisco Masdeu,[13] an eighteenth-century Catalan, who both cast doubt on the preaching of the Apostle Santiago in Spain and even greater doubt on his burial in Compostela. Castro also answers the non-Catholics like Morayta,[14] in the nineteenth, and Juan Larrea,[15] in the twentieth century, who identify the grave of the Apostle Santiago with Priscillian, the first prominent heretical leader in Western Europe, beheaded in Trier, Germany, along with two of his disciples, by order of the Roman emperor Maximus. Priscillian was then taken from Germany to Galicia by some of his faithful disciples so he could rest in the land where his doctrine had most fruitfully taken root and where he had many followers.

It was with these masterful phrases quoted above that Américo Castro took part in one of the oldest and most persistent polemics in Spanish history, the question of the value and authenticity of the Jacobean legend, placing the myth of Santiago in the living reality of Spain's historical process rather than in the remote mist of the history of Christianity. For he perceived in it one of the most authentic and influential realities:

> Santiago's shrine arose to face the Mohammedan Kaaba as a display of spiritual force, in a grandiose "mythomachia" or struggle between myths. The city of Santiago aspired to rival Rome and Jerusalem, and not only as the goal of a major pilgrimage. While Rome possessed the bodies of St. Peter and St. Paul, and the Islam that had submerged Visigothic Hispania fought under the banner of her prophet-apostle, the ninth-century Hispano-Christians unfurled in their small Galician homeland the ensign of a most ancient belief, magnified in an outburst of defensive anguish. The presence of a powerful race of infidels over almost the whole face of Spain would necessarily enliven the zeal to be protected by divine powers in the Galicia of the year 800.[16]

The link between Christian Spain and the myth of the Apostle Santiago was so deep and so strong that Spain, and Galicia in particular, was for allies as well as enemies the Land of Santiago, the *Jakobsland* as it appears in Scandinavian sagas. It had the same significance for the pilgrims who journeyed along the Jacobean roads to the grave of the Apostle and to the crusaders who began to arrive in the Peninsula around the end of the eleventh century to participate in the enterprise of expelling the Muslims from occupied Christian territory. Christian Spain was also the Land of Santiago for the Arabs who launched their great summer attack (*aceifa*) led by Almanzor against Galicia and succeeded in destroying the apostolic city in 997. The only thing the Arabs respected on this occasion was Santiago's tomb. And so it was also for the Vikings, who came down from their frigid countries of the far north of Europe to invade these Galician lands. In the course of three centuries they destroyed the main bishoprics (Britonia, Iria Flavia, Tuy, Orense), and one of the bishops of Compostela, Sisnandus, even died fighting against them in the tenth century:

The Spanish Santiago is inseparable from the sustained longing of those who sought and found in him a support and meaning for their existence; it is inseparable from the lives of those who lived their belief, a defensive faith worked and reworked by the very need of the people to hold fast to it. The Moors in al-Andalus felt this so acutely that when Almanzor, at the height of his power, judged it necessary to strike the coup de grâce against the Christianity of the north, he destroyed and dispersed the religious communities of León and Castile and finally destroyed the temple of the Apostle (997).[17]

As extraordinary as the direct influence of the myth of Santiago was on the undertaking of the Christian reconquest of Spanish soil, this influence was even broader and deeper, since it included all forms of culture, from the very beginnings of belles lettres in Latin. And a fundamental part was played by the "French Road" or "Way of St. James" in this cultural and social labor. This "Road" was, in fact, a network of roads that crossed the various regions of northern Spain and converged at the border of Old Castile, after which the road passed through León and entered Galicia on its way to the shrine at Compostela.

The reformed Benedictine order of Cluny is also intimately linked to the French or Jacobean Road. Cluny first settled in Navarre in the eleventh century in order to undertake the arduous task of spiritual and material rebuilding in Christian Spain, an area that had been laid waste by the summer attacks of Almanzor, who had destroyed Pamplona and other Christian capitals. The Jacobean Road was the real riverbed of the European cultural current that came to fertilize Christian Spain, and it was also a part of the channel of another, lesser current of Judeo-Arabic culture that flowed back to Europe along the same Road.

Cluny was the first order of an international nature to be organized within the Church; it had a central house and under it a series of abbeys in every Christian country in Western Europe, especially in Spain. It was the first order to devise a social, political, and cultural plan within the society of its time; and the vehicle for this plan was the grave and shrine of the Apostle, the myth of Santiago, which projected its enormous attraction on Cluny. The Order put itself at the service of the Apostle and took charge of the Jacobean routes that led to

Compostela. Eventually it became so inextricably identified with the pilgrimage roads that the Way of St. James developed and flourished under the watchful protection of the monks. It was Cluny who sheltered the pilgrims at inns and hospitals and provided music and songs to comfort them on their long and arduous journey. And all the while, Cluny grew in international power and wealth, particularly in Spain, thanks to the Way of St. James.

> The shrine of Galicia stood out in various perspectives. To the Saracens it seemed to be a Christian Mecca, whose efficacy they sensed and sought to destroy. For the Spanish Christians we now know what it was. For foreigners who knew the strength and splendor of al-Andalus, the tomb of the Apostle became a place of pilgrimage as venerable as Rome. In the struggle against the infidel, one of the Lord's Apostles was making war in behalf of the good cause, and this miracle was taking place in the land of Galicia, a place hospitable to miracles and that also provided an opportunity for the improvement of material fortunes. When the monks of Cluny, in furthering the secular interests of the dukes of Burgundy, undertook the task of restoring scourged Christianity, they must have quickly seen the value of the pilgrims' route as a means of international expansion for the order. Through the diplomacy of the spirit, France got more effective results than she did by fighting the Moors. The crusade into Spain never won the hearts of the French people.[18]

Américo Castro points out the transformation undergone by Cluny upon its arrival in Spain and its swift awareness of the vital religious reality of the myth of Santiago in the form of a continual stream of pilgrims marching along the Jacobean routes:

> The new Christian states in the northern part of the Iberian Peninsula were bound to attract the attention of Cluny very soon, especially the Hispanic March (primitive Catalonia), which had been politically joined to the Carolingian Empire. But the later foundations in Navarre, and afterwards in Castile, resulted from the attraction exerted by the great miracle of Compostela, whose occurrence was known in northeastern France almost a century before the foundation of Cluny. Even though the presence in Hispania of a powerful Muslim state kept pontifical Rome in a constant state of alarm, it had not given rise to any crusade to liberate so many oppressed Christians. Yet, for one reason or another, the fact that the sepulcher of an Apostle of Christ had

appeared in a zone already liberated from the infidel must have aroused the interest of the abbots of Cluny, who were very eager to develop a spiritual and economic policy that was not practicable for Rome under the circumstances of the times. Abbot Odilon (994–1048) had sent to the altar of St. Peter (the one belonging to Cluny, not the altar in Rome) the gold and silver collected from the Moors which the kings of León and Castile paid to his order as a spiritual tribute.[19]

The religious and political intervention of the abbots of Cluny was motivated as much by the ideal of catholicity held by those monks as by the desire of the Christian kings of Navarre, León, and Castile to check the inevitable cultural pressure of the Muslims.

In this close identification between the Order of Cluny and the Jacobean pilgrimages—so fruitful in every aspect of the political and cultural life of the northern Christian kingdoms—Castro confines his discussion to the political aspects which led to the formation of both the Castilian-Leonese-Galician and the Portuguese nations. But he overlooked the effects of that identification on culture, as important as they were, because they do not fit within the bounds or purpose of his study:

> A religious order is an institution tied to worldly concerns, and the Cluniac monks were first and foremost at the service of the political interests of the duchy of Burgundy. History cannot be constructed out of sighs of lamentation and humns of joy, and the truth is that the most important consequences of the coming of Cluny to Spain were, regrettably, political. The Abbot of Cluny promoted the marriage of Alfonso VI to Constance, the daughter of the Duke of Burgundy; later the daughters of the king, Urraca and Teresa, married the Counts Raymond and Henry of Burgundy. León and Castile escaped from the provincialism (with an Islamic accent) of the Mozarabic tradition only to fall into an inadequate Europeanism—the net of Cluniac and Burgundian interests. While the Spaniards, under the protection of Santiago, were fighting against the Almorávides, the dioceses were being populated with French bishops, most of them of Cluniac origin, and the crown of Alfonso VI was about to pass to the head of a foreigner, Raymond of Burgundy. For Cluny, Spain was a second Holy Land in which she could create a kingdom like that of Jerusalem, only very near to the Pyrenees.[20]

One of the most important effects of this strong tie between the Order of Cluny and Compostela occurred early in the twelfth century when the famous Diego Gelmírez was bishop of Iria Flavia (the old name for Compostela). At this time this bishopric became the metropolitan church of Lusitania, thanks to the support that the powerful international religious order of Burgundy lent to the petition. Oddly enough, this change never attracted Castro's attention, despite its eminent political character and its great importance for the land now known as Portugal.

In 1119 Archbishop Guy of Vienne was elected pope, taking the name Calixtus II. He was the brother of the late Raymond of Burgundy, governor of Galicia, and uncle of Alfonso Raimúndez. Gelmírez, who worked tirelessly to see his dream of Compostela as the metropolitan church become a reality, took full advantage of an opportunity that was so favorable to his plans. He sent Gerard, a canon of Compostela to Rome. Like Guy, Gerard was French, and he entreated the new Pope, even before he had officially assumed his duties, to elevate Santiago to the rank of archbishopric. The pope kept the matter in abeyance, waiting for the Council to be held in Toulouse that same year. But just when everything seemed to be going well, Gerard's efforts were obstructed by a letter sent by Alfonso Raimúndez to his uncle, the pope-elect, through the archbishop of Toledo, the Frenchman Bernard, complaining about Gelmírez's actions which, it seemed, were intended to deprive him of the kingdom of Galicia. Calixtus, who dearly loved his nephew, wrote to Gelmírez demanding that he give his unconditional support to Alfonso Raimúndez's cause if he wanted Compostela to be recognized as an archbishopric. Alfonso Raimúndez was, of course, the man whom the bishop himself had proclaimed king of Galicia in the basilica of Santiago. In view of such a favorable attitude on the part of the pope, Gelmírez sent the Frenchman Hugh, bishop of Oporto, the person in whom he had the greatest confidence, to assure the pope of the unswerving support of the bishop of Compostela for Alfonso Raimúndez. Convinced by these avowals, the pope issued a bull on February 20, 1120, conceding to the Compostelan church the rights of the ancient ecclesiastical province of Mérida, which was still in Muslim hands, until such time as it was reconquered. In another bull the pope named Gelmírez pontifical legate in the districts of Braga and Compostela.

The new metropolitan church of Compostela supposed an anomaly in the ecclesiastical organization of Spain, inasmuch as its jurisdiction did not extend to the territory of Galicia, in which Compostela was embedded. The reason for this was that Calixtus II did not dare to wound the rights and financial interests of the old Galician metropolitan church of Braga, united at that time to the Order of Cluny as well as to the powerful Burgundian families who were related by marriage to the pope.

With the bull issued by Calixtus II creating the new archbishopric of Compostela, there were now two archbishoprics in the western part of the Peninsula: Braga, whose jurisdiction extended through what had formerly been Galicia, including the county of Portugal and the section north of the Miño, except the diocese of Compostela; and Santiago, which included the dioceses of León, Salamanca, Avila, Coria, Ciudad Rodrigo, Plasencia, and Badajoz, in present-day Spain, as well as those of Coimbra, Lisbon, Idaña (Guarda), Evora, and Osanova (Silves) in what is now Portugal. The future of Braga, the symbol of Galician tradition and history, was completely eclipsed in the shadow cast by Santiago de Compostela. This was also true of Lisbon and Coimbra, whose bishops were subordinate to Compostela rather than to Braga. This latter city, which at one time actually rivaled Toledo as the seat of the first church in "the Spains," saw itself stripped of ecclesiastical authority in Galicia and Portugal by the archbishop of Compostela. Gelmírez's decision also thwarted Braga's ambitions by taking all the bishoprics of the old Lusitania—among them Viseo and Coimbra in Portugal—away from her ecclesiastical jurisdiction and forbidding her from extending that national jurisdiction to others like Lisbon that were about to be reconquered.

Braga, the head and see of the old metropolitan church of Galicia, had suffered the humiliation of not being able to rely on her own bishop for four centuries, from the beginning of the eighth century when it was reconquered by Alfonsi I until the end of the twelfth century when the king of Galicia, Don García, named the first official bishop of his diocese. Consequently, "Braga, faced with a threat to her very existence, became the center of the movement for Portuguese independence. The bishop of the former Galician metropolitan see was one of the prime movers of this movement."[21]

One of the aspects of Hispanic history dealt with most extensively by Américo Castro is contained in the chapter "Santiago, an International Attraction," in the section entitled "The Independence of Portugal as the Indirect Result of Santiago." In this study Castro puts the accent of Portuguese independence on international factors. At the same time, he subordinates internal factors to these outside ones and does not give them the importance they had in reality.

> Burgundy tried to bring about in Castile what the Normans had done in England some years before; that is, she tried to install a foreign dynasty. The struggles with Islam and Castilian vitality caused the project to miscarry, but they did not prevent the birth of a kingdom on the west side of the Peninsula. That kingdom did not arise out of its own existence—as happened in the Castile of Fernán González—but out of exterior ambitions. The proof of this is that the Hispanic-Galician tradition of Portugal remained intact; the eloquent sign of this is the total lack of epic poetry. If the initial rebellion of the Portuguese had proceeded from the inner will of the people, as in Castile, Count Henry, or his son Afonso Henriques, would have been converted into epic themes. But the foreigners who came to populate the land were unable to create any kind of national epic, and the Galicians who came from the north went on being lyrical dreamers. Their will to fight came to them from the outside. The only poetic aureole surrounding Afonso Henriques is fitted to a model drawn from Galicia and Santiago: the victory of Ourique (1139), after which Afonso was proclaimed king, took place on July 25, the feast of the Apostle; Christ himself appeared in the course of the battle, and left the imprint of his five wounds in the form of the five *quinas* of the Portuguese coat of arms. Portugal came into being by struggling against Islam on her southern border (led and helped by northern European people) and against Castile with her rear guard. That little detached piece of Galicia developed the spirit of a besieged city which the Spain of Philip II with its grandeur among the clouds could not assimilate.[22]

Castro perceptively points out the difference between material and spiritual conditions in Galicia and Portugal at the very time when the separation of the two regions and the same language occurs—the former remaining as an integral part of Spain, and the latter starting down the road of its national expansion within the Peninsula and in lands across the seas:

> Missing the ferment provided by the Templars and the Burgundians and not forced to go outside himself to extend his land at the price of his blood, the Galician did not become a conqueror like his Portuguese brother. This is not to say that the Galician, beginning with his archbishops, did not fight bravely in the army of the kings of León and Castile, as he had once done against the Norman invaders. Clerics and knights were present, and to their honor, in the major battles: Almeria, Cordova, Seville, Tarifa. But they always participated as *auxiliary* troops of the king. Nor did the Galician language conquer new dominions as Portuguese was doing, because Galician imperialism was receptive and not aggressive, or, one might say, it consisted in irradiating the prestige of the Apostle throughout all Christendom; that prestige kept alive the special characteristics peculiar to Galacia.[23]

But without denying the value of the Burgundian stimulus, we should point out the presence of other expressly Portuguese factors that operated in a direct way as determinants of that separation. First and foremost among them, as I have already stated, is the rivalry between Braga and Compostela, which was also a more direct than indirect consequence of Santiago and her apostolic Jacobean shrine:

> A number of forces and factors intervened in the creation of the kingdom of Portugal, as is usually the case with great historical events. On the one hand, there were the reclamations demanded by Braga's bishop, the head of the Church in the western part of the Peninsula who saw his rights being threatened by the pretensions of the metropolitan in Compostela. On the other hand, there were the aspirations of the feudal lords in Portugal, the legitimate heirs of Galicia's insubordination first against the kings of Asturias and later against those of León and Castile. At that time, Castile and León were governed mostly by Galicians, the most prominent among them being Diego Gelmírez, bishop of Compostela, the metropolitan that was Braga's great rival. Both Count Henry of Burgundy and his wife Doña Teresa—who continued his policies of making Portugal independent of Castile— depended on these two elements, the ecclesiastical and the noble estates, which together made up the representative forces of the Portuguese nation. One of the most important factors in this movement was the attitude of the bishop of Braga; and, in turn,

the attitude of the Braga metropolitan was, to a great extent, determined by the ecclesiastical and civil expansionist policies of Diego Gelmírez.[24]

The serious blow dealt her now by Compostela was only the culmination of a series of offenses committed by the Galician bishops against Braga since the beginnings of the Reconquest. At first it had been a blessing for Braga that her bishop could take refuge in northern Galicia when the Arabs took over the whole north of Portugal. But that initial blessing became the source of her future undoing, because as soon as the first bishop from Braga to take refuge in Britonia or Bretaña (the diocese of the Bretone emigrants in northern Galicia, the first one to be reconquered), later to become Mondoñedo, died in exile there, the bishop of Britonia assumed the title of bishop of Braga. Later, the bishop of Lugo was the one who assumed the title of bishop of Braga and took charge of the reconstruction of the very city that had been reconquered by Alfonso I, the Catholic. At that time, however, the bishop of Lugo had not evinced the slightest desire to undertake the necessary reconstruction of the metropolitan see of Galicia, undoubtedly because this territory was very vulnerable to raids by the Arabs during the early centuries of Muslim dominance.

The repopulation of Braga was not completed until the end of the eleventh century, during the brief era of King García of Galicia (1065–1070), who was stripped of his crown first by his brother Sancho II of Castile and, upon his death, by his other brother who became Alfonso VI, king of a united Castile and León. In order to bring about the proposed repopulation, Don García had to overcome the opposition of the two most influential bishops in Galicia, those of Lugo and Compostela. These two opposed the plan, fearing that the reconstruction of Braga would harm the interests of their respective dioceses. According to Pierre David,[25] Don García took special pains to restore Braga and to name for this see a different bishop from the one in Lugo, who up to that time had retained the title of bishop of Braga.[26] Don García expended so much effort on this project that he managed to win the support of Bishop Vestrarius of Lugo, and Cresconius of Iria Flavia or Compostela.

In spite of her reconstruction and the naming of a bishop who was the metropolitan of all Galicia (including not only present-day Galicia, but also the reconquered part of the north and central Portugal and the diocese of Astorga in León), Braga continued to suffer insults at the hands of the bishops from Compostela. The most famous of them, Diego Gelmírez, as was already mentioned, was put in charge of inflicting the gravest damages. First, he was successful in having his church at Compostela declared independent from the metropolitan of Braga (1120), thanks to her apostolic fame; then, he managed to deprive Braga of her most famous relics of Galician saints which had been kept in the churches of Braga because of their connection with the former capital of Galicia.

Anselm Gordon Biggs maintains that as soon as Gelmírez had obtained pontifical recognition of his rights of ownership in the Braga diocese, he promptly moved to Braga itself in order to take advantage of them. In Braga he visited his possessions in the company of Gerard, the metropolitan of Galicia. With a large retinue, Gelmírez moved first to the church of São Victor, which had been ceded to Compostela by Alfonso III of Asturias in the ninth century and to which half of Braga belonged.[27] Gelmírez wound up his visit by carrying back to Compostela the relics of St. Fructuoso, St. Silvestre, St. Cucufate, and St. Susana which had been in their respective churches in Braga. These relics were the most valuable ones kept in the old metropolitan city as symbols of her tradition and prestige. Some of the relics, for example, that of St. Fructuoso, even signified past religious glories. The archbishop of Braga, along with the entire population of the former capital of Galicia, raised their voices in protest to the pontiff himself. They all felt great reverence for the relics of their saints and so felt understandably offended when the archbishop from Compostela wrested them from Braga. Pascual II did order Gelmírez to return to the church of Braga the portions of the city that Compostela continued to keep unlawfully, even after the exchange agreed on during Don García's reign.[28] The pope did not, however, force Gelmírez to return to Braga her most cherished relics. They remain in Compostela to this day.

The most humiliating blow of all was the recognition by Pope Calixtus II (uncle of the Spanish king Alfonso VII, the Emperor, born in Galicia when his father Raymond of Burgundy and his mother Urraca were governors of that region) of Compostela as the metropolitan church of Lusitania.[29]

It was Payo Méndez, bishop of Braga, who broke this pattern of hostilities against Galician influence in the affairs of Portugal, when he disregarded not only Gelmírez's authority as legate, but also his jurisdiction over Coimbra, a continual bone of contention among the mitered of Compostela, Toledo, and Braga. Payo Méndez consecrated the new bishop of Coimbra, a diocese that Compostela correctly considered subordinate to her because of its having belonged to the old metropolitan of Mérida. Gelmírez immediately sought support from the pope, complaining about Braga's conduct. Pope Honorius sent a letter to Payo Méndez reminding him of Compostela's rights over Coimbra. The bishop of Braga must not have responded to the letter because Honorius was forced to send him two additional reminders. The bishop of Braga persisted in his silence.[30]

To the influence of the Galician church of Compostela in much of Portugal, we must also add the considerable power of the Trava family of Galician nobles, especially the sons of Pedro Freylas, Count of Trava and Trastamara, who had been the tutor of Alfonso VII the Emperor. In 1121 the eldest of the Trava brothers, Fernán Pérez de Trava enjoyed such favor at the small Portuguese court of Doña Teresa, the widowed countess of Portugal, that he became governor of the counties of Oporto and Coimbra which, together with Braga, were the most important territories in the country.[31] His brother Bermudo Pérez de Trava was married to Urraca, the daughter of Teresa and sister of Afonso Henriques, the first king of Portugal. It was about this time that the love affair between the widow Doña Teresa and Fernán Pérez de Trava must have begun.

The battle of San Mamed (1128) was fought near both Guimaraes and Braga. That battle is unanimously considered by Portuguese historians as the beginning of their country's independence. Neither royal troops representing the Castilian king Alfonso VII, the Emperor, nor for that matter, Castilian or Leonese troops of any kind, fought on the Spanish side. It was a battle between Galicians and Portuguese. The first were under the command of the verger of the church of Compostela, Fernán Pérez de Trava. On the Galician side there were troops belonging to Diego Gelmírez, the feudal armed retinues of the Trava brothers, and some Portuguese troops loyal to the widowed Doña Teresa, who in this battle was an ally of her Galician paramour. Opposing these forces were the Portuguese troops commanded by Afonso Henriques, the son of Henry of Burgundy and Teresa, along with Braga's bishop Payo Méndez and almost all the feudal lords of Portugal.

The Portuguese were victorious in this battle and forced the defeated Galician troops to retreat to their territory. Doña Teresa went with them to Galicia where she died, although later her remains were returned to Portugal where they were placed in the cathedral of Braga to rest alongside those of her husband, Henry of Burgundy.

Portugal gained its ecclesiastical and feudal independence from Galicia and even more so from Compostela in the first step toward total independence from Spain. The archbishop of Braga won his freedom from the Church of Compostela as well. In the final analysis, it was Compostela rather than the Burgundian court of Castile or the metropolitan church of Toledo that was defeated in the battle of San Mamed, which became the symbol of Portuguese independence.

<h2 style="text-align:center">NOTES</h2>

1. Antonio López Ferreiro, *Historia de la Santa M. Iglesia de Santiago de Compostela,* 11 vols. (Santiago de Compostela: Seminario Conciliar Central, 1898-1919).

2. Miguel de Unamuno, *En torno al casticismo* (Madrid: Biblioteca Moderna de Ciencias Sociales, 1902).

3. Angel Ganivet, "Idearium español" in *Obras completas,* 7th ed. (Madrid: Victoriano Suárez, 1944), first published in 1897.

4. R. Menéndez Pidal, Introducción a la *Historia de España* (Madrid: Espasa-Calpe, 1962) I, IX-CIII.

5. José Ortega y Gasset, *Obras,* III (first published in 1921).

6. *SIH*, p. 381. The chapters on Santiago first appeared in *ESH* (1948) and were augmented and revised in successive Spanish editions of *RHE* and the two English editions. All quotes are taken from *SIH*.

7. *SIH*, pp. 382, 384.

8. *SAN*, p. 121.

9. Ibid., pp. 133-134.

10. *SIH*, p. 387.

11. Ibid., pp. 403-404.

12. Juan de Mariana, *Historia general de España* (*Obras*, Biblioteca de Autores Españoles, XXX, XXXI). The complete text in Spanish of his *Historia* appeared in 1601.

13. Juan F. Masdeu, *Historia crítica de España y de la cultura española*. 20 vols. (Madrid, 1783-1805).

14. Miguel Morayta, *Historia general de España*, 9 vols. (Madrid: Biblioteca Ilustrada, 1889-1899).

15. Juan Larrea, *La religión del lenguaje español*, lecture delivered at the University of San Marcos, 4 September 1951 (Lima, 1951).

16. *SIH*, p. 404.

17. Ibid., p. 418.

18. Ibid., p. 420.

19. Ibid., p. 423.

20. Ibid., p. 433.

21. Emilio González López, *Grandeza y decadencia del reino de Galicia* (Buenos Aires: Citania, 1957), p. 136.

22. *SIH*, p. 436.

23. Ibid., p. 442.

24. González López, op. cit., p. 137. See n. 21.

25. Pierre David, *Études historiques sur la Galicie et le Portugal du VIe au XIe siècle* (Paris, 1947).

26. Harold V. Livermore, *History of Portugal* (Cambridge: The University Press, 1947), p. 45.

27. Anselm Gordon Biggs, *Diego Gelmírez. First Archbishop of Compostela* (Washington, D.C.: The Catholic University of America Press, 1949), p. 43.

28. Ibid., pp. 121-122.

29. Luis García de Valdeavellano, *Historia de España. De los orígenes a la baja Edad Media*, 3d ed. (Madrid: Revista de Occidente, 1952) I, pp. 889-890.

30. Biggs, op. cit., p. 215. See n. 27.

31. Fortunato de Almeida, *Historia de Portugal* (Porto, 1942), p. 185.

6

A COMPREHENSIVE VIEW OF MEDIEVAL SPAIN
Julio RodríguezpPuértolas

One definition of Américo Castro's task might be a phrase coined by Manuel Azaña, the old liberal intellectual who served as president of the Second Spanish Republic: "tradition corrected by reason."[1] Américo Castro waged an incessant battle against the monolithic "giants" that plagued Don Quixote as well as against the intellectual dwarfs he found along his way. In the fifteenth century Antonio de Nebrija remarked, "I have never ceased to think of ways to drive out that barbarism which has established itself so firmly in all parts of Spain."[2] The noted grammarian's words are, doubtless, more applicable to Américo Castro than to their author. The starting point for all of Castro's meditations seems to be summed up in the following lines: "The greatest difficulty, the greatest cause of confusion I can discover in current historical studies, is their failure to incorporate the notion of 'human life' into their theory."[3] Castro's explication and interpretation of Spanish history was to be constructed primordially on this vitalistic foundation.[4]

Manuel Durán sums up Américo Castro's work in this way:

Beginning with the Middle Ages, he has steadily advanced toward the modern period . . . and in the process he has had to confront three different static interpretations of Spanish history: the one that seeks to erect an "eternal Spain" whose essence was fixed before the beginning of time, the one that interprets the Spanish Middle Ages as an exclusively Christian phenomenon and ignores the coexistence of Jews and Moors, and finally the "idyllic interpretation of the Golden Age.[5]

Castro's efforts are of unexpected importance in another sense, as the novelist Juan Goytisolo perceptively observes: "For the scholar or anthropologist who may some day be attracted to the subject, the attitude of a vast sector of Hispanic intelligentsia toward the man Castro and his work should provide a valuable indication of the usages and customs, the taboos and rules which for five, ten, perhaps a hundred years have maintained the cohesion and structure of that remarkable species intact, robust, and astonishingly alive."[6]

After this brief introduction I shall attempt to provide a compendium of Américo Castro's ideas on the Peninsular Middle Ages, the true touchstone of all that follows in the history and culture of Spain. Castro has rewritten the history of medieval Spain around the circumstance, unique in Europe, of the coexistence of three peoples, three cultures, and three religions. Most of what has happened in Spain since 1492 is incomprehensible, if proper attention is not paid to its roots in the Middle Ages. But let us begin at the beginning.

Don Américo starts by attacking the traditional reactionary idea that there exists a "millenium-proof" essence of that which is Spanish, the idea that endows the prehistoric cave painters of Altamira and the pre-Roman inhabitants of the Peninsula with the consciousness of their own "Spanishness." As Juan Goytisolo remarks: "We have been taught since childhood that the earliest inhabitants of the Peninsula exhibited the same traits we can observe in ourselves, proof of the permanence of certain indelible ethnic characteristics, a subterranean current running like the Guadiana, from Saguntum and Numantia, passing through Pelayo, the Cid, and Isabella the Catholic, to the epic defense of the Alcazar of Toledo in 1936."[7]

We should not think that the belief in "eternal" Spain and Spaniards is a phenomenon of outdated historiography, for the following lines were penned quite recently:

In spite of the passage of three thousand years (one hundred generations), few differences can be noted between the Tartessians and the modern Andalusians, not merely in their physical appearance, which must be practically the same, but in their temperament as well. It is enough to recall that the buoyant personality, the facility for dancing, and the fascination with bulls so characteristic of presentday Andalusians were qualities which already adorned them in Antiquity. What will the Tartessian texts tell us when they can speak, or I should say, when we come to understand them? I do not know, but of this I am sure: they will describe a perfectly Spanish society.[8]

Common sense and logic impelled Castro to reject this mythifying attempt to push the phenomenon of Spanishness back in time to that moment when *Pithecanthropus erectus* first made his appearance on the Iberian Peninsula.[9] Castro observes that the acceptance of this belief implies a corollary "that the Spaniard belongs to a species which exists outside time and circumstance, with an immutable being and psychic structure, unaffected by the need to confront himself, his fellow man, or his spatial and temporal circumstance."[10]

But now we come to the Roman conquest of Iberia, and we observe something truly remarkable. The great figures of Roman life born in the province of Hispania are quintessential Spaniards! This was the belief of Marcelino Menéndez y Pelayo and of many who have come after him. Roman emperors from Hispania bring the eternal characteristics of Spanishness to the imperial administration. Thus, for example, Trajan, who was born not far from a Roman city called *Hispalis*, after the Muslim invasion *Isbilia*, and finally, much later, Sevilla, was so Spanish that we are told *he spoke Latin with an Andalusian accent*. But it is the Stoic philosopher Seneca, *another Andalusian*, who really represents eternal Spanishness, in spite of Castro's belief that "only a hallucination explicable in terms of collective psychosis could transform Seneca and his philosophy into a Spanish phenomenon."[11] Angel Ganivet, who has been called a precursor of the Generation of 1898, affirms roundly that Senecan philosophy "is Spanish, and it is so Spanish that Seneca did not even need to invent it, because he found it already invented."[12] And Ramón Menéndez Pidal writes: "the Spaniard . . . carries within himself a particular instinctive or elementary Stoicism. He is a born Senecan. Seneca himself, the great refiner of Stoicism, owes a great deal to his having been born into a Spanish family."[13]

As Américo Castro has remarked:

Spaniards receive a terrible grounding in history. For centuries they have been bestowing upon themselves a retrospective imperial category. The idiocy of calling Trajan, Hadrian, Seneca, St. Isidore, and the rest Spaniards has made idiots of our young people. No one would call Augustus, Lucretius, or Boethius Italians, nor would anyone consider Charlemagne a Frenchman. As a result of this absurd historiography, the young Spaniard is educated in the simple-minded belief that his forefathers had already been everything it is possible to be in this world.[14]

But Don Américo perhaps forgot that there was a time in Italy when an attempt was made to teach that Augustus was an Italian, as Manuel Durán recalls: "Mussolini's rhetoric attempted to convince the Italians of our time that in fact they were the heirs to the Roman virtues and that they deserved to inherit the glory of the Roman Empire as well. The concrete and tragic circumstances of the last world war demonstrated the fallacy of that argument."[15] Thus we are led by a somewhat circuitous route to perceive the apparent ideological relationship between Fascism and traditional Spanish historiography.[16]

And after the Romans came the Germanic peoples—the Visigothic kingdom in the Peninsula. The traditionalists obsessively defend the idea of Germano-Visigothic Spanishness, an idea that José Ortega y Gasset carried to the extreme in *España invertebrada* when he affirmed that ever since the eighth century, with the destruction of the Visigothic state by the Muslims, Spain has been in a state of decadence, and that Spain actually is a decadence.[17] A fundamental result of this line of thought is the belief that Castile, as the faithful heir to "Visigothism"—evident in its literature, customs, and legal system—transformed itself into the militaristic, imperialistic country we all know, that is, into the nucleus of all that is Spanish. Unwilling to begin at zero, and desirous of creating some "noble" origins for themselves, traditionalistic Spaniards have sought them in the Roman past, the Germanic past, or in both at once, for as Castro has remarked, "the nostalgia for the idealized Visigothic kingdom nurtured the belief that Christian Spain had had an illustrious past."[18] But Castro has conclusively demonstrated that the Visigoths were not Spaniards any more than the Romans were. I shall cite here only one of the examples he adduces in support of his thesis, that of the rebel prince Hermenegild, a Catholic who revolted against his father, King

Leovigild, an Arian heretic. St. Isidore of "Seville" and many others condemned the rebel who was duly executed by the authorities. He was canonized, appropriately, during the reign of Philip II, at the personal request of the "Prudent Monarch." The story of Hermenegild indicates that the Visigoths had

> a not-yet-Spanish disposition of life, and a hierarchy of values that would have been unthinkable later on. No Spanish bishop has ever affirmed, publicly and solemnly, his support of a heretic, nor have bishop and heretic ever sought shelter together under the principle of the supremacy of a secular state. The Spaniards, who began to exist only later, could not comprehend the motives of the Goths; they made Hermenegild into a martyr and his father a monster.[19]

The phenomenon is a simple one: "The 'Gothic' in the tenth, eleventh, twelfth, and thirteenth centuries is nothing more than a survival. It does not renew itself nor act positively upon Christian life . . . The famous Spanishness of the Goths is simply an anachronism and a fantasy, founded upon retrospective anxieties and on nostalgia."[20]

But historians such as Menéndez y Pelayo have written that "the true and only Spanish race" is the Gothic,[21] while others such as Menéndez Pidal, who base their ideas on the indubitable relationship between what is Germanic and what is Castilian, abandon themselves to the dangerous game of tracing an uninterrupted line which wound up with the elevation of "Castilian" to the equivalent of "Spanish." This line of thought begins with the belief in the alleged structuring and "vertebrizing" function of the Visigoths in Roman Hispania before the Muslim invasion and the corollary belief that their courageous, nationalistic imperial spirit was inherited directly by Castile. And thus Castile, toughened up by her Gothic inheritance, enters the category of what the modern Germans have called *Herrenvölker*. Menéndez Pidal's Germanistic traditionalism thus reaches its greatest heights.[22]

But in the far-off year of 711 there occurred what the traditionalistic historians can only consider the maximum tragedy. Literally overnight, the Muslims invaded the Peninsula, destroyed the Germano-"Spanish" empire and orientalized everything in sight. What to do, then, with these Muslims, who, ever since then "are present in our strivings"? Menéndez Pidal believes that the Islamization of what he calls Spain was more apparent than real, that Hispano-Arabic culture was in fact rather unimportant.[23] Professor Emilio García Gómez, a distinguished Spanish Arabist, in speaking of the Alhambra of Granada, that extraordinary manifestation of the civilization of al-Andalus, refers to what he calls "the penetrating tragedy of many peoples who must live amid monuments which are not their own."[24] But we should not believe that only Spanish critics are guilty of saying this sort of thing. Consider these lines published, significantly in 1944, by the eminent German Romance scholar Karl Vossler: "The Spanish people struggled, from the Arab invasion of 711 until the expulsion in 1492, against Islam, defending their Christian faith, their national essence, and their liberty against the religion and the imperialism of Mohammed and his Afro-Asiatic hordes."[25] The same hordes that built the mosque of Cordova and the Alhambra of Granada, and who civilized and brought a new sense of culture to Western Europe.

Thus there began in 711 a long historical period that ended only in 1492 with the unification program carried out by the Catholic Monarchs and the formation of the first modern political state. But between the two dates lie eight hundred years of what is popularly known, in defiance of all logic, as the Reconquest. This spectacular name is based on the assumption that between the few groups of Christians who had taken refuge in the mountains at the northern extreme of the Peninsula and the conquerors of Granada at the end of the fifteenth century, there existed a continuous line of aims, ideals, and lived experiences and that both groups were, at the same time, the direct heirs to the "historic mission" of continuing the Visigothic state destroyed by the Muslim invasion. Ortega's remark about how something that lasted eight centuries could be called a "Reconquest" is well-known. Instead of the traditional term, Américo Castro uses the phrase "a long struggle between two uncertainties."[26] From this prolonged contact, which was by no means always violent, the concept of Spanishness began to sprout. With the progressive triumph of the Christian caste and from its contact with the Muslim caste, the notion of Spanishness began to take on decidedly religious connotations.

The Muslims were characterized by their being animated and sustained by a religious faith. This was an entirely new phenomenon in the West. For those who waged war against them, year after year and century upon century, religious faith also came to be the ultimate line of their vital horizon. . . . When peoples are believers rather than thinkers (and in this the Christians of the Peninsula were no different from the Moors), what is established by traditional consensus becomes the real and the true.[27]

Let us not fall into the trap laid by traditional criticism. I shall cite simply one passage in which Castro brilliantly sums up *a part* of the Muslim contribution to Hispanic forms of life:

The belief of certain Spanish Arabists that the Muslims "invaded" and "destroyed" a preexisting Spain which returned to its pristine state after evicting such undesirable tenants is simply untenable. A glance at the topography of the Peninsula will suffice to demonstrate the falseness of this assertion. "Pillagers" and "invaders" do not leave in their wake mountains, rivers, and cities whose names reveal the presence of a civilizing force, in the language and in every other aspect of culture as well. *Guadalquivir* is an Arabic name, and *Tajo* (Tagus) is Arabized (it should otherwise have been *Tago*). Without the Arabs there would be no cities with names like *Alcalá, Medina, Almunia, Alcolea, Alcázar, Madrid, Almansa. . . .* A Spanish house has an *aljibe* (well), *zaguán* (entryway), *alcobas* (bedrooms), *alféizares* (windowsills), *baldosas* (flooring tiles), an *azotea* (flat-roofed terrace), an *albañal* (drain). . . . Were not these houses built by workers called *albañiles* (bricklayers) and *alarifes* (architects), whose language was originally Arabic? In a Castilian or Andalusian dwelling there were *tabiques* (interior walls), *azulejos* (ornamental tiles), *argollas* (iron rings for hitching), *arambeles* (wall hangings), and other articles that served to *alhajar* (adorn) the house. *Alacenas* (closets) with *anaqueles* (shelves) were built into walls to hold objects kept in *azafates* (baskets). Water was kept cool in an *alcarraza* (unglazed jug) and was drawn up from the well in an *acetre* (bucket). Money was placed for safekeeping in an *alcancía*. The *algorza* was where grain was stored. The *almotacén* (inspector of weights and measures), the *albacea* (executor of a will), and the *almojarife* (royal tax collector) all needed a knowledge of accounting in their professions. *Cifra* (cipher) and *guarismo* (number) are also Arabic words.[28]

A good portion of Américo Castro's enormous work is devoted to the study of the Muslim-Arabic contribution to the culture that may now be called Spanish.[29]

The Visigothic past as an operative reality, began to recede into the distance. From this time on, history will be made in the form of an independent movement toward the south by six human groups—Galicians, Leonese, Castilians, Basques, Aragonese, and Catalans—who, like six horsemen begin their journey armed with their respective languages and life-plans. From the intersection of their lives, under the strong hand of Castile, would emerge the Spanish experience, the "dwelling place" of their existence.[30]

The Spanish people emerged from this constant dialectic over a period of eight hundred years—and we must not forget that the Christians of the north were and felt themselves to be no more and no less Spanish than the Muslims of al-Andalus or the Jews of Sepharad who mingled with both. The matter is, to say the least, extremely complex.

Let us consider the word *español*. In a work published in 1948, the Swiss scholar Paul Aebischer demonstrated with appropriate philological rigor that the term *español* is of Provençal and not of Peninsular origin, and that it did not appear south of the Pyrenees until the thirteenth century.[31] The repercussions of Professor Aebischer's discovery were nil; suffice it to recall that Joan Corominas omits the etymology of the term *español* from his great *Diccionario,* nor does it appear in the dictionary of the Real Academia Española. In view of this we might wonder, just as Castro did, "if this silence is because the subject was unimportant to those known as *españoles* or because it was too important?"[32] The question is not at all Byzantine, for it happens that a country—or groups of countries—was without a distinctive name at a time when England and France were already known by their present-day names. In the Peninsula, on the other hand, each "nationality" had a specific name: Castilians, Galicians, Leonese, etc. Together they were called Christians and not Spaniards. Now if all Europe was by definition Christian, it was meaningless for the pilgrims going to Santiago to distinguish the inhabitants of the Peninsula from themselves by calling them Christians. Thus, for very practical reasons, the Peninsular Christians came to be called *españoles* by the visitors from beyond the Pyrenees. The concept of Spanishness, then, appears enveloped in misty confusion literally from its very origins. Américo Castro fought to clear up this confusion indefatigably.

But what really upsets the traditionalistic historians is the presence of the Jews and the consequences of their participation in medieval Peninsular life. The Jews normally appear in histories of Spain on only two occasions: in connection with King Alfonso the Learned and his School of Translators in Toledo, and in connection with their expulsion from Spain in 1492. Inexplicably, in 1492 we suddenly find ourselves, almost as if by magic, endowed with a numerous and apparently dangerous Jewish community in the Peninsula, which Ferdinand and Isabella, spurred by their extraordinary religious zeal, had expelled. Of course, the histories point out movingly that a good percentage of these Jews had converted often en masse to Christianity. That is all we are told about a fundamental episode and a key period in Spanish history, a period that conditioned everything to come afterward. A truly surprising simplism is revealed as the norm in which so many Spaniards have been "educated" in recent years. In many cases the subject is reduced to the grossest Hollywood terms of good guys and bad guys— Christians and Muslims respectively.

The Jews, as we have seen, appear suddenly, first as translators and then as strange beings with no history during the preceding eight hundred years who are suddenly and inexplicably visited with the terrible punishment of exile. It is as though Fernando de Rojas had not written the *Celestina,* as if Juan de Mena, Hernando del Pulgar, Juan de Gato, Fray Iñigo de Mendoza and so many others had not expressed in their works the tormented life of fifteenth-century Castile from the unique perspective of their Jewish origins. It is as though King Ferdinand *the Catholic,* no less, had no Jewish blood in his royal veins. But the reality is different: "From the eighth century onward, the nuclei of Christian resistance had as their inevitable horizon and their fascinating model the life that was lived in the enemy's land, a land not simply Islamic, but above all *the setting for an Islamic-Christian-Judaic conglomeration.*"[33]

This conglomerate is precisely the foundation of what we call Spain, a Spain appropriately characterized as Mudéjar, crisscrossed by different racial-religious castes and by their various combinations:

The future Spaniards were made possible as a ternary combination of Christians, Moors, and Jews. The Christian caste could not have survived without the support and the impulse of the other two, and there came a time when all three considered themselves equally Spanish. Don Diego de Mendoza called the war against the Moriscos of Granada a war of "Spaniards against Spaniards." The Jews who labored and prospered in the presence of royalty and nobility felt themselves to be Spaniards.[34]

The situation appears in this way in the *Poema de Alfonso Onceno*:

> Knights throwing their lances
> all with great gaiety;
> and playing on horseback
> taking up shield and spear.
>
> And the Moorish people
> made great rejoicing
> the Jews with their Torahs
> received these Kings well.[35]

And in the *Libro de Buen Amor*:

> Powerful Don Carnal, by the grace of God,
> sends greetings to all Christians, Moors, and Jews.[36]

Ideas fundamental to Castro's system are, for example, that caste consciousness had a religious basis,[37] or that the Hispanic form of life consisted in the integration of the individual personality and in the absence of objectifiable thought.[38] We must limit ourselves to only a few examples from the forest of data generated and handled in order to avoid lengthening this essay intolerably. Let us recall, for example, the remarkable fact that the kings of Castile officially protected Jewish orthodoxy and persecuted the Karaite heretics, who accepted biblical revelation but not rabbinical tradition.[39] To Castro we owe the explanation of how and why Castilian prose in the period of Alfonso X (the Wise) was made possible by learned Jews;[40] the literary work of the Rabbi of Carrión, Sem Tob, and its relationship to later Christian thought and culture;[41] and finally the activity of the Medieval Hispano-Jews, present and participating significantly in all aspects of Peninsular life.[42] And with respect to the Hispano-Muslims, on the influence of Islamic tradition and customs on Spanish life, it is enough to recall Américo Castro's fascinating pages on the concept of holy war,[43] or on *hidalgo* and *hidalguía*,[44] on the Islamic roots of the Christian military-religious orders,[45] and, naturally, everything that refers to the cult of Santiago of Galicia: "If Spain had not been submerged by Islam, the cult of Santiago of Galicia would never have prospered. But the anxiety of the eighth and ninth centuries strengthened the faith in a Santiago, the brother of Christ, who, like a reborn Castor, would achieve innumerable victories, mounted on his white and radiant steed."[46] The need for drawing a parallel is obvious, since "the Moors considered Santiago a rival of Mohammed."[47] In the *Poem of the Cid* the Moors called on Mohammed and the Christians on St. James when they went into battle.

The intersection of the three castes reaches its maximum literary expression in the *Libro de Buen Amor*.[48] Castro considers it: "a Castilian reflection of Arabic models of an erotic literature of which this songbook of Juan Ruiz is a splendid example. His art consisted in giving Christian meaning to Islamic themes and customs."[49] It is a book which "moves dialectically, less between the notions of sin and virtue than between the experiences of vital impulse (effort, levity, agility, joy, etc.) and the obstacles encountered (rejection, disillusion, sorrow, etc.)."[50] In short, a Mudéjar book, in which "Castile, with her three religions, flowers as never before nor since."[51]

The peaceful coexistence and unique interlacing of mutual influences of the three Hispanic castes were broken at the end of the fourteenth century. The problem really dates from before that, however, from the period of civil war between King Peter I of Castile and his step-brother Henry of Trastamara, in which the side of the latter was triumphant and carried out its anti-Semitic program with fire and sword. This was an important aspect of the policy which opposed the real sovereign King Peter, a well-known protector of the Castilian Jews. Sem Tob had already invoked, in verses as prophetic as they are beautiful, a comprehension and a coexistence that were soon to be shattered:

> The rose is worth no less
> because it is born among thorns,
> nor good wine because
> it comes forth from a withered vine.

> The hawk is worth no less
> because it is born in a rude nest,
> nor good moral tales because
> it is a Jew who writes them.[52]

In the year 1391, as a result of a confluence of economic, social, political, and religious "reasons," all of them basically irrational, Jewish quarters all over the Peninsula were razed and their inhabitants murdered in great numbers. The Hispano-Jewish poet Jacob Albeneh relates the sorrowful events thus:

> Ay for the synagogues,
> transformed into ruins,
> where hawks and vultures nest
> since the children of Israel are flown!
> The great Synagogue itself
> was destroyed in a moment:
> raise your voice in a wail,
> synagogue of Israel.
> Its doors lie flat on the ground,
> and the Christian and Muslim hordes
> that penetrated its interior
> have erased from that place
> the children of Israel.[53]

The pogroms of 1391 had an immediate result which was of profound, definitive, and unsuspected consequences for the future: the conversion of a great many Jews to Christianity, thus creating a new caste, that of the *conversos,* that would expand throughout the fifteenth century. The most amazing case is that of the learned rabbi of Burgos, Solomon Levi, who became Pablo de Santa María, and was later ordained as a bishop in the very city where he had formerly directed the spiritual life of the Jewish community.[54] Thus begins another fascinating phenomenon: "the converted Jews become the spokesmen of 'what should be' in Spanish life."[55]

Here I should like to make a brief digression. In spite of incontrovertible facts such as the above, a complete silence has been maintained concerning the true structure of the Spanish Middle Ages, so that Américo Castro has been able to write that "the written history of the Spaniards has been placed under a kind of statute of 'purity of blood.' The presence of Moors and Jews in the very texture of Spanish life is acknowledged by modern professionals of history only with great difficulty. Historians want an 'honorable' image of the past, or more properly, they want a past that 'maintains honor.'[56] Even in the eighteenth century the Count of Peñaflorida, a keen observer of Spanish life, could talk ironically of the old caste manias and say in jest that Aristotle was an "old Christian"; Descartes and Newton "heretical dogs, atheists, and Jews"; and Galileo Galilei, "to judge by his very name, must have been some arch-Jew."[57] The fact that some of the greatest glories of Spanish culture, Santa Teresa de Jesús, for example, are of Jewish origin, is fraught with ominous forebodings for the defenders of Hispanic purity. Thus, a critic opposed to Américo Castro's viewpoint, Eugenio Asensio, confronted with what for him seems to be an unpleasant truth, attempts to "save" the saint by pointing out that she had only "a quarter of Jewish blood."[58] This sort of cultural purity of blood can lead to curious situations, as I can testify from personal experience. A well-known poet and intellectual of the Falangist "old guard," since repented of his political past, remarked to me upon learning that the author of *Don Quixote* might be *ex illis*: "This is the limit! Don't let them touch our Cervantes!"

But let us return to the fifteenth century. The process is clear. In spite of its internal political problems, Castile gradually asserts itself as the dominant kingdom in the Peninsula and begins to lay the foundation for the first modern, that is, absolutist state, whose premises would be established by the Catholic Monarchs. At the same time, however, the routes of intercaste tolerance are closed off ominously one by one. In this sense the establishment of the Inquisition in 1480 is of the utmost importance, since, as an institution it served the cause of unification in every imaginable sense. It would be erroneous to believe that the Inquisition was well received by the majority of Spaniards. The assassination of the Inquisitor Pedro de Arbués in Saragossa and the riots in many other places prove the contrary, but once it was operative, nothing could stop the sinister machinery. Sinister not necessarily for its bloody consequences, or at least not only for that, but much more because through it a fundamental insecurity was created in the Spanish mentality, from which it is possible that we have not yet recovered. The Jesuit Mariana wrote in the seventeenth century: "What was particularly strange was that the sons should pay for the sins of their fathers. . . . Those secret investigations did away with their freedom to hear and speak among themselves."[59]

We come by this route to the spectacular year 1492 with its well-known events: the conquest of Granada, the expulsion of the unconverted Jews, and the discovery of the New World. With his genius for observation of significant detail, Castro studied the tomb of the Catholic Rulers in Granada, in which the triumphs and glories of their reign are reduced, with startling brevity, to a single element:

> Mahometics secte prostratores
> et heretice pervicacie extinctores
> Fernandus Aragonum et Helisabetha Castelle
> vir et uxor unanimes
> Catholici appellati
> marmoreo clauduntur hoc tumulo.

> (Destroyers of the Mohammedan sect
> and the annihilators of heretical obstinacy [i.e., of the Jews],
> Ferdinand of Aragon and Isabella of Castile,
> husband and wife undivided in opinion,
> called the Catholic [Sovereigns],
> lie enclosed by this marble tomb.)[60]

According to this inscription, the only thing worthy of eternal memory is the annihilation of the Jewish and Muslim castes by the Christians. This is all the more shocking if we compare, as Castro did, this epitaph with the one of King Ferdinand III (1252) in four languages: Latin, Castilian, Hebrew, and Arabic, in which not a trace of the later intolerance can be discerned.[61] In sum, "An abyss separated the two situations—1252 and the beginning of the sixteenth century—even though the subject-agent of both was the awareness and the will that directed the collective life of the Spaniards."[62]

The tearing asunder of the traditional forms of Peninsular life, the total rupture of the old harmony of the three castes, and the consequences of the process may be observed clearly in fifteenth-century Castilian literature. It will suffice to cite two cases of exceptional importance in the panorama of Spanish letters: the ballad tradition and *La Celestina*. As we know, the fifteenth century is the great period of popularity and dissemination of the ballad:

> The unlettered Castilian populace—the "rustics," as Juan de Mena calls them—had conferred upon themselves a certificate of collective nobility by preserving from one generation to the next all that was worthy of being remembered in beautiful and melodious verses. The populace constituted itself as such as it relived its own history through the uninterrupted line of its ballads. . . . The "people of low and servile condition," [as the Marquis of Santillana called them] had passed in a few years from levels of semi-darkness to the brightness that illuminated, with their ancestral ignorance, the counselors of the Emperor. Having four grandparents who had never left the farm opened the way to the highest honors.[63]

That is, the Castilian populace manifested itself in the ballads, which propagate, significantly, at precisely the same time as the new intolerance, the "caste-ism" of purity of blood, and the Inquisition. People of the *lower* class triumphed, as they have in other periods of Spanish history—in the first half of the sixteenth century with the annihilation of the Erasmist minority—and in the eighteenth century with the failure of the Enlightened minority when the *lower* class also imposed its racist myths and obsessions over the possibilities of pluralism and rational organization for Spanish life. And *The Celestina*? The first edition of that work of genius appeared in 1499. Fernando de Rojas poured into it all the anguish, pessimism, and nihilism of a *converso* who has lost the religion of his fathers but has been unable to integrate himself within the compass of Christian belief. Rojas subjects the Castilian society of his time to a corrosive analysis, destroying with a spirit that has been called "destructive" all the traditional values and mental schemas of the new, intolerant system.[64] Beginning with literature and proceeding to religion, passing through all the "values" of institutionalized caste-ism—honor, valor, love—everything is perversely pulverized.

The popular ballads and *The Celestina* thus beautifully express in literature the two extremes of the conflictive Castilian social situation in the fifteenth century. Between them exists the entire gamut of possibilities: the anti-Jewish fanaticism of a *converso* such as the Inquisitor Torquemada, the noble plea for tolerance of an Old Christian such as Fernán Pérez de Guzmán, the terror and anguish of some and the servile complacency of others; the insecurity of all those caught up in an inexorable march toward imperial absolutism. In these circumstances it would be puerile to try to schematize and typify the reactions of the *conversos*, as some of Don Américo's detractors have attempted to do, guided either by honest misunderstanding or willful distortion of his thought.[65] There is obviously an abyss between a *converso* like Torquemada and one like Fernando de Rojas. It is clear, however, that what Américo Castro called *Messianism* is a fifteenth-century constant, shared by Old Christians as well as innumerable *conversos*, no matter what their motives for this belief: the desire to integrate and disavow "troublesome" background or the fascination exerted by the new and spectacular sociopolitical events. The machinery of imperial "gigantism" began to function, to trap Hispanic minds and imaginations: "The Spanish Empire, founded by Ferdinand and Isabella was not a felicitous happenstance. It was, rather, an expanded form of the Castilian vital experience at the time when Castile was acquiring an awareness of its own identity vis-à-vis the other European peoples, a consciousness that the Hispano-Semites had been expressing and expanding since the time of Alfonso the Learned."[66] All of this is happening at the same time as Church and State become progressively and inevitably allied:

> Thus we begin to realize that the peculiar identification established in Spain between Church and State is inseparable from the Islamic-Christian-Judaic social and religious context . . . My idea, that Spanish Christianity became more fanatical in direct proportion to the disappearance and Christianization of the Jews is not, therefore, a paradox, but an elementary reality. The official Spanish State-Catholicism of the sixteenth century has little in common with that of the Middle Ages, the rest of Europe, or, for that matter, with Pontifical Rome.[67]

The new situation at the end of the fifteenth century which we have been examining will be transmitted to and will constitute the basis for what is traditionally referred to as the Spanish Golden Age, and which Castro rechristened with a more realistic and accurate term, "The Age of Conflict," in which the myths

of Hispanic casticism—religiosity, purity of blood, honor, etc.—
appear omnipotent and unchallenged.[68]

But what lurks beneath the imperial superstructure? Why is
it that the plaintive testimony to the disintegration of the social
fabric coincides in time with the beginning of Spanish expan-
sionism? What accounts for the coexistence of literary genres as
radically opposed as the picaresque and the pastoral? Why was
Fray Luis de León really persecuted? What is the true significance of the Baroque? What accounts for the almost complete
lack of Spanish science, in spite of Menéndez y Pelayo's heroic
efforts to demonstrate its existence? What of Spain's economic
and material decadence? Many questions could be added. The
answer? Traditional historiography proposes several answers,
summed up in the sonorous and well-known pronouncements on
the hatred of the English and the French, the "Black Legend,"
the inefficient administration of the colonies and the metropolis.
Theological explanations have also been advanced. But Américo
Castro has found the real answer, and it stands revealed in the
authentic meaning of words and concepts rooted in the Spanish
mode of being, words such as *castizo, honor, sosiego, religiosi-
dad,* all joined irremediably in the conflict between Old
Christians and *conversos,* and in the need felt by the former to
affirm themselves in their identity as Old Christians and the
latter group's need to adapt to the social structure by attempting
to erase their origin from consciousness. These four words, we
are constantly reminded, are indicative of the purest Spanishness, and as such have long stood in need of clarification. Now,
after Castro's definitions, they can no longer be distorted and
used capriciously. But the events of the Age of Conflict fall
outside the bounds of this study.

Let us conclude by returning to our point of departure.
Américo Castro, like Nebrija, attempted to "drive out that
barbarism which has established itself so firmly in all parts of
Spain." Some ingenuous spirit might believe that things have
changed since the time of the first Castilian grammarian. But
let us see, rapidly, if what Unamuno euphemistically called
ramplonería (vulgarity) has really changed, and we shall thus
be able to understand what and who were Castro's lifelong
antagonists. Not long ago, in a Madrid newspaper there

appeared an erudite article which raised the disturbing question: "Was one of the three Magi an Andalusian?"[69] Even more recently, the long-suffering reader of the Spanish press had the opportunity to learn that the process of beatification of Isabella the Catholic had begun, and that the appropriate committee had taken a survey to determine whether "Isabella of Castile has been venerated as a saint in Granada."[70] Upon the arrival (on the significant date of 12 October) of a film crew in Madrid to begin work on a film about the Catholic Monarchs, the English actress who was to play Queen Isabella declared— *horresco referens*—that she was an agnostic. An alert and alarmed reporter posed the question: "Is it possible for an unbelieving actress to portray Isabella of Castile, the very quintessence of religious sentiment, with any degree of accuracy? With no chauvinism whatever intended, we believe that an intensive search should have been made for Spanish actresses to incarnate the great protagonists of the best Spanish history."[71] On the occasion of the four-hundredth anniversary of the battle of Lepanto, heroic voices were raised in warning: "If we pass from then to now, and leave the flag the same color [red] and instead of the Turk we contemplate another menace from the East, if we substitute the jet bomber for the galley, modern weapons for the cannon and blunderbuss, the situation is virtually the same."[72]

Let us attempt to reach a higher level. Juan Goytisolo states:

> In a country where people still write with impunity about the "Sevillian" emperor Trajan and the "Spanishness" of Seneca (Ortega y Gasset, Menéndez Pidal), about the "temporary" importance of the Muslim conquest (Menéndez Pidal), where it is still maintained that the Muslims—those same Muslims referred to as "pillagers" and "invaders" by the Arabist Emilio García Gómez— were not an "essential ingredient" in Spanish history (Ortega y Gasset), and where people construct the most exquisite theories about the Spanish Christian knight, "champion, defender of a cause, righter of wrongs and injustices, who moves through the world subordinating every reality to the imperative of a few supreme, absolute, unconditioned values" (García Morente)— lucubrations and entelechies repeated to the point of paroxysm every day by so many irresponsible penholders—in such a country the work of Américo Castro is bound to cause a scandal.[73]

There is no need to continue. As Martín González de Cellorigo remarked in 1600, "it seems as though this kingdom has voluntarily reduced itself to a republic of enchanted men who live outside the natural order of things."[74] This, finally, was what Castro fought against. He believed in a better future, and all his demythifying work had as its object to enable us Spaniards to understand our past and our present, to stop killing each other and to begin to construct our future in a rational manner. We might say of Don Américo what has been said of Don Quixote, that he wanted "to disenchant the enchanted world, that is, to humanize it, to return it to an existential condition governed by human forces."[75]

NOTES

1. Quoted by Guillermo de Torre in "Américo Castro y su interpretación de España," *La realidad histórica de España. Juicios y comentarios* (Mexico: Porrúa, 1957), p. 28. Previously published in *Imago Mundi* II, 8 (Buenos Aires, 1955) p. 64.

2. *Apud* Castro himself in *LEL*, p. 141.

3. *RHE* (1962), p. 115; *SIH*, p. 105.

4. See *RHE* (1962), chap. iv; *SIH*, chap. iv. See also n. 1 in Guillermo Araya Goubet's contribution to this book.

5. "Américo Castro y la identidad de los españoles," in *Estudios*, p. 88.

6. "Supervivencias tribales en el medio intelectual español," in *Estudios*, p. 143.

7. Ibid., p. 145.

8. Luis Pericot García, *Las raíces de España* (Madrid: C.S.I.C., 1952), pp. 52-53.

9. Let us not forget that Castro has been proudly characterized as a 'national mythoclast." See Paulino Garagorri, "Un mitoclasta nacional: En torno a la tarea desmitificadora de Américo Castro," *Revista de Occidente*, Año IV, 2ª época, no. 41 (1966), pp. 234-244.

10. *RHE* (1962), p. 4; *SIH*, p. 24.

11. *RHE* (1962), p. 146; *SIH*, p. 177.

12. Angel Ganivet, "Idearium español" in *Obras completas*, 7th ed. (Madrid: Victoriano Suárez, 1944), I, 6; see also p. 52.

13. Ramón Menéndez Pidal, *España y su historia* (Madrid: Minotauro, 1957), I, 15; see also pp. 23, 24, 31:II, 615 (introduction and translation by Walter Starkie: *The Spaniards in Their History* [N.Y.: W.W. Norton, 1950]).

14. Interview in the newspaper *ABC* (Madrid), 17 May 1972; see also "Discrepancias y mal entender," in *DEN*, pp. 55-58.

15. *Estudios*, p. 89. See n. 5.

16. Historians of the stature of Jaime Vicens Vives coincide with Castro in his vision of "un-Spanish" Hispania; cf. his *Aproximación a la historia de España* (Barcelona: Ed. Vicens-Vives, 1960), pp. 43 ff. and 185 (trans.: *Approaches to the History of Spain* [University of California Press, rev. ed., 1970]).

17. See Vicens Vives, op. cit. in n. 16, p. 186 and Ortega, *Obras*, III, 118 on the Visigoths.

18. *RHE* (1962), p. 163; *SIH*, p. 198.

19. *RHE* (1962), p. 153; *SIH*, p. 185.

20. *RHE* (1962), pp. 149, 151; *SIH*, pp. 180, 182.

21. Marcelino Menéndez y Pelayo, *Historia de los heterodoxos españoles* (Madrid: Victoriano Suárez, 1917), II, 135, n. *b*.

22. See William Reinhart, "La tradición visigoda en el nacimiento de Castilla," in *Estudios dedicados a don Ramón Menéndez Pidal* (Madrid: C.S.I.C., 1950), I, 535-554; A. García Gallo, "El carácter germánico de la épica y del derecho en la Edad Media española," *Anuario de historia del derecho español*, XXV (1955), 583-679; C. Sánchez-Albornoz, "Tradición y derecho en León y Castilla," *Cuadernos de historia de España* (Buenos Aires), XXIX-XXX (1959), 244-265; and, of course, R. Menéndez Pidal, *Los godos y la epopeya española* (Madrid: Espasa-Calpe, 1956). See finally Julio Rodríguez-Puértolas, "*Poema de Mio Cid*: nueva épica y nueva propaganda," in *Poema de Mio Cid Studies* ed. by Alan Deyermond (London: Tamesis). In press.

23. See, for example, Menéndez Pidal, *España y su historia*, II, 752.

24. Emilio García Gómez, *La Alhambra: la Casa Real* (Granada-Florence: Albaicín-Sadea, 1966).

25. *Escritores y poetas de España* (Madrid: Espasa-Calpe, 1944), p. quoted by Juan Goytisolo in *El furgón de cola* (Paris, 1967), p. 163. In a more modest vein, Spanish television, in a program entitled "La noche de los tiempos," offered its viewers: "Saracens, Moors, unknown and enigmatic beings who in a few weeks violated the stupendous Celtic-Iberian-Phoenician-Carthaginian-Roman-Visigothic Spain only to lose it little by little, for they were uncultured, indolent, maladroit, unbelievers . . ." See Antonio de los Reyes, "Lucha de razas," in *La Verdad* (Alicante), March 1972.

26. *ECS*, p. 121 and chap. iii; *SIH*, chap. v.

27. *ECS*, pp. 89, 90.

28. *EPE*, pp. 10-12; *SIH*, pp. 255-259.

29. See especially *ESH, SSH, RHE* (1954).

30. *RHE* (1954), p. 86; *SSH,* p. 78.

31. Aebischer, op. cit.; see Araya Goubet, p. 54, and note 28.

32. *EPE,* p. 15.

33. *ECS,* p. 160.

34. See *ESH,* chap. xi; *SSH,* chap. xv; *RHE* (1962), chap. ii; *SIH,* chap. iii; *RHE* (1962), p. xx; *ECS,* pp. 163-164.

35. *Poema de Alfonso Onceno,* Yo ten Cate, ed. (Madrid: C.S.I.C., 1956), stanzas 1267-1268.

36. *El Libro de Buen Amor,* (Madrid: Clásicos Castellanos, 1959), II, stanza 1193.

37. *RHE* (1962), pp. 29-41; *SIH,* 49-63.

38. *ESH,* pp. 604-621; *SSH,* pp. 614-628.

39. *EPE,* p. 18; *SIH,* p. 547.

40. *RHE* (1954), pp. 478-587; *SSH,* 473-491; *DEN,* pp. 63-74.

41. *RHE* (1954), pp. 561-581; *SSH,* 551-558.

42. *RHE* (1954), chap. xiii; *SSH,* chaps. xiii-xiv.

43. *ESH,* pp. 204-225; *SSH,* pp. 219-221; *RHE* (1962), pp. 419-429; *SIH,* pp. 487-498.

44. *ESH,* pp. 71-78, 621-634, 686-689; *SSH,* pp. 100, 628-635; *RHE* (1962), pp. 219-223, 266-271; *SIH,* pp. 266-271.

45. *ESH,* pp. 188-204; *SSH,* pp. 202-218; *RHE* (1962), pp. 407-419; *SIH,* pp. 471-486.

46. *RHE* (1962), p. 328; *SIH,* p. 382.

47. *RHE* (1962), p. 356; *SIH,* p. 418.

48. *ESH,* chap. ix; *SSH,* chap. xii; *RHE* (1954), chap. xii.

49. *ESH,* pp. 371, 376; *SSH,* pp. 393, 402. See also Dámaço Alonso, "La bella de Juan Ruiz, toda problemas," in *De los siglos oscuros al de Oro* (Madrid: Gredos,, 1958), pp. 86-99; María Rosa Lida de Malkiel, *Two Spanish Masterpieces: the "Book of Good Love" and "The Celestina"* (Urbana: The University of Illinois Press, 1961), pp. 18-50; Julio Rodríguez-Puértolas, "Del 'Poema de Mio Cid' al 'Lazarillo' " in *Literatura, Historia, Alienación* (Barcelona: Labor, 1976).

50. *RHE* (1954), p. 383; *SSH,* p. 397.

51. Lida de Malkiel, op. cit., p. 11. See n. 49.

52. *Proverbios Morales,* I. González-Llubera, ed. (Cambridge: The University Press, 1947), p.70.

53. "Elegía" stanzas 32-34; adaptation by Francisco Cantera Burgos, in *Sinagogas españolas* (Madrid: C.S.I.C., 1955), pp. 36-37.

54. The conversion of Rabbi Salomón took place in 1390, not long before the great pogrom. See F. Cantera Burgos, *Alvar García de Santa María. Historia de*

la judería de Burgos y de sus conversos más egregios (Madrid: C.S.I.C., 1952).

55. *RHE* (1962), p. 81-85; *SIH*, p. 147 ff.

56. *ECD* (1962), p. 91.

57. *Los aldeanos críticos,* 1758; *apud* Paulino Garagorri in "Xavier de Munibe en la filosofía española," *Revista de Occidente,* Año II, 2ª época, no. 21 (1964), p. 340.

58. Eugenio Asensio, "En torno a Américo Castro, polémica con Albert A. Sicroff," *Hispanic Review,* XL, no. 4 (Autumn 1972), 378. A good example of Asensio's position is to be found in one of his opening statements: "Dificultan nuestro diálogo no mi condición de cristiano y la suya de hebreo—aunque puedan influir en nuestras predilecciones—" (p. 366). See also A.A. Sicroff "Américo Castro and his critics: Eugenio Asensio," *Hispanic Review,* XL, no. 1 (1972), 1-30.

59. *Apud ESH,* p. 550; *SSH,* p. 534; see also *ESH,* pp. 551-560; *SSH,* pp. 521-544; *RHE* (1962), pp. 44-45; *SIH,* pp. 66-68.

60. *RHE* (1962), p. 169; *SIH,* p. 205; see also *RHE* (1962), p. 247; *SIH,* p. 295; *ECS*, pp. 100-102.

61. *RHE* (1962), p. 38-39; *SIH,* pp. 59-61.

62. *RHE* (1962), p. 170; *SIH,* p. 206. The importance of these royal epitaphs is also pointed out by Guillermo Araya, *Evolución,* pp. 33-35.

63. *EPE,* pp. 58, 60-61.

64. *CCL,* p. 147. See also Rafael Lapesa, "*La Celestina* en la obra de Américo Castro," in *Estudios,* pp. 247-261; Julio Rodríguez-Puértolas, "*La Celestina* o la negación de la negación," in *Literatura, Historia, Alienación.* See note 49.

65. Cf., for example, Eugenio Asensio, note 58.

66. *RHE* (1962), p. 89; *SIH,* p. 156; see *AVH* (1970), pp. 21-45.

67. *RHE* (1962), pp. 52-53; *SIH,* pp. 77-78.

68. See *ECD* (1963).

69. *Apud* Juan Goytisolo, in *Estudios,* p. 150.

70. *La Verdad* (Alicante), 10 June 1972.

71. *La Verdad* (Alicante), 14 October 1971.

72. *Información* (Alicante), 8 October 1971.

73. Goytisolo, *Estudios,* pp. 147-148.

74. Martín González de Cellorigo, *Memorial de la política necessaria, y útil restauración de España* (Valladolid, 1600), Biblioteca Nacional, Madrid, fol. 29.

75. Werner Krauss, *Miguel de Cervantes. Leben und Werk* (Berlin: Luchterland, 1966), p. 145.

Part III
On Spain's Age of Conflict

7

THE SPANISH JEWS: EARLY REFERENCES AND LATER EFFECTS
Joseph H. Silverman

In 1922 Américo Castro, who at that time was specializing in Hispanic dialectology, among other varied interests, visited the Jewish quarters of Morocco in order to collect linguistic and folk literary materials. During that same year, he published a brief article on the Spanish language in Morocco which scarcely hinted at the wealth of data he had collected there.[1] Unfortunately, interests of another sort were soon to absorb Don Américo's attention and he would never again return to these materials in order to give them the final form required for public consumption. Some forty years later, having learned of our work among the Sephardim of the United States, he presented to Professor Samuel G. Armistead and me his entire collection of Moroccan texts as well as his extremely valuable field notes.[2]

And yet, his sojourn in Morocco was to mean far more to the history of Spain and its culture than the preservation of precious linguistic and literary documentation; in Morocco, in the cities of Tetuán, Xauen, and Larache, Professor Castro was to experience at first hand a dynamic association of peoples belonging to three great religions. This multireligious confrontation and collaboration had also been intrinsic to the fabric of Hispanic life in centuries past. And, in Morocco, he would come in contact with a society, not unlike that which had existed in Medieval Spain, wherein almost every aspect of reality—political, economic, communal, and individual—was conditioned by considerations of a religious nature.

Less than a year later, the profound impact of his Moroccan experience, in conjunction with his scholarly meditations, was to find expression in words that lamented the tragic dissolution of what might have been a truly great society. In January 1923, writing about the notable Bible of the House of Alba—translated from Hebrew to Spanish by Rabbi Moshé Arragel, between 1422 and 1433, with the advice and assistance of two Catholic priests, at the behest of Don Luis de Guzmán, Grand Master of the Order of Calatrava—Don Américo remarked that few episodes could provide a more authentic reflection of Medieval Spain than this enduring collaborative effort. Had Spain continued in this way, forging a special kind of culture out of the opposing elements of different civilizations that were striving to adapt to one another, it might have reached modern times with a great spirit, a spirit incompatible with that tribal mentality which would make of the nation one vast village, even before the end of the seventeenth century.

In the accompanying commentary to his translation, Rabbi Arragel explained that "in many places of this work it will be said that the Son of God, the true Messiah, will come to liberate Israel from its trials and tribulations. Christians believe that these words refer to Jesus Christ, and Jews assume that they refer to the Messiah, whom they still await. In such cases, each one should embrace the articles of his own faith." For Professor Castro, it was this attitude of fruitful tolerance that allowed individuals like Rabbi Arragel and his collaborators to bring together, in an undertaking that was meaningful to all, whatever remained outside the dogmatic limits of each select individuality. In this way, dogmas gradually were narrowed down to a minimum of irrational conventionality and did not prevent the birth of new and valued forms of culture. From the thirteenth century on, the court of Alfonso el Sabio had been an example of how national differences in culture and religion could be resolved in creative harmony, giving rise to scientific and historical works that were veritable wonders, if we bear in mind the date at which they were conceived. But, regrettably, the collaborative enterprise supported by the Master of Calatrava was one of the last expressions of that aristocratic spirit, already an anachronism for a society that, in religious matters, was gradually sinking to the lowest level of popular thought.[3]

Still in 1923, in an essay devoted to Golden Age theater, Don Américo would continue to write in a bitterly elegiac vein about the history of his country and the tragic flaw in its official faith. Catholicism, he maintained, denies its very essence when it declares itself incompatible with other beliefs. In Spain during the Middle Ages, three civilizations lived together, and from this living-togetherness there blossomed a valuable civilization. When the rabble—for it was not Ferdinand and Isabel—expelled the Jews from Spain, many of them took refuge in the very capital of Christendom.[4] And they have never ceased to live in Italy. Their synagogues still stand in the city of St. Peter. A considerable number of Jews from the north of the Peninsula settled in Bayonne and Bordeaux, and these communities still exist, and Spanish was preserved there for a long time. What accursed germ provoked religious madness on the Spanish side of the Pyrenees? History has not yet supplied an answer.[5] But it was Castro's intention, during the next fifty years, to provide some explanation that would satisfy himself and his disciples and that might be meaningful to his countrymen in understanding their past and in facing their future.

In the first issue of *La Gaceta Literaria,* an important Madrid journal that would give sympathetic attention to the Sephardic Jews of Morocco and the Balkans, Don Américo published a fragment of a pathetic visionary letter, sent from Istanbul by the secret Jew David Ebrón to King Philip II on December 9, 1597. Ebrón pleaded with the King to take pity on the Jews and allow them to return to Spain, to live there with freedom of movement as they were living in Italy, not only for their sake, but for his own, for the riches they would provide his country and for the favor that such an action would find in the eyes of Jehovah. In his fawning despair, Ebrón—not unlike Ricote (*Don Quixote,* Part II, chapter liv)—even justified the need for the Inquisition and, in a self-flagellating jeremiad, praised its scourging activities against false converts to Christianity, Lutherans, heretics and practitioners of sodomy.[6]

Writing with an urge to promote unity and understanding among the various elements of the Hispanic world, Professor Castro also reproduced a passage from King Alfonso el Sabio's legal code, the *Siete Partidas:*

> Jews are a kind of people who, though they do not believe in our
> Lord Jesus Christ, have been allowed by great Christian lords to

live among them. . . . And since the synagogue is a house wherein God's name is praised, we forbid any Christian to dare desecrate it or to remove anything from it by force. . . . We order that no judge shall exert pressure on the Jews to bring them to trial on the Sabbath, nor shall they be imprisoned nor made to suffer any punishment on that day; for there are days enough in the week in which to demand of them what may legally be expected.

The conclusion to this article is a small measure of Don Américo's humanity:

> The *Gaceta Literaria* directs its uncertain voice, like that of a new-born child, to our brothers in Morocco and the Balkans who share our language and tradition. Our program is to unite and understand. And we should not wish to exclude the Spanish Jews from this circle of love and understanding. It is our fervent wish that the song, once so tragic for them,
>
> Hey there, Jews, pack up your things;
> you must cross the sea, say the Catholic Kings!
>
> may resound anew, but this time in the other direction, with good faith and optimism, revealing a desirable goal to many Jews, since in their heart of hearts, despite all the grief they've endured, they continue to look upon Spain as their cruel and forgetful mother.[7]

In a study written in 1931, he could still lump together, as Establishment conformists, Mateo Alemán—a New Christian of Jewish background—and two so-called quintessential Old Christians, Lope de Vega and Calderón.[8] Obviously, he was not yet aware of the subversive qualities and subtle ironies that were hidden away in the pages of the *Guzmán de Alfarache*. He had not yet perceived the individualizing nuances of *converso* style. But by 1934 he had come to recognize that Mateo Alemán was a fiercely resentful man, bilious and sagacious, at times a prodigious writer, one more victim condemned to live out the bitter destiny of those families who were descended from Jewish converts, those unfortunate people who played such an important role in Spanish life from the fifteenth century on. Whatever else they might have been, or continued to be surreptitiously, Castro understood that the *conversos* were Spaniards, as Spanish as any Old Christian.[9]

In the famous essay, "Lo hispánico y el erasmismo," written in 1939, Professor Castro allowed us to see the tentativeness of his thought, his near reluctance to accept the validity of his own recent discovery of the special significance of the *converso,* the New Christian, in Hispanic literature:

> If one were to adopt a fragmented view of history, it could be maintained that the picaresque novel owes much to the fact that Mateo Alemán belonged to a family of converts, and that from that circumstance emanated the bitterness, rancor and social strife which pervade the pages of the *Guzmán de Alfarache.* Moreover, one might assume that the unknown author of the *Lazarillo* was also a convert. But I fear that by proceeding in this way, trying to explain history in a logical manner, we would end up explaining too little and too much. Could so many outstanding manifestations of Spanish spirituality and Spanish art be either directly or indirectly reflections of an anguished Jewishness . . . a *semitismo atormentado?*[10]

It would seem that the question he posed was an expression of his own insecurity, as well as a kind of trial balloon to gauge the reaction to this revolutionary hypothesis. By 1949, however, when the study appeared in book form under the title of *Aspectos del vivir hispánico,* the passage was no longer needed. The answer to the rhetorical question was a resounding YES. And, in a preface to the 1970 edition of the work, the earlier version is described as a kind of preliminary exercise, written when his idea of the Spaniard was not yet fully formed.[11]

Having given this bird's-eye view of the early development of Professor Castro's interest in Jews and *conversos* as an integral part of Spanish life and his at first tentative, then forthright, acceptance of their importance in Spanish literature, I prefer to avoid the polemical aspects of his theories, offering instead a demonstration of how his writings have taught us to see works of Golden Age literature in new ways, from richer and more vital perspectives.

In the study of the Spanish seventeenth-century *comedia* very little attention has been given to the human situation, the complex social circumstances from which Spain's Golden Age literature emerged. For the most part, *comedia* research has shown little or no interest in profound social analysis. And, as for aesthetics, since the work of A. A. Parker, students have been happy to demonstrate that in Spanish theater, treated within a kind of artistic vacuum, there is a primacy of action over character portrayal, theme over action, dramatic unity achieved through theme rather than action, and theme itself subordinated to a moral purpose through the all-important principle of poetic justice, illuminated by means of dramatic causality. But nowhere amid all these neat abstractions was there time or place to show that the Golden Age was an age of terror, social injustice and repression, and that these conflictive circumstances—this tragic yet fecund collision of lives and value systems—were indeed reflected in the theater.[12]

I should now like to examine a *comedia* by Lope de Vega which I first came to understand in 1968, while teaching a seminar at UCLA on Lope's honor plays. The work, entitled *El galán escarmentado (The Suitor Who Learned His Lesson),* is not, properly speaking, an honor play. Still, honor is a central problem of the work. It was mentioned by José F. Montesinos because it includes two sonnets published subsequently, one in Pedro de Espinosa's *Flores de poetas ilustres* (1605), the other in Lope's own *Rimas* (1602), and because the third act has a passage reminiscent of the *Celestina.*[13] María Goyri de Menéndez Pidal found in the first act allusions to one of Lope's early love affairs[14] and William L. Fichter cited it as a typical drama of conjugal honor.[15] Finally, Edward Nagy comments suggestively on a significant sonnet fragment, but identifies Julio, the wealthy husband of the heroine, as a servant.[16] This is the extent of commentary on the play. Here is its plot.

Celio and Ricarda are in love, but during an absence of three years, in which Celio fights heroically with the Spanish forces of the Marqués de Santa Cruz against the French, Ricarda decides to marry Julio, a wealthy gentleman. It is stressed that Celio is not only of honorable parents but of well-born (i.e., pure-blooded) grandparents. Of Julio we learn, on more than one occasion, that he is very rich and gives generous gifts of bracelets, necklaces, and jewels.

To elucidate the juxtaposition of these characteristics and their possible importance in the play—Celio an impoverished Old Christian, Julio a wealthy gentleman—I cite a passage from *El valiente Juan de Heredia,* published under Lope's name, but of doubtful authenticity, in which the protagonist is bragging of his lineage, his *calidad*:

> I have been born
> only a poor Old Christian;
> but I think there's
> no quality like being one,
> although even a man
> of the lowest birthright,
> of the most humble blood,
> may aspire to be a gentleman,
> or make himself out to be
> an *hidalgo* through money
> or by currying favor,
> and more so nowadays.
> But, however much one may try,
> only God can make
> an Old Christian. You tell me,
> then, if the Heavens or
> money and favor can give
> a more honorable lineage.
> Who can be more of a gentleman
> than he who can boast
> of Old Christian parents and grandparents!
>
> (*Ac. N.,* II, 633b-634a)

Shortly after the marriage takes place, Julio discovers some of Celio's old love letters to Ricarda and is convinced that the affair has not ended. He feels that his honor has been compromised and decides to kill his wife, even though she may be innocent.

JULIO: You with love letters? By God,
          I'm going to kill you.

RICARDA:

                    Julio,
          Is this love or is it madness?
          If it's love, then kill me.

JULIO: How can it be madness
          if I found them in your chest?
          I insulted? You with a lover?
          I honored? With you my wife?
          Ricarda, today you will die!

Ricarda tries to explain that they are old love letters, that her relationship with Celio has long been at an end, but Julio, a Spanish surgeon of his honor, tells Ricarda that she must die. Ricarda asks for a few minutes to pray for her soul and enters her room to do so. While waiting, Julio recites a sonnet, and not only because "the sonnet is suitable for those who wait," said Lope, but because it is an ideal vehicle for the portrayal of insecurity, emotional ambivalence, and tormented introspection. The sonnet that Julio declaims seems to be communicating on more than one level. It is, on the surface, an attack against love letters or, perhaps, letters in general and the harm they have caused throughout the world. But the emotional intensity with which he describes the destructive powers of a written message suggests that he may be thinking of other matters at the same time, even more poignantly involved in the circumstances of his own life.

> Oh, accursed papers, how much harm
> have you wrought in the world! There is no
> figure to include it! May you be consumed by fire
> for all the occasions you have given for deception!
> How many individuals, both at home and abroad,
> have you raised to meteoric heights
> only to bring crashing down in the course of time!
> How many guiltless ones have you brought to ruin
> because the evidence was concealed?
> What great power there is in a written page!
> You are the silent witnesses of sin
> and, being the panderers of a crime committed,
> you are also the proof of the transgression.

It is certain that Julio laments the fact that he has discovered his wife's infidelity, but at the same time he may be expressing a fear and hatred of the informer, the dreaded *malsín*, ever ready to spy and denounce to Inquisitional authorities, anonymously or for a fee. It is surely no coincidence that in the very next scene informers are discussed from another point of view, with a fairly transparent allusion to Judas and to the odious commercial instincts of Jews.

Unlike the typical cuckolded or possibly deceived gentleman, Julio regrets his fury and decides it would be best to discuss the matter further with his wife. When his servant enters Ricarda's room, he discovers that she has fled. This, of course, convinces Julio of her guilt. The next time we see Julio, he is at the home of his father-in-law, Tácito, accusing him of hiding his adulterous daughter. Tácito, in turn, accuses Julio of having killed her without proof of her guilt. The argument becomes more and more heated and the introduction of seemingly tangential material leads to acts of violence. When mutual recriminations begin, Tácito says,

> I am to blame for giving my daughter
> in marriage to someone of tainted blood.

Julio responds,

> I am an *hidalgo,* an *hidalgo* of established
> reputation and distinguished ancestry.

To which Tácito retorts,

> Distinguished ancestry! You mean the kind
> that is being forged these days on the dungheaps of Madrid?
> How high-toned you can speak because you're rich!
> But no doubt your coat of arms is hanging in some church.

Tácito, of course, is suggesting that his son-in-law is of Jewish descent, a fact that is publicly displayed in church as a *sambenito,*[17] an ineradicable testimony of his infamy. With this, Julio loses control of himself and, in his rage, strikes the aged Tácito:

> I am not punishing your gray hair,
> old man, only your tongue;
> for it has made you young again and it has cut deeper
> than your sword could when you were young.

There is something wonderfully electrifying, Unamunesque about this scene, which in one epiphanic moment has revealed with almost unbearable intensity what Julio has done all in his power to keep hidden.

Tácito falls to his knees and, fearing for his life, begs Julio to forgive him. The old man's tears and cringing disarm him completely. When Julio bends to lift and embrace him, Tácito seizes Julio's dagger and stabs him to death. As the play progresses, Tácito is to be tried for Julio's death, particularly since he cannot produce his daughter's body to prove that Julio had killed her. At the end, to be brief, omitting an enumeration of the half-truths perpetrated by Tácity and the devious lies invented by others to protect him, Ricarda and Celio turn up together, get married and live happily ever after. And Tácito? After all, he is now clearly guilty of killing Julio without just cause . . . or is he? Well, not really. Despite the fact that Julio dies with a plea for confession on his lips, that he exclaimed, on lifting Tácito from the ground:

> Jesus, sir, for God's sake, get up!
> You at my feet and weeping such bitter tears?
> Dry those venerable eyes
> and forgive me; for it is I who should weep
> with heart and soul for having offended you.

and that Tácito had murdered him through guile, as he himself recognized; despite all this, Julio's death was justifiable. He was expendable. His blood was mixed; he was of Jewish extraction; and he did strike his father-in-law, "dishonoring his hoary head." To have killed him was to extirpate the blemished husband of his daughter, thus restoring his family honor and winning a battle for honor itself, by killing an intruder, an outsider, who deserved no share in the official system. So, Tácito is an Old Christian hero. And what of the important principles of poetic justice and moral purpose? Are they operative in this play? Indeed they are! The message could not be clearer. Jews and converts are expendable to the system. It does not pay to have Jewish blood. And if you hide the ignominious fact, you will get caught in the end . . . or in the middle, if necessary to the proper functioning of the plot. In other words, "the moral machinery of life" may occasionally be stopped by "social solidarity, resting on the buoyant force of a collective life that transcends particular mistakes"[18] like Tácito's murder of Julio.

As if to prepare us ritualistically for Julio's death, the scene that precedes his encounter with Tácito takes place in the countryside, the mythical refuge of purity of blood. Here are a few words from a conversation between a villager and the local mayor:

ARMENTO: Will we be having a production this year?

MAYOR: What? What do you think I am?
I'm so devoted to religious plays (*autos*)
that if it were possible I'd have
an auto-da-fé in our village!

El galán escarmentado (The Suitor Who Learned His Lesson) offers yet another view of the Hispanic honor code, one that closely resembles seventeenth-century Spanish life according to a certain *Memorial de algunas razones para quitar los estatutos de limpieza (Petition Concerning the Abolition of the Statutes of Purity of Blood)*. In it we learn that the existence of these statutes provoked murders—"muertes violentas"—in order to put an end to the familial infamy of mixed marriages, like that of Julio and Ricarda, and to avoid the potential danger of having tainted offspring.[19] In this play, then, Lope de Vega did invest the New Christian with traditional Hispanic traits and preoccupations. His willingness to present such a figure, and with no small amount of humanity, is much to his credit as a dramatist and allows me to inform the intransigent José Antonio Maravall—for whom Américo Castro's name is anathema—that he is falsifying Spanish history and theater when he generalizes that "references to blood [in Golden Age drama] do not allude to the tainted blood of converts from Judaism, but rather to the difference—fundamental in all social regimes based on hereditary nobility, *as was Spain's and that of all European countries*—between the good blood of nobles and the base blood of plebeians."[20] Still, and the insanity behind it forever haunts me, it was ethically and aesthetically beyond Lope's reach—despite his great gift for creative empathy—to allow a convert to survive in dramatic form as an honored member of the system.[21]

I wonder how easily we might have recognized the true significance of this play and others like it, just as nationalistic and as patriotic as *Fuenteovejuna* or *Peribáñez y el Comendador de Ocaña*, had Américo Castro not written *La realidad histórica de España* and *De la edad conflictiva*. Thanks to these works and the awareness they have helped to create, we can understand why in Ruiz de Alarcón's *La verdad sospechosa (The Truth Suspected)* the engagement of Don Juan and Jacinta dragged on for two years. Finally, after an intense investigation, Don Juan was admitted to the religious-military order of Calatrava, thus confirming the "purity" of his blood. Had he not been granted membership, it is most unlikely that he would have been accepted as a proper husband for the status-conscious Jacinta.[22] In Golden Age theater, literary convention and life are not always as removed from each other as we have been led to believe.

In one of the most entertaining chapters of *Don Quixote,* Part II, a courier enters with a sealed communication which must be delivered to Sancho personally, as Governor of the island of Barataria, or to his private secretary:

> Hearing which Sancho asked: 'Who here is my secretary?' And one of those standing by answered: 'I, sir, for I can read and write, and I'm a Basque.'
> 'With the last qualification,' said Sancho, 'you could well be secretary to the Emperor himself. Open this envelope and see what it says.'
>
> (Chapter xlvii)

Any reader of *De la edad conflictiva* will recall Don Américo's discussion of a document he considered decisive for a proper understanding of Spain's social reality during the sixteenth and seventeenth centuries.[23] In it are presented the results of an investigation conducted by the eminent jurist Lorenzo Galíndez Carvajal concerning the various members of Emperor Charles V's Royal Council. It is obvious, almost at a glance, that Galíndez Carvajal was less interested in the intellectual capacities and moral integrity of the Emperor's counselors than in the purity of their blood. Intellect, learning—"buenas letras"— could be more of a drawback than a virtue for an advisor to the Emperor. What counted most in order to advise and govern properly—"para saber bien gobernar"—was to be of peasant stock, the ideal being "de todas partes de linaje de labradores." Reading and writing were potentially dangerous activities and were suggestive of a Jewish background.[24] But how do the commentators of *Don Quixote* clarify Sancho's remark? The general consensus is that Basques, Biscayans in particular, are very discreet and loyal. Edition after edition stresses this view and some provide quotations to support it. Clemencín suggests, however, that Sancho's remark might have been satirical.[25]

Cortejón and Rodríguez Marín disagree, the former rather violently, with assistance from Julián de Apraiz, an impassioned Bascophile.[26] Schevill-Bonilla support the notion of fidelity and cite the following passage from Covarrubias' *Tesoro de la lengua,* s.v. *Cantabria:*:

> It is said that the Biscayans are a ferocious people who are not content unless they are making war. And this is the way they must have been in those remote times when they had neither refinement nor religion. Now they are possessed of gentlemanly valor and are great soldiers on land and sea. And in matters of learning, government, finance and administration, Biscayans are superior to all other Spaniards. They are most faithful, long-suffering and persevering in work.[27]

There is, of course, no reason to question the fidelity or ferocity of the Basques, nor even to dispute their special gifts as secretaries and scribes.[28] In a *Loa de los oficios y naciones,* Lope de Vega observed that "it is certain that Biscayans are very fine clerks."[29] But, in his play, *La villana de Getafe,* we read that "these *hidalgos* / do not hunt with dogs [= Moors], / since they come from Biscay" (p. 395b). And this adds another very different dimension to Sancho's words, directly related to Galíndez Carvajal's investigation of the Emperor's counselors. It begins to tell us what was *behind* their fidelity and valor. Basques were renowned not only for their courage and devotion but for the mythical purity of their blood, never sullied by intimate contact with Jews or Moors.[30]

St. Ignatius of Loyola, free of the anti-Semitism that he had known among his own Basque family, claimed that he would have considered it a divine gift to have been born of Jewish lineage, since in that way he would have been related to Christ and the Virgin Mary. But, a few years earlier, while studying in Alcalá de Henares, he claimed not to know anything about Jewish customs, since there were no Jews in his land. Before the ecclesiastical authorities of the city, Ignatius would insist on the legendary purity of the Basque regions, their freedom from the taint of Judaism. And this haloed facet of their character was simply neglected by all the editors of *Don Quixote.* They were unaware of its significance. The most dramatic evidence of this is to be found in a sentence from Covarrubias' *Tesoro de la lengua,* which Schevill-Bonilla chose to omit as unimportant for the elucidation of the cited passage: "Gente limpíssima, que no han admitido en su provincia hombres estrangeros ni mal nacidos" ('Extremely clean people, who have allowed neither foreigners nor individuals of inferior birth to settle in their province'). Covarrubias is alluding here to *limpieza de sangre,* purity of blood, and to the meticulous care with which the Basques excluded Semitic peoples from their land. He is recalling those ordinances, one of which was raised to the category of law in 1483 by the Councils of Guipúzcoa, which were promulgated against the entry of Jews and Moors into their region and prohibited intermarriage with New Christians and their descendants. But don't such ordinances suggest that Basque purity of blood was more illusory than real? More often than not there is an abyss between reality and desire.

From a letter written by Fernando del Pulgar to Don Pedro González de Mendoza, Cardinal of Spain, we get a *converso's* view of the relationships that prevailed among the Old Christians of Guipúzcoa and the New Christians of Castile:

> Illustrious and most reverend sir:
> You have probably learned about that new statute passed in Guipúzcoa which ordered us not to go there in order to marry or take up residence, etc., as if there were nothing better to do than to settle that fertile tableland and abundant farmland. It is not unlike that ordinance issued by the stonecutters of Toledo, which forbade their members to teach the craft to any convert. May the Lord preserve me, sir, but on careful consideration I have never seen a more ridiculous thing for one who knows the quality of that land and the character of its inhabitants. Isn't it laughable that all or almost all of them send their sons here to serve us, many of them as grooms, and yet are unwilling to become related through marriage to the very people they would serve? I certainly do not understand, my lord, how one can justify such behavior: to reject us as relatives but to choose us as masters. And I understand even less how they can accept on the one hand an ordinance prohibiting contact with us, while on the other they fill the homes of [*converso*] merchants and notaries here with their sons. At the same time, these very fathers formulate offensive laws against those who raise their sons for them and instruct them in trades and sources of income just as they did for them when they were young. As for me, sir, I have seen more of these [Guipuzcoan] young men in the court clerk's house, learning to write, than at the Marquis

Iñigo López's residence, learning how to joust. I also assure your worship that there are more Guipuzcoans living at the homes of the secretaries Fernand Alvares and Alfonso de Avila than at your home or at the Constable's even though you're from their land. By my faith, sir, I'm bringing up four of them in my own home, while their fathers pass laws like those I've mentioned. And more than forty honored and married men, whom I raised and educated, but certainly not to make such ordinances, are living in that region now.[31]

In the light of such information, Sancho's remarks take on a new meaning. And it is now clear why his secretary might have served Charles V himself, even with the enthusiastic approval of Galíndez Carvajal. Basque loyalty and valor, genetically based in Old Christian purity of blood, served to enhance and render innocuous the stereotypical Judaic skills of reading and writing. But literature and life are more complex and subtle than the reductionist version provided by official propaganda. Basques may well have been competent notaries and secretaries, but—how wonderfully ironic!—they owed their success and renown to the excellent training they received in the homes of Judeo-Christians.

Is it likely that we would have been able to discern the different levels of meaning in Sancho's words without the preparatory work of Professor Castro? Who more than he has taught us to be sensitive to the multiplicity of possible meanings in a Cervantine text, to recognize that ultimately meaning in literature implies layer upon layer of meaning, some invented, inherited or deliberately acquired, presented with varying degrees of "clarity,"[32] held together by an authorial intention, but always retaining a partial autonomy, so that the author's intention remains only one element—the presiding element, but still only one—in a complex federal association, including author and audience, ethics and aesthetics, personal life and sociohistoric circumstances, etc., etc.?[33]

In a similar vein, I wonder if we could have fully understood why as late as 1758 Galileo—the quintessential scientist—was considered an arch-Jew in Spain or why a certain student was so devoted to Aristotle—an honorary church father since the days of Thomas Aquinas—that every night without fail he said an

Our Father and a Hail Mary on his behalf. It is not likely that we would have appreciated, without Don Américo's insistent help, the *tragic* humor in the fact that this same student was heard to say, speaking of modern philosophers: "Allá se compongan con sus patrañas y embelecos; más nos vale jugar a lo seguro y andar piano, piano, a la pata la llana, siguiendo las pisadas de nuestro cristiano viejo Aristóteles." ('The Devil take them with all their humbug and tomfoolery; we'd better play it safe and go real slow, like plain folks would do, following in the footsteps of our Old Christian Aristotle.')[34] A few days before he died, Don Américo repeated this text to me, which I had heard him cite and elaborate upon many times during 1972.[35]

I can testify as well as anyone—having been with him to the very end—that he died as he had lived. His curiosity was still insatiable, his lucidity of mind unmarred, his arrogantly humble quest for perfection in the expression of his doctrines—what Rafael Lapesa called his "never satisfied striving to surpass himself"[36]—intact. Nothing, perhaps, is more characteristic of his special kind of humility than the title *Hacia Cervantes* and the fact that at the age of 86 he could have written with new insights and renewed expressions of reverence and love *Cómo veo ahora el Quijote,*[37] that a few weeks before his death he wrote four or five additional pages for the English version of this study, and that—when I showed him a little article of mine on Galdós[38]—he could have apologized profusely for not having written about Galdós's genius, although he was quick to point out that he had devoted classes to him at Princeton. His urge to write, to communicate—inspiring, nagging, scolding, suggesting, demanding—remained unabated. In fact, as his few vacation possessions were being loaded into a taxi at Lloret de Mar, the last item I saw was his ever-present typewriter.

He died loving life, remembering with undisguised emotion his disciples and friends. He died cherishing the memory of America and his American citizenship,[39] speaking Spanish, English, French, German and Italian, with adults and children at Lloret de Mar, giving the lie to Richard Herr's recent suggestion that Don Américo envisioned Spain as a monolithic and unchanging entity and that he seemed "to exclude his country forever from contemporary Western life."[40] In an interview published a few months before his death, Professor Castro concluded with an answer to the following question:

> Do you feel pessimistic about the possibilities of young Spaniards in the mastery of History?
>
> Although I will not live to see it, I have faith that Spanish youth—despite the universal disdain in which History is held nowadays—will come to understand fully how complex and difficult it was for authentic Spaniards to achieve their identity. When these truths appear on the pages of honest books, then both affluent and indigent youth can become capable of facing at the same time their past and their future. . . . While Spaniards remain stultified by the image of an illusory and falsified past, they will never be able to spread the wings of their scientific curiosity, nor will they reach the level of Western culture, sought after by so many on the Peninsula since the fifteenth century.[41]

In Wallace Stevens' "Notes toward a Supreme Fiction," there are five lines that I find most appropriate to describe the life and works of both Cervantes and Américo Castro:

> He had to choose. But it was not a choice
> Between excluding things. It was not a choice
> Between, but of. He chose to include the things
> That in each other are included, the whole,
> The complicate, the amassing harmony.[42]

At the California Palace of the Legion of Honor, the fine arts museum of San Francisco, there is an armorial tapestry, dated 1550, with the coat of arms of Don Diego de Córdoba, Primer Marqués de Santillán. Its motto reads: *Sine ipso factum est nihil* ('Without him[self] the deed is nothing'). This Hispanic truism[43] may not be accurate with regard to the intellectual achievements of Don Américo, for they are destined to endure on their own, but, for those of us who were privileged to know him and to experience the irresistible imperative dimension of his person, it is irrefutable.[44]

NOTES

1. "Entre los hebreos marroquíes: La lengua española de Marruecos," *Revista Hispano-Africana,* I, no. 5 (May 1922), pp. 145-146.

2. For more details about these materials, see S. G. Armistead and J. H. Silverman, "Un aspecto desatendido de la obra de Américo Castro," in *Estudios,* pp. 181-190.

3. "La Biblia de la casa de Alba," Folletones de *El Sol,* January 26, 1923. Don Américo had already recognized by this time that the Sephardim were as Spanish as the Old Christians, that Spain was as much theirs as of any other Spaniards.

Concerning Rabbi Arragel and the Alba Bible as a unique expression of religious syncretism, see Margherita Morreale, "La Biblia de Alba," *Arbor,* nos. 177-178 (1960), pp. 47-54, "El glosario de Rabí Mosé Arragel en la *Biblia de Alba,*" *Bulletin of Hispanic Studies,* XXXVIII (1961), pp. 145-152, and Carl-Otto Nordström, *The Duke of Alba's Castilian Bible: A Study of the Rabbinical Features of the Miniatures* (Uppsala, 1967).

There is an interesting reference to anti-Semitism in *PCer,* p. 294, n. 1; see now the revised edition (1972), pp. 281-282, 321, n. 142.

4. In 1927 Professor Castro called the expulsion of the Jews from Spain a sterile victory of the lower classes, whose inordinate pressure, above all in Andalusia, caused King Ferdinand to agree to the edict of expulsion—that "brutal exradicación"—after ten long years of indecision. See "Judíos," *La Gaceta Literaria,* I, no. 1 (1927), p. 2, reprinted in *ENC,* vol. 1, 205-211: p. 209.

5. "Sobre el teatro clásico español," *Nosotros,* 44 (1923), pp. 549-559. The article was first published in *El Sol,* but I do not have the specific date.

6. Some time ago I had the good fortune to locate the complete text of David Ebrón's letter as the result of a marginal note written by Don Américo on one of his books now at the Dean E. McHenry Library of the University of California at Santa Cruz. In July 1972, Mrs. Carmen Castro de Zubiri, following an unwritten wish of her father, and with the consent of her brother Luis, gave to the Santa Cruz library the books and reprints that her father had in Madrid at the time of his death, including several volumes from the library of her mother, Mrs. Carmen Madinaveitia de Castro. I take this opportunity to thank her and Mr. Luis Castro publicly for this most precious legacy and for their expression of confidence in the young Santa Cruz campus.

Ebrón's letter, identified in the article "Judíos" only as being found in the archive of the Duke of Alba, was published by the Duquesa de Berwick y de Alba in the *Documentos escogidos del Archivo de la Casa de Alba* (Madrid, 1891), pp. 228-235.

7. In a note added in 1969, Castro states that he had not yet realized by 1927 how important the Jews had been in the cultural history of the Iberian Peninsula. (*ENC,* I, 211).

8. "Erasmo en tiempo de Cervantes," *Revista de Filología Española,* XVIII (1931), pp. 329-389: pp. 367-368, n. 2. In *HCer,* 2d ed., the note continues to join the names of Mateo Alemán, Lope de Vega and Calderón (p. 198, n. 1; 2d ed., p. 224, n. 1), but in the considerably revised third edition Mateo Alemán is removed and the note concludes: "Nothing similar is to be found—nor do I believe it can be found—in the works of Lope de Vega, Calderón or Salas Barbadillo" pp. 254-255, n. 1).

9. See his detailed review of Ludwig Pfandl's *Historia de la literatura nacional española en la Edad de Oro* in the *Revista de Filología Española,* XXI (1934), 66-77: pp. 73-74.

10. I translate from the separate printing of "Lo hispánico y el erasmismo" and "Los prólogos al *Quijote*" (Buenos Aires, 1942), first published in vols. II-IV (1940, 1942) of the *Revista de Filología Hispánica*. See pp. 4-5.

11. *AVH*. The passage should have appeared on page 16 of both editions.

12. Don Américo once wrote that great literature has not infrequently been born in the most disagreeable human circumstances. See "Literatura y sociedad, 2," *Revista Mexicana de Literatura*, no. 8 (1956), 25-30: p. 27.

13. See *Estudios sobre Lope* (Mexico, 1951), pp. 223, 225-226, 268 and pp. 112-114 or *Estudios sobre Lope de Vega* (Salamanca, 1967), pp. 112-114, 239 and pp. 101-103.

14. María Goyri de Menéndez Pidal, "Los romances de Gazul," *Nueva Revista de Filología Hispánica*, VII, (1953), 403-416: p. 406.

15. *Lope de Vega's "El castigo del discreto", together with a study of conjugal honor in his theater* (New York, 1925), p. 41, n. 54. Fichter also noted that its plot was "somewhat similar" to that of *Las ferias de Madrid*, but missed crucial similarities and differences (p. 64, n. 116).

16. *Lope de Vega y La Celestina: Perspectiva seudocelestinesca en "comedias" de Lope* (Xalapa, 1968), p. 30. Erna Berndt Kelley cites the play in passing, since it includes a fragment of the popular ballad *Mira Nero de Tarpeya*. See "Popularidad del romance *Mira Nero de Tarpeya,*" *Estudios dedicados a James Homer Herriott* (University of Wisconsin [Valencia], 1966), pp. 118-126: p. 125. Camille Pitollet noted that *El galán escarmentado* might have been the source for John Dryden's *The Wild Gallant*: "La question de décider si Dryden—qui devait savoir l'espagnol; témoins . . . son *Wild Gallant*, emprunté (?) à *El galán escarmentado*, pièce actuellement perdue . . . —a été influencé par les défenseurs espagnols du drame libre, n'a pas encore été définitivement résolue" ("La poétique de Lope de Vega," *Feuilleton du Siècle*, November 16, 1906). On the basis of this tenuous observation, Milton A. Buchanan repeated that *El galán escarmentado* was lost, but was "known as the source of Dryden's *Wild Gallant.*" See "Chorley's Catalogue of Comedias and Autos of Frey Lope de Vega Carpio," *Modern Language Notes*, XXIV (1909), 167-171, 198-204: p. 199b. In Hugo A. Rennert and Américo Castro, *Vida de Lope de Vega* (Madrid, 1919), we read that *"El galán escarmentado* es la fuente de *Wild Gallant* de Dryden,"* p. 543, n. 482. The remark is perpetuated in the recent re-edition of the work (Salamanca, 1969), p. 514, n. 465, as well as an irrelevant reference to *Modern Language Notes*, XXXIII (1918), 115, unless one were looking for a review of H. W. Church, *Friedrich Rückert als Lyriker der Befreiungskriege* (Rennert-Castro, 1st ed., p. 482; 2d ed., p. 465).

It is obvious that none of these critics took the trouble to read Dryden's play, which is not at all reminiscent of Lope's *Galán escarmentado*. Moreover, Pitollet must have misread W. Harvey-Jellie, *Les sources du théâtre anglais à l'époque de la restauration* (Paris, 1906), since this critic had suggested that *The Wild Gallant* was derived from an unpublished, lost drama by Lope de Vega entitled *El galán bobo*. Buchanan and Rennert-Castro dutifully repeated this bit of nonsense, including Pitollet's erroneous variant of the Spanish title. For more details about this confusion and a demonstration that *The Wild Gallant* does not have a Spanish source, see Ned Bliss Allen, *The Sources of John Dryden's Comedies* (New York, 1967), pp. 2-8. A note by Federico Sánchez Escribano suggests that Dryden did have some knowledge of Lope and his revolutionary

156   ON SPAIN'S AGE OF CONFLICT

dramatic precepts ("Lope de Vega según una alusión de John Dryden," *Hispanófila*, no. 16 [1962], pp. 101-102). There is an interesting, well-documented discussion of this possibility in John Loftis, *The Spanish Plays of Neoclassical England* (New Haven and London, 1973), pp. 5, 9-11, although he is strangely unaware of Allen's useful study. For a few other passing references to *El Galán escarmentado*, see S. Griswold Morley and Courtney Bruerton, *The Chronology of Lope de Vega's "Comedias"* (New York, 1940), pp. 130-131 or, in the Spanish version, *Cronología de las comedias de Lope de Vega* (Madrid, 1968), pp. 223-225, and Noël Salomon, *Recherches sur le thème paysan dans la "comedia" au temps de Lope de Vega* (Bordeaux, 1965), pp. 103-104. See Juan Millé y Giménez, "Lope de Vega en la 'Armada Invencible'," *Revue Hispanique*, LVI (1922), 356-395: pp. 370-371, for an early discussion of possible autobiographical allusions in the play.

17. For an interesting discussion of the etymology of *sambenito*, see Américo Castro, "Sambenito," *Revista de Filología Española*, XV (1928), 170-181, included in *ENC*, III, 235-238, also Julio Caro Baroja, *Los judíos en la España moderna y contemporánea* (Madrid, 1961), I, 327-335, for details about the nefarious practice.

Although his etymologizing might have been inaccurate (Castro, p. 237), Sebastián de Covarrubias managed to include a subtle defense of those condemned to wear the ignominious *sambenito* in his definition of the term: ". . . although it may be a source of humiliation and disgrace, if those who wear it endure with patience the insults of the common people, they will merit much in the eyes of God" (*Tesoro de la lengua castellana* [1611], M. Riquer, ed. [Barcelona, 1943], p. 925a). In the words of a Sephardic Jew from Tetuán: "We are obliged to submit in this world to every species of indignity, but in the next we shall shine forth the chosen people of the Most High" (see Caro Baroja, op. cit., III, 262, n. 22). Is this veiled support of the vilified *conversos*— Covarrubias was writing in "an occupied language" (the phrase is Juan Goytisolo's)—further testimony of the distinguished lexicographer's own probably "tainted" background? See José Gómez-Menor Fuentes, "Nuevos datos documentales sobre el licenciado Sebastián de Horozco," *Anales Toledanos*, VI (1973), 249-286. Professor Castro saw the *sambenito* as an expression of the collective belief that national honor and unity of faith were one and the same thing. See *ECD*, 4th ed., p. 92.

At the December 29, 1970 meeting of The American Association of Teachers of Spanish and Portuguese held in San Francisco, I read a paper on "Los conversos en la vida y en la literatura" in the Peninsular Literature Session devoted to Golden Age Literature and Social Concern. In that paper, which I intend to publish in expanded form, I analyze the deleterious effects of the statutes of purity of blood and the institution of the *sambenito* on life in seventeenth-century Spain.

18. C. L. Barber, *Shakespeare's Festive Comedy* (Princeton, 1972), p. 186, in a discussion of "The Merchants and the Jew of Venice: Wealth's Communion and an *Intruder*" (emphasis added).

"The auto-da-fé eliminated a heretic, an *intruder* in the midst of the only possible faith" (my emphasis), Américo Castro, *ENC*, I, 20. In this sense, *El galán escarmentado* constituted a kind of secular version of the religious spectacle.

Concerning Julio's wealth as a cause in itself for suspicion about his lineage, see my "Los *hidalgos cansados* de Lope de Vega", *Homenaje a William L. Fichter* (Madrid, 1971), 693-711: p. 710, n. 42. In Lope de Vega's *Servir a señor discreto*, we read that to save money is for "base people": "a gentleman must be a bridge over which money can pass" (i.e., he doesn't hoard it). (*BAE* [Biblioteca de Autores Españoles] vol. 52, p. 77a).

19. See Antonio Domínguez Ortiz, *Los judeoconversos en España y América* (Madrid, 1971), p. 222, or the *Memorial* (Archivo Histórico Nacional. Ordenes Militares, 1320, C), fol. 113v. Selma Margaretten was kind enough to locate this manuscript for me in Madrid.

Marcelino Menéndez y Pelayo observed that the brutal intolerance behind the mania of purity of blood was a motive for rancor and revenge, an unending source of discord. See his *Historia de los heterodoxos españoles* (Madrid, 1965), I, 644. In an essay entitled "How Jewish Were the Marranos?", to be included in the volume *Hispania Judaica*, edited by S. G. Armistead, J. H. Silverman, and J. M. Sola-Solé, Ellis Rivkin has noted that "the concept of purity of blood had devastating effects, for it deprived the *converso* who had escaped the Inquisition of his Christian rights. He was doomed, however Christian he might be, to a pariah status because Old Christians would refuse to intermarry, lest they and their progeny become tainted with Jewish blood."

20. José Antonio Maravall, *Teatro y literatura en la sociedad barroca* (Madrid, 1972), p. 94, n. 57 (emphasis not in original of quotation). This is yet another manifestation of Maravall's chimeric urge to make Spain identical to all other European countries. See my *Hidalgos cansados*, p. 703, n. 33. To the texts cited there, add these remarks which are appropriate despite their reference to an earlier historical period: "Not to attempt to grasp those profound national differences that lie beneath a surface unity is not to realize that our great distance from the observed phenomena, our meager familiarity with them, is the reason we perceive so dimly the numerous differences between them that reality presents. And so we fall into the ingenuous simplicity of the observer who cannot recognize the differences in individuals of a race he is unfamiliar with and concludes that all Chinese look alike. The *medievality* common to the various peoples of western Europe prevents us from perceiving the individual *nationality* of each one of them" (R. Menéndez Pidal, "La épica medieval en España y en Francia," included in *En torno al Poema del Cid* [Barcelona, 1970], p. 76).

A curious way of avoicing the awkward matter of purity of blood can be seen in recent translations of Fernando de Rojas' *La Celestina*. Lesley Byrd Simpson renders the phrase "tu limpieza de sangre e fechos" (Act 12), said by Calisto to Melibea, as "your pure intentions" (*The Celestina* [Berkeley and Los Angeles, 1955], p. 132). Phyllis Hartnoll offers "your sincerity" (*Celestina* [London, 1959], p. 139), which J. M. Cohen repeats (*The Spanish Bawd* [Baltimore, 1964], p. 175). Only Mack Hendricks Singleton has been faithful to the original with "the purity of your lineage and your actions" (*Celestina*[Madison, 1958], p. 178. This phrase has been conveniently overlooked by those who insist on Melibea's Jewish background.

As late as 1805 it was still necessary to provide, in addition to a baptismal certificate, documentary proof of purity of blood as one of the rigorous selection criteria for enrollment at the Nautical School of La Coruña. See *Origen y progresos de la Escuela Náutica de La Coruña* (1790–1825), an address delivered by Antonio Meijide Pardo before the Galician Royal Academy (La Coruña, 1963), p. 27.

21. "In the auto da fé, the bullfight, and the plays of Lope de Vega, the popular masses had the opportunity to participate collectively and to reinforce their own pride as Old Christians. On these occasions Spanish unanimity wore its finest clothes. No matter what the denouement of Lope de Vega or his followers' plays might be, these works echoed the beliefs, expectations, sentiments, and value judgments of their audience." (Américo Castro, *SIH,* p. 599).
El galán escarmentado and other plays related to it thematically are given detailed treatment in my forthcoming *El otro teatro nacional de Lope de Vega.* At the University of Kentucky's 21st Foreign Language Conference, April 26, 1968, I read a paper on *El galán escarmentado* entitled "Un caso insólito de la honra en Lope de Vega."

22. Don García, the supposed target of Alarcón's moralizing, recognized that in all likelihood the lengthy delay had been caused by some invidious scandal-monger—"algún pecho de envidia emponzoñnado"—the very same kind of individual evoked by Sancho Panza with such penetrating irony that his remarks were judged to be apocryphal ·(*Don Quixote,* Part II, chapter 5); an informer filled with that "envidia emponzoñada," "envidia ponzoñosa," of which Fray Luis de León bitterly complained during years of inquisitional persecution, or the "embidia venenosa" that precipitated the exile of Antonio Enríquez Gómez from Spain and would become a plaintive constant of his fictional and doctrinal writings. See my "Plinio, Pedro Mejía y Mateo Alemán: La enemistad entre las especies hecha símbolo visual," *Et Cætera,* no. 14 (1969), 23–31: pp. 28, 30–31, n. 14, and Constance Hubbard Rose, *Alonso Núñez de Reinoso: The Lament of a Sixteenth-Century Exile* (Rutherford-Madison-Teaneck, 1971), pp. 77, 119–125, and "Antonio Enríquez Gómez and the Literature of Exile," *Romanische Forschungen,* 85 (1973), 63–77: pp. 73–74. For Núñez de Reinoso, envy is the "destruction of familial honor . . . provoking lawsuits, discord, hardships, misfortunes, allowing no chance for rest or serenity." Envy leads to "false and perverse accusations against which the defense of the accused is to no avail" (p. 77; remember Julio's sonnet on written messages). Lope de Vega, although most often a voice of popular opinion, clearly understood the dangers and injustices of the Inquisition and its network of informers and *malsines:*

> With sinister information
> he has convinced Don Pedro,
> and thus have I lost Elena,
> my honor and my reputation.
> I suspect that he has accused me
> of some impurity in my blood,
> and if I allow the charge to stand,
> my blood will one day be considered
> completely tainted; for from such deceits
> arise untold dangers which impede
> the entry into prestigious orders
> and result in the total loss of one's honor.
> How many individuals have served
> as false witnesses in more than one investigation
> against the enemies who once maligned them!
> How many reputations have been destroyed,

> nobilities lost, by dint of the unreasoning
> passion in family feuds!
> May the Lord free you from the weight
> of a charge against your honor,
> for once it has been lodged,
> not all the water in the sea
> can wash it away.

(Lope de Vega Carpio, *La buena guarda, Obras dramáticas escogidas,* edited by Eduardo Juliá Martínez [Madrid, 1934], vol. I, pp. 154-155; also his *La villana de Getafe, Acad. N.* X, 393b, 398a-b).

For Mateo Alemán's remarks about malicious informers who take pride in their activities and believe that they can achieve salvation through spreading "aquella ponzoña," see "Los *hidalgos cansados,*" p. 701, n. 30. In the dream world of Don Quixote, with his undaunted vision of a Spain that might have been, lineage, purity of blood, Jewish or Moorish ancestry, meant nothing. There was no Inquisition and there were no relentless investigations:

> I am . . . content to imagine and believe that the good
> Aldonza Lorenzo is lovely and virtuous; and the question of her
> lineage is of little importance, for no one will investigate that
> for the purpose of investing her with any order, and for my part
> I consider her the greatest princess in the world.

> (*Don Quixote,* Part I, chapter 25)

23. He reiterated his position in the lengthy prologue to *ENC,* I, 30 (completed in June 1970), in *SIH,* pp. 550-551, and, for the last time, in the fourth edition of *ECD,* p. 181.

24. It is worth recalling at this point Cervantes's *La elección de los alcaldes de Daganzo (The Election of the Daganzo Aldermen)* and the qualifications of Humillos to be one:

PESUNA: Do you know how to read, Humillos?

HUMILLOS: Certainly not, and you can't find that any member of my family was ever so unbalanced as to try to learn those silly hentracks that bring men to the stake and women to the whorehouse. I can't read; but I know a lot of things more useful than reading.

PESUNA: And what are they?

HUMILLOS: I know all four prayers by heart, and I say them four or five times a week.

RANA: And you think that's enough to make you alderman?

HUMILLOS: With that, and my being an Old Christian, I dare to be a Roman senator.

In an important article on "San Ignacio de Loyola y el problema de los *cristianos nuevos,*" *Razón y Fe,* nos. 696-701 (January-February 1956), 173-204, Father Eusebio Rey, S. J., refers to an inquisitor who would give no position of authority to a convert, however saintly and learned he might be (p. 191). Antonio Enríquez Gómez, writing from a convert's point of view, lamented that they should be excluded "from among the ecclesiastical dignitaries and nobles of the Republic, putting in the place of such learned and scholarly individuals, crude farmers, unschooled peasants, and boorish shepherds." See

I. S. Révah, "Un pamphlet contre l'Inquisition d'Antonio Enríquez Gómez: La seconde partie de la *Política Angélica* (Rouen, 1647)," *Revue des Etudes Juives,* CXXI (1962), 81–168: p. 145. Luis de Góngora, on the other hand, assuming the voice of a mock-patriotic simpleton, writes in his *romance* "Ensíllenme el asno rucio":

> If your sadness were to increase,
> you could cut yourself a slice of ham,
> which would certainly know how to
> change your grief to merriment.
> Oh, how much more a slice of ham
> knows (how much better a slice of ham tastes)
> than all who know how to read,
> and pigs' tails more than the tongues of scholars!

Góngora is playing with two meanings of *saber*: 'to know' and 'to taste.' A slice of ham, then, tastes better and is worth more than anyone who knows how to read. Pork products—the very essence of Hispanic Christianity—are juxtaposed with learning—a Jewish characteristic—in order to ridicule the latter. In *Servir a señor discreto,* a lackey proclaims from the depths of his folk prejudice:

> . . . exquisite preserves,
> I consider them vile things.
> . . . .
> Oh, if only you made pork sausages,
> large sausages and hams!

Naturally! There was something dangerously Semitic about exquisite preserves, as compared to the Christianity and fervent patriotism to be found in a good ham or pork sausage. The limits of this dietary nationalism are reached by a lackey named Lope:

> I am the one
> who invented bacon.
> I engendered pigs;
> the invention was mine.
> (*La villana de Getafe,* p. 395a)

For other examples of the virtue of illiteracy, see my "Some Aspects of Literature and Life in the Golden Age of Spain," *Estudios de literatura española ofrecidos a Marcos A. Morínigo* (Madrid, 1971), pp. 131–170: p. 157, n. 28.

25. "Apparently a satirical note, as Pellicer already indicated when mentioning the many secretaries of the King as well as of Councils and high-level organizations who were Biscayans by birth or origin, and who served in the times of Charles V and his son Philip II" (*El ingenioso hidalgo Don Quijote de la Mancha.* Edición IV Centenario. Ediciones Castilla [Madrid, n.d.], p. 1788, n. 32).

26. *El ingenioso hidalgo Don Quijote de la Mancha,* Clemente Cortejón, ed. (Madrid, 1911), V, 427–428.

27. *Don Quixote de la Mancha,* edited by Rodolfo Schevill and Adolfo Bonilla (Madrid, 1941), IV, 428, n. 101-2. I cite the Covarrubias text from Martín de Riquer's edition of the *Tesoro* (Barcelona, 1943), p. 288b.

28. Clemencín, however, reminds us that the Biscayans have never been reputed to be particularly competent in writing Castilian. In fact, he suspects that the

entire passage might be ironic, harking back to the early satire of Biscayans (Part I, chapter 8) and their ludicrously garbled Spanish (op. cit., p. 1789, n. 41). An interesting confirmation of this sixteenth-century linguistic reality is found in Julio Caro Baroja's *The World of the Witches* (Chicago, 1964), p. 155: "On this occasion [1575] one of the major problems of the whole business cropped up once more: the language difficulty. The inquisitors could not understand the prisoners, who doubtless spoke nothing but Basque." For the Spanish original, see *Las brujas y su mundo* (Madrid, 1966), p. 200. I am grateful to Professor Theodore R. Sarbin for this reference.

29. Lope de Vega, *Obras sueltas. El ayre de la almena*, XXII. Ed. Antonio Pérez y Gómez (Cieza, 1969), II, 115.

30. See my "Judíos y conversos en el *Libro de chistes* de Luis de Pinedo," *Papeles de Son Armadans*, XXIII, no. 69 (1961), 289-301: pp. 295-297; A. Castro, *OSE*, pp. 62-63; *ECS*, pp. 175-177; *SNQ*, pp. 282-283.

31. Fernando del Pulgar, *Letras. Glosa a las Coplas de Mingo Revulgo*. Edited by J. Domínguez Bordona, Clásicos Castellanos, vol. 99 (Madrid, 1929), pp. 149-150.

32. "A writer must beware of . . . censorship, and on its account he must soften and distort the expression of his opinion. According to the strength and sensitiveness of the censorship he finds himself compelled either merely to refrain from certain forms of attack, or to speak in allusions in place of direct references, or he must conceal his objectionable pronouncement beneath some apparently innocent disguise. . . . The stricter the censorship, the more far-reaching will be the disguise and the more ingenious too may be the means employed for putting the reader on the scent of the true meaning" (S. Freud, *The Interpretation of Dreams* [New York, 1961], p. 142).

33. These words on meaning in literature paraphrase and extend a statement by Graham Hough. Regrettably, I have misplaced the exact reference.

34. See Paulino Garagorri, "Xavier de Munibe en la filosofía española," *Revista de Occidente*, II, no. 21 (1964), 335-347: p. 340 or *Españoles razonantes* (Madrid, 1969), p. 48. For the complete text, see Padre José Francisco de Isla, *Obras escogidas, BAE*, XV (Madrid, 1945), p. 375a. In 1923, probably unaware of Munibe's satire, Don Américo would duplicate his tone and the grotesquerie it evoked: "El aborrecimiento tradicional de las inteligencias pedía ser católicos, en la forma que eso se entendía aquí. Y para poder estar con comodidad, en familia, a la pata la llana espiritual, echaron a judíos y moriscos, que por azar histórico y por su desdicha vinieron a España." ('The traditional hatred of intelligence required that one be Catholic in the way that it was understood in Spain. And in order to live comfortably, with one's own kind, at a folksy level in spiritual things, they expelled the Jews and Moriscos, who by some accident of history and for their misfortune had come to Spain'; "Sobre el teatro clásico español," p. 558). Already in 1926 M. Núñez de Arenas recognized the value of Munibe's (Count Peñaflorida) caustic *Los aldeanos críticos* and even cited a passage that Garagorri would also emphasize about Newton, Descartes, Leibniz, and Galileo as "heretical dogs, atheists, and Jews." But Núñez de Arenas did not grasp its profound significance for a holistic understanding of Spanish society. See "Un problema histórico: La heterodoxia de los caballeros vascos," *Boletín de la Biblioteca Menéndez y Pelayo*, VIII (1926), 163-184: p. 175, and A. Castro, *SIH*, p. 577.

35. Thanks to a Senior Fellowship from the National Endowment for the Humanities, I was able to spend a year in Spain (1971-1972), during which time I had the unforgettable good fortune of speaking with Don Américo on numerous occasions in Madrid and Lloret de Mar.

36. "*La Celestina* en la obra de Américo Castro," in *Estudios,* pp. 247-261: p. 261. Don Américo's death, at the height of his intellectual powers, brings to mind the death of Cervantes—"who tried to go even beyond death in realizing his intention"—and the way Don Américo had described it: "And now, precisely now, he had to die. But Cervantes died holding fast to the preoccupations of his life, dependent upon himself alone, rooted in the consciousness of what he could and couldn't do, as if he were a major character in one of his greatest works" (see his introduction to *El ingenioso hidalgo Don Quijote de la Mancha* [Mexico, 1960], p. LXVIII). Toward the end, Don Américo was acutely aware of the gnawing truth that "anything we want to do must be accomplished within a certain, constantly decreasing, period of time" (José Ferrater Mora, *Being and Death: An Outline of Integrationist Philosophy* [Berkeley and Los Angeles, 1965], p. 187).

37. It appeared as a preliminary study to a popular edition of *Don Quijote*: Colección Novelas y Cuentos, no. 100-101 (Madrid, Editorial Magisterio Español, 1971).

38. "Unos judíos admiradores de Galdós," *Amistad Judeo-Cristiana,* no. 42 (1972), p. 3.

39. In a recent open letter to Claudio Sánchez-Albornoz (*ABC,* May 3, 1974, pp. 36-37), Pedro Laín Entralgo indicated that Professor Castro had returned to Spain because he wanted to die there, because he had a vital need for a piece of Spanish soil as his final resting place. However neatly this may fit the image of the exiled Spaniard who must go home to die, it is not the case as I knew it. Don Américo returned to Spain above all to please Doña Carmen. Over and over he insisted, while speaking English, that he was "doing time" in Madrid, a prisoner in a country scarcely his own. He dreamed of returning to America, and a favorite fantasy of his last days was to be back in Princeton once again, where he might live out his days in the home of some quiet American family, near the beloved library at which he had worked so fruitfully during his mature years. This is the truth as I heard it. An old man is capable of many daydreams and, in the company of his Spanish friends, Don Américo's may have been different than the one that I, as an American, had proudly shared. In 1961 he mentioned his American citizenship with pride and gratitude. His words on that occasion—honoring the great humanist Marcel Bataillon— deserve to be repeated in this homage volume: "I should like to say that I am particularly pleased to have been invited to say these words in Washington, as a citizen of this country which has refined the Hispanic spirit of my Spanish soul and my consciousness of the common destiny of the Hispanic peoples. Those peoples need freedom and the chance to give increasingly worthy expression to their desire to be free. For freedom is not a magic virtue, floating in the clouds of Utopia. It is, rather, a means of giving expression or form to what is deserving thereof. Words are of value for what they say, and freedom is important in that it permits the unhindered airing of questions which have a right to circulate in human society. There are many of us who regret the absence of freedom in some Hispanic nations, thinking of the values which remain mute

or which fade away for lack of means of expression. There are many of us too who regret that tyranny should be so free to assert itself over peoples. It makes no difference whether such tyranny be exercised from above or from below: the result is the same. . . . If blind, tyrannical dogmatism, imposed from above or from below, were ever diabolically to prevail, our world would fall into barbarity of the dullest and most sinister type" ("The 1961 Serra Award of the Americas," *The Americas*, XVIII [1962]. 394-396: pp. 395-396).

40. *Spain* (Englewood Cliffs, 1971), p. 31. A more than adequate response to Herr's words can be found in the final section of *SNQ*, entitled "Ultimos escritos, año 1972" (pp. 375-404): "The authentic historiography of a people conscious of having a history is always based on the dual hope of having had a past worthy of attention today, and of creating a future that can remedy the shortcomings of the past and exist *in its own time*," (p. 390; emphasis in the original). See also *SIH*, p. 94; *ENC*, 1, 49-50, p. 98. The entire article "La reflexión sobre España y el espíritu de la escuela," *Revista de Pedagogía*, no. 139 (Madrid, 1933), pp. 289-293 (1-8 in offprint pagination) is worth reproducing here, but a few sentences must suffice: "Spain in its history [the great *España en su historia* appears in 1948] was essentially a struggle, a conflict, within itself. Side by side with the predominant tendencies, there exist the efforts of dissenting observers who, since the fifteenth century, have been trying to alter the direction that the governing masses had chosen for the country. It seems to me that this sustained tendency and the very existence of a difference of opinions and preferences that extends from the fifteenth century until the present is something as essential to the history of Spain as the battle of Otumba or the Inquisition. And Spain is as much the country of the majority and its leaders as it is of the dissidents and nonconformists" (p. 5). Cf. the brilliant essay on "Jovellanos" included in *SEE*, pp. 405-411, particularly the moving discussion of "hispanidad discrepante" (p. 406).

See also the valuable study of Paulino Garagorri, "Un mitoclasta nacional: En torno a la tarea desmitificadora de Américo Castro," *Revista de Occidente*, IV, no. 41 (1966), 234-244 and Oriol Pi-Sunyer's excellent "The Historiography of Américo Castro: An Anthropological Interpretation," *Bulletin of Hispanic Studies*, 49 (1972), 40-50. A quotation he provides from Claude Lévi-Strauss— "But actually our ultimate purpose is not so much to discover the unique characteristics of the societies we study, as it is to discover in what ways these societies differ from one another. As in linguistics, it is the *discontinuities* which constitute the true subject matter of anthropology"—recalls these decisive words of Don Américo: "The ways in which individuals and peoples are alike are comparatively easy to discern. I am interested in the more elusive problem of how they are different. . . . *The Structure of Spanish History* rests upon the assumption that differences in style, whether in life or in art, are meaningful, that a distinctive style of collective life is the expression of a reality" ("A Note on *The Structure of Spanish History*," *Speculum*, XXXII [1957], 222-223: p. 223).

Pi-Sunyer observes that Castro's conception of history resembles the anthropologist's view of culture and that there is in both "a similar recognition that societies are *not static entities*, but rather evidence certain directional qualities" (p. 42; emphasis added). And, like Franz Boas, Castro would claim that the genius of culture—its configuration—"has often remarkable permanency" (Introduction to Ruth Benedict, *Patterns of Culture* [New York, 1951], n.p.).

41. Manuel Cerezales, "Américo Castro: La literatura fuente de la historia," *ABC* (Reportaje), 17 May 1972, n.p.

42. *Selected Poems* (London, 1960), pp. 99-125; p. 124. See my "Sobre el arte de no renunciar a nada," *Papeles de Son Armadans,* XIX, nos. CCXXI-II (1974), 129-142. (Page 133, lines 19-21, should read: "Se ha dicho que el *Lazarillo,* a diferencia de la sátira erasmista, no critica el mal creer sino el mal vivir.") It will also appear as prologue to Joseph V. Ricapito's *Bibliografía razonada y anotada de las obras maestras de la novela picaresca española.*

43. In a bitter proleptic vision of industrialized society's dehumanization, Mariano José de Larra wrote that "in progressive countries civilization had convinced society that only things, only facts are something, persons nothing" (1837). This vital interest in the individual integrity of human beings is thought to have emerged in Spain from the multisecular *convivencia* of Arabs, Christians and Jews. In a fascinating articcle by Lawrence Rosen, "A Moroccan Jewish Community during the Middle Eastern Crisis," *The American Scholar,* 37 (1968), 435-451, we learn that in Morocco "the locus of every level of organization is the single individual, whose status is based not on some innate position in a fixed set of social categories but on his ability to maneuver within the rules of the game to consolidate and extend his personal power within and beyond his own kinsmen. Through the arrangement of his alliances and the sheer force of his own personality each man can, according to his abilities, mold the pliable social fabric into a pattern as distinctive and ephemeral as himself. . . . Throughout their lives, Berbers and Arabs alike will have judged others and themselves been judged according to the principle T. E. Lawrence once referred to when he said: 'Arabs believe in persons, not in institutions' " (p. 444). See A. Castro, *The Meaning of Spanish Civilization; RHE,* pp. 250-254; *ECD, 4th ed., pp. 137*-138, and *SIH,* pp. 39-40.

I was pleased to find among Don Américo's papers a note which harks back to the Larra quotation of 1837: "We still live with the prejudice that nobody is more than anyone else except through his works. We still do not esteem men except for what they have been able to transform from their personality into things and material works. But a new humanism is dawning, one that decries the supremacy of things and affirms that of persons, who will be valued more for what they were than for what they did." These words—an affirmation of Don Américo's *man in himself, essential man*—were part of a necrology for Laureano Díaz Canseco, prepared in 1930 by Blas Ramos, for publication in the *Anuario de Historia del Derecho Español.* It was, however, not published until 1967, when Jorge Guillén had it privately printed: Blas Ramos, *Necrología de Canseco* (Málaga, Imprenta Dardo, 1967). According to Don Américo's note, the cited passage appears on p. 48.

In a brilliant study of the "Jewish struggle with modernity," John Murray Cuddihy demonstrates how *Western* Christianity, the Protestant Ethic in particular, with its code of *"impersonal* service of an *impersonal* end" and its esthetic manifestation in "restraint and self-effacement," goes against the grain of *Jewish* living and writing. Such puritanical dictates of good taste made Leslie Fiedler feel that as a student at City College of New York he was writing in an "occupied country" (remember Goytisolo's "occupied language"), for his Freshman Composition teacher exercised rigorous censorship against Yiddishisms and taught "a language capable of uttering only the most correctly tepid Protestant banalities no matter what stirred in our *alien* innards." See Cuddihy's *The Ordeal of Civility* (New York, 1974), pp. 220-221, 185 (emphases added).

44. In *SNQ,* see the essay "Dimensión imperativa de la persona" (pp. 300-326). Elsewhere, Professor Samuel G. Armistead and I will take up other aspects of our conversations and correspondence with Professor Castro during 1971-72, particularly concerning the *Romancero* and the concept of hyphenated culture, a subject I have recently examined in lectures at the Universities of Cincinnati and Kentucky.

8

A NEW PERSPECTIVE
OF CERVANTES' WORK

Antony van Beysterveldt

According to 1959 statistics there are over two thousand editions
of Cervantes' most famous work, *Don Quixote*. Such a clear
sign of the continuing popularity of the *Quixote* with an
undifferentiated mass of readers all over the world cannot help
but intrigue the historian of literature who must take into
account the ever-growing wave of criticism that has accompanied
the triumphal march of Cervantes' work from the very beginning.
Consequently, the one single factor we can derive from the mul-
titude of most diverse judgments that critics have pronounced
on the *Quixote* seems to be its difficulty of interpretation.
According to Roland Barthes, in his controversial essay, "Histoire
ou littérature,"[1] it is convenient to differentiate between two
clearly separate facets of the task of the literary historian. The
interpretation of the work itself is, naturally, the most essential
part. But prior to this comes the analysis of sources, influences,
and the linguistic aspects of the text. This is where Cervantine
scholars have tread on firm ground and where the reader of the
Quixote can surrender almost completely to the triumphal erudition of a Francisco Rodríguez Marín. Unfortunately, though,
the high degree of accuracy and irreproachable honesty that
characterize this initial phase fade away when we come to the
critical moment in the interpretation of the work itself. Until
recently, Roland Barthes' skepticism seemed well-founded in
regard to Cervantes' greatest work when he declared that the
literary historian, after giving proof of scientific rigor in his
preliminary research, is satisfied with "a purely magical interpretation of literary creation" in the essential aspect of his
task.

167

It is true that any work of art, in order to be enjoyed to the fullest, demands a co-creative effort on the part of the reader or the viewer. But the fact is that, alongside the legitimate inhabitants of Cervantes' universe, outsiders have intervened to take over those literary specters to the extent that there were moments in a not very remote past when the characters created by Cervantes' genius seemed to speak only through the mouths of those intruders. But these voices have been stilled and after a brief eclipse the authentic characters of the *Quixote* have reappeared, more enigmatic than ever, and behind them, the indispensable presence of Cervantes himself. In the broad field of Cervantine studies, the most extreme statements confront each other, more irreconcilable, perhaps, than in any other field of Spanish literary criticism, and the most flagrant contradictions coexist as to the meaning of this capital work in Spanish and in world literature. It is a bitter and false consolation to recommend to the budding scholar of Cervantes, disoriented by the overwhelming amount of critical material published on the *Quixote* that, if he were to discard from all those commentaries only the ones that mutually cancel each other out because they are contradictory, he would drastically reduce the amount of material he has to deal with. But the matter is not so simple. The enormous number of erudite opinions, all respectable but contradictory and mutually exclusive, which weight down the "science" of literature, seem to jeopardize the very scientific nature of the professional task of the literary historian. There are many who feel that the attitude of complacent tolerance toward incompatible judgments that swell the manuals of literary history has become somewhat anachronistic. According to this view, the history of a literary period ought to be something more than a collection of personal value judgments, because what that concept seems to imply ultimately is that the search for objective truths in matters of literary criticism is not only impossible but irrelevant.

Others, in contrast, hold that the multiplicity of literary interpretations is inevitable and even necessary insofar as it is an expression of the sociohistorical changes that have been operating on successive generations of readers who have thought

about their common cultural heritage. If many of these judgments have been rejected by the succeeding generation, some
have definitely found their way into the small heap of accumu-
lative cultural treasures toward which the interminable controversies of literati progress at a snail's pace. Cervantine criticism,
as a collective critical task, has followed this arduous path,
recording the objectifiable values of each individual vision and
discarding value judgments that are too subjective. Nevertheless,
in Cervantes' case the fruits of those continuing endeavors have
led to a better understanding only of very partial aspects of the
Quixote and have hardly raised the level of our perception of the
work in its entirety. This is because critics prior to Américo
Castro, and even he himself in his 1925 edition of *El pensamiento de Cervantes,* had only succeeded in defining many
elements in the life and works of Cervantes. But there were very
few sure steps that criticism, with the aid of these elements,
could take in the search for the meaning of the work and the
relationship between it and the personal circumstances of
Cervantes' life. Thus, most of the attempts to interpret the
Quixote are fragmentary. With his usual intellectual honesty,
Ortega y Gasset seems to have expressed what many critics must
have felt as a personal sense of frustration when he said apropos
of the *Quixote*: "No other book has as great a power to create
symbolic allusions to the universal meaning of life, nevertheless,
in no other book do we find fewer hints or indications as to its
own interpretation." Ortega, with his unfailing literary intuition,
called Don Quixote "the guardian of the Spanish secret, of the
ambiguity of Spanish culture."[2]

The only theoretical explanation capable of elucidating the
total meaning of the *Quixote* seems to be the one explicitly
indicated by Cervantes himself: his intention to satirize the
novels of chivalry. Even today there are still scholars who insist
blindly and stubbornly on clinging to that guideline—the only
legitimate one for them—and led by it they have arrived at a
very narrow vision of a "quixotesque world." What is significant
about the growing underground current of the vague ways of
interpreting the *Quixote* is the fact that many commentators
have stubbornly rejected the idea that the *Quixote* was merely

an invective against the novels of chivalry because, in their own readings of this great book, they had perceived allusions and references that seemed to point towards much deeper and more mysterious secrets of the mind. This rejection, therefore, was founded on a few tentative efforts made within the world of the *Quixote* on the basis of vague impressions and intuitions. Nevertheless, these probes constitute the most valuable aspect of the fragmentary critical explanations of Cervantes' work because they have cut off the hasty generalizations that might have upset the delicate balance in the problematical explanations of Cervantes' multifaceted work. Thus, before arriving at the great synthetic vision of Américo Castro, it was already possible to see the positive, productive efforts of these cautious and increasingly more perceptive approaches to the wealth of material in Cervantes' novel. In this regard Richard Predmore's theory on the composition of the *Quixote* should be mentioned, although, as an example, it is not entirely pertinent since it concerns a technical aspect of the novel.[3] However, it will serve to illustrate what we have said until this point.

It is common knowledge that Cervantes calls himself the "stepfather" and not the father of the *Quixote*. In the course of the narration he constantly refers to the authority of other writers, sources, and *archives*. Furthermore, in chapter ix of Part I he introduces *Cide Hamete Benengeli*, the "Arabic historian" whose *History of Don Quixote de la Mancha*, duly rendered into Spanish by a *translator*, enables Cervantes to continue with the narration of the adventures of his hero. In Part II this shifting perspectivism becomes even more complicated by presenting Don Quixote and Sancho as *literary characters* whose exploits were already recorded in Part I, and at the same time, as real people in search of new adventures that will give a new historian ample material for another book. In addition, many scholars have taken up the complex problem of literary perspectivism posed by the composition of the *Quixote*. In *La ambigüedad del Quijote*,[4] Manuel Durán illustrates the protagonists' awareness in Part II of their own adventures with the eloquent example of a Steinberg cartoon showing an arm in the process of drawing its head on the very stump of which it is a member. This graphic comparison is as revealing as the many reflections by which critics have attempted to come to grips with the problem, to pinpoint its elements more accurately. But it was not until Predmore's *El mundo del Quijote* that these partial explanations would be fused into an overall, definitive vision. Cervantes succeeded in creating the illusion of the autonomous reality of Don Quixote and Sancho, Predmore tells us, thanks to the literary devices mentioned earlier (archives, Benengeli, etc.). This, then, is Predmore's formula: *Cervantes established two levels of fiction, separated in such a way that the distance between the two appears to the reader to be the difference between life and literature.* Thus he formulated in words a truth whose elements, already coated with a clear intention, had been evident to everyone. In this way Predmore's contributions have shed new light on this technical aspect of the *Quixote.*

América Castro's new ideas on the way of interpreting the history of Spain and Spanish culture have also provoked a similar revelation, but this time on an infinitely broader scale, because of the light they shed on the entire literary panorama of Cervantes' work. Castro writes: "The peculiar 'casticism' of Cervantes only serves the purpose in these pages to see more accurately *what was only glimpsed or falsified prior to this time.*"[5] As the italicized words indicate, it is a matter of projecting a new perspective onto what we have called the "elements" of the *Quixote.* The far-reaching implications of Castro's theories are actually so broad that they have shed new light on much of what was already known or believed about the life and works of Cervantes. In the following observations on Américo Castro's decisive intervention in the reappraisal of Cervantes' works, I have taken into account the essays collected in *Estudios sobre la obra de Américo Castro* and particularly those contributions that touch upon the theme that Zamora Vicente has called "Castro's Cervantine task."

In 1925 Américo Castro published his fundamental study, *El pensamiento de Cervantes,* a book that many scholars consider to be the best study ever written on Cervantes. It was, in effect, not only the most profound and thorough study on Cervantes until that time, but even then it was considered as a model for what literary investigation could and should be. But the most perplexing and paradoxical aspect, particularly for that sector of Cervantine scholars who subsequently rejected the new historico-literary theories postulated by Castro, is the fact that the author himself left vacant his eminent post as *maestro de los hispanistas*, which he justly deserved, in the opinion of both Spanish and foreign Hispanists, because of his great work published in 1925. Since his "second period," whose beginning coincides with the Spanish Civil War and Castro's ensuing expatriation, the author has referred to his work only to show how blind, disoriented, and mistaken he had been in this first phase of his Cervantine explorations. Without the slightest display of pride or affection for this magnificent product of his vast erudition and analytic abilities and perhaps unscrupulously, Castro left Cervantes orphaned and imprisoned within the pages of his famous 1925 work, and his most fervent supporters, who wanted to speak of no other Cervantes but that one, were left alone and abandoned. Why did Castro later reject the fame he so justly deserved? What was there in his new approach to the historical and literary reality of Spain that caused him to reject his previous work with a gesture of impatience and almost irritation, which has left more than a few of his most devoted followers perplexed? The problem had already been posed by scholars who asked if there was a complete break between *El pensamiento de Cervantes* (the most representative work of his first period) and his works after 1938.[6] Obviously those who refused to recognize Castro's new ideas gave an affirmative answer to this question. But Francisco López Estrada and Juan Marichal, who by no means could be included in this group, also held the same opinion.[7] In contrast, those who believe that there was not, in the long run, a break in the continuity of Castro's long labor of investigation, belong, if I am not mistaken, to the small circle of the most well-known and oldest followers of Américo Castro: Stephen Gilman, Guillermo Araya, Vicente Llorens, Julio Rodríguez-Puértolas, Francisco Márquez Villanueva, and others. Later we shall briefly discuss this matter, which is intimately related to the very form in which we are evaluating the new stimulus that Américo Castro has given to Hispanic studies.

Now I should like to point out a few problems in *El pensamiento de Cervantes* that, at first glance, seem to be the forerunners of ideas and concepts developed by the author much later. According to Stephen Gilman: "If we examine the work of Castro's first period, not from the point of view of its usefulness then and now, but as if it were the larva of a hitherto unsuspected butterfly . . . then we are in a position to detect the first symptoms of an imminent metamorphosis."[8]

Even though it was always couched in purely literary terms in *El pensamiento de Cervantes,* a clear vision already begins to develop of the differentiating elements that separate the dramatic world of the *comedia* from the novelistic universe of Cervantes. Castro comments that "Cervantes' world vision is diametrically opposed to Lope's. All these concomitances with the literary science of the period served as the basis for Cervantes' discourse on the way things are and the way they ought to be; and we already know that Lope is not noted for raising questions of that nature, at least in a serious manner."[9] Later on Castro states: "Cervantes knew very well that he was not the type of person to throw himself naively and gallantly into the heroic saga of the ideals that made up the drama of his time."[10] Remarks like this abound in his 1925 work, often illuminated by the brilliant flashes of Castro's magnificent intuition that was to lead him later along such innovative paths. He speaks, for example, of the discretion and moderation that Cervantes' culture reveals: "This absence of a pedantic attitude has not been thoroughly appreciated by some Cervantine scholars who are unaware of the fact that one of the important traits of the author was precisely this intention of leaving us mere incandescent substances that would conceal their humble origins, as happens so often in Lope de Vega."[11] Castro could not possibly have suspected what a different light, so different from the one that shines in the 1925 pages, would eventually illuminate those incandescent substances in Cervantes' work in the burning molds of his new historico-literary interpretations. The last quotation, along with many others, illustrates the author's constant concern with the contrast between the two great literary manifestations of the period, Lope's theater and Cervantes' novel.

In *El pensamiento de Cervantes,* Castro's preoccupation with the traits that distinguish the Hispanic mentality from others, as reflected in Cervantes' works, still plays a secondary role, although it will become the anguished core of his writings after 1938. But this is not surprising, since one of the author's aims in that book was precisely to show how Cervantes' work was linked to the great currents of European culture (Renaissance, Erasmus, Counter-Reformation, etc.). The footnotes, which always betray an author's second thoughts, scruples, impressions, sources, and readings he has left undeveloped, reveal in *El pensamiento de Cervantes* a broad knowledge of European literature together with a tendency (albeit restrained because of the aim of the book itself) to compare his readings critically with works in Spanish literature. But his always profound inquiries into certain nonconformist attitudes of Cervantes in regard to the general tone of his time usually do not go beyond the bounds of the strictly literary, and only on very few occasions does he inject into these perceptions something like a hint of those lengthy historical meditations that Castro would later devote to the peculiarity of the Hispanic mode of living. This is exemplified in the way the author discusses Cervantes' attitude toward the expulsion of the Moriscos in 1609: "Cervantes must have bowed his noble head thoughtfully before the same question that has mortified the most reflexive Spaniards since the sixteenth century. Why have we not applied European solutions to the gravest problems of our nation?[12] At that time Castro undoubtedly was already one of those thoughtful Spaniards who reflected on that question. But evidently he was also far from looking for a satisfactory answer to the very question that, years later, was to occupy such a prominent place in the thought of the *homo novus,* the new Castro born as a result of his exile. For the moment, Castro's avid desire to provide explanatory notes in his 1925 work is aimed at proving that both the unique and ambiguous factors in Cervantes' work are conditioned by the high quality of Cervantes' genius. For Castro, he is one of the most eminent and universal figures of his time, comparable to Galileo, Bruno, Montaigne, and Descartes. Like those outstanding representatives of the spiritual currents of that period, Cervantes saw the need to harmonize his enthusiasm for

Renaissance ideas with his respect for Catholic tradition. But in Counter-Reformation Spain even this attempt to reconcile religious feeling with Renaissance desires was considered suspect. Hence, Cervantes' constant recourse to disguises, pretenses, ambiguities, in short, to an attitude that Castro, in 1925, did not hesitate to call *hypocritical.* This last term reveals the religious-literary nature of the criteria Castro uses to account for Cervantes' inability to conform to the commonly held beliefs of many of his contemporaries. Thus, according to Castro in 1925, Cervantes' hypocrisy can be explained as a concession to the imperative of old religious traditions, on the one hand, and as a sign of his belonging to that elite group of universal men of European humanism, on the other.

The concept of literary reality *as an absolute* is the theoretical framework that serves as the basis for *El pensamiento de Cervantes.* After 1938, as we already know, Castro's literary investigation, intimately linked to his task as a historiographer, takes a radically different turn. His attention is diverted from the literary figure of Cervantes in order to concentrate on the extraliterary aspect of the man Cervantes. If we apply the new analytical tools invented by Castro in his second period to some of the judgments we have previously discussed, we can see that what was mere conjecture, "glimpsed" by Castro in 1925, now takes on a hitherto unsuspected meaning in his new interpretations.

In 1925 there is a marked contrast between the dramatic world of Lope and the novelistic world of Cervantes, but now Castro *explains* this contrast as a literary reply to the real opposition between the majority of Old Christians and the minority of New Christians within Spanish society of the Golden Age. The predominance of the Old Christian caste tended to exclude the group of *conversos* from any participation in public life, forcing it to retreat into a remote corner of society from which there was no escape. "Drawing strength from weakness" (weakness meant his origin as a *converso*), the genius of Cervantes springs precisely from the vital experience of all those frustrations brought on by his marginal position, from the creative effort to wrap in enduring forms of art the solidarity rebellion of a New Christian, conscious of his own worth but unable to grasp everyday reality in the face of the devastating power of the "gigantism" of the dominant caste of Old Christians. If it is true that references to this original design are sometimes diffuse in the *Quixote* because these allusions have become confused with the artistic intent subordinated to the internal logic of the work of art, it is also true that absolutely everything in the *Quixote* becomes obscure and chaotic if we lose sight of its original plan. But we shall come back to this matter later. Within the broad perspective from which it is possible to discover the real meaning of the opposition between the theater of Lope and the novel of Cervantes, his hypocritical attitude (based on religious motives according to Castro's opinion in 1925) appears to us now as the manifestation of a fundamental tendency in Cervantes to conceal his truths, intentions, and opinions. This tendency to hide, disguise, and cover up is a device that many Golden Age authors in Spain have used to criticize in a subtle way the numerous abuses and injustices in the society of their time. But this attempt to cover up, this ever-present desire to throw the reader off the track, to cover up the markings that the creative mind has made, is a trait so deeply ingrained in Cervantes' genius that it almost seems like a state of mind. More than in any other writer of this period, Cervantes forces us to read between the lines, to accept as possibilities the most extravagant associations that his fabulous memory enables him to establish between two incredibly distant points.

For example, one of the passages in which the "quixotization" of Sancho takes on an almost solemn dimension is in Part II, chap. liii, where Sancho takes leave of his Isle of Barataria. The last cruel joke played on him by the Duke's servants has finally exhausted his patience; he wants to return to his "former freedom." Sancho's last moments on the Isle are impressive when "in deep silence" and surrounded by his executioners of only a moment before, but who now do not know what to make of his sudden transformation, Sancho gets ready to leave. After dressing himself, and in that same sepulchral silence, Sancho slowly goes to the stable to look for his ass. Everyone follows him. When Sancho finally breaks his long silence, it is to greet his faithful donkey with a speech that solemnly sums up his disenchantment, his disillusion, after he had finally fulfilled his long-sought ambition from his first sortie with Don Quixote: "Come here, dear companion and friend of mine, my fellow-partner in my trials and sorrows. When I went along with you and had no other thought but the mending of your harness and the feeding of your little carcase, happy were my hours, my days and my years! But since I left you and climbed the tower of ambition and pride a thousand miseries have pierced my soul, a thousand troubles and four thousand tribulations."[13] It seems to me, beyond any shadow of a doubt, that Sancho's words are a deliberate paraphrase of the following passage in St. Augustine's *Civitas Dei*: "Colligens me a dispersione in qua frustratim discissus sum, dum ab uno te aversus in multa evanui." It is not a matter, here, of a covert aggressive attempt on the part of Cervantes, but what is puzzling about this passage is the free adaptation, not devoid of a certain irreverence, that Cervantes makes of St. Augustine.

At this point I should like to glance back at the previous pages. After analyzing some of Castro's thoughts on the unique and at the same time ambiguous nature of Cervantes' creation in *El pensamiento de Cervantes,* we have shown how these points of view have expanded later in a much broader vision, thanks to Américo Castro's new historico-literary theories. On making this sketch of a comparative study, we have adopted the conventional point of view of the literary critic "qui prend son bien où il le trouve," an attitude apparently justified by the obvious assumption that every one of Castro's studies on Cervantes has contributed to a fuller understanding of that author's work. Nevertheless, if we assume this ambiguous attitude in the light of Castro's entire scholarly production, I believe that we misunderstand, with unpardonable superficiality, the idealistic aspect of his doctrine. To accept a schism, a complete break between the two phases of Castro's life, seems to me to postulate an analogous break in the evolution of his thought, as I shall attempt to show later on.

Between *El pensamiento de Cervantes* and Castro's work after 1938 there is a barrier never surmounted by the author himself in the second phase of his life. After 1938 he never again returned to frequent this territory of his initial efforts. The reason for this seems clear to me: the basic assumptions formulated by Castro in his 1925 book were diametrically opposed to the new direction of his thoughts on Spanish culture later on. His entire interpretive effort in 1925 was bent on fitting Cervantes into the humanistic framework of the European culture of his time. Castro abruptly removed Cervantes from the framework he had so carefully constructed in his early work to turn the creator of the *Quixote* into the major exponent of the particular form of Spanish life that he has called *intercastiza*. In other words, Castro's Europeanist point of view has become a decidedly anti-Europeanist attitude: "We must accept the fact of Spain's non-parallelism in relation to Europe and the fact that its cultural and economic isolation cannot be explained by cultural or economic causes, but rather by an individual attitude of *casticism*."[14] Until now we have been satisfied with a very superficial explanation of Américo Castro's radical turnabout, which is legitimate enough, considering how amazingly fruitful this change in attitude has been. But it is obvious that the cause and effect are reversed in this attempt at justification. I am certain that without the painful, yet fertile stimulus of Castro's exile, with all the circumstances that motivated it and the consequences that followed, the space ship of the great thinker would never have left the orbit it had followed in its investigations prior to 1938. Here we must bear in mind that his intellectual activities and habits until 1938 were conditioned by his association with that tightly closed group of intellectuals who constituted the Centro de Estudios Históricos in Madrid. In his evocative and suggestive essay,[15] Vicente Llorens also holds that Castro probably would not have detached himself from the mental discipline that tied together the members of this group without the corrosive action of exile that unexpectedly was going to desintegrate those former bonds. According to the unanimous testimony of his oldest and closest friends: Lapesa, Bataillon, Gilman, etc., the catastrophe of the Civil War had a profound effect on Castro's sensibility. In order to better understand the decisive changes this sorrowful experience must have produced in Castro's "Weltanschauung," it would be fitting,

I think, to apply to Castro's first years in the United States the phrase of Léon Bloy recalled by Graham Greene at the beginning of one of his books: "Man has places in his heart which do not yet exist, and into them enters suffering in order that they may have existence."

The disheartening impressions that the refugee experienced in his initial contacts with the new university atmosphere at Princeton must have left an indelible impression on the scholar. Vicente Llorens tells how Castro soon realized what little interest people had in matters concerning Spain. The ignorance of and disdain for Spanish culture contrasted intensely with the brilliant prestige enjoyed by other European cultures, and France in particular. Impressions of this type, multiplied innumerable times in the daily life of the expatriot and combined with the anguishing repercussions the national catastrophe had on his spirit, undoubtedly acted as a catalyst on the mysterious chemistry of his emotional life. Thus it is here that we must look for the non-rational basis for Castro's new attitude toward Hispanic culture. There are few direct accounts about this decisive change in his work itself, but in the prologue to the 1962 revised edition of *La realidad histórica de España* Castro mentions the feeling of dissatisfaction and heartbreak that he and other Spanish intellectuals experienced at this unauthentic approach to the history of Spain and Hispanic culture. Referring to his work prior to 1938, Castro writes:

> At that time I tried to bring to light what there was in Spain of Europeanism . . . without first plunging into the depths of collective feeling, without realizing that we were continuing to complain, we were cursing our hard luck, denying our destiny, daydreaming, and making ourselves blacker inside even more than the black legends had done; *we were piling up facts, editions, anecdotes, or coming out with statements of a synthetic nature, but without the slightest analytic base.*[16]

What was unauthentic about the activities that we have italicized is that they tended to eliminate, in an inoperative area of the mind, the real vital problems elicited by everything that is different, individual, and peculiar in Hispanic forms of life. The content of these vital concerns is impervious to the probings of the so-called intrinsic critics who have tried to define the essence of other European cultures, which, according to Castro, have a more rational view of the world. I have always been attentive to the accents of vital concern that mark Américo Castro's style and give such a tremendous authenticity to the expression of his ideas. Behind that expression we intuit the tense presence of a man for whom *l'univers de discours* and *le monde vécu* of Merleau-Ponty are two closely intertwined realities. For this reason I am inclined to see a certain anti-thetical parallelism between Castro's and Cervantes' circumstance. If Cervantes had succeeded in his repeated attempts to go to the New World, we would not have the *Quixote*. But the famous *Búsquese por acá . . .* , so beautifully symbolic of the retrospective vision, confined the author to the narrow boundaries of his country, and thanks to this, the *Quixote* was made possible. For Castro, in contrast, it was his estrangement from his own country that caused him to discover, on the alien soil of exile, the unsuspected possibilities that he was able to achieve so splendidly in his work during the remaining years of his lifetime. In conclusion, what I should like to point out here is the hidden affinity between Castro's own marginal situation as an outsider and that of Cervantes and other sixteenth-century *conversos*. For the greatest of them, as for Castro himself, the frustrations of their marginal condition, a phenomenon similar to what is known as "alienation" today, gave them access to the most intimate depths of their being, "a port both near and far, and difficult to enter," as Castro once called that realm of the mind. Seen in this light, the following passage would confirm what we have already said about the non-rational basis for Castro's new attitude. And note that the italics are the author's, not mine: "In the sixteenth century there existed a literature of souls walled-up in a castle, who discovered themselves through *non-intellectual* ways, and from this vantage point contemplated the world around, above, and beyond them."[17]

In short, I should like to emphasize the fact that not one of the major problems arising in Cervantes' work and formulated in *El pensamiento de Cervantes* could have been solved within the perspective and with the means Castro had at his disposal in 1925. In other words, if there were any solutions, Castro discarded them as false or inadequate in his second period.

In the previous pages I put forth some arguments for my thesis that there was a break between Castro's first works and the ones he wrote after 1938. It seems to me that this question should not be considered as interesting from a purely academic standpoint. On the contrary, I believe that if we lose sight of this dividing line between Castro's life and his work, there is the risk that we might also overlook the lesson of "humanology," to use Castro's own term, implied in the theories of the man who is, according to Gilman, "perhaps the greatest humanist of our time." I would stray too far from the theme of this essay if I attempted to examine the idealistic message that discreetly but persistently finds its way into Américo Castro's great work. Moreover, I share with other disciples of Castro certain modest reservations about all the implications of this message. But I am aware of its content, which nowadays seems to provide the best antidote for those dehumanizing tendencies that have invaded the very field of literary studies. The prestige of the exact sciences whose applications have radically transformed the life-styles of modern technological societies is so great that it has affected the visual field of those professional men dedicated to cultivating the humanities. Under such conditions it might even seem tempting to follow the "charlatanism" of those who offer us their learned abstractions, devoid of any practical application or human ties with the aloofness and conceit of the physicist or biologist who knows that his contribution, no matter how slight, will be incorporated into a coherent body of doctrine, with the mathematical precision of its qualitative relevance. If the applications of science cause the scientist's own security to become increasingly illusory, then the assurance of the interpreter of literature who stubbornly insists on moving about *in a literary "ether" without descending to the lower levels of breathable atmosphere* (according to Castro's words) is, if not comical, at least unjustified and irresponsible.

To conclude our reflections on Castro's work on Cervantes in its entirety, we recall that *El pensamiento de Cervantes* presents us with a Cervantes immersed in the major European problems elicited by the Renaissance and the Reformation. Cervantes' hypocritical attitude, no matter how shocking it seemed to many readers at that time, was merely the covert manifestation of a discrepancy, not very serious in the long run, with the prevailing forms of religious feeling in Spain. But this very phenomenon, seen in the light of Spanish *casticismo,* becomes a transcendental state of mind in Cervantes' personality, something that he acquired in his prolonged isolation in that marginal state to which the exclusivism of the Old Christian caste had relegated the minority group of *conversos.* From the vital experience of this difficult situation that Cervantes shared with many of his contemporaries, there came forth the great work of art, the literary creation of a true counterworld in which Cervantes, as Guillermo Araya Goubet says, enabled "an old Christian (Sancho) to join up and get along with a New Christian (Don Quixote)."[18]

Partisans of the so-called intrinsic criticism, alert only to the inner, measurable phenomena in the literary vision of the work of art, have censured Castro's systematic recourse to extraliterary factors that may have intervened in the evolution of Cervantes' work. But we already saw earlier that, without Castro's theories, it is impossible to formulate an accurate explanation of the meaning of the *Quixote* as a whole. We shall see in the following section that it is also imperative to follow the itinerary indicated by Castro's new methods and ideas to explain the great artistic originality of the *Quixote.*

It is well-known how Castro found the analytical instruments he needed to formulate his new ideas about Spain's past in the philosophical systems of Spengler, Toynbee, and Dilthey, in particular. Moreover, this application of conceptual and analytical tools inherited from Dilthey is, to a certain extent, responsible for the very originality of Castro's new historical theories. Much of the discursive effort in Castro's work demonstrates the irrefutable nature of the concepts with which he worked. Once the author explained to me that he wanted to make his new edition of *La realidad histórica* "a prueba de tontos," which sounds much stronger in Spanish than the English "foolproof." This almost obsessive concern for the unfounded resistance that his arguments might encounter in the prejudiced minds of some ill-intentioned readers is very apparent in his works. In *'Español,' palabra extranjera,* one of his last works, we can still read: "In present-day science what can be proved and made evident prevails; but in the field of human knowledge, the evident sometimes becomes obvious, and for that very reason it is rejected as bothersome and even odious."[19] But today, since an ever-growing number of critics have made use of resources developed in other disciplines to evaluate literary phenomena, there is really no need to take so many precautions to legitimize them. For example, our understanding of Erasmianism in Spain, a particularly controversial subject in relation to Cervantes, can profit a great deal from the ideas on the historicity of human existence formulated by philosophers such as Sartre, Merleau-Ponty, and R. C. Kwant in Holland. Now Erasmianism can be seen as a phase in what those philosophers call "the progressive collective enlightment." And given the irreversible nature of the new vision of essential aspects of reality achieved, thanks to this progressive and collective enlightenment, we can now provide a much stronger conceptual support for the theory that the reactionary form of religiosity reinstated in Spain in the second half of the sixteenth century became problematic for Cervantes and other great thinkers of his time. The remarkable climate of religious tolerance that had prevailed in Spain for decades was repressed by the coercive methods at the disposal of the State. This means that the entire mechanism of Inquisitorial surveillance was incapable of destroying the desire for a reformation of the religious spirit, once it was firmly implanted in the hearts of men. These aspirations made up a part of the overall spiritual climate and were present in the atmosphere of the time. It seems absurd, therefore, from a methodological point of view, to restrict the study of Cervantes' Erasmianism to a few inquiries into the possible contacts the author had with prominent Erasmians. This would be like trying to determine the degree of probability with which a patient might have run the germ-infested course of a contagious disease.

Erasmianism, as it appears in Cervantes' work, is a form of religious sentiment with roots in the same historical period that gave Cervantes the ideals of a courageous and heroic life that he pursued for a brief period in his life and later transformed into literature. According to Bataillon, "Cervantes' work is that of a man who remained to the last faithful to the ideas of his youth, to ways of thought that the era of Philip II had inherited from the Emperor."[20]

Cervantes' life shows a clearly marked ascending line beginning with the evidence of his sojourn in Italy, his glorious participation in the battle of Lepanto, and his years of captivity in Algiers. But this line would be cut short prematurely in 1580 when he returned to Spain at the age of 33, filled with the illusion of reaping the well-deserved reward of service to his country. To what extent those just expectations were frustrated is shown by Cervantes' attempt to go to the Indies, first in 1582 and again in 1590. These were the attempts of a desperate man. In *El celoso extremeño (The Jealous Extremaduran)*, he calls the Indies "refuge and shelter of the desperate of Spain, church of the destitute, safeconduct of murderers . . . common deception for many and personal remedy for a few." The lot that fell to the "one-armed man of Lepanto" by chance upon his return to Spain was by no means an honorable post at the Hapsburg court, but rather the tiresome hustle of an itinerant, anonymous existence as a tax collector and purveyor of grain to the Armada. And while Cervantes spent those arduous years in menial activities in Andalusia, Madrid was celebrating the successes of Lope de Vega's drama, the triumph of a theatrical formula that monopolized for the "Fenix" and his followers all the glories of a genre in which Cervantes had placed all his hopes, after the scant enthusiasm aroused by the publication of his novel *La Galatea* in 1585.

There is a total absence of autobiographical data or any other type of evidence that could shed more specific light on the repercussions that all these adverse circumstances probably had on the brilliant author's state of mind. In spite of the hermetic nature of Cervantes' work, if we add to the literary reality of the *Quixote* the famous "reactive" of Américo Castro's precisions on the vital dwelling place of the Spaniards in the sixteenth century, it is possible to interpret the experience lived by Cervantes as one of an outsider in the society of his time. But this alienation, caused either by socioreligious elements as in the case of Cervantes, or by more or less psychological peculiarities, as in the case of Marcel Proust, or perhaps García Lorca, is merely a fertile and temporary stage for the creator of genius.

Artistic creation, conditioned by the frustrations inherent in a marginal situation, is the splendid way an artist succeeds in breaking out of his isolation and integrating himself into the fullness of the life of his time. His period is what offers the artist the existential field with all its possibilities and restrictions, but it is in the creation of artists of genius like Cervantes where the possibilities of this field are revealed and its limitations magnificently overcome.[21] In Cervantes' case, the irremediable condition of emptiness, loneliness, and desperation—all the essential ingredients of the phenomenon of alienation—have found both a powerful palliative in the nostalgic recollection of those brief youthful years when Cervantes participated fully in the life of his time, and a supreme compensation in his immortal work, the *Quixote*. The many nostalgic allusions to an extraliterary reality, to the bygone era of Charles V, provide practically the only firsthand information we can extract from this great work in which all the elements of the author's vital experience have been rigorously subordinated to his artistic aims. For any further inferences we must resort to the "reagent" of Don Américo's theories in order to reveal to us their hidden links with the actual life of that time. Among the many passages we cite the following one in which Don Quixote implores heaven to "make you see how beneficial and necessary knights errant were to the world in past ages and how useful they would be in the present, *if they were in fashion. But now, for the peoples' sins,* sloth, idleness, gluttony, and luxury triumph."[22] The vices he points out here are precisely the ones censured by many contemporary writers who are afraid that the lack of bellicose objectives during the time of Philip II would cause the Spaniards to lose their former vigor. Let us compare the italicized words above with others in Part I where the Captive laments that the Spaniards, after the famous battle of Lepanto, missed their opportunity to completely destroy the Turkish armada. The Captive concludes: "But Heaven ordained otherwise, through no fault or neglect of our commander, but *for the sins of Christendom,* and because God ordains that there shall always be some scourge [*verdugos,* hangmen] to chastise us."[23] With almost identical words, Cervantes alludes in these passages to the fact that it was the Spaniards' own fault that the historical events had taken on such a catastrophic aspect under Charles V's successors who had refused to make use of the services of their finest vassals. In this context it is very clear that the *verdugos* (scourge, hangmen) should be identified with enemies inside, and not outside Spain.

Cervantes was a straggler left behind from the heroic days of the Emperor, clinging wholeheartedly to the ideals of that period and deeply regretting the changes that had taken place in the Spain of Philip II and Philip III, such as the waning of the martial spirit, the decline in faith in Spain's missionary role, and the recurrence of social conflicts provoked by the suspicion of impure blood.

But the most revealing reference to the glorious epoch of the Emperor Charles V is found in a part of the *Quixote* where one would least expect it: in the "Sonnet on the legend of Pyramus and Thisbe" composed by Don Lorenzo, the son of Don Diego de Miranda, the Knight of the Green Coat. Don Quixote and Sancho are enjoying the knight's hospitality as a respite from their wanderings (Part II, chapters xvi, xvii, and xviii). Without stopping to analyze the theme of the loves of Pyramus and Thisbe, which was so popular among the Spanish poets of the Golden Age, we reproduce only the last tercet, which is pertinent to our discussion:

> Both of them in a moment— strange sight!—
> *One sword, one sepulchre, one memory*
> Kills, covers, crowns with immortality.[24]

The last line irresistibly recalls another very famous passage in the sonnet to Charles V by Hernando de Acuña, *Al rey nuestro señor* in the second quatrain:

> Ya tan alto principio en tal jornada
> os muestra el fin de vuestro santo celo,
> y anuncia al mundo, para más consuelo,
> *un monarca, un imperio y una espada.*

These lines in which Hernando de Acuña had sung the grandeur of the Spanish Empire at the time of Charles V were famous even in the reign of Philip III. Compare the two:

> One monarch, one Empire, and one sword.
> (Un monarca, un imperio y una espada.)

One sword, one sepulcher, one memory.
(Una espada, un sepulcro, una memoria.)

Considering Cervantes' extraordinary memory, it is frankly unthinkable that the author was unfamiliar with the lines by Acuña when he was composing the last tercet of his sonnet to produce the final unexpected effect.[25] But if this is true—and I do not see how it could be otherwise, unless it is through the usual ostrich method—we would have to recognize the tremendous repercussions of this explosive line, skillfully hidden away by Cervantes in the poetic exercises of the young Lorenzo to entertain his father's houseguests. This single line by itself, echoing the one by Acuña which it unmistakably evokes, reveals Cervantes' lucid vision of that very moment when Spain began her political decline. In a nostalgic, yet resigned tone Cervantes bears witness to the failure of those ideals that were indelibly imprinted on his soul since the heroic years of his youth when he fought in one of the finest regiments in the Spanish army.

If the *Quixote* enables us to establish accurately that the time longed for here is actually that of Charles V, then it is in *Los trabajos de Persiles y Segismunda* where we see to what extent the longing for a courageous life and the ideal warrior of Charles V's time had remained intact in Cervantes' mind. The following passage is so significant that we should like to quote it at length. It deals with Periandro's (Persiles') speech to his fishermen friends after the corsairs have made off with the fishermen's wives and with Periandro's fiancée, Auristela:

Base fortune was neveer remedied by sloth or indolence: good fortune was never harbored in timid souls; we alone have forged our own fortune and there is no soul so dull and heavy that cannot rise to fortune's seat, and cowards, although born rich, will always be poor, and misers will always be beggars. This I say to you, my friends, to encourage and incite you to *leave the miserable dowry of a few nets and narrow boats,* to better your lot and to look for the treasures prized in noble work. By noble, liberal, magnanimous work, I mean the kind of occupation engaged in great things. A man who tills the soil hardly earns a daily wage from it, and earns no fame at all. *Why should he not take up a lance instead of a hoe, and not fearing the sun or the inclemencies of heaven, earn with it the fame that ennobles him above all other men? War is the stepmother of cowards and the mother of courage, and the rewards to be gained from her may be called "otherworldly."*

We call the reader's attention to the warlike spirit that directs the protagonist's ambitions. The italicized passages enable us to discern something like an intermediate stage in the process of literary development or progress that would culminate in the creation of the *Quixote* where those same aspirations, now divested of their bellicose impulse would be carried to their full artistic maturity. In effect, in the *Quixote* we see how that warlike impulse disappeared in the mission of the mad knight to give way to the noble desire to accomplish and carry out by sheer willpower and courageous action, a handful of ideals of justice and solidarity with mankind within the framework of an inadequate everyday reality. Through the magic of the work of art Cervantes succeeds in incarnating in an imaginary person the poetic essence of his ardent longing for a bygone era and ideal, already entombed (*sepultados*) and transformed into mere memory (*memoria*) when the hero of Lepanto returned to Spain in 1580. In this way Cervantes' arduous but extraordinary destiny finally offered him the unexpected way of letters, "the otherworldly rewards" that he had dreamed of attaining in his lifetime through arms. His own personal failure was redeemed through the sublime story of Don Quixote and Sancho. Thus the book's artistic originality springs from the full awareness of the redeeming power of the work of art that Cervantes acquired when he conceived the *Quixote*. André Gide has said that there is no problem that cannot find its supreme solution in the work of art.[26]

The merit of Américo Castro's great Cervantine venture lies in having clarified the complex interweaving of the concrete circumstances of the time with Cervantes' life and *El ingenioso hidalgo don Quijote de la Mancha*. If we cannot grasp the extraliterary reflections of Cervantes in the world of the *Quixote,* the true meaning of the work will elude us. But at the same time, Castro warns us that "we should never lose sight of the fact that Cervantes was more interested in his own art than in any extraliterary finality which is present in the work as nothing more than material for an artistic construction."[27] These words are significant. Américo Castro's most pressing task, and the one that he alone could accomplish, was to interpret the greatest work of Spanish literature from the viewpoint of a more authentic vision of the structure of Spanish history. Once this task has ended, and "with one foot in the stirrup," Castro seems to invite us to turn our sights once more to the artistic beauties and the universal values of Cervantes' immortal work.

NOTES

1. See Roland Barthes, *Sur Racine* (Paris: Seuil, 1963).

2. J. Ortega y Gasset, *Meditaciones del Quijote* (Madrid: Revista de Occidente, 1956), pp. 75-76. (First published in 1914.)

3. Richard L. Predmore, *El mundo del Quijote* (Madrid: Insula, 1958), p. 31-33 (English edition: *The World of Don Quijote,* Cambridge, Mass.: Harvard, 1967). Predmore seems to open the way to a much broader interpretation when he says that "Don Quixote's madness consists precisely in his inability to distinguish between life and literature." But he does not develop this line of thought with much consistency. Some of his judgments, such as his analysis of conjectural language in the *Quixote* are very sound; others, however, such as his interpretation of the role of the enchanters in the work are completely untenable.

4. Manuel Durán, *La ambigüedad del Quixote* (Xalapa: Universidad veracruzana, 1960), p. 89.

5. *CCE* (1966), pp. 131-132.

6. See Araya Goubet, p. 43.

7. See Francisco López Estrada, "La literatura pastoril en la obra de Américo Castro," in *Estudios,* p. 281.

8. Stephen Gilman, "Américo Castro como humanista e historiador," in *Estudios,* p. 137.

9. *PCer* (1925), p. 35; (1972), pp. 63-64, no. 38. (This essay was written before the publication of the 2d edition of *El pensamiento de Cervantes* [Madrid: 1972], which the author was unable to consult. Although the original text is essentially the same, the revised edition was enlarged and updated with notes by the author and Julio Rodríguez-Puértolas. Editor's note.)

10. Ibid. (1925), p. 49; (1972), p. 45.

11. Ibid. (1925), 112; (1972), p. 105.

12. Ibid. (1925), p. 298; (1972), p. 285.

13. *The Adventures of Don Quixote,* translated by J.M. Cohen (Middlesex: Penguin, 1956), II, chap. liii, pp. 813-814.

14. *CCE* (1966), pp. 231-232.

15. Vicente Llorens, "Los años de Princeton," in *Estudios,* pp. 291-292.

16. *RHE* (1962), p. xiv.

17. *CCE* (1966), p. 343.

18. Guillermo Araya Goubet, "Evolución y proyecciones del pensamiento de Américo Castro," in *Estudios*, p. 50.

19. *EPE*, pp. 29-30; *SIH*, p. 4.

20. Marcel Bataillon, *Erasmo y España*, 2d ed. (Mexico: Fondo de Cultura, 1966), p. 778.

21. Cf. R.C. Kwant, *Fenomenologie van de taal* (Utrecht, 1967), Hfst. vi. This author uses the term "existential field" which we prefer in this context instead of *morada vital* or *vividura* (vital structure), concepts that Castro specifically applies to the Spanish circumstances.

22. *Don Quixote*, Cohen, trans., II, chap. xviii, p. 583.

23. Ibid., I, chap. xxxix, p. 349.

24. Ibid., II, chap. xviii, p. 586.

25. In 1971 when Castro was reading the proofs of his introductory study to a new edition of the Quixote, "Como veo ahora el Quijote," I called his attention to the antithetical analogy between the sonnets by Don Lorenzo and Hernando de Acuña. Acknowledging the validity of my suggestion, Castro included it in note 55, p. 86, of his study. A short time ago I discovered that this analogy had already been pointed out over ten years ago by Alberto Sánchez in "El Caballero del Verde Gabán," (*Anales cervantinos*, IX (1961-1962), 169-201. Following the concepts established by Dámaso Alonso, Sánchez points out the two "pluralidades trimembres" of Don Lorenzo's sonnet and mentions the "remarkable similarity" of the last line with the one in the quatrain by Hernando de Acuña. But I am surprised at the incredible fact that Sánchez explains this analogy as the result of an involuntary and unconscious recollection of Cervantes. Rarely has Freud's well-worn authority been so abused as in this remark by Sánchez in his very learned style: "the psychopathology of everyday life, analyzed by Freud, shows us a multiplicity of examples with the oblique transmission of dormant perceptions" (p. 200). In his lengthy essay Alberto Sánchez gives us a description of the personality of Don Diego de Miranda. The author comes to the conclusion that in this portrait of the country gentleman, who lives aloof from the noisy confusion of the court, "in the marvelous silence of a comfortable country mansion," there might be "some hidden longing" of Cervantes himself.

The episode of the Knight of the Green Coat is one of the most controversial in the *Quixote*. Counter to the authoritative opinion of the great French Hispanist, Marcel Bataillon, an opinion shared by most of the critics who have taken up the matter, like Sánchez here, Américo Castro holds that Don Diego de Mirando did not have anything to warrant Don Quixote's attraction to him. They are two completely incompatible characters. Castro writes: "For several years I have thought that Cervantes made the target of his greatest sarcasm, the life of that knight, the symbol of Spain's spiritual and intellectual quietism which Cervantes tried to shake up and inflame by every possible means." (*CVQ*, pp. 93-94). I am inclined to think that one of those means was perhaps the explosive line that Cervantes left as a parting gift in the "peaceful house" of Don Diego de Miranda. As for Cervantes' intention to present Don Diego as a person who has nothing in common with Don Quixote, which I think is very apparent, I call the reader's attention to the episode of Don Quixote's first encounter with Cardenio. We are in the presence of two kindred souls, destined to understand and to love each other from the very beginning. Cervantes' art makes this spontaneous current of mutual attraction vibrate, and like some magic potion, envelop this first meeting of two extraordinary characters: "When the youth came up he greeted them in a rough and toneless voice, but very courteously. Don Quixote returned his greetings no less politely and, charmingly and graciously dismounting from Rocinante, advanced to embrace him, and held him for some time clasped in his arms, as if he had known him for a long while. The other . . . after allowing himself to be embraced drew back a little and, placing his hands on Don Quixote's shoulders, stood gazing at him, as if to see whether he knew him, being no less surprised, perhaps, to see Don Quixote's face, figure and armour than Don Quixote was to see him." (Part I, chap. xxiii, 191.)

26. In this respect it is curious that Cervantes' work presents some similarities with that of Garcilaso "El Inca," another marginal figure of almost the same period. See my article, "Nueva interpretación de los *Comentarios reales* de Garcilaso El Inca," *Cuadernos Hispanoamericanos,* no. 230 (February 1969), pp. 353-390.

27. *CVQ,* p. 58.

9

THE CLASSICAL THEATER AND ITS REFLECTION OF LIFE
Carroll B. Johnson

Castro published his first study on the classical theater—the *comedia* of the Golden Age—in his twenty-fifth year, and he never lost interest in what he described as "the spontaneous manifestation of the inclinations and preferences of the Spanish people."[1] I should like to begin with an outline, certainly sketchy and probably incomplete, of the chronology of Don Américo's encounters with that fundamental genre, so monumental in its presence yet so elusive in its substance.

1910 (1) Tirso de Molina, *El vergonzoso en palacio* and *El burlador de Sevilla,* edited by Américo Castro. Ediciones de "La Lectura," Clásicos Castellanos I (Madrid: Calpe, 1910).

1916 (1) Américo Castro, "Algunas observaciones acerca del concepto del honor en los siglos XVI y XVII," *Revista de Filología Española,* III (1916), 1-50; 357-386.

    (2) Américo Castro, "Obras mal atribuidas a Rojas Zorrilla," *Revista de Filología Española,* III (1916), 66-68.

1917 (1) D. Francisco de Rojas Zorrilla, *Cada cual lo que le toca* and *La viña de Nabot,* edited by Américo Castro. Ediciones de la Junta para la ampliación de estudios, Teatro Antiguo Español II (Madrid: Sucesores de Hernando, 1917).

1919 (1) Américo Castro and Hugo A. Rennert, *Vida de Lope de Vega* (Madrid, 1919); 2d ed. of Américo Castro and F. Lázaro Carreter (Salamanca: Anaya, 1968). 584 pp.

(2)   Tirso de Molina, *El condenado por desconfiado,* edited by Américo Castro. (Madrid: Calpe, 1919).

(3)   Lope de Vega, *Fuenteovejuna,* edited by Américo Castro (Madrid: Calpe, 1919).

(4)   Américo Castro, "Por los fueros de nuestro teatro: *El castigo sin venganza* de Lope de Vega," *La Unión Hispanoamericana* (Madrid), III (1919), no. 36, p. 15.

(5)   Américo Castro, "El autógrafo de *La corona merecida* de Lope de Vega," *Revista de Filología Española,* VI (1919), 306–309.

1922 (1)   Tirso de Molina, *El vergonzoso en palacio* and *El burlador de Sevilla,* edited by Américo Castro, 2d ed., very revised, with a general introductory study on the theater (Madrid: Espasa-Calpe, 1922).

(2)   Américo Castro, "Una comedia de Lope de Vega condenada por la Inquisición," *Revista de Filología Española,* IX (1922), 311–314.

1923 (1)   Lope de Vega, *Selección (Amar sin saber a quién; El mejor alcalde, el Rey; El caballero de Olmedo; Peribáñez y el Comendador de Ocaña),* Junta para la Ampliación de Estudios (Madrid: Centro de Estudios Históricos, 1923).

(2)   Américo Castro, *Conferencias dadas en el Salón de Honor de la Universidad* ("Lope de Vega: su vida" and "Lope de Vega: sus obras") (Santiago de Chile: Imprenta y Litografía Universo, 1924). The lectures were given the previous year.

(3)   Américo Castro, "Sobre el teatro clásico español," *Nosotros* (Buenos Aires), 44 (1923), 549–559.

(4)   Américo Castro, "Don Juan en la literatura española," in *Conferencias del año 1923* (Buenos Aires: Imprenta del Jockey Club, 1924), 144–168.

1932 (1)   Tirso de Molina, *El vergonzoso en palacio* and *El burlador de Sevilla,* edited by Américo Castro, 3d ed., very revised, with notes (Madrid: Espasa-Calpe, 1932).

1933 (1)   Lope de Vega, *Selección,* edited by Américo Castro, 2d ed., with notes (Madrid: Centro de Estudios Históricos, 1933).

1935 (1)   Américo Castro, "Tricentenario de Lope de Vega,"
           La Nación (Buenos Aires), 25 August 1935. Re-
           printed in *ENC,* III, pp. 157–168.
1939 (1)   Américo Castro, "El Don Juan de Tirso y el de
           Molière como personajes barrocos," in *Hommage à
           Ernest Martinenche. Études hispaniques et améri-
           caines* (Paris: Artrey, 1939), 93–111.
1953 (1)   Américo Castro, "El Don Juan de Tirso y el Eneas
           de Virgilio," *El Nacional* (Caracas), 3 August 1953.
           Reprinted in *SEE,* pp. 397–401; and in *ENC,* III,
           pp. 149–155.
1961 (1)   Américo Castro, *De la edad conflictiva. El drama
           de la honra en España y en su literatura* (Madrid:
           Taurus, 1961); 2d ed., corrected and augmented,
           1963; 3d ed., very modified, 1967.

This impressive bibliography, which spans the whole of
Castro's long and productive scholarly life, may be divided for
convenience into three phases. These are first the editions of the
plays themselves, with introductory studies, in the years 1910–
1924. During roughly the same period Castro dedicated himself
to varied studies on the *comedia,* ranging from three-page notes
in the *Revista de Filología Española* to the monumental biography of Lope de Vega with Hugo A. Rennert, passing through
such seminal contributions as the 1916 *Revista de Filología
Española* paper on honor and two general studies, attempts to
come to grips with the uniqueness of the *comedia* as a genre,
in 1922 (prologue to Tirso de Molina) and 1923 (*Nosotros*).
From 1925 to the mid 1950s his contributions to the study of the
theater are less frequent, and the theme of Don Juan is
dominant. Here the study of Tirso's and Molière's Don Juan is
probably the most important. The 1953 paper on Don Juan and
Aeneas has an importance all out of proportion to its length,
for it documents a radical change in Castro's habits of thought.
We can discern a hiatus in theatrical studies until 1961, when
the theater is again considered en bloc, in light of the theories
of caste conflict which had come increasingly to dominate
Castro's writings from 1948. There are no more studies of
individual plays. We find instead an attempt first to illustrate
caste conflict by the relatively few direct references to it in the

plays, and second to elucidate the famous "honor code" in relation to caste conflict. The key work here is of course *De la edad conflictiva,* but in addition there are scattered, almost schematic references to the *comedia* (usually in opposition to the novel) in *La realidad histórica de España* (1962) and *Cervantes y los casticismos españoles* (1966). The studies published in the 1960s have laid Castro open to charges of dilettantism and disdain for erudition. In this context it is well to recall that the global insights of the later years would have been impossible without the massive and detailed erudition acquired and demonstrated play by three-act play between 1910 and 1924.

The motivation for the early editions of particular *comedias* is manifold, and springs finally from the tradition of the great Renaissance humanists and their passion to make the authentic texts of Holy Writ available for study and commentary. In the most direct way this enterprise engaged Castro's professional training as a philologist. It should be noted that in addition to various *comedias,* Castro made available to his countryment other difficult classics of the national literature, notably Quevedo's picaresque *Vida del Buscón,* which together with Tirso's *Burlador de Sevilla* may be classed as perhaps the most corrupt and most vitiated texts of the Golden Age. In addition, Castro's activity as editor of texts is related to his association with the Centro de Estudios Históricos, which grouped together a number of younger anti- or at least extra-Establishment scholars and stood in opposition to the official literary history emanating from the Spanish Academy. Castro addresses himself to this point in the most explicit terms. He refers, for example, to the Academy editions of the complete works of Lope de Vega, under the direction of Emilio Cotarelo y Mori as the "detritus of the scientific vacuity of the nineteenth century," which consists in publishing hundreds of *comedias* "without understanding them, without explicating them, in the belief that the scholar who makes them public must of course comprehend their meaning."[2] The few plays painstakingly edited in the "Teatro Antiguo Español" collection published under the aegis of the Centro de Estudios Históricos stand in eloquent contrast to the shelves of massive tomes issuing from the Academy. The careful work of young men like Américo Castro and José Fernández Montesinos, late of the University of California, Berkeley, offers a silent but devastating reproach to the oceanic output of Cotarelo and his employees, who committed, Castro estimates, an average of at least one hundred linguistic errors per play edited. The careful editing of texts and their publication with intelligent commentary constitutes the first major aspect of Castro's continuing involvement with the *comedia*. The one I should like to consider next is the overwhelming presence of Lope de Vega. Castro insists at both the beginning and the end of his career on Lope's status as the creator of the *comedia*. In his 1910 edition of Tirso de Molina he remarks Tirso's devotion to Lope and refers to the inclusion by the former, in his *Cigarrales de Toledo* (1621) of a *comedia* and a discourse characterized as "the most brilliant apology on record" of the dramatic formula Lope had invented and imposed.[3] Here Castro is especially concerned with Lope's willful violations of Aristotelian precepts as formulated in his *Arte nuevo de hacer comedias en este tiempo* (1609). When he returned to the theater much later, Castro again insisted on the uniqueness of Lope's formula, this time in opposition to its immediate predecessor, the sixteenth-century Spanish theater of such playwrights as Lucas Fernández, Torres Naharro, and Lope de Rueda. Their work, he insists, could not and did not evolve into Lope de Vega's *comedia*.[4]

Obviously, Castro's most comprehensive treatment of Lope is his revision—a revision so radical as to constitute a new work— of the biography published in English by Hugo A. Rennert in 1904. When the combined version appeared in Spanish in 1919, Castro presented himself at first as a translator who could not resist availing himself of the enormous bibliographical treasures of the Madrid libraries in the preparation of his translation. As his prologue progresses, however, and he details his own contributions, it becomes evident that it is he who is making available whole episodes of Lope's life—his relationship with Micaela de Luján, for example—and their relevance for his work. In his prologue to the edition of 1968 he confesses that not only had he written the sections he admitted in 1919, but indeed everything connected to the aesthetic appreciation of the plays, poems and novels of the "monster of Nature."[5]

Because the presence of Lope—in life and art—is so overpowering and complex it is impossible to do justice here to Castro and Rennert's biography, except to remark that it continues to be the standard source of information on the subject. Instead, I should like to point out just one of Castro's fundamental ideas concerning Lope and its evolution in his writing. In 1919 Castro insists on the identification of Lope with the ideals and aspirations of the vast majority of his fellow Spaniards: "Lope does not raise himself above the contemporary ideal; the foundation of his artistic construction rests on the vulgar, popular ideas of his time."[6] In 1935 Castro defines "that which is Spanish" as consisting of "vital and ideological postures in harmony with majoritarian Spain," and continues that "Lope unchains the freest human impulses and then limits and reduces them in consonance with the supreme exigencies of the ideas dominant in that singular society. This limit on Lope's impulse is the perimeter that encloses 'popular' and 'official' Spain simultaneously. Through the innumerable acts of the *comedia* we discover what the great mass of Spaniards was thinking and dreaming. In this sense it is unjust to speak of 'Lope de Vega *and his time*' [the title of a then-recent book by Karl Vossler]; we should say rather that Lope *is* his time."[7]

In his additions to Rennert, Castro speaks of an almost mystical collaboration between the poet and his people, in defining the *comedia* as a massive national poem:

> The theater leaves Lope's hands as an immense national deed of epic proportions, a variegated compendium of popular songs and sayings, a compilation of poetic, erudite, and vulgar material both national and foreign. The dramatists who came after him solidified or intensified certain aspects, but really added nothing essential to the genre Lope had invented. In this way the theater stands before us as an immense collective poem in which everyone demanded his right to participate. . . . After Lope, the genre was, so to speak, predetermined, and although literary science still does not allow us to understand the techniques of this mystical collaboration between poet and race, the fact of it is no less potent for all that.[8]

The image of the grandiose collective poem resurfaces again, much later in Castro's career, when he identifies the *comedia* explicitly with the *romancero*—the vast Peninsular ballad tradition—as the two majoritarian genres *par excellence*: "Both poetic genres kept alive in the majority caste the memory of its glorious past, the legacy of Philip II's universalized Spain."[9]

He goes on to oppose Lope's *comedia* (for the majority) to Cervantes' novel, a private genre of minoritarian stance. He further remarks that the two writers use the material of the *romancero* in exactly opposite ways. Finally, in the 1968 edition of *Vida de Lope de Vega* Castro simply refers to Lope as "the genial organizer of the majority sensibility and value system in Spain, the creator of a poetic vision still valid in the eighteenth century."[10]

If Lope de Vega is the maximum national poet, it is Don Juan, the creation of his follower Tirso de Molina, who is best known outside Spain. As early as 1910 Castro was involved in pondering the relationship of the *comedia*—specifically Tirso's Don Juan, and the play in which he appears, *El burlador de Sevilla*—to the extra-Hispanic national theaters. In part these efforts may be considered a kind of schizoid attempt to demonstrate simultaneously that the *comedia* belongs to the European tradition and that it is uniquely Spanish. In this respect some of the studies on Tirso and Don Juan offer a remarkable continuity, always tinged, however, with the restless questioning that sets Castro apart from so many of his fellow Hispanists. This is generally the tenor of the brief prologue he wrote for his edition of the *Burlador* in 1910. The *comedia* is seen as Romantic, in the sense that it derives from "the most intimate part of the individual, from his honor." This in turn is related to the Romantics' passion for things medieval—indeed, the *comedia* was "discovered" by the German Romantics—which allows Castro to conclude that the *comedia* as a genre is essentially dependent on medieval patterns of thought which persisted, thus preventing the "modernization" or "Europeization" of the genre because Spain had turned her back on the rest of Europe.

With the publication of the second edition of the *Burlador* in 1922 Castro's tone becomes more shrill and nationalistic. He remarks that until that time it had been impossible to demonstrate that the text of the *Burlador* had indeed been preserved intact, and that what Tirso wrote was in fact an excellent play on its own merits. Heretofore it had always been possible to see Tirso's Don Juan as an insignificant creation, the raw material from which other dramatists in other countries would fabricate works of genius. In the same article he denounces the deficiencies of Spanish scholarship, remarking that Calderón's *La vida es sueño* had been edited and studied in depth in Germany, Italy, France, England, and the United States, but not in Spain. There is, he says, no tradition of serious philological studies in Spain—only rhetoric and sacred cows.[11]

In the prologue to the third edition, dated "Berlin, 1931," Castro continues his efforts. He affirms that one of the features of the *comedia* is the insistence on the woman's freedom to choose her own husband, and remarks that the Spanish presentation of this issue clearly anticipates *L'école des femmes* and *L'école des maris*. He rails against "insipid Neoclassical criticism with its demands of verisimilitude, gradual development of character and the like." It is not difficult to see here a reference to the French critical tradition. In his treatment of the character of Don Juan he is even more explicit. Tirso's character has a certain tragic grandeur because he believes in God and challenges His system, whereas Molière's character "believes only that two and two make four."[12]

In the last of what we might describe as the chauvinistic presentations of Tirso's Don Juan, Castro is concerned with two fundamental themes, the demonstration of the existence in European art of a moment and style called Baroque, and the comparison within this general frame of Tirso's amd Molière's Don Juan. Baroque art, for Castro, is characterized in part by a confusion between real values (love, heroism, etc.) and their counterfeits. This leads in turn to the systematic destruction of substance in favor of a shifting play of surface contortion. In this sense Castro calls attention to the triviality of the characters and actions dramatized in *El Burlador,* remarking for example that in fact Don Juan is not the great lover we like to see in him. Because the women in the play are prey to their passions, as he is to his, real conquest becomes virtually impossible. Duquesa Isabela, for example, cannot wait for her wedding night, Tisbea is "nothing but an amorous coquette who delights in arousing the passions of her suitors." Aminta abandons her rustic husband for Don Juan in the belief that she is about to move up the social ladder. Don Juan himself dies crying for confession "like any neighbor's child." All this, Castro suggests, is typical of the new Baroque sensibility that can no longer accept the Renaissance ideal of *dignitas hominis*. The phrase of Tirso's Don Juan, "I wear myself out in vain,/ throwing blows at the air," is symbolic of this sense of instability, of vain effort expended in a substanceless vacuum. Molière's contribution was to have raised this intuition by the character to the level of full consciousness. As Castro describes him, Molière's Don Juan is "force and impetus flailing about in an unfillable void, a movement that reabsorbs its own energy."[13]

For Castro, Tirso and Molière belong to the same spiritual tradition—Baroque—within which Tirso's priority is firmly established. Besides the two Don Juans, Castro observes that the attitudes of Tirso's Aminta, and his Doña Ana, who refuses Don Juan but is willing to bed down instantly with her cousin the Marqués de la Mota in order to avoid a disagreeable marriage, clearly anticipate *L'école des maris*. Analogous relationships are posited between Juan Ruiz de Alarcón (*La verdad sospechosa*) and Corneille (*Le Menteur*).

The principal difference that remains, or appears to remain, between the two Baroque national theaters is that of style and poetic diction. The Spanish plays are characterized by a "Baroque" style that cannot fail to strike every reader as violently artificial, in contrast with the elegant clarity of the French works. This difference, Castro concludes, is more apparent than real, for in fact Corneille's poetic diction is extremely artificial— certainly as far removed from actual speech as Tirso's, for example. The difference lies not in the poetic diction itself, but in the education of authors and audiences in the respective societies. "The ritualistic traditionalism of French education has the effect of causing the artificial to seem natural, while the constant fissures in the history of Spanish life have created a situation in which, for example, Menéndez y Pelayo could experience Gongora as 'empty' and 'demented.' For those Spaniards who have not enjoyed the advantages of French education, the tragic style of the *grand siècle* is unbearably pompous and affected."[14]

One phase of the dynamics of these Don Juan studies is clear. On the one hand, Castro seeks to minimize the qualitative differences between the Spanish and French versions by insisting on their common identity as products of the pan-European moment of crisis whose characteristic artistic style is Baroque. On the other, he suggests that the "bad press" the Spanish plays have traditionally suffered is due not to any real qualitative inferiority but to a perverse combination of foreign chauvinism and national ignorance. It is in this context that Castro's continued attacks on the poverty and superficiality of the Spanish intellectual establishment, his jokes at the Faculties of Letters and at the Academy, take on their real meaning. The French can be forgiven for minimizing or misunderstanding the importance of a Tirso; they have a Molière to glorify. What is intolerable is the fact that the Spaniards themselves, uncertain first of all as to whether what they are reading is actually what Tirso wrote, are content to put the text aside and repeat the conventional wisdom, thus basing their evaluation of his work and place in literary history on the most abysmal ignorance.

Castro's studies of Tirso and Don Juan are by no means limited, however, to the simultaneous pushing and pulling into some kind of alignment with French tragedy that we have just seen. Again, beginning in 1910, we can discern in his work the presence of a mind concerned above all with the formulation of those questions, which, when answered, will open the doors of understanding. For example, in the first *Burlador* prologue Castro wonders how it is that a friar of the Order of Mercy, whose natural habitat is his cell, could have known so much about the emotional states, as well as the overt actions and reactions, of men and women in society. He offers a tentative answer based on Tirso's contacts with high society, his travels in Spain and to America, and his studies. This particular answer, I think, is less important than the question. Castro pounces on an anomaly, a discrepancy, an inconsistency, in this case the paradox of the cloistered friar whose plays are the worldliest of his age—and formulates the essential question: "How was this possible?"

A corollary aspect of this same problem becomes the subject of a meditation in the 1932 *Burlador* prologue, where Castro wonders how it is that Tirso, a respected priest who held important offices in his Order, could write the most sexually liberated descriptions of women to be found among his contemporaries. For Castro, this implies the larger and more fundamental question of the essence and meaning of religiosity in the seventeenth century. "In what, then, did the religiosity of many seventeenth-century intellectuals consist? What zones of life fell within the purview of religion? And what was that which was not religion?"[15] He further remarks that Lope, Tirso, and Calderón were all priests and all wrote plays incompatible with twentieth-century moral conventions. He suggests that what is important in contemporary religiosity—the matter of sexual control—may simply not have been a great issue in the seventeenth century. The ruling theocracy, he concludes, was satisfied with the solemn and exterior practice of religion—the endless cycle of processions and celebrations that fill the ecclesiastical calendar—with the exercise of political and intellectual control, and with the security of being invulnerable. The theocracy simply had no need to intervene in any area of human behavior that did not threaten its policies. Thus there is no contradiction between writing serious theology and in another work describing the form and color of a woman's breast.

The 1953 study of Don Juan and Aeneas is important first because it is predicated upon structural concepts we shall examine later, and second because of its content. Castro here abandons his more or less invidious comparisons of the *Burlador* and its descendants in France and elsewhere, and addresses himself to the structure and meaning of Tirso's play. The original Don Juan is conceived on the pattern of Aeneas, not as his image, but as his antithesis. This relation, Castro confesses, had remained inaccessible to him precisely because Don Juan himself makes a pejorative allusion to Aeneas. After he seduces the fisher girl who had rescued him after the shipwreck, his servant comments on this ungenerous payment for her hospitality and Don Juan retorts: "You fool! Aeneas did the same thing to the Queen of Carthage!" That is, Don Juan makes a positive identification of himself with the founder of Rome, and the audience is thus invited to ponder the discrepancies between the two. Tirso's use of preexisting literary tradition, then, is central to the meaning of his own play, for it allows us to perceive the grandeur—a negative grandeur grounded in emptiness and the absence of values—of the protagonist and the society in which he exists. As Castro states: "Tirso (as opposed to Cervantes) seeks after grandeur and majesty, only to knock them to pieces without, however, destroying them. Don Juan is pure *air,* but he struggles heroically to the end against his fatal inanity. He begins his dramatic existence with the declaration: 'I am the wind,' and ends it with words that are grandiose insofar as they express an invincible spirit, but minimal with respect to their objective content: 'I wear myself out in vain,/ throwing blows at the air!'"[16]

In 1954 Castro suggested, in contrast to what he had mockingly decried in 1910, that the peculiarities of Don Juan might be explained by the absorption of some Semitic—and in this case specifically Moorish—experience in the fabric of Spanish life.[17] In 1962 Don Juan is seen as an example of that peculiarly Spanish method of inserting oneself in life Castro came to call "*vivir desviviéndose*"—living by denying the reality of one's existence—after his great theories as to the uniqueness of Spanish life had been formulated and solidified.[18] It will be observed that all the examples we have just considered involve the relation between art and life. Castro seeks constantly to explore the relation, in all its shifting ambiguities and disguises, between the work of art and its relevant historical context, and to explain the former with reference to the latter. He attempts to discover and isolate the peculiar combination of circumstances that created the possibility—never the fact, for that is the ultimate secret of the creative process—for a particular phenomenon (*Don Quijote,* Lope de Vega) to come to exist. This is the question Castro formulates time and again: "¿Cómo fue posible . . .?", a question we should properly translate as: "How did this *become* possible?"

There are two notions implicit here. The first is the crucial importance of the relevant historical context and the second is the idea of process. With this in mind I should like to turn now to the relation of the *comedia* to the other national dramas, this time from an undefensive and unchauvinistic perspective, Castro's attempts to answer the question of what is uniquely

Spanish in the Spanish *comedia*. The most obvious answer is the convention of the bloody code of conjugal honor, and Castro was by no means the first to focus on it as the most distinctively Spanish trait in the Spanish national theater. He has been, however, the most insistent seeker after the structural function and ultimate meaning of the so-called "honor code." In terms of our understanding of the *comedia,* this is Castro's most important contribution. It is also his most controversial. For this reason I should like to examine the evolution of his ideas on honor across time and to conclude by relating this to the evolution of his ideas in general.

The first and most obvious area of concern is the relation between stage honor and real life. Any consideration of "real life" in the sixteenth and seventeenth centuries leads inevitably to consideration of the substantial matter of the growing importance conceded to the phenomenon of caste: Christian, Moors, and Jews in the Middle Ages, and the Old Christian-New Christian dichotomy of the sixteenth and seventeenth centuries. Finally we must not undervalue the methodological revolution in Castro's thought, the change from refining out abstractions and "concepts" to dis-covering underlying structures. Instead of a triumphal procession from darkness to light, we have a history of anticipations and retreats, some detours and not a few contradictions.

Castro confronted the problem of honor in a systematic way first in 1916, in a study that many Hispanists, principally those who do not agree with his more recent theories, still consider impressive and useful. It is impressive in its erudition, the vast and intimate knowledge it displays of a genre composed of thousands of individual members. Its usefulness, however, is vitiated by its methodological biases. It is preoccupied with surface phenomena. Passages from many, many plays are analyzed and the characters' speeches taken at face value. From this massive accumulation of data Castro abstracts out and arrays a series of principles or concepts that float like Hegelian ideas above the individual facts. Furthermore, there seems to be a tacit assumption that the plays faithfully reflect social reality, so that the former can be used to study the latter. Thus, for example, the study is subdivided into such sections as: "The

Concept of Honor is Not Exclusively Calderonian," "The Concept of Honor in the Sixteenth Century," "The Concept of Honor in Lope," "Honor: Patrimony of the Nobility," "Honor: the Highest Good," "The Loss of Honor," "Honor and the King," "Honor and the Romances of Chivalry."

The status of Castro's thought in 1916, and the direction it was subsequently to take, is summed up in the relationship between a paragraph of the text and an accompanying footnote. "Honor is innate in the nobility, and it might be added that honor is the exclusive property of the noble class. In the theater the right to honor is typically denied to the peasant. He is ridiculed when he exhibits pretensions to honor, and in the rarest of cases, when a villein is considered to have honor, the dramatist feels obliged to provide an explanation."[19] Now the note to this passage contains examples of what in 1916 were doubtless considered "exceptions" to the conclusions derived from examination of the data, but which in 1961 had come to be the "rule." The texts from *Peribáñez,* for example, which constitute the cllimax of *De la edad conflictiva* appear here, in miniscule type, as examples of "sporadic" appearances of peasants with honor. It is a tribute to Castro's intellectual honesty first that he should have included the information contained in the note in his 1916 essay, where it tends to undermine the principal thesis, and second that he should have been perturbed enough by the incongruity to return to it again and again in search of a resolution.

Let me offer one final example, drawn from the same article, of Castro's early tendency to raise fundamental questions in the process of answering the more obvious ones. In his discussion of the "honor code" Castro refers to the characteristic homogeneity of Spanish society in the Golden Age. "In Spain there existed, in the seventeenth century, an extraordinary degree of social cohesion. In religion, in government, in the establishment of those principles that confer value on the individual within the collectivity, there was unanimous agreement. For an individual to manifest discord in any of these areas meant social infamy."[20] Within this description of collective unanimity is the tacit recognition of the existence of some form of conflict, a majority opinion forced onto an oppressed minority and enforced with the sanctions of honor. At the end of the essay Castro makes this explicit. "We should not conclude, however, that there were no manifestations of points of view opposed to the foregoing, especially in the sixteenth century." This suggests that a more open society prevailed in the sixteenth century, that certain actions and opinions were possible then which became impossible later. In the years between 1916 and 1961 Castro would ponder the reasons for this shift. Here he seems to be still in the process of discerning that a problem exists.

In his 1917 study of Rojas Zorrilla, Castro is still moving in a realm of abstractions, although without entirely succeeding in taking up permanent residence there. He bemoans the lack of "scientific studies of the character and origin of the ideas reflected in the classical *comedia*," probably thinking of something like his own massive *El pensamiento de Cervantes*, which would correlate the speeches in the plays to the ideological currents of the Renaissance.[21] He insists on the abstract character of the *comedia* as a genre, when he remarks apropos of the allegorical religious plays known as *autos sacramentales*: "and the same abstract personifications contribute to reveal to us more clearly the tendency toward abstraction which informs the technique of the *comedia* itself—ideological conceptions (honor, gallantry, friendship) that envelop the characters like a kind of hieratic vestment."[22] And yet in the same study Castro ponders the relation of stage honor, which he describes on the one hand as an abstraction, to real life in the seventeenth century, and cites the case of a certain Miguel Pérez de las Navas, notary, who on Holy Thursday, 1636, executed his wife by hanging, on the suspicion that she had been unfaithful.[23] Indeed, Castro can here never escape entirely from the social milieu in which the *comedia* was created and in which it existed. He remarks that the play he is editing was a popular failure because it offered an unacceptable solution to a problem of conjugal honor: the wife avenges her dishonor herself. According to Castro, this action "totally subverts the normal principles of honor." In his more recent terminology he would say that the play must fail because the wife deprives her husband of his most crucial exercise of *hombría*. This change in terminology reflects a change in orientation, from abstractions such as "the normal principles of honor," to the experiential dimension of the most intimate aspects of human life projected onto and then rejected by the audience whose passions are collectively engaged. What is crucial here in 1917 is the insistence, in spite of the tendency toward abstraction, on the relationship between the play, the life of which it is some kind of slice, and the lives of those onto which it is projected and who see themselves reflected in it.

This web of relationships is the core of Castro's 1922 study of the *comedia* as a genre. He insists that it is impossible to understand or enjoy the *comedia* without understanding its historical context, and that the Spanish university system makes virtually no provision for the study of national history or the history of national literature.

> It is obvious that the interest offered by the theater increases in relation to one's knowledge of Spain and its past. This type of knowledge is exceptionally rare among us Spaniards, and usually limited to a few anecdotes and commonplaces. The classical theater ideally defines Spain in an essential moment of its history. Without it the Spanish past would exist in a vacuum, as inaccessible as the moon. It is, therefore, practically impossible for the plays to have any meaning unless the reader brings to them a clear desire to penetrate the history of Hispanic civilization.[24]

In this study he comes to grips with the relation, or possible relation, between conjugal honor on the stage and what happaned in life. There is, he says, a kind of springboard movement in the plays from what the audience knew from experience to what he calls "la cosa extraordinaria, la aventura.' This latter is the dramatization of cases of conjugal honor. "Lope de Vega's art consisted in discovering what were, so to speak, the ideal trampolines from which it was worthwhile to cause the fantasy of his audience to jump"[25] The proliferation of "honor cases" on stage, then, does not necessarily imply their existence in any significant number in life.

The thesis that there is any correlation between reality and the stage was challenged by the novelist and essayist José Martínez Ruiz (Azorín), who averred that the *comedia* was the purest fantasy, and that any other kind of popular literature was rendered impossible by the pervasive presence of the Inquisition. In his rejoinder to Azorín, Castro insists again on his concept of a well-known reality serving as springboard for the flight of fancy that finally engages the passions—"moves with force," in Lope's words—of the spectator. "The perfect *comedia* for a Spaniard of 1600 is one which, offering him at first a real, usual and ordinary base, applicable in every way to his daily experience, suddenly propels him into the regions of fantasy, where life offers all its possibilities in maximum tension. The artistry of Lope de Vega and of those who adopted his dramatic formula is rooted in this abrupt shift from reality to poetry."[26] Later in the same essay he describes the structure as triangular, beginning in reality, taking flight in fantasy, and then returning to reality, to the world of the audience to whom it belonged.

Here in the 1920s Castro's thought is remarkably consistent in its insistence on the fact and importance of a positive relation between what happens on stage and what occurs in life. He sees clearly too that this relation is not that of a mirror image. Instead of positing some transitional or transformational phase between the stage situations and the drama of real life, however, he posits a flight of poetic fantasy within the plays themselves. That is, once again we are confronted by a tendency toward abstraction even as Castro insists on the experience—real or vicarious—of life, what he calls the *vivencia,* of characters and spectators alike. There is no question as to the fact of a relationship between stage honor and real life. It is the cornerstone of Castro's interpretive edifice. The question now becomes that of determining the precise nature of that relationship. A change in methodology, accompanied by massive new insights into the historical reality of Spain, will allow Castro to posit an answer.

The 1953 article on Don Juan and Aeneas assumes pivotal importance because in it Castro specifically rejects the process of abstracting conclusions above and away from the data and replaces it with the notion of structure. He speaks of the relation in the play between what he calls its *aspecto* (surface appearance) and its *transfondo* (literally "transdepth"), clarifying immediately that the *transfondo* is present in the work, that it is not the sources, the historical period, or the biography of the author. He further states that the degree of difficulty the reader encounters in his attempt to experience and understand a work is a function of the clarity of the relation between *aspecto* and *transfondo*. The two do not necessarily look alike—hence the reader's difficulty. Implicit here, of course, is the notion of some transferential or transformational element between them, which, when discovered, allows their relation to be perceived as well. And although Castro explicitly rejects Freud in the next sentence, his thought is not out of harmony with Freud's—nor, I should add, is it at odds with that of Marx, Saussure, or Chomsky.

What these thinkers have in common is their insistence that observable phenomena are constructed upon and determined by some underlying facts that are not visible and are accessible only by a process of analysis. Engels demonstrated, for example, that urban planning and architecture are determined by the economic infrastructure of capitalist society, and that cities are in fact laid out *in order to* mask the existence of the poor. The enterprise of modern transformational grammar is precisely that of dis-covering, by rearranging the elements of discourse, the hidden rules, often of astounding complexity, which govern speech and assure, for example, that no speaker makes a mistake in his native language. Saussure had made possible this train of thought when he discovered the distinction between *langue* and *parole*. Chomsky has further elaborated this into the notion of surface structure (what is visible) and deep structure (what determines the shape of the surface structure). Of all these, Freud is doubtless the most important, for he discovered first that the two levels do not necessarily look alike or even resemble each other—the manifest content of a dream is a disguised version of the latent content—and second that the individual is frequently (usually) unaware of the real motivation for his behavior, staunch a believer in free will as he may be, because it lies below the surface of consciousness. Chomsky's insights, for example, would be impossible without this knowledge. When Castro in 1953 considers a *comedia* in terms of its *aspecto* and *transfondo,* he is coining Spanish equivalents of such pairs as "surface and deep structure," "*langue* and *parole,*" "infrastructure and superstructure," and finally "behavior and motivation (conscious and unconscious)." He is simultaneously placing himself in the company of thinkers he himself consciously rejects because of what appears to be their anachronistic determinism. Nevertheless, and as I hope to show, his own later thought—the crowning achievement of a long career studded with important accomplishments—acquires unity and coherence only if it is considered in light of the concepts of structure discovered by thinkers Don Américo considered his intellectual antagonists.

Now, from approximately 1948 to the early 1960s Castro was discovering and clarifying the crucial importance of intercaste harmony and conflict in Spanish life. This, finally, is what is uniquely Spanish about Spanish life, without parallel anywhere in Europe, and this is what determined, finally, the shape of Hispanic civilization, art, and culture. The major revelations of these discoveries, too well-known to bear further description here, are: *España en su historia: moros, cristianos y judíos* (1948), significantly translated as *The Structure of Spanish History* (1954; *La realidad histórica de España* (1954); *De la edad conflictiva* (1961); and *La realidad histórica de España,* 2ª edición renovada (1962).

Returning with this new knowledge and new method to the consideration of the *comedia,* we can illuminate two separate areas, one of which had remained uncharted, and the other undiscovered. Understanding the overriding importance of caste conflict in the period that interests us enables us to make sense out of a welter of apparently nonsensical episodes and passages in a number of specific *comedias.* Lope's *La dama boba,* for example, opens with a discussion between two quite serious characters—one of them indeed is one of our heroes—concerning, if you will, the nobility of bacon.[27] In a society composed of a majority of Old Christians (those whose families had always been Christian) and New Christians or *conversos* (the descendants of converted Jews) demonstrating one's membership in the Old Christian caste is of paramount importance. Avoidance of pork products suggests Jewishness. Praise of bacon therefore becomes an affirmation of one's caste. Castro cites several other examples, as this one from a *comedia* by Juan Ruiz de Alarcón, *Quien mal anda, en mal acaba,* where one gentleman says to another: "because I have watched you eat,/ and I saw you drink no wine,/ nor have you tasted bacon,/ And I am now ashamed to speak to you,/ for he who eats no bacon/ and drinks no wine, is unworthy/ to speak or even to spit in public." He then cites a text previously quoted by Albert A. Sicroff, whom he credits, a letter from Benito Arias Montano (a well known sixteenth-century *converso*), to a royal secretary named Gabriel de Zayas:

> I beg your Grace not to send me the hams, but to please me by making use of them yourself and eating them, for that would give me more pleasure. For I ate ham in your house, and I shall again, if it please God. I have not tasted meat except for the day I purged myself, and it was like a second purge, and the ham they had sent me from Llerena disappeared from where it was when Monte left. I wasn't keeping it to eat myself, but in case some guest should come.[28]

Castro remarks that Arias Montano ate ham when he was someone's guest, or when he had guests, only in order that his own purity of blood (*limpieza de sangre*) would not come under suspicion, certainly not because he liked it. The passage from the *comedia,* we now see, has a direct relation to the caste conflict that pervaded real life—except that the play contains an accusation of Moorish blood (the failure to drink wine) as well as Jewish.[29]

Understanding the caste conflict also permits us to comprehend the strange phenomenon, impossible outside Spain, of illiterate peasants who came on stage and presented a valid claim to more honor than titled noblemen. During the Middle Ages noble Christian and wealthy Jewish families had intermarried for their mutual advantage, and indeed, it was felt, the entire urban population was suspect of having intermarried with Jews. The only social group, therefore, whose membership in the Old Christian caste was beyond question were the tillers of the soil—and the more rustic, the better. As Castro states: "Country life was a theme of primary importance in the art of Lope de Vega not only because of some Virgilian resonance, or because the Renaissance had exalted Nature and the Golden Age, but because the farmer was considered the foundation of the dominant caste."[30] Or, accentuating the distinction between social *classes* and *castes,* he characterizes the peasants of *Fuenteovejuna* as "low in class, but of high caste, by the simple fact of their being Old Christians, with no mark of Jews or Moors in their lineage."[31]

Castro goes on to relate the Old Christian peasants and their honor to the dramatic conflicts on the stage.

> The farmers were the seat of honor in the popular mind because of their presumed freedom from the taint of Jewishness, but in Lope de Vega's theater the honored consciousness of the rustic comes to the surface in his clashes with the decadent nobility. Although the farmer comes on stage supported by his Old Christian pedigree, his encounters with the nobles are projected against the common memory of the opposite relation of the two groups to the Jews. The nobles had traditionally protected the Jews, and in their contacts had become "contaminated."

He then cites as examples the confrontation between the peasant Old Christian city councilman and the Comendador in *Fuenteovejuna,* in which the former quite openly questions the purity of the latter's blood, and the face-off between the company of peasant soldiers and that composed of *hidalgos* (nobles) in *Peribáñez y el Comendador de Ocaña,* where the former refer to the latter first as "tired *hidalgos*" (tired of waiting—for the Messiah, a common anti-Semitic joke) and then simply as "these Jews."[32]

To be a peasant was good, to eat bacon was good, and to be illiterate was also good, an Old-Christian caste-marker, because of the traditional association of Jewishness with the learned professions and what the Old Christians referred to as *agudeza* or "sharpness." Castro quotes Cervantes' burlesque playlet *La elección de los alcaldes de Daganzo,* in which a rustic buffoon declares not only himself but all his forebears innocent of literacy, that chimera "that carries men off to the stake." This citation appears among a welter of similar demonstrations taken from learned treatises of the period, in which references to this absurd state of affairs abound.[33]

Tirso addresses himself to the matter of the learned professions, and counsels the king to choose "wise and noble physicians, well born and with a title to some land, without 'race,' note or hint of any alien or contrary law. I speak in this from experience, and I know that in any endeavor, Christianity can accomplish more than any science" (*La prudencia en la mujer*). After remarking that in the play the Queen's Jewish doctor had indeed almost poisoned her son, Castro observes: "But science itself, because it was 'Jewish,' was considered poisonous. The idea floating in the air in the seventeenth century was simply that all science was suspect and risky, because any intellectual occupation was traditionally the province of Jews."[34]

The caste conflict underlies the presentation of wealth and poverty, associated with different castes and valued accordingly, in the *comedia*. In Lope's *La pobreza estimada* a poor but Old Christian *hidalgo* (Leonido) and a wealthy New Christian (Ricardo) are rivals for a certain Dorotea. The *converso* sends her a sack of money and she upbraids his messenger: "I shall have you killed! Get out of here, and give back the money you got for selling out your master Leonido to that Jew!" Here Ricardo is cast in the role of Caiaphas, the messenger as Judas, and Leonido as Christ himself. Castro remarks: "What is noteworthy here is that Lope, so attuned to the sentiments of Spanish society, makes being rich coincide with belonging to the Hispano-Jewish caste. Lope demonstrates that the *converso*'s money does not confer any social dignity, and is certainly not the way to a young lady's heart."[35]

Clearly, the new knowledge of the caste conflict enables us to understand a good many passages that formerly either made no sense at all or could be subsumed under some pan-European cultural rubric, and to grasp their essential and peculiar Spanishness. Yet for all that, such references are scanty and comparatively insignificant in the thousands of three-act plays that together comprise the genre. The plays are simply not dramatizations of what Castro refers to as the "sterile and infecund debate over whether one was or was not an Old Christian." Rather, the characteristic theme of the genre is conjugal honor. On the basis of the insights gained since the late 1940s concerning the real nature of Spanish society and social conflict, Castro can now formulate much more precisely the fundamental question he had attempted to answer in 1922 and 1923. Instead of simply pondering the relation between stage honor and "reality" he can now confront the social drama—caste conflict—and the stage drama—conjugal honor—and ask two related questions. First, if the *comedia* is based in reality, as it must be, how is it that the real social issue is never dramatized? Second, how is it that cases of conjugal honor can come to replace the "real" theme of caste conflict? The investigation of these issues is the subject of *De la edad conflictiva*.

In this work Castro offers a radically reordered version of the "springboard" theory he had developed in 1922 and 1923, with the important distinction that what was previously explained as a "flight of fantasy" is now seen as a transference from a reality of conflicct so oppressive as to be unmentionable to one or more subjects about which reasonable men may certainly differ, and which engage the passions of the audience, but which ultimately serve to preserve the inviolability of the real source of conflict. This operates, according to Castro, on two levels. The first concerns the conflict between peasants and feudal lords dramatized in such plays as *Fuenteovejuna.*

> The conflict between "clean" and "dirty" Christians is seldom alluded to directly in literature. It is understood that the peasants' Old Christianity authorizes him to present himself as the antagonist of his lord. The latter, in turn, is not depicted as evil because of the possibility of carrying Jewish blood in his veins, but because he abdicates his reponsibility and wreaks violence upon those it was his duty to support. In short, the social conflict made the literary conflict possible—without being mentioned directly (fortunately for art).[36]

The second level is the transference of caste conflict to conjugal honor. After insisting once again that the artistry of the artist resides in his ability "to transform the paralytic and fecund debate over whether one was or was not an Old Christian into axiological perspectives capable of stirring men's souls," he observes—and this is the kernel of his thought—that it was easier to "move the audience with force," as Lope said, with conjugal honor situations than through the subtle ironies of a Cervantes, even though the latter sometimes refers directly to the matter of *limpieza de sangre.* He finally exemplifies this thesis by reference to *Peribáñez,* a play whose theme is conjugal honor but which insists again and again on the presentation of the married couple as Old Christians. The unstated implication, of course, is that the threat to Peribáñez's husbandly honor, the Comendador, is not a Christian. In this way the real, social conflict between Old and New Christians is transformed into the dramatic conflict between husband and would-be lover. Peribáñez's assertion of *hombría,* his murder of the Comendador with a (symbolic) sword dripping (impure) blood, becomes in this way a metaphorical or displaced assertion of his irreducible essence as Old Christian.

Castro's thesis has by no means been universally accepted. Arnold Reichenberger, to mention only one example, confesses his inability to accompany Don Américo in what appears to be a leap in logic which makes the demonstration of one's manhood (*hombría*—conjugal honor) dependent upon one's race (*sangre limpia*).[37] The explanation for the breakdown in communication lies, I believe, in a situation created by the history of Castro's own philosophical underpinnings. In his earlier period, dominated as we have seen by belief in the validity of abstract concepts, he could still feel the pulse of vital experience, as his discussion (1917) of the popular failure of *Cada cual lo que le toca* suggests. Later, when his thought centered on the individual's consciousness of existing in a particular situation, as opposed to being the toy of some "concept," Castro is not entirely successful in explaining away the presence of underlying structures. His accounting for the fact that the real social conflict is never dramatized in the *comedia,* for example, by saying that Lope conceived of life pictorially, with the implied suggestion that conjugal honor is somehow more "pictorial" than intercaste conflict, is not really satisfactory. In my view it springs from Castro's unwillingness to concede the existence of unconscious forces—operating individually or collectively—in the belief that to do so would vitiate the thesis of the primacy of consciousness and will. In a way his dilemma resembles Sartre's circular polemics with psychoanalysis.

Castro in fact discovered and isolated the underlying structure of Spanish life, the intercaste conflict, which determined the visible manifestations of art and culture, but because of his antideterministic philosophical posture he was unwilling to shore up and systematize his explanation with appropriate analogies to structuralist—notably Freudian—thought. Because Freud demonstrated that what we do (conscious behavior) is frequently a disguised and distorted version of what we would like to do but which for some reason is intolerable (unconscious motivation), he provides a model for the rational explanation of the strange and apparently illogical relationship between caste conflict and conjugal honor. The real conflict is experienced as intolerable and must be repressed, that is, banished from consciousness. But the repression is only partially successful, and the repressed material rises to the surface, but in a disguised form. This allows the psychic energy cathected to the repressed material to be harmlessly released and simultaneously avoids the necessity to deal with the explicit content of the material. This is a circular way of saying that the psychic energy is displaced from its real object onto a substitute object, which can then absorb it. We can begin to discern how repressed concern for intercaste conflict (the underlying structure, or in Castro's terminology the *transfondo*) might surface in the form of concern for conjugal honor (Castro's *aspecto*).

But we need not content ourselves with this schematic formulation, for the fact is that we can, thanks to Castro's studies, chart the intermediate or transformational phases of this massive displacement with some precision. There are three points to be made. First, in order for the displacement to be effective and not precipitate the formation of neurotic symptoms, the substitute issue must be one of sufficient magnitude and real concern to actually engage the individual's interest and absorb the psychic energy. To attempt to displace intercaste conflict onto something too trivial—wearing one's hair long or short, for example—would only exacerbate the conflict. Conjugal honor obviously has the power to engage the individual's interest, as Lope knew when he wrote: "los casos de la honra son mejores,/ porque mueven con fuerza a toda gente" (Honor cases are the best, because they move *everyone* strongly). Indeed, if we could imagine issues existing in a vacuum, conjugal honor would appear at least as "engaging" a matter as purity of blood. Of course the *comedia* does not exist in a vacuum, and what attests to the direction of the displacement is the fact that the society was not composed of psychopathic wife-murderers.

Second, there is a conceptual or perhaps semantic analogy between the notions of purity and contamination, sanctity and violation, and integrity and fragmentation which are present as contrasting possibilities referable both to caste and to marriage.

Finally there is a rational and immediately observable link between the two, which is the phenomenon of honor itself. Honor exists first in a public context, where it is measured by such things as membership in a military-religious order (marked by special insignia worn on clothing), legal authorization to carry offensive weapons,, membership in a *colegio mayor* (a remote ancestor of the American college fraternity) at the University, exemption from paying taxes, such semihonorary civic positions as that of *familiar* of the Inquisition, membership in a cathedral chapter or indeed in practically any prestigious corporate body. In the sixteenth and seventeenth centuries this form of honor was reserved for those who could prove their Old Christianity. That is, public recognition, honor in this sense, became an outward and visible manifestation of an inner grace called purity of blood. Phrased another way, the entire honorific apparatus was designed in order to keep *conversos* out. Honor also exists in private, in the intimacy of the conjugal relationship and is a function of the husband's *hombría*. The transference from *limpieza* (the real social conflict) to *hombría* (the stage conflict) can thus be traced through the middle ground of public honor, already defined as a matter of *limpieza*. Private honor therefore becomes a plausible substitute.

Castro's lifelong relationship with the *comedia*, which began in 1910 when he asked how Tirso de Molina was possible, thus concludes by embracing the literary genre within its broadest social and historical context. The question has finally become: "How is the Spanish *comedia*, with its characteristic theme of conjugal honor, possible?" The answers he provides may not be definitive; indeed, there may be no such thing as a definitive answer. Castro's hypotheses and explanations, like those of Freud in his discipline, are the essential foundation, the indispensable point of departure for any future attempts to explain the Spanish *comedia*.

NOTES

1. "Sobre el teatro clásico español," *Nosotros,* 44 (1923), p. 558.
2. Ibid., p. 551.

3. Tirso de Molina, *El vergonzoso en palacio y El burlador de Sevilla,* edited by Américo Castro (Madrid: Calpe, 1910), pp. xv–xvi.

4. *ECD* (1963), p. 252.

5. "Advertencia," *VLV* (1968), p. 11–12.

6. Ibid., p. 381.

7. "Tricentenario de Lope de Vega," *La Nación* (Buenos Aires), 25 August 1935. Reprinted in *ENC,* III, 166.

8. *VLV* (1968), p. 263.

9. "Cómo y por qué fue dualmente conflictiva la literatura del siglo XVI," *Papeles de Son Armadans,* 42, no. 126 (1966), 234. Reprinted as a prologue to *ECD* (1967).

10. "Avertencia," *VLV* (1968), p. 11.

11. "Sobre el teatro clásico español," p. 51. See n. 1.

12. Tirso de Molina, *El vergonzoso en palacio y El burlador de Sevilla,* edited by Américo Castro, 3d ed. (Madrid: Espasa-Calpe, 1932), pp. xvi–svii; xxv.

13. "El Don Juan de Tirso y el de Molière como personajes barrocos," in *Hommage à Ernest Martinenche* (Paris: Artrey, 1939), p. 106.

14. Ibid., p. 110.

15. *El vergonzoso en palacio,* 3d ed., p. xii. See n. 12.

16. "El Don Juan de Tirso y el Eneas de Virgilio," first published in *El Nacional* (Caracas), 3 August 1953; reprinted in *Semblanzas y estudios españoles* (Princeton, 1956); and in *ENC,* III, 149–155.

17. *RHE* (1954), p. 431.

18. *RHE* (1962), p. 81.

19. "Algunas observaciones acerca del concepto del honor en los siglos XVI y XVII," *Revista de Filología Española,* III (1916), 21–22; reprinted in *Semblanzas y estudios españoles,* p. 336.

20. Ibid., 358.

21. F. Rojas Zorrilla, *Cada cual lo que le toca y La viña de Nabot,* edited by Américo Castro (Madrid: Centro de Estudios Históricos, 1917), p. 195. My deepest thanks to my colleague Enrique Rodríguez-Cepeda, who graciously loaned me his copy of this rare book, which is permanently missing from the UCLA library.

22. Ibid., p. 254.

23. Ibid., p. 195.

24. "El teatro clásico," originally in Tirso de Molina, *El vergonzoso en palacio y El burlador de Sevilla,* 2d ed. (Madrid: Espasa-Calpe, 1922); reprinted in M. Benardete and A. del Río, eds., *El concepto contemporáneo de España: Antología de ensayos* (Buenos Aires: Losada, 1946), pp. 591–610: 609.

25. Ibid., p. 600.

26. "Sobre el teatro clásico español," p. 555. See n. 1.

27. The importance of this scene was first noted, according to Castro, by Alonso Zamora Vicente, "Para el entendimiento de *La dama boba,*" in M.P. Hornik, ed. *Collected Studies in Honour of Américo Castro's Eightieth Year* (Oxford: Lincombe Lodge Research Library, 1965), pp. 447–460.

28. See Albert A. Sicroff, *Les controverses des statuts de pureté de sang en Espagne du XVe au XVIIe siècle* (Paris: Didier, 1960), pp. 269–270.

29. *ECD* (1961), pp. 61–62.

30. *RHE* (1962), pp. 93–94.

31. *ECD* (1961), pp. 48–49.

32. Ibid. pp. 205–206. See also Joseph H. Silverman, "Los 'hidalgos cansados' de Lope de Vega," in *Homenaje al profesor William L. Fichter* (Madrid: Castalia, 1971), pp. 693–711.

33. Ibid., p. 162.

34. Ibid., pp. 154–155.

35. Ibid., p. 298. See also a passage from *El premio del bien hablar* in which a character "justifies" his involvement in maritime commerce, p. 323, n. 80.

36. Ibid., pp. 203–204.

37. A.G. Reichenberger, "Review of *De la edad conflictiva,*" *Hispanic Review,* XXXI-2 (April 1962), 166–170.

Part IV
On the Modern Period

10

THE SPANISHNESS OF
THE EIGHTEENTH CENTURY
Enrique Rodríguez-Cepeda

Many years ago I was impressed
to find these words that a hand
had indelibly engraved on the
wall of the seminary in Vergara
(Vizcaya) in the eighteenth
century:
"¡Oh, qué mucho lo de allá!
Oh, qué poco lo de acá!"[1]

Everything that has happened in the Iberian Peninsula since the
sixteenth century seems to respond to a vital interweaving of
causes and effects which has made up in a unique way every
moment lived by the Spaniards in the last four hundred years.
Historiographers like Ortega y Gasset and Américo Castro do
not take as their point of departure the Age of Enlightenment,
the nineteenth, or even the historifiable dimension of the
twentieth century because the dominant aspects of our modes of
living and certain forms of coexistence had already been determined in a more distant past. The spiritual tangle that has
surrounded the Spaniards since the "Golden Century," actually
a period of over a hundred and fifty years, is still present in
everything today. That so-called Golden Era has now acquired
names such as "Tibetanization" and "Age of Conflict," and
recent centuries still bear the well-defined mark of those two
contrasting expressions, programmed so wisely by Ortega and
Castro. The fundamental and operative element in the historiographic discoveries of these thinkers is how Spanish history has
been paralyzed by the reversible action of these contrasting
characterizations (*Tibetanism* and *conflictiveness*), which have
put everything Spanish in an "occupied" state of stereotypes
and outlines. In recent years these types and shapes have
become all too familiar to us. Those obviously antiquated

223

structures mark and retard the disastrous rhythm of Spanish history and even in the twentieth century they still extend their tentacles to crush it. It is impossible to understand, for example, what a Spaniard living in Madrid experiences right now without considering his immersion in and projection onto a past with terrifying limitations or recalling the latent insecurity of Don Quixote whose experiential awareness of life is conceived of as "change and exchange." It is very significant that Juan Goytisolo increasingly stresses the need to free the Spanish language from its marginal state as a means of communication and art in the world as a whole.[2]

Returning to the eighteenth century, we can quickly assure ourselves that in Américo Castro's thoughts on Spanish history we will not find any rhythm, organization, or key expressions referring to the secondary, less important moments in our last three centuries. This is logical because the eighteenth century could not explain the sixteenth or seventeenth centuries, and the nineteenth century could do so even less. Such successions, however, ought not to eliminate the uniqueness and originality of each age. What we are going to explore of Castro's ideas about the eighteenth century is, then, any results, similarities, and counterpoints in terms of the central idea of the conflictive origin of Spain. Moreover, we should not be surprised if this analysis does not directly contribute to a greater understanding of the Enlightenment. We ought to be content with a balance of ideas and clear and precise viewpoints over a period of more than forty years of intellectual inquiry.

It is no sign of nationalistic pride to say, first of all, that Spain has always belonged to Spain, because it is discouraging to try to defend that position. It means that Spain has never completely belonged to Europe. For some reason, neither Don Quixote's "change and exchange" nor the terrifying frontier, the latent unease of the conflict, the critical fatality of things Hispanic has ever been overccome. We have not mixed our history well with the rest of the world and, if Spain by necessity has always been Europe's neighbor, she has "never been a joiner," as Don Américo said.[3]

The Age of Enlightenment is a special case because, apparently, some Spaniards, at least an important minority, resolutely wanted and planned to belong to Europe as the only way to counterbalance and assimilate their past. The big problem was that Europe, and France in particular, neither admitted nor understood the sincere cooperative intentions of the Spaniards and treated us very poorly.

These foreign reactions obliged us, to some extent, to adopt a defensive attitude, to return to our past in an unfortunate way, and also to go back to living in that old indecisive land between two waters. Consequently, in spite of the irrefutable rapprochement of a certain sector of Spain with the universal movement, terms like "Frenchified" and "Frenchification" have always seemed remote and devoid of meaning for us. Basically they are damning stigmas to cover up ancient intellectual and social caste differences in the Peninsula. The philosophy of *social imitation* (fashions, appearances, taste) that set the tone for the bourgeois culture of eighteenth-century Europe is perceptibly dampened in Spain because there is still no relation between culture and masses, politics and society, reason and belief, science and bread. Our eighteenth century is linked to the past in a way that is defined by our own and others' obligations, and it is no longer possible to believe—since it is so un-Spanish and so strange in our history—that it is not very closely related to the Age of Conflict and Tibetanism. We must banish the rather feeble notion that naively justifies all of Don Américo's work, namely, that his ideas work well up to the seventeenth century, but after that his theories fall down because of the near miracle of the liberal eighteenth century—as if anything had really changed in function or meaning. There was nothing new about the enlightened miracle, since the intent to improve and renew Peninsular coexistence was, in many ways, quite old, although none of those attempts had succeeded as they did at this time. Nor was the eighteenth century any less miracle-working than others in Spanish history, even though it was mixed with more rational elements to counterbalance our beliefs.

The famous "1965 Introduction" seems too superficial to some critics, but carefully appraised, it is still the most thoughtful writing on our Enlightenment and the most sensible way of blotting out the false notion of the uninterrupted flow of "possible Spains" that Spaniards have lived throughout their

history. Don Américo says: "What was imported in the eighteenth century changed nothing essential in Spain, since everything was an exterior incrustation and not organically absorbed.
Without this knowledge, the usual studies about the so-called
eighteenth-century Enlightenment are raised on a fallacious
base. Everything turns out to be just as it was."[4] Later on he
calls this type of thinking a "vain exercise" and quotes a
contemporary critic who talks about "the enormous efforts that
were made during the eighteenth century, especially during
the reign of Charles III, to open Spain up again, to incorporate
her into Europe, to which she has always belonged, and so to
let her be herself."[5] He regrets that this "placid way of looking
at history" which is so acceptable to many thinkers, puts certain
Spanish intellectuals on that naive borderline of *the possible,* if
only to confront Marcelino Menéndez y Pelayo's uninspired idea
that the eighteenth is the least Spanish century in our past.

If Spain has always belonged to Europe, it has belonged in
the same marginal way for five hundred years, and the eighteenth
century is neither the golden dream nor the black sheep of the
Peninsular conflict. Don Américo was called a "possibleist" in
a homage to his work because he did not think that the
eighteenth century was either the most or the least Spanish and
because he showed that it supposed a dramatic continuation of
the ideas of Tibetanization and conflict. The average twentieth-
century Spaniard, living immersed in the Peninsula, is not likely
to notice of his own accord—thanks to the mere fact of living
there—the latency of that frontier state which is still present in
every one of the individual and collective acts of his life.

We Spaniards cannot solve our problem of living-togetherness
by looking at Spain's harmony with Europe, by believing that,
in the eighteenth century we had "Frenchified people" (*afrance-
sados*) and a large share in the universal Enlightenment; nor
should we think that the same is true in the twentieth century
because of tourism, a free Republic, the Common Market, a
million young people sold to foreign countries "to learn the
language" in specialized factories, and a superior way of life
thanks to the miracle of "social security" and "a plot of land."
In an historical structure as closed, repetitive, and dense as
Spain's, such obviously grandiose generalizations fall flat and
overwhelm us with the tragic conflict of the terrible frontier.

The eighteenth century, then, is no different from the rest of our past, nor is it more or less Spanish, nor do we know it better or worse than other periods. What attracts us today about this age is its cultural complexity, the figure of Godoy, journalism, the good sense of those who believed in Spain in a healthy way, the great Spaniards who lived outside Spain and set an admirable example with their social and literary talent, and the world of Goya and Moratín. It is an indisputable fact that in the first thirty-five years of the twentieth century very few scholars, with the exception of Don Américo in the 1920s, had taken an interest in the eighteenth century; this neglect is also true of Menéndez Pidal's *Revista de Filología Española* and Ortega's *Revista de Occidente.* The most cogent reason for this neglect is probably that other aspects of our culture seem to be more odious to unmask and thus it is more urgent to study their problems before taking up the eighteenth century. In 1924 Don Américo talked about the eighteenth century only to show that it was no less known than other portions of our past and that it was as Spanish as any other. And he talked about this same century in 1965 because there was beginning to be born in Spain the desire to find an exemplary age, more golden than the first, an age that would liven up the current stage of national history a little and, at the same time, justify the idea of still having to be Spanish above all else. The eighteenth century could thus be the solution to the search for a new *face* value on the other side of the coin. Don Américo had to come out to call this spiritual bluff in order to rechannel the waters we spoke of earlier back to their old boundaries and to explain why it was not possible to divide the Spaniards' ideals and beliefs into two distinct phases, one before and another after 1700.

If the ideas of Tibetanization and the Age of Conflict had been expressed before 1930, now was the time to approach the gaps that a disciple of Ortega and Castro, José F. Montesinos no less, found in 1969: "In order to have a complete understanding of modern Spain, it is imperative to trace a thorough outline of this uneasy, imaginative, curious, non-conformist figure of the Spaniard of the last two hundred fifty years."[6] Until now we have considered only one problem, but let us talk about a few others. The eighteenth century does, however, have some particularly interesting aspects that distinguish it from the outstanding elements of other periods. It has also been singularly attractive to foreign critics, such as the French. Unfortunately, until now there has not yet been any timely reaction in American university circles.

Around 1924 Don Américo assured us that "our nineteenth century represented, relatively speaking, a serious step backward from the previous one insofar as historical science is concerned," which indicates the thoroughness and broad perspective some enlightened Spaniards upheld when it came to sciences of the Spirit.[7] The critical function of society in regard to certain Spanish clichés and beliefs was actually a program of many people in the eighteenth century. That century was "an attempt we made to reincorporate ourselves into the universal forms of 'culture.' . . . The entire eighteenth century movement was basically nothing but a preparation for rebuilding the country; if the movement that reached its height at the court of Charles III had continued organically against the background of international culture, the Spanish way of living would have come out on top."[8] It is apparent that Castro had not yet discovered the conflictive trajectory of Spain's inwardness, but he does point out that the eighteenth century is the touchstone of our past where we have all gone to worship and fall. We must recognize that the men of the Enlightenment brought better ways of saying things, a certain imposition of the common welfare, a reordering of cultural and literary values, more politeness in our treatment of each other, in addition to a revitalization of more practical matters.

Negatively speaking, however, the attitude of the Spanish people in general did not change much, since, apart from the plebeianization of the most well-to-do, the social scars of the past conflict were never really healed. The nation went on more or less Tibetanized, and only that minority who were not easily manipulated by a few were saved from it, and then only in part. The confrontation between Jovellanos and Godoy is still a mystery, the defections of Moratín and Goya are still controversial and obscure, the caste problem continued underground as Paulino Garragorri has discovered in Xavier de Munibe's philosophy, France's attitude was deceptive as always, and England's was chilly. Nothing and nobody helped our most promising age. Good minds, healthy national intentions, great artists, and a clearer social and economic view were just not enough. Internal divisions and obstacles had not been overcome; successive bouts with inflation throughout the century did not solve the problem of the lack of mutual cooperation, nor did the new jobs, the emerging middle class, or the new ideals of the petite bourgeoisie that imitated and was influenced by Europe. First Hamilton and later Vilar commented on Spain's advantageous development and her economic rapport with the other great powers; but today we believe that this was just another illusion, imposed by the necessities in common with the rest of Europe, similar to what happened at other times in history and again in the twentieth century when it is actually easier and more economical to modernize than to try to preserve the past immobilized. There were changes, but not enough of them were made. There were increases in salaries and prices, new administrative posts, the new idea of the value of money, greater prestige for artists and scholars, opportunities to travel abroad, etc. But as Don Américo has said, "What was imported in the eighteenth century changed nothing essential about Spain itself, since everything was an exterior incrustation and was not organically absorbed." The problem of interrupting this stifling historical continuity was still pending, and the questions of latent insecurity and mutual cooperation between an "I" and an "Other" remained without answers. In his essay on Jovellanos in 1930s, Castro had already intuited the burden of the conflict of Tibetanization when he said that "the utopian and, at the same time, tragic desire of those eighteenth-century men consisted in wanting to reject what Spain really was, in order to forge another country in its place, with other assumptions, and a different sensibility. They wanted to be what they were not."[9] How advanced that was, and what progress for Don Américo since 1921, and what a solid basis for the even greater advance of 1965! Even though the illustrious Asturian was straightforward, steadfast in his convictions, and well-meaning, Castro must classify Jovellanos' personalism, always genuine and honest, as the "essential Jovellanism of our history," because the social and vital solutions he proposed for the Peninsula did not lie either in literature or in "the echoes of Montesquieu, Condorcet, Rousseau, Locke, or Adam Smith."[10]

In terms of literature, Spain never did lose her bright star of liberal arts, and literary production never implied anything decadent compared to the preceding century. The art of writing changed a great deal during this time, even though no really great novelists, dramatists, or poets contributed to world literature. The three major literary genres were in crisis because they were in the process of being renovated, and in the new art of the essay and journalism, exposition and great scope were sought. Clavijo's *Diario de los Literatos, El Pensador matritense,* Cañuelo's *El Censor,* and other newspapers compare favorably with what was being published outside the Peninsula. Cultured people like Feijoo and Torres Villarroel are not common in Europe. Instead of imitating Molière, who is basically a direct descendant of Lope de Vega, the playwright Moratín came to influence drama, first in France and later in England; and excellent editions of his works were published in Spanish in these two countries even during Moratín's lifetime. Allowing for obvious differences, Father Isla contributed as much to the Spanish novel as Lesage did to the French picaresque genre, which is essentially a product of the depths of the Spanish character. The short plays and farces of Ramón de la Cruz also have their good qualities. Goya's painting had an enormous influence on art in general and on the European Romantic movement from Victor Hugo to Delacroix, in particular. Moreover, the historian of the Inquisition, Llorente, along with two other friars, the abbot Marchena and Blanco White, all gained universal prominence, although for different reasons. Maíquez was a well-known actor and Teresa Cabarrús' beauty was legendary. All of these figures, each at his or her own level, signified something special in the European history of the time. And Godoy's policies would have had more influence in the world if his own nation had not excoriated his personal gifts in such a highly irrational way. France took advantage of all this even more than is customarily acknowledged.

Other European countries may very possibly have come to respect Spain's cultural past more accurately and sensibly than the Spaniards themselves. Good judgment and common sense prevailed beyond our borders in regard to the Cervantine novel and Lope's theater when, contrarily, we ourselves were making every effort to dislodge permanently Lope's fundamental innovations and to refute the apparent lack of consideration for others, didacticism, and rational judgment of Don Quixote. Many eighteenth-century intellectuals tried to forget the seventeenth century because, for them, the previous era implied irrationality, concealment, and close-mindedness, with an excessive use of the imagination in literary genres. This tendency had to be corrected precisely because it did not educate or help a man to share in a common aesthetic good; it did not include social teaching, but it did encourage individual and private thinking, and was a serious obstacle toward attaining the *integral spirit* that all enlightened men of Europe were pursuing.

Spain was no less herself in the world of eighteenth-century imitation, although a critic born in that century, Antonio Alcalá Galiano, can already point out that "owing to special circumstances, Spain was still inferior to other civilized nations in many respects."[11] Undoubtedly those "special circumstances" are related to Don Américo's assertion, "being a joiner, never"; and those "special circumstances" have existed in the Peninsula since the time of the Catholic Rulers. Our misunderstanding of what happened in the eighteenth century was not due to a lack of information, but rather to the fact that until we could localize the contrasting processes of our history—Tibetanism and conflictivism—we could not decipher anything else. Even before he published *El pensamiento de Cervantes,* Castro had already observed around 1924 that "the eighteenth century is no less well-known than the sixteenth or fifteenth," and that "it is amazing that people complain about the lack of information about Feijoo's century, but they almost completely overlook the absence of a readable book about Cervantes."[12] And to think that it was not until the thirties that definitive studies on Lope, Góngora, and Quevedo began to be published in the *Revista de Filología Española.* The nineteenth century studied the eighteenth more carefully than other aspects of our culture; Castro recalls that in just a few years, the Biblioteca de Autores Españoles edited works by Moratín (father and son), Isla, Feijoo, Jovellanos, and Quintana, in addition to three volumes of poetry. Paradoxically, the eighteenth century, with so much negative reflection on the seventeenth, was the century that best edited our past literature. I refer not only to the editions of the *Poema de mio Cid* and Berceo by Tomás Antonio Sánchez (1778), but also to the support of our old theater by García de la

Huerta and Trigueros, the editions of Cervantes' work by Ibarra and Sancha, in addition to the magnificent and still unsurpassed twenty-one volumes of Lope de Vega, the ten volumes of Quevedo, the *Parnaso español* by Sedano, and the twenty volumes of poetry published by Ramón Fernández (a pseudonym of Pedro Estala). Furthermore, the men of the Enlightenment, completely free from any spiritual responsibility, paid particular attention to the cultural-religious conflict of the Spaniards and carefully edited previously unpublished works by St. Theresa, Luis de León, Fray Luis de Granada, and even by the *converso* Luis Vives.

In short, Don Américo was right. In 1921 he could define the cultural outline of the eighteenth century much better because there were more reference works and material available than ever before. Still unaware of the burden of the "Age of Conflict" he could say:

> The eighteenth century is a period of criticism and intellectual combat, to the point that mere literary values pale and fade into the background. . . . A reading of any of the choice works of that period attracts the critical spirit: the clarity, modern tone, and noble purpose that issue from any page by Feijoo or Jovellanos contrast strikingly with the confusion and arbitrary nature of many of our earlier prose writers, so much so that we naively rush to seek a poetry and drama that would be their equal. And when we discover we have been deceived, there are those who believe that the reason for the failure is to be found in our inadequate information about the eighteenth century. This attitude is an outcome of the sympathy of those who ask of that century perhaps more than it can give.[13]

In the eighteenth century some thinkers did appear whom Spain could not match, but most writing everywhere was directed to a select minority because the experimentation and mannerism of the preceding two centuries had already come to an end after a fantastic "assembly line" or "mass production" output. Literary art in the eighteenth century demanded a more academic, personal, individual, and less popular approach. Writers sought balance, proportion, and the proper social level in addition to good manners, civic improvement, and education for the common good; Moratín's best plays set a good example for drama in many countries.

Don Américo also pointed out in 1924 that "a naive view of history makes us say that all this is nothing but an imitation of the French," when, in truth, there simply could not be very many admirers of France in a basically marginal country where this imitation was criticized in such a derogatory term as "Frenchified."[14] And if the French Revolution had its repercussions all over the world, it did not frighten the Peninsular petite bourgeoisie any more than it did in other countries, including France herself. More or less following the universal rhythm that ideas, new forms of industry, commerce, and economy and fashions imposed on a country was not really succumbing to French influence. For Spain, all this was superficial. The expulsion of the Jesuits in 1767 was not an internal revolution because the causes were rooted in specific grievances of the particular religious orders involved, which in no way affected the "frontier" beliefs of the Spaniards. The stand that Castro reiterated in 1970 still holds true:

> I have analyzed that process which began in the sixteenth century and reached a climax in the eighteenth in *De la edad conflictiva*. The Inquisition petrified anti-Semitism, and injected religious meaning into the fact of being or not being an Old Christian and, as such, worthy of nobility. The absurd aspects of current history in vogue, just like those of Inquisitorial vigilance against scientific innovation in the eighteenth century, will be put in their proper perspective only when we accept the fact that Spanish ignorance (*incultura*) is the result of a particular attitude or *stance*.[15]

If the term "Frenchification" (*afrancesamiento*) is used to describe the attempt to make a complete turn about in regard to certain vices of Spain's historical conscience, then the explanation is very naive and only adds to the confusion. France has never helped Spain to understand its problems, and did so even less on that occasion. If Spain, or at least a small, undetermined minority of Spaniards, tried to recover what could not be retrieved, the solution was not in France. As at other times in our history, France was the deceptive name that helped some ill-informed souls to add to the already existing confusion. The experience of these two countries in that century of lights stems from different problems and implies a different attitude towards their past and present. In the same way, if we compare ourselves to England, similar differences arise. Our ills really did not come from abroad, and Castro is one of the few who have not been satisfied with the naive explanation that Spain was different under the men of the Enlightenment, when he saw perfectly well that everything was going on just as before and that our behaviour in general indicated nothing new, positive, or noteworthy from that period on. We failed to create a healthier living situation for everyone; we also failed to implant or establish logical ways of living and thinking like other progressive nations. Today it is very clear that the miracle of "Charles III's possible Spain" could not happen the way it did of its own accord. There is no serious justification for this situation. It was not enough that at a certain level there were attempts to reorganize national ideas and beliefs, to recommend more liberal policies, and to define a broader ethical code. Nor was it enough that Spaniards could perceive their virtues and vices more subtly or control their passions to a greater extent. Nothing good was kept with Ferdinand VII and his horrible anticonstitutional coterie. The shadow of the frontier once again rose in fury and the spell was broken. It was as if nothing had ever happened.

Another problem that Don Américo raised during the twenties was the idea that "the men of the eighteenth century saw Spain's defect as the result of her lack of science and discretion."[16] It is hard to understand the full implication of this idea; it seems that in eighteenth-century Europe this was a common notion about Spaniards, even though in the arts Cervantes' talent, Lope de Vega's theatrical ingenuity, Calderón's dramatic philosophy, and Moratín's plays were in fashion, along with the great line of Spanish painters from Velázquez to Goya. This means, more or less, that our artists do not exactly represent an accurate reflection of our political and social history. The indiscretions and irregularities of the past and the scientific restrictions that Philip II imposed on the Spaniards, to the point where it was dangerous to know how to read and write in Spanish, were all too apparent in the Enlightened world. It is possible that our lack of *modern* education—in other words, the absence of eighteenth-century science and education—was not congenital to our entire cultural past, but rather something we had acquired at the time of the Catholic Monarchs and stamped upon those two conflictive centuries. There is no doubt that Spanish science and good judgment (freedom of thought and action) had a good reputation in the fourteenth century. This was precisely the period of coexistence of three faiths, Moors, Jews, and Christians. In spite of all the precious absurdity of our Golden Age, the conflictive society had decisively influenced Europe, and nobody at that time would have believed that Tibetanization was going to convert us into a "European minority" of displaced persons. As early as 1924 Castro noted that the serious error made by the eighteenth century Peninsular intellectual was "to have established a solidarity that was all too intimate or private" with those obligations from the immediate past. And art paid twice for the same mistake because none of the Neoclassical artists anywhere accepted the immediate past; they sought even older models in the Renaissance, in line rather than in color. At least it seems that way to the intellectual eyes of the nineteenth and twentieth centuries. At any rate, the Neoclassicists imagined that the preceding age in Spain, with its bigger-than-life stereotypes, was overly exaggerated. This too might have seemed like another indiscretion to European eyes, but today in the twentieth century it seems like the only salvation. The new idea of an "Enlightened Renaissance" did not achieve any great artistic results because the application of reason to everything was another esthetic absurdity.

Castro refers to an important passage quoted by Domínguez Ortiz on the eighteenth century concerning Philip V's admonition that "nobody would lose his nobility just because of his commercial dealings . . . , but that popular opinion, stronger than any laws, had not been changed; [business] was largely in the hands of foreigners, just as it had previously been in the hands of the Jews."[17]

In religious matters Don Américo is forced to admit that "a change of life styles inspired in secular, earthly ideas and beliefs never came about from within the life of the Spaniards. Something as minimal as freedom of religion" never came about because of the continuing imitation of the cleric's life and his examinations of conscience, without realizing that there is another fundamental examination of conscience, both social and civic, which brings about order and mutual understanding. On the same level Castro had to reexamine the useless aspects of the university reform ordered by Charles III, the partial and fragmented state of learning in the provinces and regions, besides which "the spirit of the Old Christian caste reigned" as always in the university colleges. In conclusion, "it would be overly naive to expect the uprooting of traditional values overnight," since certain sectors of society such as those progressive Spaniards "always wanted everything to change and at the same time to continue exactly as it was."[18]

What Don Américo does not adequately explain in his 1965 essay on the eighteenth century is his statement that "some eminent personalities illuminated those retarded and backward circumstances with reflected and not original ideas. Feijoo, Azara, Jovellanos, and other illustrious figures were planets and not stars with their own light."[19] I believe, however, that these men, as well as Goya and Moratín were indeed stars in their own right. The eighteenth is not a century of artists in general because, at least in literature, the genres were already structured in the way they would be understood in the future. Nobody surpasses Cervantes in the novel, Lope de Vega or Shakespeare in the theater, and even less the tradition of Petrarch and Dante in poetry. Furthermore, the persistent marginal character of the Peninsula only accentuated its special stamp and the peculiar aggressiveness of all Spanish art. We must never forget that *La Celestina, Lazarillo de Tormes,* and *Don Quixote* grew out of the tragic stump of Tibetanization and the Age of Conflict, and that these works are very different from those of countries without any concept of isolation. The most outstanding aspects of our art continued to be found in its marginal nature, as Galdós in his writings, Picasso in his paintings, and Buñuel in his films were later to demonstrate.

Castro returned to the subject of the eighteenth century in *La realidad histórica de España,* but without developing a theme which seems to merit additional commentary.[20] He draws an important parallel between the "similarities" of our past and "how our future was being sealed off hermetically, the seventeenth century vis-à-vis the sixteenth, the nineteenth vis-à-vis the eighteenth," to conclude that "the exclusivism and obstinacy of the *inner man* have failed," because "our history is like a being who carries in the open wound of its side the arrow of its perennial discontent."[21]

In conclusion, we can see how all the fundamental ideas of this eminent historiographer fit together rhythmically from 1921, considering what he wrote in 1924 and 1930, all the way up to 1965 and 1970. The themes he deals with seem valid as a whole, namely: the eighteenth century is no less well-known than other centuries, nor is it the most or the least Spanish, but it does coincide perfectly in its isolationist and marginal attitude with the past and future (Tibetanism and conflictivism); it is not Spain's century of unbounded promise because the entire past history of the Peninsula was always "possibilist" and not just Castro's thought as today's "liberal" intellectuals have believed. The social and vital structure of Spain never really fitted in with the rest of Europe. There were no real "Frenchified" men in the Peninsula, nor were there any clear imitations of the British. Nevertheless, we must understand why the Spaniards never went beyond the superficial imitation of fashions and integral spirit that the European atmosphere gave to every Enlightened movement in the world. Conversely, those who read Voltaire and Rousseau did not always recommend their works unreservedly. Spain continued to be a European country with everything of Europe, but without Europe, without being a European nation.[22]

NOTES

1. "Oh, how great is all beyond this world; oh, how little the things of this world!" *AVH* (1949), p. 19.

2. See Julio Ortega, "Preguntas a Juan Goytisolo," *Triunfo,* no. 592 (Madrid, 2 February 1972), pp. 35-37. In a magazine interview the novelist talks about the betrayal of his native language by Spain's social and political history. He takes as his starting point Blanco White's reaction when he decided to write in English on the grounds that his mother tongue was a repressed language and unsuitable for the exercise of intellectual liberty. The death of the language is becoming more imminent every day with the use of illusory clichés like "being the bearer of eternal values," "a destiny in the universal order of things," or the Spaniards' conviction that they can say with mere words that they are virtually

"the spiritual reserve of Europe" and actually believe that it is true. This semantic dream-world undoubtedly signifies the amputation of the living meaning of a language and inhibits its logical objective, esthetic, and communicative development.

3. *CCE,* p. 241.

4. *RHE* (1966), p. 21.

5. Ibid., p. 34.

6. José F. Montesinos, Prologue to *El Censor (1781-1787),* edited by Elsa García (Barcelona: Labor, 1972. Textos Hispánicos Modernos, no. 17), p. 17.

7. "La crítica filológica de los textos," in *LEL,* p. 172.

8. "Algunos aspectos del siglo XVIII," in *LEL,* pp. 291, 333; reprinted in *Españoles al márgen,* pp. 45-71.

9. The article "Jovellanos" is dated in Madrid, October 1930, but was published first in *La Nación,* (Buenos Aires, 2 November 1930), p. 16; it was published again in *El Sol* (Madrid, 21 July 1933, p. 4) with the meaningful subtitle "Asunto más que actual." Reprinted in *ENC,* II, pp. 203-210.

10. Ibid., p. 203.

11. Antonio Alcalá Galiano, *Literatura española siglo XIX. De Moratín a Rivas,* translation, introduction, and notes by Vicente Lloréns (Madrid: Alianza, 1969), p. 21.

12. "Algunos aspectos del siglo XVIII," *LEL,* p. 283.

13. Ibid., p. 283 ff.

14. Julio Rodríguez-Puértolas comments on the same term in "En los ochenta años de Américo Castro," *Revista Hispánica Moderna,* XXXII, no. 3-4 (1966), p. 234.

15. *EPE,* p. 109.

16. "Algunos aspectos del siglo XVIII," *LEL,* p. 296.

17. "Alguna claridad sobre el siglo XVII," in *RHE* (1966), pp. 21, 32. The work referred to is A. Domínguez Ortiz, *La sociedad española en el siglo XVIII* (Madrid: C.S.I.C., 1955), I, 185-186.

18. *RHE* (1966), pp. 21, 36, 33-34.

19. Ibid., p. 31.

20. *RHE* (1962), pp. 251, 306, 312, 313.

21. Ibid., p. 318.

22. A very modest little book by Raynal's translator, Pedro de Luxán, Duque de Almodóvar (pseud. of Francisco María de Silva), entitled *Década epistolar sobre el estado de las letras en Francia* (Madrid: Antonio de Sancha, 1781), explains this to us in an absolutely marvelous way.

11

AN APPRAISAL OF THE IMMEDIATE PAST AND PRESENT
Rubén Benítez

It seems only fair to recognize in Américo Castro a body of thought racked with national suffering. The anguish of the Civil War (1936–1939) takes precedence over any intellectual reasons that might otherwise have impelled him to seek, in the intimate structure of Spanish being, the explanation for so many similar crises. He himself is aware of this: "It was toward the end of 1943 when the BBC in London returned my record with my words on 'Castilla la gentil' which it deemed unwise to broadcast in Spain. It was then that I began to investigate what there might be above and below, behind and in front of that killing of Spaniards by other Spaniards which was so senseless in my opinion."[1] So it is that Castro's vision of the past is a result of his experience of the present. Only in this way can we better understand the dramatic meaning of his ideas about the nineteenth century. He cannot speak to us about the Carlist Wars without projecting onto them the specter of 1936 or talk about Romantic liberalism without referring to twentieth-century liberalism. In his review of Vicente Llorens' book, *Liberales y románticos,* published in *Cuadernos* in 1956, he comments on the emigration of 1823, but he addresses himself to today's exiles in order to make them see the causes of similar events in Spain's past. The fault is not in *the Other,* in that which is not oneself. He rejects the idea of two Spains: "The spurious notion of two Spains is common: the reactionary Spain and the progressive one which is always crushed in the end. Traditional and spontaneous customs are considered 'reactionary,' just as certain ideas not born in Spain but imported from outside are called 'progressive.'[2] Castro's single most significant contribution to nineteenth-century studies consists precisely in that estrangement from the dichotomy "tradition and progress"; instead, he analyzes the conflicts as an indicator of a vital structure underlying those differences.

The problem of two Spains concerned Castro many years before. In the early part of the 1930s when he wrote about Jovellanos, he perceived in him something more than the disillusion of a progressive whose explanations are not solutions. Jovellanos is the supreme example of a constant *Jovellanism* in Spanish history. This attitude wishes to reject what Spain really is in order to build another country in that void, with other assumptions, with a different sensibility. In short, it is "the desire to be what one is not, in a way one is not." That profound discrepancy constitutes an essential fact of Spanish history, and is not a result of whim or accident: "Spain's history is that of a being who carried the arrow of eternal discontent in the open wound of its side."[3] This is what the Spanish nobleman's "tranquility" (*sosiego*) and purity of blood came down to, as Don Américo tells us at this early date.

Thus, for Castro, Jovellanos unexpectedly becomes the symbol of "life as a denial of itself, or the process of simultaneous affirmation and rejection" (*vivir desviviéndose*). In *Hacia Cervantes* he discovers the specter of Jovellanos in Son Armadans: "the one who was burned without a bonfire." No Hamlet perceiving the real meaning of his apparitions, this ghost neither drags chains nor moans. "The great man of Asturias is too much of a gentleman to voice his complaints. Seen up close, his grimace is only one of discreet surprise and his words a simple 'Why?' repeated like a drop that has fallen every midnight since 1811."[4]

Castro read Jovellanos in surprising depth. It is more than a question of a literary study. Jovellanos' existential drama became Castro's own when the Civil War brought all the hopes of Spanish progressivism tumbling down. He remembers himself in his youth, embarked on the same course as Jovellanos and Feijoo, bent on changing the direction of Spanish life.[5] Just like Jovellanos faced with a similar crisis, Castro demanded more

profound responses. He did not find them either in the traditionalism that conceives of the national spirit as something
eternal and inalterable, or in a liberalism oriented outside the
country's borders and concerned only with material progress.
The answer lies in the development of a new spirit rooted in
the reality of Spain. Castro considered liberalism a dimension
of humanism, embodying political and religious tolerance, a
return to a way of being which had been profoundly altered
since the time of the Catholic Monarchs.

In this context it is easy to see the influence exercised on him
during his formative years by some nineteenth-century thinkers.
In his contacts with Giner de los Ríos and Cossío, Castro, "the
philologist of an institutional stripe,"[6] learned not only the
means to surpass in theory the bipolar nineteenth-century
ideology, but also the practical example of a broader and more
understanding liberalism. He tells us that Catholics and free-
thinkers, rich and poor, all gathered around Giner de los Ríos,
who, according to the unimpeachable testimony of Rafael
Altamira, "always attempted to lead his disciples toward the
most scrupulous respect and rigorous practice of the principle
of tolerance."[7] In Castro's review of "El movimiento científico
en la España actual" [1918], published in 1919 in *La Rassegna,*
he points up in Giner the candor and sensitivity that always set
him apart from exclusivism and violence.[8] In 1937 he considered
Giner to be the leading exponent of an ascetic humanism that
did not reject the world, but accepted the achievements of
modern thought and promoted them for the benefit of the
individual, with emphasis on spiritual values. Giner encouraged
the young people of his generation to investigate carefully any
new truth—he is responsible for the increase in Spain's scientific
knowledge at the end of the nineteenth century—but taught that
the interest in rigorous data ought not to exclude the passionate
search for an inner, personal truth with a humanitarian and
ethical base. Giner preached "the forgetting of precise and
measurable relationships, the threshold of rational nihilism"
in order to tend instead towards a "reduction of the world to
pure values that matter to me without my necessarily knowing
them or being able to define them."[9] From then on Castro

rejected positivism and Hegelian categories that reduce human richness to abstractions devoid of meaning. As a teacher, he continued Giner's stance. He accepted Giner's pedagogical ideas from his first polemic in 1935 in *El Debate* in defense of Giner's Institución Libre de Enseñanza. He always maintained an interest in pedagogy as applied to the teaching of language, literature, and history.

Giner and Cossío also examined Spain's past through historical and literary texts in order to uncover evidence of a national way of being and thus to understand better the reality of their own time. Giner tried to understand the reasons for the expansion of the Empire in the fifteenth century and its almost complete paralysis in development for four centuries after that. He reminds his students that in the fifteenth century Spain imposed on Europe a concept of man and life exemplified in the idea of being a man with honor (*hombría de bien*), which had a purely Hispanic origin. He sought an explanation for history in the Spaniards' psychological characteristics and in their cultural manifestations. Cossío revitalized literary texts and Spanish works of art in search of expressive traits that would reveal the Spanish way of being and feeling. Castro was later to use those teachings and to give them meaning when he postulated the "vital dwelling place" (*morada vital*) of the Spaniards as the structure that explains the unique nature of their actions and expressions.[10]

Joaquín Costa also examined Spanish history, but along somewhat different lines and with keener insights, and he put together a series of observations on national psychology that anticipated some of Castro's ideas.[11] Don Américo not only takes Costa as his point of departure, but he also explains him as an exponent of the Spanish experience of living (*vividura*). Costa's personalism can be better understood in the light of Castro's works and his concepts of the "vital dwelling place."[12] Costa, Giner, and other thinkers from the past are helpful to him in two ways: first, they directly point up certain concrete facts of the Hispanic mode of living; and second, they indirectly express an ongoing, continual process that coincides with old ways of being "having their origin in the tension created by the conflict between the inner, personal law of belief (one *was* a Christian, Moor, or Jew) and the outward aspect of that law."[13]

Castro received a treasure of important ideas from Costa, some of which he comments on in *La realidad histórica de España*. Costa intuited the Islamic nature of certain Spanish institutions and even believed that the tolerance for things Islamic, accepting the Muslims as an integral part of the nation, undoubtedly made up a part of the Cid's political program. That is the real Cid, the one in the chronicles, not yet corrupted by official ideology; the other one should remain locked in his tomb with several turns of the key. Castro transformed the symbol: it is the tomb of the Catholic Sovereigns, whose inscription is a motto of intolerance, and not the tomb of the Cid, which should be locked forever.

Like Costa, Castro conceives of rule by a strong man (*caudillismo*) as the result of a way of structuring Hispanic life; once the dependence on a king has disappeared, the towns group together under the leadership of strong men who are both desired and sought after, as though they were following a basic drive. This is his explanation, for example, for the breakup of the Empire in the wake of the Napoleonic invasion. Costa is the source for his appraisal of the political ideas of Fray Luis de León, a spiritual libertarian, and the relationship between those ideas and nineteenth-century anarchism. Castro asserts that Costa is not an anarchist, although he does approach that same essential libertarianism. Finally, Castro makes use of Costa when he studies the juridical institutions that point up the conflict between the individual and the coercion of law, organized authority, and official justice, as, for example, the court of water-rights and communal convents.[14] At times Castro's prose even betrays the pained and prophetic tone of Costa, "maddened by his love for Spain and his anguish over being a Spaniard."[15]

Castro was also influenced by traditionalist Spain, not as the result of such a personal and direct contact, but rather through assiduous reading. He read Donoso Cortés attentively—the reactionary Donoso, that is—in whom he discovered "luminous flashes." Donoso had already observed that Spanish Catholicism is filled with oriental influences. Furthermore, he considered that the Spaniards' disdain for civilization began during the wars against the infidel; the Christians, sunk in poverty and ignorance but proud of their true faith, denounced as false the refined culture of the Muslims.[16]

Menéndez y Pelayo best represents the thought of the other Spain: "The *other* Spain was not radically different from the other one opposed to it. Menéndez y Pelayo, a prominent layman and a reactionary, contributed to the developing tolerance in the small-town mentality that prevailed around 1890, as much as Giner de los Ríos and Pérez Galdós, only from opposite shores."[17] Castro continually accepts Menéndez y Pelayo's opinions. It could be no other way. He admires the critic "With his good intuition of artistic values."[18] It is more important that he raised the same questions as Menéndez y Pelayo about the historical enigma of Spain, the meaning of heterodoxy in Spanish thought, and the value of Spanish science. Of course they do not agree on the answers. Menéndez y Pelayo is blind when he runs up against areas of Spanish life that he does not wish to probe or that he cannot explain to himself in accordance with his orthodox ideas. For Castro, the problem of *La Celestina* is typical. Menéndez y Pelayo senses in the work a lack of solid moral principles and attributes it to the religious and moral skepticism of converted Jews such as the author of the work, Fernando de Rojas. But that fact becomes for him merely "an infraction of the social code." His critical perception thus stagnates in that area of ideological friction. About *Don Quixote,* Castro bemoans the fact that Menéndez y Pelayo payed tribute to Romantic criticism and judgments of Milá y Fontanals and Valera, but that he did not see in the "lay genius" the dimension of his solid foundation in humanistic studies.[19] A certain concept of history like the expression of a national spirit—unchanging and eternal—prevents Menéndez y Pelayo and others from understanding Spanish life in its most profound sense. A concept that, according to Castro, precedes Romanticism in Spain.

That concept does not change in more recent thinkers. Castro rejects, in similar fashion, Ganivet's concept of the Spaniard as eternally Senecan, as well as Unamuno's equation of "authentic tradition" (*casticismo*) with "Castile"; on the other hand, he accepts some of their partial judgments based on an intuition of Spanish life. Like Ganivet, Castro sought in history an essential structure of Spanish being that would explain individual character. The difference is that for Ganivet that structure has an ethnic and sanguine nature, whereas for Castro it is a matter of a vital cause arising out of a concrete historical event. Both do point out, however, the non-European nature of Spanish being—African, for Ganivet. For both Ganivet and Castro, mysticism and a certain ascetic reign on sensuality are causes of very strange ways of life in Spain. Spaniards are adept at practicing a sharing of wealth with an ideal goal in mind, but they are unable to associate will and capital in a practical sense. Ganivet noticed as a symptom the prosperity of religious communities in contrast to the failure of secular corporations. In Ganivet, Castro could confirm his idea that the Spaniard does not trust any type of state machinery; hence, the difference between the European community-oriented city and the kind of city typical of Spain.[20]

Castro shows Unamuno's fascinating influence very early in his career. As early as 1918 he distorted his resume of the state of Spanish science in order to include Unamuno in it:

> Unamuno is not actually a scientist; although his official position is that of professor of Greek at Salamanca, classical philology has not made him famous. But in spite of this, we must refer here to this admirable author—imbued with mysticism, personalism, and arbitrariness—as one of the greatest living figures of the Spanish spirit. His literary production and his personal behavior are, and have been, an element of renovation and stimulus for the country. His intense and vibrant campaigns on the side of greater modernity in public life are indirectly influencing the resurgence of Spanish culture that is evident today in the most diverse ways.[21]

Unamuno is the "great intuiter" of Hispanic reality. He abandons conventional history in order to probe the deepest layers of Spanishness and discover in them the "latent possibilities for life," that Castro considers potential history (*historiable*). In *En torno al casticismo* Unamuno foresaw Spain's problem: "The Castilian caste, composed of conquerors ill-disposed toward work, never got along well enough to question and analyze perceptible reality or work in empirical science. They only drove themselves to conquer (with hardships, yes, but not with work) a final truth pregnant with all the lesser ones. It was not by reasoning that they proceeded from one step to the next."[22] Unamuno knew how to read literary texts with an eye out for vital causes. Nevertheless, Castro criticizes certain aspects of his interpretation of *Don Quixote* because Unamuno considered the literary character as though it created itself spontaneously, without seeing in it the projection of its author's life and ideology. In his opinion Unamuno saw what he wanted to see in Don Quixote and he preferred him to be a seeker of eternal truths.[23]

But at the same time Unamuno is for Castro a great disorienter. His idea of spiritual history underlying the conventional body of historical data (*intrahistoria*) turns into a nebula appropriate for literary creations, but one that adds nothing to the science of history because he tends to seek out in it the permanent human quality of a social group instead of the unique characteristics born out of specific circumstances. In the foreword to *De la España que aún no conocía,* Castro blames Unamuno along with Ganivet and Rubén Darío for the confusion among the Spanish youth who were seeking past glories and even losing their lives in defense of a false tradition.[24]

Castro also read Azorín enthusiastically and considered him to be the creator of a new sensibility. On two different occasions he asserts that Azorín deserves credit for recognizing the delights to be found in the classics. "His vision of our literary past, both loving and critical, has had more than a little influence on the spiritual formation of our generation."[25]

Each one of the aforementioned contacts warrants a separate, more careful study in greater detail. But they are adequate to define the background of dissatisfaction created by teachers and writers of the second half of the nineteenth century in the thought and sensibility of Américo Castro. Against that background later readings of Dilthey and Ortega, for example, were to have their effect. In fact, they gave him the tools with which to capture the reality of life without excluding real historical events or appealing to abstract formulas. But the basic impulse came from farther away. Twenty years before the new century began the keenest observers of Spanish life were already asking themselves what exactly Spain was, how its vital uniqueness could be explained, and what profound messages its literature and art were transmitting. Jovellanos' attitude of questioning, wonder, and amazement had been becoming clearer as the century progressed. Castro would attempt to give a coherent and lucid answer from the vantage point of his own living experience.

We are now ready to discuss Castro's views on nineteenth-century history and ideology. His opinions after 1948 are particularly important since this is when he defined his concept of the *vital dwelling place*. After that date he reexamines Spanish history in search of any evidence that will confirm his ideas. He observes an anomaly in the treatment of nineteenth-century history: some Spaniards, and among them Giner de los Ríos, consider the entire century a parenthesis or accuse it of being invalid, in the same way they treated the seventeenth and eighteenth centuries. Thus, they escape the very question that Castro was concerned with clarifying: what were the root causes of the conviction held by so many that the nineteenth century in Spain and Spanish America was a human community devoid of science and in need of outside help even in the most insignificant matters? In *La realidad histórica de España* he points out the inferiority of the Hispanic world compared to Europe and the United States in technical ability, industry, energy, coinciding with the lack of resignation in the face of the inescapable truth that "it was a century of backwardness, one that lost much blood in the never-ending battle between its refusal to change and its insistence on not resigning itself not to change."[26]

From the sixteenth century on it was felt that cultural and economic activities stained the status of the Old Christian.[27] The doctrine of purity of blood persists to a certain extent into the nineteenth century. In this regard Castro recalls that even Bolívar boasted of his pure blood and that authors like Antonio Gil y Zárate spoke of a similar concern.[28] In short, "that doctrine was what there was of Jewishness at the core of Spanish society from 1500 until well into the nineteenth century, and in isolated Mallorca until recently (sometimes one thinks it is so even today)."[29]

Although the caste system does not appear to be as much of a force in the nineteenth century as it was in the sixteenth, its effects still show up in an exclusive, intolerant faith and in a disdain for material wealth and technology. Castro finds a reference to castes in Galdós' novel *Gloria,* although he admits that it is more of a novelistic device than a reflection of an historical or sociological reality. Nevertheless, "the incompatibility of castes is the wall of impassible reality against which Gloria and Daniel are shattered."[30]

As a result, the Spaniard still tends to direct his will inward toward the center of his being rather than toward the periphery.[31] Attention is focused on the intrinsic worth of a person and not on what he has acquired. Thus, a vacuum results which must be filled with technical expertise supplied by foreigners, or, as Unamuno proposes, "let the rest of the world do the inventing." Castro believes that even in literary expression Spaniards cannot resist the temptation to make the supremacy of the individual the highest value, as in versions of the Don Juan myth where Don Juan dares to be the antagonist of God Himself.[32] In *Cervantes y los casticismos españoles* Don Américo describes the nineteenth-century Spaniard as uncertain about material prosperity and exempt, therefore, from the placid happiness of the European. He is affirmative, however, about his ability to create expressive forms in relation to self-awareness and the problematic aspects of life.[33]

According to Castro, those who cannot comprehend the background of the Spaniards' way of organizing their vital structure are mistaken in their judgments about the nineteenth century. On several occasions he opposes both economic and sociological criticism that takes into account only concrete facts or external circumstances. In *Cervantes y los casticismos* he discusses Vicens Vives' ideas on Spanish life between 1815 and 1868, which Vicens sees as affected by elements outside of Spain only because of political circumstances, the failure of the old regime, and the culmination of the liberal ideology, thanks to a favorable moment for economic expansion, the advent of the Industrial Revolution, and the spiritual movement of Romanticism. For Castro these are mere fictions born of Spain's desire to see itself develop in parallel fashion with the rest of Europe. But Spain is different from the other European countries.[34]

An analysis of specific facts will help us to prove Spain's

uniqueness. Don Américo pays particular attention to the breakup of the Empire at the beginning of the century and to the programs associated with the liberals. The new ideologies succeeded only insofar as they authentically reflected the Spanish way of being. The French Revolution and the Napoleonic invasion, however, modified the appearance of Spanish society; without them, "it is quite probable that the Spanish nation would have kept its ecclesiastical, nobiliary, and rural outlook for some time."[35] But that change did not really alter the fundamental attitude because the war against the French also took on certain characteristics of a holy war and was made in defense of the king's sovereignty. Common faith in the doctrine and in purity of blood maintained cohesion in the realm during the invasion. The notion of regional loyalty had little value. Once this fleeting cohesion was lost, the Empire came tumbling down.[36] The division of the New World into fourteen republics was a result of the loss of the shared faith and the almost religious allegiance to the figure of the king. There is no other explanation for this fragmentation, which cannot be rationalized by references to geographical characteristics. The Incas maintained a homogeneous empire within the same geographical boundaries.[37]

He deals with what happened in the Iberian Peninsula in similar terms. When the prestige of the monarchy wanes, the various regions dissociate themselves from the central power. From then on the tendencies toward regionalism only become more marked. During the twentieth century many people in the Basque provinces, Catalonia, and Galicia have preferred to identify themselves first as Basques, Catalans, and Galicians rather than as Spaniards.[38] In *La enseñanza del español en España,* Castro declares himself a proponent of a republic that would look with favor on the rights of the various regions to keep their own language and assert their local character. He believes that the liberals ought to accept the real facts and allow Catalonia, for example, to establish an independent state if a majority of its people vote to do so.[39]

Castro wonders why the Spaniards did not seem to be aware of the breaking up of the Empire until 1898. Before 1824 he finds only the faintest echoes of it. He does not believe that this fact should be attributed to Ferdinand VII's tyranny, but rather to the indifference with which Spaniards tend to observe problems not intimately tied to their personal destiny.[40]

Given that fundamental reality, the outbreak of civil wars can begin to be understood. Just as in 1936, according to Castro, the Carlist War was fought by the old caste religiosity on one side and a new religiosity that combined the "I'll do this because I damn well want to" syndrome with a universal utopian felicity, on the other.[41] The Carlist Wars further point up the difficulty Spaniards have in going from the plane of what one is to the plane of what one does.[42] These wars are provoked by a private or personal dimension rather than by external facts, and for this reason, they are difficult to explain. Castro is concerned to observe that the Spaniards do not know the causes of their wars, as if they were the victims of a nuclear catastrophe without being aware of the nature of those weapons or the spirit that set off the conflict.[43]

Spain's disdain for material wealth and technical know-how prevented her from forming a solid bourgeois class in the nineteenth century.[44] The ideal of progress is thus transformed into a deceptive fantasy. The liberals, especially those who emigrated in 1823, lived their ideas as if they had no relation to themselves. At the time of the French invasion they experienced a contradictory impulse; they were both adversaries and debtors of the new Vandals. Later the Spaniards in London failed to take advantage of their leisure to learn new modes of living, or even the language. To return, therefore, did not mean a change in their work habits or ideas about coexistence. The liberal of that period, like today's liberal, blames all his ills on the other fellow, on forces outside himself, without realizing that he himself is a part of those same flaws that he recognizes in others.[45]

Castro's criticism of nineteenth-century liberalism creates an obvious area of conflict. Claudio Sánchez-Albornoz, in a distinctly antagonistic article (published in the airmail edition of *ABC*, 28 February 1974) discusses various points of view about the nineteenth century from the liberal vantage point, and he accuses Castro of having imputed "a foolish lack of ideas to the nineteenth-century liberals." Don Américo does not go so far. He does observe, though, that the nineteenth century lacks an intelligent liberalism of national origin. The mutations associated with the early part of the century seem superficial or only slightly effective to him.[46] The constitutional system that some individuals, like Martínez de la Rosa, tried to attribute to medieval Spain was never very influential either in the Peninsula or in the Spanish American colonies. Parliamentarianism did not have any impact either. The problem is not a *lack of ideas,* but rather an incompatibility between those ideas and the national reality.

Castro emphasizes two factors in Romantic liberalism that confirm his opinions. In 1835 there was a slaughter of monks, a new display of religious intolerance, although under a contradictory banner. Mendizábal's confiscation of church property only managed to produce negative results or no results at all. The decree was nil as a benefit to the public treasury and negative because of the destruction of cultural centers where Spain's artistic treasures were found.[47] These measures meant to Castro that the liberals believed in the need to eliminate the other Spain, without taking into account that in other countries like France, revolutions and reactions to them, religious tolerance, religious and even antireligious rationalism, philosophies, and several types of science were able to coexist: "The variety of positions and contents in human communities does not necessarily create the need to break up the homogeneity of a people's vital structure when these people appear rooted in their history as a selfhood (*ipseidad*), as an entity that completely identifies conscience with values."[48] The type of civilization defended by liberalism does not succeed in convincing Spaniards that objective facts are more important than people. Castro bases his theory on comments made by Larra in his obituary for the Count of Campo Alange. The issue remains unsolved, precisely as Larra had left it.[49]

Don Américo draws on accounts written by the most intelligent observers of the nineteenth century who, like Sarmiento, for example, see in Spain the absence of a legitimate civilization. Thinkers explain it in a variety of ways. Referring to the freedom of religion as scandalous, Balmes exalts the strength of Spanish Catholicism that refuses to admit such a "seed of death" in its vigorous breast. Donoso Cortés intuits the Eastern European nature of that Spanish trait. All these men coincide in lamenting the downfall of Spain's former splendor.[50]

The kind of liberalism associated with the second half of the nineteenth century attempts to find a better interpretation of Spanish reality and, therefore, proposes better solutions, beginning with the introduction of Krausism. Castro does not consider Krausism a foreign ideology, or rather, he deems whatever foreign elements may be present as unimportant. There must be a deeper explanation for its success in Spain, over and above other doctrines such as the philosophical systems of Kant and Hegel that became well-known in the nineteenth century but never exerted the fascination of Krausism on Spanish intellectuals. According to Castro, Krause's philosophy has had such a lasting influence because it exalts the value of the individual over state institutions, the family over the group, and individual collective bodies over the nation. In Krause, Castro asserts, the structuring movement of reality moves upward, like an ethical impulse and a hope. Krause's metaphysics are less important than their ethical, pedagogical, and legal derivations. This philosophical movement deserves the credit for revitalizing Spanish culture at the end of the century.

Krausism was instrumental in activating individual awareness and, in that sense, it combined perfectly with the traditional concept of life. It affected vital areas; it was an outlook on life, a lay form of piety, and, at the same time, a school of conduct.[51]

The importance of Spanish anarchism in Castro's thought can be explained in a similar way, if it is seen in opposition to Marxism and Communism; anarchism is more respectful of individual conscience and identity than the other ideologies. It is also a foreign ideology, but it is based on a vital structure that has its roots in the sixteenth and seventeenth centuries. The doctrine was one that could indeed be molded onto a Spanish way of being and experiencing: "The anarchist idea caught on particularly in the southern and eastern regions where a tradition of fantasy is deeply engrained—the promise of freedom proffered by people with unimpeachable reputations, found an echo in those thirsting after a new justice, a communal, fragmented, and cooperative regimen." The anarcho-syndicalist organization is patterned on the model of religious communities of a cooperative stamp, like the ones described by Joaquín Costa.[52]

The rest is recent history. Castro considers the Generation of 1898 as the culmination of the process begun at the turn of the century. The breakup of the Empire was intensely experienced at that time. Spain emerged from the Spanish-American War "dry and wasted; it remained alone, although without exterior bonds of any kind."[53] Once again Spain came into intimate contact with its painful reality. In the idea of Europeanizing Spain Castro observes the whole drama of Spanish life; on one hand, it is another attempt to escape current realities; on the other, it is the straightforward admission that Spain is not Europe. With that verification and with a feeling of ruin and desolation, the trajectory of the century comes to a close. As a young Spanish student in 1898, Castro bears witness to the feeling of frustration and disillusion he experienced when confronted with the nation's history:

> I remember the effect that the inadequate vision of the past had on those of us who were studying the history of our country in 1898. They made us contemplate an incredibly vast horizon, and all that worldly vastness had been ours, so they said. Then, suddenly, we began to see that this whole dominion was empty; it began to disintegrate, just as the ruined grandee began by losing his palaces and ended up by being confined to the loneliness and austerity of his family manor. After a rapid flight to the heights, we descended and finally were pushed over the edge into the depths of the valley—all without subtlety or moderation—leaving in our impressionable souls the germ of everlasting anguish, that even the most aware Spaniards would abandon only with the greatest difficulty.[54]

Castro asserts at least once that if the nineteenth century did not create new ways of living, it at least succeeded in formulating original modes of literary expression. I should now like to analyze his opinions on Romantic literature and the nineteenth-century novel.

In 1920 he published an article in the *Revista de Filología* entitled "Acerca de *El diablo mundo* de Espronceda" in which

he studied the influence of Voltaire's *L'Ingénu* on that work.
At that time there were only a few general works on Romanticism: the studies by Father Blanco García, Boris de Tannenberg,
Enrique Piñeyro, and Valera's *Florilegio*. Menéndez Pidal had
already done sensitive studies on some Romantic works in *La
epopeya castellana a través de la literatura española*. Castro
makes use of that bibliography and adds another one on French
translations of Rivas, Espronceda, and Zorrilla, in a slim volume
from his early years, now unjustly forgotten, *Les grands romantiques espagnoles* published in Paris in 1922 in the collection
Cent Chefs-d'oeuvre Étrangers directed by Professor M.
Wilmote.

I shall discuss this book later, but here I shall simply point
out Castro's broad knowledge of Romantic philosophy and
criticism which dates from this period. He reexamines that
philosophy and criticism in relation to his study of the *Quixote*.
He is familiar with the texts of German philosophers mostly
through J.-J.A. Bertrand's work, *Cervantès et le romantisme
allemand,* 1914, translated into Spanish as *Cervantes en el país
de Fausto* in 1950. Even in *El pensamiento de Cervantes* Castro
emphasizes the fact that "the work of the German Romantics
is admirable, and a good many of the viewpoints projected onto
Don Quixote have their origin in the sporadic, but enthusiastic
effort undertaken by those eminent men."[55] Some years later,
in his book *Cervantès* published in Paris in 1931, he insists that
it is thanks to the Romantic movement that *Don Quixote* begins
to be seen in its entirety as a profound and melancholy, entertaining and novelesque work.[56] Romanticism is credited with
the creation of a critical literature interested in Spanish culture:
"Scholars from abroad threw themselves wholeheartedly into the
studies of Spain's glorious ruins spurred on by the ideology of
a few German philosophers eager to illuminate the mystery of
national spirit."[57] He cites the histories of Ticknor and Prescott
as proof of foreign interest in Spain. He also acknowledges the
efforts of Spanish critics such as Clemencín, Fernández de
Navarrete, Valera, Milá y Fontanals, and Menéndez y Pelayo
in connection with Cervantes.

Castro accepts the literary concept of Romanticism, but he
attempts to explain it within the framework of Spanish identity.

Literature, as he says in *De la edad conflictiva*, 1963, when discussing the Baroque period, is not determined by hackneyed external "Hegelian" circumstances but rather, by real-life situations expressed in a direct or indirect way.[58] The writer does not respond to external norms but to concrete situations, to political and social circumstances that interest the human group he represents.[59] This is why Castro never uses any of the terms coined by European criticism such as *Baroque, Neoclassicism, positivism, realism,* or *naturalism,* terms that do not always correspond to the Spanish experience. But *Romanticism* is different because, in this case, it is a question of accepting an international philosophy also adopted by Spain, as well as a whole new view of the world.[60]

For Castro, Romanticism begins with the rise of a new sensibility in the eighteenth century, and in this sense, he anticipates very recent studies on that new sensibility (for example, Sebold). Jean Jacques Rousseau, one of the European figures who most attracts him, created that sensibility when he turned the insights of his emotional metaphysics to the contemplation of the Alps. From that time on, European thinkers begin to doubt the strict rules of reason and feel misgivings about their culture. Rousseau, "the man of genius," taught men to reject earthly limits for the sake of higher aspirations toward infinity: "Snow-capped peaks and sealed-off forests served as a great symbol of that desire for immense boundlessness."[61] From then on, the Romantic landscape is surrounded by a frame of pantheistic spirituality. In this regard Castro cites a line from Victor Hugo: *C'est Dieu qui remplit tout, le monde c'est son temple.* Following the line of Castro's thought after 1948, we might wonder if Romanticism in Spain coincides in its yearning for the infinite with the unique way of facing life that began in the sixteenth century. But he could not confirm this before that date. Spanish Romanticism, always interpreted from the outside in, from a foreign point of view, could now be seen from a much broader and hitherto unsuspected vantage point.

In *Les grands romantiques espagnols,* Castro considers Spanish Romanticism to be an extension of the new sensibility that first appeared in Neoclassicism with Jovellanos, Meléndez Valdés, Cadalso, and Cienfuegos. He is the first person to confer any importance on the versious of the Spanish classical theater of the Golden Age adapted for modern taste by Cándido M. Trigueros, versions to which only the most recent criticism has turned its attention.[62] What we call Romanticism is thus fixed as a change in individual consciousness; it is a new metaphysic, a concept of the universe whose center is the self. There is also a change in the collective consciousness. Castro seems to discover a weakening in religious faith exemplified by the expulsion of the monastic orders and the expropriation of ecclesiastical property. In 1922 he still believed in the advances of liberalism and referred to those events approvingly.

Romantic traits are evident in poetry as early as the first thirty years of the nineteenth century. Castro disagrees with Valera who believed that this type of poetry was in no way different from the Neoclassical; the confusion arises because of the continuation of a preference for narrative poetry and the use of certain techniques reminiscent of Neoclassicism, but the base is Romantic. This is his justification for including Espronceda's "El Pelayo" in the anthology portion of the book. Castro's judgments on the Romantic movement are decidedly enthusiastic. It represents for him an essential period in Spanish literary history; it is necessary to go back two centuries or ahead to the "splendid" art of Rubén Darío and his successors in order to surpass the qualities inherent in Romantic poetry.

His brief reference to the relationship between Romanticism and Golden Age literature is full of valuable suggestions. But literature prior to the eighteenth century is not sufficient to explain the Romantic impulse. Besides, the works of 1835 are fundamentally different from the seventeenth-century ones: "À mon avis, ce qui sépare profondément ces deux époques, ce sont les différences qu'on observe dans leur conscience collective et individuelle."[63] In spite of these differences, Castro believes that earlier Spanish literature offered the Romantics, especially the theoreticians of the movement, a picture of poetic and emotional motifs that could help to shape a Romantic outlook on life and art. The Romantics did not, however, take advantage of the variety of emotion generated by *La Celestina,* in scenes comparable, for example, to *Tristan and Isolde* and *Romeo and Juliet.* Castro does not accept the notion that collections of old

Spanish ballads—as influential as they were in Romanticism—represented merely a return to the past in Spain. He supports this theory when he deals with Calderón's influence on the Romantics, an influence that lasted until Schopenhauer's time: "Pour Calderón, le monde n'est ni la 'volunté ni la 'représentation' de ses héros. Il y a au contraire des régles très sévères qui répriment les élans en aparence les plus personnels et les plus indomptables."[64] In the Duke of Rivas' play *Don Alvaro,* he makes a fundamental distinction between Romantic drama and Calderón's type of theater: "jamais un héros d'alors [Golden Age drama] n'aurait pu se précipiter du haut d'un rocher en maudisant le genre humain, après avoir vécu une vie qui était la négation de la Providence."[65]

In the Duke of Rivas' theater Castro discovers the inspiration of the great classics of the seventeenth century, but mixed with his own pessimistic view so characteristic of the sensibility of his time. More than anything else, Castro praises the quality of his language; he is the Romantic with the greatest linguistic sensitivity. His style is both precise and laconic, a rarity in that period. When Castro studies the traditional sources for "El moro expósito," he criticizes the lack of historical accuracy as well as the frequent anachronisms in the poem.

Don Américo's reading of Espronceda shows more enthusiasm. He understood this author better than other members of his generation. Even in his 1920 article he has high praise for Espronceda, in whom he saw the Romantic sensibility existing alongside a background of readings in eighteenth-century criticism.[66] In *Les grands romantiques espagnols* he classifies Espronceda as a poet only superficially linked to the national tradition, but he also rejects any close relationship between Espronceda and Byron, as critics like Pujals have pointed out. He viewed Leopardi in the same light, even though his influence seems less doubtful to Castro. In short, Espronceda is a highly original literary personality, especially in *El diablo mundo*: "L'éclat de la langue et des métaphores, l'intense émotion de plusieurs strophes du 'Chant à Thérèse,' cette charmante Salada qu'on dirait descendue d'une toile de Goya, quelques traits d'un fin humorisme, Adam lui-même dont le caractère invraisemblable finit par nous sembler naturel, voilà des raisons plus que suffisantes, pour aimer ce gran essai d'ardente poésie."[67] His study of the "Canto a Teresa," which makes us live "a vast, intimate tragedy," is equally perceptive. The encounter between Adam and Salada partakes of an erotic intensity rare in Spanish literature except for *La Celestina,* according to Castro. In fact, Américo Castro should be considered one of the first scholars of Espronceda in modern criticism, if not because of the volume of his studies, then for the originality, accuracy, and fairness of his judgments.

In contrast, he adds little to our understanding of Zorrilla; he judges him to be a superficial poet, a virtuoso in the handling of the mechanics of verse. His comments on Father Arolas, whom he includes in the appendix, are more original. All of his poetry is the vague expression of a fantasy elevated to the heights of morbid exaltation; but the delicacy, humility, and gentleness of his complaints lend a certain undefined charm to his poetry. In a footnote, he even manages to include a brief but accurate opinion about Larra.

The texts translated into French by Castro himself attempt to convey the musical and rhythmic charm of the original poems. He succeeds often, particularly in his translations of Espronceda.

Castro obviously read the Romantic authors with uncommon enthusiasm; on the other hand, he looks down on Núñez de Arce and his followers who he thinks will ultimately be nothing more than a literary curiosity.[68] There are no references in Castro's work to Bécquer, although he did contribute to at least one important thesis on this author, Edmund L. King's *From Painter to Poet.* Castro's poetic preferences waver between the Romantics and the Modernists. On several occasions in his later work, he refers to Rubén Darío who, in his opinion, was responsible for the loss of solemnity and affectation in Spanish poetry. Darío eliminated the naive, provincial, domestic, intellectual, and prosaic tone from the poetry written at the end of the century: "In order to do this, it was necessary to invent a new poetic language, a new style in which literary currents from other countries could fit, and the music of the rhymes and the harmony of each line could play upon the senses in a new way."[69] Elsewhere he criticizes the ideology expressed in "Canto a Roosevelt" in which the poet invites the Hispanic orb to fight in the name of God, as a kind of hint of the Fascism to come.[70] He scarcely refers to the more modern poets such as Antonio Machado, but he does deal at some length with Juan Ramón Jiménez, whose poetic purity he associates with the ethical ideas of the Institución Libre de Enseñanza.[71] He also praises the poetry of Jorge Guillén in the introduction to his *Cántico*.[72]

Castro also makes a valuable contribution to the study of the nineteenth-century European novel. His works on the structure of the Cervantine novel shed some light on the characteristics of the modern novel. He shares with Lukács his estimation of Cervantes' art as the creation of an internal form and a dynamic and meaningful structure. Like Lukács, he sees in *Don Quixote* a problematic hero, a character in a state of liberty. The novel duplicates the structure of life; the hero projects himself onto the world in the completion of his vital plan (*proyecto vital*), and he modifies it as he modifies himself, in a dialectical relation. As the creator of the modern novel, Cervantes profits from the previous tradition and projects and broadens the new form: "He invented for himself a literary form of the widest scope which served as the basis of the great nineteenth-century novels."[73] For Castro, Cervantes' influence on the European novel occurs when Romantic ideology loses its vigor and other ways of narrating fact and fiction have been exhausted; he does not detect Cervantes' influence on Sir Walter Scott.

The reasons for the success of the Cervantine formulary are already apparent in Romantic philosophy. From Fichte on, the self is conceived in the practical sphere as needing an opposing force in order to continue existing: "Along these lines, the vital arena in which every man shapes himself will continue to acquire a significance that becomes ever more primary." For that reason the Cervantine character makes such an impression, split as he is, between *who he is* and the problem of *what he wants to be*:

Thus, the incalculable efficacy of *Don Quixote* when, during the Romantic period, the time was ripe for the emergence of the modern novel in which the central characters are anything and everything they want to be and furthermore, are a poetic projection of themselves (Balzac's kindly "père Goriot" is a pasta manufacturer and a reincarnation of the imprudent and desperate King Lear; Julien Sorel, in Stendhal's *Le rouge et le noir*, is both the boy who saws wood and a projection of the hero of the *Mémorial de Sainte Hélène*).[74]

He studies the traces of Cervantes in European novelists. In *Cervantes y los casticismos,* he refers to Richardson who, along with Rousseau, made emotions an acceptable part of literary creation. The English novel, which broke with the traditional concept of man as something abstract and rational, was what was needed in order to take full advantage of Cervantes' discovery: the representation of life as an open and dynamic process.[75] In Goethe, and even in his *Wilhelm Meister* where Castro finds some influence of *Don Quixote,* life is still conceived as something outside the character: "the puppets do not 'puppetize' Wilhelm Meister in the way that Don Quixote was 'bookified' by the books he read and which held his mind in thrall."[76] In contrast, in Stendhal's work, *Mémorial de Sainte Hélène* affects Julien Sorel in the same way that the novels of chivalry affected Don Quixote: "But the Cervantine aspect of this splendid novel is, in the final analysis, the continuous dialectical link between the level of imagined experience and that of immediate experience; it is the constant transition, in Julien Sorel as well as in the secondary characters, from 'rêverie' to the rude awakening to the real world."[77] The same thing happens in works by Balzac, Dickens, Galdós, Flaubert, and Dostoyevsky and even in *Don Segundo Sombra* by Ricardo Güiraldes:

> If the reader thinks back, he will undoubtedly observe that this type of phenomenon has no equivalent in post-Renaissance literature—that is, that the internal structure of a seventeenth-century work could affect nineteenth-century literature. I am talking about profound and stimulating presences and not about 'imitations.' The famous example of Dostoyevsky is an obvious one, because even though he did not 'imitate' Don Quixote, I think it is justifiable to claim that without Cervantes his artistic creation would have been very different.[78]

Regretfully, Américo Castro never analyzed the relationship between the Cervantine novel and Galdós' work, a study which cries out to be done. He always cites Galdós with praise and, for Castro, Galdós is a brilliant seer or prophet who succeeded in identifying with the spirit of his time and who saw what there was of real life underlying conventional chronicles.[79] In 1922 he already recommended the *Episodios nacionales* as required texts in high school.[80] Later he rates as "stupendous" novels like *Nazarín, Gloria,* and *Fortunata y Jacinta.*

He does, however, indicate some important points of contact between the art of Cervantes and Galdós. Before Galdós, he says, the Spaniards "did not know what to do literarily with that new art of making novels in 1600."[81] Galdós returns to Cervantes' work once the European novel had been taken over by the Cervantine pattern. In *Gloria* he notices this connection "in the character's inability to follow a pattern of life which is only apparently possible on the surface and only gives the illusion of being one's own."[82] Generally speaking, Castro says that Galdós did not allow himself to sink down into the dull, grayish life of his century; like Cervantes, he also saw a light beyond the present, and like Cervantes, he too created "solid, yet sparkling figures, issuing from formless, popular sources."[83]

There are not many references, but, nevertheless, Galdós synthesizes the network of problems relating to life and art that gives Spain her particular physiognomy. The great symbol of heterodoxy caught a glimpse of the structure of the Spanish mode of living and intuited that the Cervantine novel was the form in which the inner workings of that life were most accurately reproduced. Thus he invented a world of characters who expressed the historico-national contradiction, and therefore, oscillate between what they are and what they want to be, trapped between harsh reality and exalted fantasy. Castro does not say it outright, but his almost unconscious association between Galdós and Giner de los Ríos allows us to intuit that he also accepts Galdós' "vital project" for Spain. Galdós and Giner agree in their concept of a future life based on an ethical and tolerant humanitarianism in which pure human values unify men over and above occasional differences.

In spite of the fact that Castro only discusses Galdós briefly, nobody has done more than he has to illuminate this author's work. It is not surprising, therefore, that some of his most eminent disciples are currently studying Galdós' novels.

According to Don Américo, the Cervantization process in the modern novel reaches its peak in Unamuno. By this time the

epic tradition had already been broken. In realism and naturalism, this tradition had made it impossible to avoid the description of costume and the details of one's surroundings as a
way of situating human lives. In Unamuno, life conforms to its
real structure without any external distractions. *Niebla*—whose
similarities to Pirandello's theater Castro is one of the first to
point out—is an "authentically Cervantine novel." The character, now endowed with complete autonomy, rises up before
his own creator.[84]

So life surpasses literature. Castro's works always offer us a
lesson filled with intense vitalism. It is our task to define more
clearly the *vital dwelling place* of nineteenth-century man. And
especially to reap the benefits from the lesson that Castro left
as a part of his comments on the nineteenth century as a cordial
legacy to the youth of Spain and Spanish America: man is a
much more valuable being than any ideology.

Even though the *vital dwelling place* may seem to some critics
to be as abstract and inalterable a notion as the "national
spirit" of the traditionalists, it does constitute, in Castro's view,
a dynamic structure loaded with potential for the future, in the
same way as Dilthey's *Seelenleben* and Ortega's *vital reason*.
In the nineteenth century, more than at any other time in the
history of Spain, Castro detects the cruel battle between the past
that still remains and the future contained in the contradictions
of the present. And with the painful confirmation, besides, that
the future is already the unhappy present of today.

NOTES

1. "Advertencia previa" to *ENC*, I, 68. This foreword was anticipated in
Estudios Filológicos, no. 5 (Valdivia, Chile, 1969), pp. 7–58. The article itself
was reprinted in *ENC*, I, 101–117.

2. "Emigrados," *Cuadernos*, no. 17 (Paris, March-April 1956), pp. 3–12;
reprinted in *ENC*, I, 181–201. The quote appears on p. 182. Castro repeats
some of these ideas in *CCE*, pp. 210–214.

3. "Jovellanos," in *ENC*, II, 204. First published in *El Sol* (21 July 1933).

4. *HCer* (1957), p. 389.

5. "Emigrados," *ENC,* I, 191; see also "Advertencia previa," p. 76 ff.

6. He is given this name in *El Debate*; see "Una historia de la educación," in *ENC,* II, 69.

7. Rafael Altamira, *Giner de los Ríos, educador* (Valencia: Prometeo, 1915), p. 69.

8. *ENC,* II, 97–98.

9. Ibid., pp. 217–218; first published in *La Nación* (Buenos Aires, June 1937). See also in the same volume "Una historia de la educación" and "Otro ensayo de terapéutica nacional" and *RHE* (1962), pp. 297 ff. His view of Giner is completed in the biographical sketches of Manuel B. Cossío and Alberto Jiménez, in *ENC,* II, pp. 221–272; also reprinted in *Españoles al margen.*

10. See Rafael Pérez de la Dehesa, *El pensamiento de Costa y su influencia en el 98* (Madrid: Sociedad de Estudios y Publicaciones, 1966), p. 125.

11. See Guillermo Araya Goubet, "Idea de la historia de Américo Castro," *Estudios Filológicos,* no. 7 (1971), pp. 7–35.

12. Pérez de la Dehesa, op. cit., p. 158.

13. *RHE* (1962), p. 257.

14. About Costa, see the numerous references in *RHE* (1962), pp. 279 ff.; *CCE,* p. 239; "Prólogo" to *Don Quijote,* 2d ed. (Mexico: Porrúa, 1962), pp. xl–xli.

15. "Prólogo," p. xli.

16. *RHE* (1966), 21–23.

17. "Emigrados," p. 199.

18. "El problema histórico de *La Celestina,* in *STE,* p. 196.

19. *PCer* (1972), pp. 16–17.

20. About Ganivet see *RHE* (1962), pp. 261–262; also see "Entrando en Portugal" in *ENC,* III, 58; *PCer* (1972), p. 17, and the "Advertencia previa," p. 64, 70.

21. "El movimiento científico de la España actual," in *ENC,* II, 114.

22. *HCer* (1957), p. 309.

23. "Advertencia previa," pp. 62–66. Other references to Unamuno in *AVH* (1949), p. 19; *STE,* p. 35, n. 1; *OSE,* p. 12; *RHE* (1962), pp. 256–262, et passim. On Unamuno as a reader of Don Quixote, see *HCer* (1957), pp. 151–152, 362–363, et passim.

24. *ENC,* I, 62–66.

25. "El movimiento científico," pp. 114–115. He refers to Azorín in a similar way in "Tricentenario de Lope de Vega," in *ENC,* III, 162.

26. *RHE* (1966), p. 39. See also "Las dos Américas," in *ENC,* III, 81.

27. Ibid., p. 32; see also *CCE,* p. 196.

28. *RHE* (1962), pp. 295, 323 n. 76.

29. *CCE,* p. 351.

30. *RHE* (1966), p. 5-6.

31. "If castes no longer exist, if we are simply Spaniards," Castro wonders when he is talking about Jovellanos, "then why do we not bend our efforts constructively toward the periphery of ourselves and not towards our irreducible centers?" *RHE* (1962), p. 262.

32. *RHE* (1962), p. 310.

33. *CCE,* pp. 210-211.

34. Ibid., pp. 204-205.

35. *RHE* (1962), p. 312.

36. "El pueblo español," in *ENC,* III, 13-14.

37. *RHE* (1962), p. 277.

38. "El pueblo español," p. 14.

39. *La enseñanza del español en España* (Madrid: V. Suárez, 1922), pp. 83, 100-101.

40. *CCE,* pp. 316-317.

41. *RHE* (1962), p. 245.

42. Ibid., p. 244.

43. "Advertencia," p. 49.

44. *CCE,* pp. 329-330.

45. "Emigrados," pp. 181-188.

46. *RHE* (1962), p. 312.

47. "Una hora en Guadalupe," in *ENC,* I, 216-217.

48. "Emigrados," p. 183.

49. "Humanidades," in *ENC,* II, 198.

50. *RHE* (1966), pp. 21-24.

51. *RHE* (1962), p. 315.

52. See "Lo español del anarquismo," in *RHE* (1962), p. 293 ff. See also *AVH* (1970), 123-124; 153, n. 51 bis.

53. "Entrando en Portugal," p. 57.

54. "Las polémicas sobre España. Insuficiente educación histórica," in *ENC,* II, 133-134.

55. *PCer* (1972), p. 20, n. 1.

56. *Cervantès,* p. 49.

57. *RHE* (1966), p. 13.

58. *EDC* (1963), p. 209.

59. Ibid., p. 244.

60. Ibid., pp. 142-243.

61. *STE,* pp. 277-278.

62. *Les grands romantiques espagnols* (Paris: Cent chefs-d'oeuvre ètrangers, 1922), p. 16.

63. Ibid., p. 6.

64. Ibid., p. 14.

65. Ibid., p. 15.

66. "Acerca del 'Diablo mundo' de Espronceda," *Revista de Filología Española,* VII (1920), 378.

67. *Les grands romantiques espagnols,* p. 111.

68. Ibid., p. 2.

69. *IHC* (1954), p. 209.

70. "Advertencia previa," p. 61.

71. "Don Francisco's book was the splendid flowing of his life, just as Juan Ramón Jiménez's unique poetry lies in the very yearning for poetic perfection, that makes him not consider any particular piece as finally and definitively completed. Poetry about writing poetry; or the process of living on a spiritual plane, like an incessant philosophy about philosophizing, in search of the human absolute, in a perennial ascesis or exercise to obtain not some final truth of a rational or scientific kind, but, rather, an approximation (ultimately, more religious than intellectual) to the infinite boundaries of the spirit of the Universe, present and active at all times and in all places. The universe as a temple. The ineffable." ("Francisco Giner," in *ENC,* II, 218).

72. "Introduction" to Frances A. Pleak, *The Poetry of Jorge Guillén* (Princeton: Princeton University Press, 1942); published in Spanish with considerable changes as " *'Cántico'* de Jorge Guillén," *Ex-Insula* (Buenos Aires), Año I, no. 1 (1943), pp. 3-16.

73. *HCer* (1957), p. 301; "Prólogo" to *Don Quijote,* p. xxxiii.

74. Ibid., pp. 389-390.

75. *CCE,* p. 160.

76. "Prólogo" to *Don Quijote,* p. xi.

77. Ibid., p. xvi.

78. Ibid., p. xvi.

79. *RHE* (1966), pp. 5-6; "La indiferencia frente a lo público," in *ENC,* I, 134.

80. *La enseñanza del español,* p. 73.

81. *CCE,* p. 180. Castro does not refer to the Spanish novel before Galdós. He mentions Valera, but as an intellectual and a critic, not as a novelist. Valera,

he says, cut himself off from the world, "creating for himself an exquisite style as much in his life as in his prose, and arming himself with skepticism in the face of any dogmatism." ("De grata recordación. Juan Valera y Alberto Jiménez," in *ENC,* II, 252–253).

82. *RHE* (1966), p. 6.

83. "De grata recordación," p. 247.

84. *HCer* (1957), pp. 477–478.

12

A PARALLEL OBSERVER
AND INNOVATOR:
JOSÉ ORTEGA Y GASSET
Franco Meregalli

Any attempt to define the place of Américo Castro and his work within the evolution of Spanish culture must eventually confront the problem of Castro's personal and ideological relations with Ortega.

From Ortega's *Obras completas* we learn that, in 1909, as a part of a polemic he was carrying on with that "wild Spaniard" (*energúmeno español*), Unamuno, he cites a letter written by Castro stating that Menéndez Pidal owed his initiation to "the rigorous method that was followed in this kind of studies outside of Spain" (the studies being Romance linguistics). Unamuno had previously cited Menéndez Pidal as an example of "Spanish science." Although Ortega was twenty-six years old and Castro only twenty-four at the time, it is clear that Ortega knew about and appreciated Castro. Ortega regarded him as "young and very intelligent," and as "a favorite student and protégé of Menéndez Pidal." Ortega refers to Castro as a "great friend," but he does not refer to Castro in his later writings, except in a very marginal way, as seen in vol. III of his *Obras Completas.*[1] Castro's name does not appear in the following six volumes, in volumes X and XI of his political writings, or as far as I can recall, in the three posthumous volumes VII–IX, this last group having no index of proper names. It is equally true of the works of Ortega not yet included in any of the published collections of his works with which I am familiar.

Evidence in fact shows that Castro's political position was for many years absolutely analogous to Ortega's, as shown in Gonzalo Redondo's extensive *Las empresas políticas de José*

Ortega y Gasset. Castro and Ortega both declare their support of the program of reform proposed by Melquíades Alvarez in October 1913,[2] and Castro appears on the list of followers of the League for Spanish Political Education (Liga de Educación Política Española), which is included in the first edition of *Vieja y nueva política* (1914).[3] A study of this list is particularly instructive because it includes some names destined to shine in the cultural and political spheres of Spain in succeeding decades. The names are mostly of Ortega's contemporaries (Unamuno had refused to sponsor Ortega's initiative[4]), but there is also a significant number of older contemporaries who apparently already accepted his precocious leadership.[5]

Later on, at crucial moments, we find Castro faithfully on the same side as Ortega even after the Republic was proclaimed.[6] However, Castro's bibliography shows that he not only remained for some time on the sidelines of Ortega's journalistic initiatives, but that he also collaborated in *El Sol* during the period (1932–1933) when and after that paper supported Azaña, a figure of whom Ortega had already become critical.[7] In short, we can state that the two men knew each other professionally and politically, but that they did not enjoy a close personal relationship.

It seems more promising to investigate the incidental and more indirect influences of Ortega's writings on Castro. In order to find a text that directly expresses his place in Spain's cultural ambience, we must go back to late November 1918 when Castro wrote his study "El movimiento científico en la España actual [1918]".[8] Every historian of Spanish culture in this century should be familiar with this article because of the balanced and objective way the information is presented, in spite of certain polemical points that anticipate those elaborated by Castro many years later.[9] Within Castro's overall view, the figure of Giner de los Ríos and the Institución Libre de Enseñanza take on an extraordinary importance, one which has no comparable place in Ortega's work of the same period, even though Ortega and the Institución Libre held the same view in common that top priority for education was a way of overcoming Spain's "backwardness." But Castro comes closer to Ortega when he identifies two essential trends in literary studies that go beyond "erudition, the upshot of the preceding century's positivism." He identifies them as the current represented by Menéndez Pidal, "the rebuilding of the past with philological methods," and the one represented by Ortega, "the most modern criticism that begins to analyze the nature of the historical and literary phenomenon." Castro comments on Ortega in the following terms:

> In this sense, José Ortega y Gasset's work comes to us full of promise. He is, after all, a professor of philosophy at the university, one of the finest minds of our time. His essays reveal a man who is conscious of the innovativeness of his style; the works themselves are characterized especially by their breadth and vigor of thought never before engaged when dealing with literary matters in Spain. His work, although not yet very extensive, includes both literature and science. . . . Like other first-rate Spaniards, Ortega cannot remain deaf to the unease of his surroundings, and from the newspaper he tries to orient public opinion by indicating new directions. But his main effort is in literary criticism and pure philosophy, the areas where our greatest hope lies today.[10]

An analysis of these lines clearly shows that they point towards a new orientation, integrating the philological methods in vogue, but at the same time, suggesting a potential substitute for this direction in the personality of Castro himself. For several years Castro continued to turn out philological "contributions" until his work *El pensamiento de Cervantes* appeared in 1925. This book marks the high point of his first period and is precisely indicative of a synthesis between philological commitment and a tendency to "analyze the nature of the historical and literary phenomenon." This fact, more than any analysis of the content itself, shows the radical influence on Castro of Ortega, who was "far ahead" even of the new literary criticism.[11]

In 1922 Castro published a pamphlet entitled *La enseñanza del español en España* (The Teaching of Spanish in Spain), which he claimed was actually written three years before in 1919: "I have only added some bibliographical references."[12] Ortega is never cited, and in fact everything in the pamphlet points to a personal culture with a more specifically linguistic and quite different orientation from Ortega's. But the coincidence in their refusal to "convert *Don Quixote* in the lower grades into a ceremonial reading" is very revealing.[13] Ortega maintains the same position, albeit for very different reasons, in *"Don Quixote en la escuela,"* an essay dated March 1920, in which his pedagogical ideas could be expressed with a phrase from Castro himself in an image of an exquisitely Ortegian stamp: "to render our children's spirits like a crossbow stretched taut."[14]

The very title, *El pensamiento de Cervantes,* presupposes a polemic. Cervantes had been considered a "layman," in the sense that his thinking was not held to be original, and that he could even be defined as "behind the times." Castro's entire introduction is marshaled against this position that directly opposed more or less arbitrary esoteric interpretations, but whose basic intent, however, had been to rescue Cervantes from any suspicion of heterodoxy. "The watchword is to deny to *Don Quixote* any possibility of an intimate study of any kind."[15] The reference to Menéndez y Pelayo (and Valera) is explicit, but there is some subterranean coolness to Menéndez Pidal, himself, to whom the book is dedicated. In fact, it is possible to apply to Menéndez Pidal the assertion that "it is always surprising that Menéndez Pelayo only occasionally concerned himself with Cervantes."[16] It is obvious that Unamuno cannot be the source for this new perspective since he put down Cervantes in favor of Don Quixote and actually came to scorn his lesser works. Contrarily, Castro talks about Cervantes and not *Don Quixote,* and he wants to attempt a study of Cervantes' works "taken together as a whole."[17] The necessary antecedent for this undertaking is Ortega's *Meditaciones del Quijote* (1915), which, as Castro remarked later, "représentent une réaction vigoureuse contre la critique traditionnelle et marquent une date."[18] In spite of this statement Castro—much more knowledgeable than Ortega about sixteenth and seventeenth-century Spain—does not approach the hasty and categorical devaluation of almost all Spanish literature from that period contained in the *Meditaciones.*[19] For Ortega the real quixotism is "Cervantes's and not Don Quixote's"; and "There was a period in Spanish life when nobody wanted to recognize the profundity of *Don Quixote.*"[20] This last phrase might well be the motto for Castro's introduction. The basis for Castro's book is precisely "the intimate study"; there is no literary value without human value. And Ortega writes: "A poetic style carries within it a philosophy and a morality, a science and a politics."[21]

The chapter on Cervantes' religious ideas is based on the belief that he was "a great dissembler" and "a skillful hypocrite," an affirmation that stuck in Spaniards' minds as an essential quality of *Don Quixote.*[22] But Castro himself cites "the heroic hypocrisy" practiced by those superior seventeenth-century men mentioned by Ortega, and he refers to it in connection with the "exemplariness" of the *Exemplary Novels.*[23] So this same essential feature really comes from Ortega, just as Ortega is the source for his remarks about needing "a comprehensive definition of that kind of novel [the picaresque] which would include not only its formal characteristics, but also the intimate inner structure of its esthetics."[24] Actually Ortega clarifies this intimate inner structure in his essay "La picardía original de la novela picaresca," quoted by Castro on the same page. Ortega says that the picaresque is an art of imitation, "a corrosive literature, composed of pure negations, driven by a preconceived pessimism," an assessment that anticipates recent studies on the relationship between the picaresque and the descendants of converted Jews.[25] In any case, Castro's book is more balanced than Ortega's *Meditaciones.* Castro was at the zenith of his forty-some years and schooled in the rigorous discipline of philology, whereas in the *Meditaciones del Quijote,* published when Ortega was thirty-one, there is a certain childish imprudence and journalistic arbitrariness.

In 1929 Castro published his *Santa Teresa y otros ensayos.* The most important essay, "La mística y humana feminidad de Teresa la Santa," precedes the rest, but was actually written some time before its publication in book form. This study signifies an important phase in the development of Castro's scholarly pursuits. Presumably he had read Ortega's articles on St. Theresa, "Estudios sobre el amor," published in *El Sol* between 1927 and 1928, in which the analogy between worldly love and mysticism is confirmed.[26] Both Ortega's and Castro's writings had undoubtedly been influenced in turn by Jean Baruzi's book *Saint Jean de la Croix et le problème de l'experience mystique* (1924). While it is significant that there is no mention of Ortega in Castro's work, he does, however, refer to Unamuno's "penetrating and incisive essay" entitled "Misticismo y humanismo."[27] Also in 1929 Ortega wrote his pages "Defensa del teólogo frente al místico," in which he states that "no intellectual benefit can be derived from the mystic vision," an allusion that seems to refer specifically to the Spanish mystics.[28] A careful study reveals the first steps in Castro's alienation from Ortega's thought, of an intellectual, "vital-reasonist," if not intellectualist stamp. The idea of the Spanish way of life as not being reducible to a European mold appears much more of an Unamunian than an Ortegian notion. He remarks on the fact that "our literary history is not usually made with concepts wrought on Hispanic forges."[29] The trauma of the Civil War was to divide Castro's intellectual life into two separate parts, if it is possible to speak of a dichotomy; this does not mean, however, that the seeds of the future were not apparent in the earlier Castro.[30] Nevertheless, in that same work, when he deals with "El problema histórico de *La Celestina,*" Castro confirms his tendency to interpret Spain as a part of Europe; for him, the "moral philosophy" of the *Celestina* "rests on ideas . . . of the Italian Renaissance."[31]

As we have seen, both Castro and Ortega left *El Sol* in March 1931. Castro wrote for *Crisol* and also for *Luz,* two publications inspired and guided by Ortega; but after these contacts, Castro went back to *El Sol,* where he continued publishing articles until 1936. Only a direct examination of these contributions in their political and journalistic context would be able to bring the intellectual relations between Castro and Ortega during this period into sharper focus. We can only say here that the July 1933 article on Jovellanos confirms, as its very theme implies, the climate of Europeanism with which Castro was still imbued.[32] However, anyone who reads the article on Jovellanos "since" the further evolution of its author can observe the idea of a "discrepant Spanishness," which is tinged with the Ortegian idea of a select minority, and actually takes advantage of Menéndez y Pelayo's *Heterodoxos* with opposite intentions. It anticipates the future Castro in such phrases as: "His theme is no mere disinterested intellectual problem, but rather that other kind of problem of a practical nature which presented him with the structure of his people's history" and "the expulsion of the sons of St. Ignatius marks the peak of that intent to unlive one's own history."[33]

In an essay on Manuel Bartolomé Cossío written near the end of 1935, Castro describes as praiseworthy and particularly Spanish traits, the "mystical, serene dignity, the knighthood of the errant spirit, the love of process over static being, the mechanics of the spirit, the value [at times exaggerated] of intuition over rational calculation, and the Spanish attributes of drive and emotion. . . . Giner saw that eighteenth-century intellectualism was not suited to Spain; opposing accomplishments were realized, but the well-springs of originality remained blocked."[34] Castro at fifty had already removed himself from *El pensamiento de Cervantes*. It is no longer reason, science, or the Spanish Renaissance defended against Klemperer that interests him.[35] Nor is he interested in "the individual's façade" that "is his work," but rather "the closed office in which that work is forged."[36]

In June 1937, after the irreparable had already occurred in Spain and Castro had gone to live in Buenos Aires shortly before leaving for Wisconsin, he published an emotion-filled portrait of Giner de los Ríos in *La Nación*. Castro recalls that Giner wrote many books, but what was particularly valuable about him was something that was worth more than all the sciences, classified or not: an attitude or stance toward the world. Each idea "is valuable insofar as it is an aspect of a vital and creative function, since this is indeed radically essential . . . Don Francisco did not try to force Spain to adopt foreign customs; he cherished, like no one else, the positive aspects of Spain's uniqueness."[37] Ortega's vital reason is the unmistakable antecedent of these statements which, in their broader national context, are perfectly compatible with the Ortegian line. But it is no mere coincidence that this vitally reasoning individual is Giner (in Don Francisco "doctrine was constantly projecting itself onto the act of living"), and that there is no explicit reference to Ortega. Neither Ortega nor Castro favored a mimetic Europeanization, but the accent falls on the uniquely Hispanic, "on what it has of worth," of course. Castro's absence from Spain and the fact that his country was fighting a "uniquely Hispanic" war undoubtedly contributed to this emphasis. The new events illuminated Spain's past in a dramatic way and encouraged him to interpret it in a different light.

Another of Castro's personality traits comes to light in this context, one which stayed with him for the rest of his life: the desire to reexamine his writings and bring them up to date. At the beginning of his preliminary remarks to the first edition of *Hacia Cervantes,* Castro wrote: "When something originally published many years earlier is reissued or when a writer allows such a work to be republished, he feels a tremendous urge to rewrite the whole thing again. Since this is not possible he reaches a compromise with himself. I have modified certain expressions which I have since abandoned, and I have added some complementary observations."[38] I believe this is a question of a mistaken method. Thinking from another period cannot be retouched; the "compromise with oneself," the adjustment, becomes a falsification in which historically different times, investigation and later reflection, are mixed. Additions can be made, but in such a way that it is possible to date each expression. I do not know whether Castro, at the end of his life, either by intuition or simply from fatigue, authorized the republication of *El pensamiento de Cervantes* without variants, although he and Rodríguez-Puértolas added notes. He republished the 1962 edition of *La realidad histórica de España* in 1966 with a new introduction. In any case, anyone who wishes to reconstruct Castro's development must distrust the reprintings and have recourse to the original editions. Unfortunately this does complicate matters.

To illustrate this facet of Castro's scholarship in connection with Ortega I shall limit myself here to a comparison between "Lo hispánico y el erasmismo" (1940, 1942), a work written before *España en su historia* and its revision, and *Aspectos del vivir* (1949, 1970), which was done after the aforementioned work and which contains "quite a few cuts and additions." A thorough critical comparison would illuminate the trajectory of Castro's thinking; but here we must confine ourselves to a few limited observations. The change in title itself diverts our attention, emphasizing the Hispanic and omitting the Erasmism,

a phenomenon of European origin. "Lo hispánico y el erasmismo" already contained in embryonic form some of the
essential traits of Castro's concept of "the Hispanic." In it we
find expressions like "the vital structure of the Hispanic
species," or "it is futile to apply methods of logical intellection
to anything Hispanic . . ." and further on: "So the Spaniard is
accustomed to inventing for himself a climate in the chimera
of illusion, idealism, or utopianism, without ever once having
attained a moment of complete, dependable, and savoured
reality."[39] The numerous revisions in the 1949 edition systemat-
ically underscore the semitic element, clearly demonstrating that
the recourse to Semitic elements to explain the uniqueness of
the Hispanic "vital dwelling place" postdates the characterization
of this dwelling place as personalism in the face of all things
European. There is a vast difference between the two editions as
seen in the additional section "Algunas deducciones de lo
anterior," where some preexisting tendencies of Castro's position
are carried to extremes. But even more important is the omission
of pages 3 to 9 of the 1940 text in which he denied what would
later be one of his most fervent convictions: "These are all forms
of inwardness, inner calling, so characteristic of the Hispanic
temperament. Was it all an indirect or remote influence of some
larvate Semitism? I do not think so . . . contrary to every
Orientalist hypothesis to explain Hispanic uniqueness."[40] Nevertheless, a certain bewilderment is apparent: "I do not know
what caused such a singular form of existence, nor to what
extent the eight centuries left over from beyond the Moorish
frontier may have contributed to explaining it."[41]

As for Castro's relationship to Ortega, we find in these
deleted pages (for obvious reasons that have nothing to do with
Ortega), an allusion to Ortega as a "thinker *more hispanico*
such has never before been seen in Spain."[42] But it is precisely
in the 1949 edition of *Aspectos* that the word "belief" appears:
'When collective life rests on unchangeable beliefs," and further
on, "using thought more than belief."[43] In the corresponding
passage of "Lo hispánico" we read: "When collective life rests
on petrified traditions" and "not using either acts of magic or
spells."[44] The entire Ortegian opposition between ideas and

beliefs seems evident here as put forth in his *Ideas y creencias,* first published in 1940. Where we originally read in "Lo hispánico": "The preceding means that the emotively personal attitudes which had come in as a foreign influence, are resolved in Spain in a desire for confidence and freedom in the face of the ultimate destiny—death," we read in *Aspectos*: "The preceding means that the emotively personal attitudes of a Christian-Islamic-Hebraic tradition were resolved in a desire for confidence and freedom within belief."[45] The terminology of Ortegian origin is mixed with the new "ideas" of Castro, even substituting the allusion to the Unamunian theme of death.

In the 1970 edition of *Aspectos* Castro corrected, as he himself states in the Foreword, everything that really needed correcting. Variants are identified by the use of brackets. Castro emphasizes the deplorable "confusion between the notions of race and caste" and he brings the bibliography up to date, but essentially he does not alter his 1949 outlook.[46]

Naturally it is much more important to study the successive transformations of *España en su historia*. In fact, Castro's original elaboration of this theme followed by a series of changes, occupied more than twenty years of his life. The prologue to *España en su historia* is dated April 1946, in other words, two years before the publication of the book itself. However we can place the genesis of the book between 1940 and 1943 in Princeton, "when Castro developed in a few intense and unforgettable seminars the revolutionary work he was forging for the first time."[47] The basis for *España en su historia* is the concept of the nation: "Within that vagueness of the 'Latin world,' Spain, France, and Italy display radically different characteristics, much more decisive than their secondary similarities."[48] Spain "is different." We are at the antipodes of *The Revolt of the Masses*. In the aforementioned prologue we found the Ortegian concept of "belief" applied to the Spaniards and characteristic of them: "Neither in the Occident nor in the Orient is there anything analogous to Spain," and Spain has acquired values both "very high and unparalleled in kind," whereas "there are European countries that figure 'at the head of modern civilization,' without an interesting physiognomy or universality of values."[49]

As for Ortega's presence, a reference is made to "a certain fundamental study on Spanish history published some twenty years ago." The allusion is to *Invertebrate Spain,* first published in 1921, even though Castro thinks it dates from 1922, which dates his own writing at around 1942. Castro states that Ortega is "a thinker in tune with the abundance of problems of his time," such as Spain had not had since Vives. He notes that *España invertebrada* is "a minor work, hastily done, within Ortega's production . . . a lyrical complaint."⁵⁰ Ortega's idea of an absence of minorities in Spain seems to him to be related to a Spanish tradition: Quevedo, Gracián, and Pérez de Guzmán all have "a feeling of vital emptiness," anticipating, in a way, Ortega's own thoughts. This is not, however, a point of departure for his meditation, according to Castro, but rather an indication of a consistant vital attitude of "life as a denial of itself" (*vivir desviviéndose*) that can only be characterized as very Spanish and that continues in the twentieth century.

Ortega is cited again in the work to affirm that "Luis Vives, Miguel de Unamuno, and J. Ortega y Gasset recall men like Averroes, Ibn Ḥazm and Ibn Khaldūn rather than Aristotle, Descartes, and Kant."⁵¹ What is Castro's basis for such a disconcerting observation? A quick look at the index of names in Ortega's *Obras completas* (volumes I-VI) actually shows that Ortega cites Aristotle 85 times, Descartes 96, and Kant 122 times; there are many more references to Plato, 147, and, significantly, 114 references to Goethe. In contrast, he cites Averroes only twice and does not mention Ibn Ḥazm or Ibn Khaldūn at all. Evidently Ortega was unaware of their relationship. But Castro explains that the Hispano-Muslim and Hispano-Judaic thinkers, like the Spaniards themselves, have only "brilliant derivations of the thought systems of other countries, whose most original element is related to the problems of living and conduct" (a scheme we could unfortunately apply to Seneca as well). Ortega's most brilliant contribution, therefore, would be in the area of ethics: "And if there is to be some great philosophy in the Hispanic world, that will be its course, and not that of the physico-mathematical sciences."⁵² Later on he states that "Ortega y Gasset, embued with Germanic thought, reacts here with a Hispanic longing for concretion and vital integrity, and he creates something new and valuable, but which sounds familiar to us after a thousand years of Spanishness."[53] And incidentally, Ortega must certainly have "amplified" in 1944 Unamuno's observation made in 1912 about the excessively slight attention that historians of philosophy pay to the "intimate biography of the philosophers."

This is not the place to discuss the relations between Unamuno's existential position and Ortega's thought. It is, however, appropriate to state that the disengagement of these two Spaniards from the vitalist and intuitionist European tendencies means contradicting not only Ortega's evaluation of his own historical position, but also the documentable intellectual presence in him of some European contemporaries, from his early loves—Renan and Nietzsche—to his rather belated discovery of Dilthey.

In *España en su historia* there is a fundamental contradiction between the initial affirmation that "a country is not a fixed entity," and the conclusion: "the history in which we find ourselves placed consisted of arranging, from a fixed position and out of a desire for eternity, a series of changes in scenery, which left the essential part of Spain unaffected." So we come, as we have seen, to the prophecy: Spain will always be this way.[54]

In order to explain the violence of Castro's attitude, we must keep in mind his own personal situation as an exiled and isolated man in the North American world.[55] Unamuno and Ortega were both right when they pointed to the vital element as indispensable to the understanding of an author's thought, and Castro asserted himself as a Spaniard; in his isolation he saw this world as something "European" (might that phrase about "European" nations that figure "at the head of modern civilization" not refer precisely to the geographically non-European United States?). Castro firmly and proudly contended that he was different in the face of this new world. This solitary assertion was a kind of compensation to him for the personal feeling of bitterness left by the Civil War and its consequences. After all, the "history of Europe would be incomprehensible without Spain's presence"; yet "at heart, the Hispanic man only gives what in English is called 'lip service' to whatever he imitates or imports from foreign countries and he ends up by destroying it or by transforming it into a tool for his vital authenticity."[56] At times Castro assesses this interpretation almost as if it were the diagnosis of some psychic infirmity whose origin he must particularize in order to be free of it. But at the deepest level, when he thought about this marginal, autonomous, even impervious situation of Spain, he was experiencing a Spain that was Castro, projected from his own dwelling place.

Between Castro's emotive standpoint and Ortega's position there is a substantial opposition. Ortega begins with a desire to exalt the pulse of Spain, but he thinks about human problems, man among men, European among Europeans. For him Spain belongs to the European culture of a classical bent.[57] After *España invertebrada,* he scarcely ever concerns himself with Spain from a speculative point of view, even though his whole work is inspired by a profound patriotism. According to Ortega, the surpassing of physico-mathematical science as an exemplary science, an event which occurred in the first decades of this century, is a European accomplishment, even though a European from Spain—Ortega to be exact—contributed to it. Contrarily, with Castro we have an opposition between a physico-mathematical science characteristic of Europe and not in crisis in its exemplariness for Europe and the Spanish "vital dwelling place."

In any case, Ortega appears in *España en su historia* as a prime example of Castro's Spaniard: "one more case of life as a denial of itself." In contrast in *La realidad histórica de España* (1954), an elaboration of the earlier *España en su historia,* in which chapters of a theoretical nature are added, and where, for that reason, Ortega's presence seems more credible, we find Dilthey cited persistently: "Not enough has been said about how much we Spanish-speaking people owe to Dilthey's thought about human life."[58] But there is no allusion to Ortega's merits at least in the dissemination of Dilthey's thought. Ortega himself appears only twice: once in a newly written chapter, in reference to the (deplorable) scheme of the "three centuries of error and heartache," with a quote from the *Pedagogía social,* written in

1910, no less; and again in a statement from *España en su historia,* which emphasizes the Unamunian derivation of Ortega's idea that it is abstract to study philosophers' ideas without taking into account their existential situation.[59] Not even in the chapter on the Visigoths "who were not Spaniards," does he see his way clear to cite the author of *Invertebrate Spain.* Castro does, however, implicitly refer to this work when he maintains that "it makes no sense to lament abstractly the absence of select minorities in Spain."[60] In reality, of course, Ortega did not lament "abstractly"; rather, he tried to give an explanation (one which does not personally convince me). Contrary to this sort of censoring of Ortega we have a significant increase in the allusions to Menéndez y Pelayo, an author Ortega had read "when he was a boy . . . shot through with faith," and had almost excluded from his scope (unjustly, in my opinion).[61]

It seems clear that behind all this there is a personal factor, as has already been observed, although from an inverted perspective.[62] The fact is that between the publication of *España en su historia* and *La realidad,* Ortega had taken up the study of Ibn Hazm, specifically when he wrote his prologue to Emilio García Gomez's translation of *El collar de la paloma* (1952). In the prologue he states that "the relationship between the two societies, the Islamic and the Hispano-Christian, has not even begun to be clarified."[63] This was written four years after the publication of *España en su historia,* a work that Ortega could not possibly have been unfamiliar with, if only because García Gómez discusses it at length in his introduction to *El collar de la paloma,* in other words, in the same book containing Ortega's foreword. Guillermo Araya, who does not refer to this introduction, assumes that Ortega's silence and implicit judgment is due to his conviction that Castro did not sufficiently recognize the Ortegian derivation of some of his ideas. Without dismissing this unflattering motive (a certain resentment does, in effect, appear especially in Ortega's later writings, for example, in some chapters of *La idea de principio en Leibniz,* against Heidegger and Sartre), it is clear that there were more intrinsic reasons for Ortega's silence. For him the problem of "shedding

light on the relationship between the two societies . . . cannot
be reduced to the boundaries of Spain." It is not entirely the
Spaniards' fault. Foreign historians have not clarified the
relationship either, and this "has been one of the main obstacles
to the comprehension of the European Middle Ages," which "is,
in its reality, inseparable from Islamic civilization, since it
consists precisely in the living-together, both positive and
negative, of Christianity and Islam in a common ground im-
pregnated with Greco-Roman culture."[64] These statements
contain a much broader perspective than *España en su historia,*
a point of view in which the Greco-Roman world is not isolated
from Spanish life, in which in a certain sense the concept of
the Middle Ages is maintained and a Spanish "vital dwelling
place" is not made into a myth to explain almost everything up
to our own time and even in the future, both in the Iberian
Peninsula and in Latin America.

Ortega's silence is also related to the content of García
Gómez's introduction, and he implicitly confirms this. García
Gómez remarks that Castro is "a devoted convert to the Arabic
theses," that "with typical neophyte fervor he accentuates,
reiterates, and carries to extremes."[65] It seems to him "highly
unlikely" that among the Arabic elements in the *Libro de buen
amor* "the *Collar* appears as basic and in a direct way," since
the *Collar* is "an aristocratic and very difficult book," which is
separated from " 'good love' real chasms of spiritual differences."[66] Castro, who cites the translation, replies to García
Gómez's remarks, as in the case of Ortega's prologue, only with
silence.[67]

The "revised edition" of *La realidad histórica de España*
appeared in 1962. This is actually an extensive elaboration of
one part of the contents of the first edition, so that the 1962
Realidad is further removed from the 1954 version than the
latter is from *España en su historia.* Castro now develops the
portion directly related to the "historical reality of Spain,"
eliminating the literary texts that he continued to publish in
separate works. This new orientation is, in part, due to his
obvious sensitivity to the criticisms of Jaime Vicens Vives, for
whom the "reality" Castro discusses pertains only to "some

minority-oriented mental circles," and therefore, "borders on the defect of ideologism (over-reliance on literary or documentary texts without effective structural support)."[68]

In the 1962 *Realidad* there is some trace of a renewed knowledge of Ortega. Castro does cite *Una interpretación de la historia universal.*[69] But this work only serves to confirm the idea that for Ortega "the notion of an almost geological Spanishness of his ancestors" was also important. For Castro, Ortega continues to be substantially the one he was in his 1922 *España invertebrada*; and Castro, accustomed to revising his works with the idea of "bringing them up to date," points out as an extraordinary thing that in 1952 Ortega republished that volume with no modifications.[70] In any case, Ortega once again becomes an example of "living by the denial of life" in 1962. Historians who have tried to explain Spain's existence as a chronic illness (for example, Ortega y Casset in his *España invertebrada*) now appear as outstanding cases of the phenomenon of living by unliving oneself; their analysis of Hispanicism (*hispanidad*) is a function of their Hispanicness (*hispanismo*).

The 1965 edition is identical to the 1962 *Realidad,* except for the addition of a second prologue. For once Castro did not redo the text, instead he added an introduction containing new considerations and reactions to new criticisms. This time he finds a support for his ideas in the last pages of Ortega's unedited and fragmentary work, *La idea de principio en Leibniz.* Ortega asserts here that the Counter-Reformation was harmful "not for its own account, but because of its coincidence with some other national vice." It was joined to "a terrible sickness in our country which coincided, in a surprising way" with the Council of Trent: the illness that Ortega calls the "Tibetanization" of Spain.[71] Ortega, Castro comments, wrote this in 1947; and "who had the slightest idea of what the inner structure of Spanish life was really like?" In that year a man named Américo Castro, of course, had the idea, "although complete insight did not come about until 1960."[72]

This is not the place to clarify this "surprising coincidence" asserted by Ortega, but it is interesting to note that Castro once again, at least briefly, recognizes himself in Ortega in one of the cases in which Ortega, as at the time of *España invertebrada,* reveals a certain tendency toward peremptory and apodictic assertions, with polemical assumptions.

Now that we have studied the trajectory of the relationship Ortega-Castro through the transformations of Castro's well-known and extensive works, we can deduce the essential line of his evolution. But while the text of *España en su historia* was undergoing the aforementioned changes, other works by Castro were appearing which have a bearing on our central theme. This is the case of *De la edad conflictiva* (1961), a book in which Castro could make good use of his long and thorough knowledge of sixteenth- and seventeenth-century Spain, and for this reason, produced one of his most vigorous and fertile works. Very little in the book is related to Ortega; he again recalls the matter of "the last three centuries."[73] He reproaches Ortega for calling Trajan "Spanish" and "Sevillian" in *Una interpretación de la historia universal,* saying that when Ortega expressed himself in this way he "reflects a belief, not a thought," with which he certainly applies to Ortega a very Ortegian distinction. Further on he says: "In the case of Ortega y Gasset, like that of Menéndez Pidal, it does not do to attribute to ignorance the belief that whoever was born in the Iberian Peninsula was necessarily Spanish. The human and historic reason for a belief unaffected by thinking beyond its own borders must be sought in the habitual approach—elegiac and lamenting—to Spanish life.[74] And Castro refers once more to *España invertebrada,* where Ortega states that "Spanish life has been both a radical abnormality and an ailment."[75] The third edition of *De la edad conflictiva* (1972) adds one more reference to *España invertebrada,* "an important work for so many reasons."[76] This insistence on quoting a fairly episodic work by Ortega after half a century demonstrates how the genesis of some of Castro's ideas of the second period have their origin in this very work. For Castro too, Spain is an "abnormality," a living by denial of life; for him too "it was becoming impossible for an intellectual minority to prevail and act," as he adds in the third edition of *De la edad conflictiva.*[77] For the single motivation proposed by Ortega in 1921, Castro substitutes another equally unique explanation: the symbiosis and later the conflict of castes. Castro's innovation is that the Spanish "abnormality" explains traits of being Spanish as very valuable in human terms, whereas that "abnormality" appeared to the young Ortega as something purely negative.[78]

In later writings of Castro we again find references to "Tibetanization," and, as far as I can recall, to nothing else.[79] There is no doubt that Ortega was not a renewed experience for Castro in those last years, in spite of his collaboration in the second period of the *Revista de Occidente*. This is understandable if we think about Castro's interest in the literature of the Age of Conflict and Ortega's withdrawal from the Spanish theme, the literary one, and naturally even more so from the theme of Spanish literature as proved by the posthumous publication of the three volumes of *Obras postumas* (1961–1962). This change prevented Ortega from revising his youthful judgment on the "mystical little friars," the "torrential dramatists," and the lyrical "deserts without flowers."

In this sense, Castro's work fits into an empty space in Ortega's thought. There are brilliant intuitions on the development of Spanish civilization in his works, with specific reference to literature. Ortega asserted that the physico-mathematical sciences were born from hypothesis rather than from observation, in other words, from an intellectual deduction, either accepted or rejected afterward by experience, which is Galileo's procedure.[80] We find something similar in Castro, a great scorner, in his second period, of mere accumulation of data. The danger of this method is that a few facts are chosen to prove a thesis, whereas others, which may actually be more numerous and symptomatic, are rejected. What one misses at times in Castro (but on another level we could say the same of Ortega) is subtlety and at the same time, the clarification of boundaries. He was not mistaken when he maintained that the formative centuries of the Castilian nation—a bit hastily identified, at least tendentially, with Spain—coincide with the "origins of Spanish." But sometimes he seems to assume that the Visigoths and men of Altamira, the Celtiberians and Hispano-Romans "were not Spanish" to the same degree. Because of his desire to make Spain unique, he ultimately rejected those elements that made and still make Spain a part of Europe.[81]

It is true that Spain cannot be understood in terms of historiographic categories used for the history of other countries; it is necessary to examine it from the perspective of its own "structure" (the word is used in the same way by both Ortega and Castro); but precisely Spain's "structure" is also in the fact of being a part of Europe. Spain speaks a neo-Latin language, which constitutes a definitive historical conditioning; she was Christianized in times and ways analogous to those of other European countries. She was invaded by Germanic peoples, also in analogous ways (not identical, which would be impossible). All this was and is projected onto the Spanish "vital dwelling place" (which certainly is a "dwelling place" even though it changes). The continuity between Goths and Spaniards, for example, was felt for many centuries by the Spaniards; it was a fact of consciousness, and, therefore, it was a real phenomenon. Seneca was not "Spanish" but he was perceived as Spanish. We should not be scandalized if Ortega talks about the "Sevillian" Trajan, as the Italians call Virgil, "Mantuan," following Dante's example. Spain, of course, "is different"; but each nation is different, different in a different way.

Américo Castro was not, however, just another historian. Thanks to him, for example, the expression "Golden Age" sounds hollow to us to talk about what is, rather, a "conflictive Age." His solutions may not completely convince, but his problems remain. And that is what counts.

NOTES

1. José Ortega y Gasset, *Obras completas,* 11 vols. (Madrid: Revista de Occidente, 1950-1969), I, 130, 132; III, 397. Hereafter cited as *Obras.*

2. Gonzalo Redondo, *Las empresas políticas de Ortega y Gasset,* 2 vols. (Madrid: Rialp, 1970), I, 86.

3. Already in Julián Marías, *Ortega. Circunstancia y vocación* (Madrid: Revista de Occidente, 1960), I, 530-532; now also in Redondo, I, 84.

4. On the position of Ortega and Unamuno in regard to the Liga, and more generally on the relations between Ortega and Unamuno, see now the last chapter "Para la interpretación de una continuidad" of Paulino Garagorri,

Unamuno y Ortega (Barcelona: Salvat, 1972), with updated bibliography. For Garagorri, who adduced the testimony of his assiduous dealings with Ortega, the spirit of the two was "divergent when not opposite" in spite of the political affinity of their attitudes, since their approximation to socialism "had a similar stamp" (p. 116). "Unamuno's political ideas are exactly the same ones I am trying to defend with the puny modern little lance of my pen," wrote Ortega in 1908 (*Obras*, I, 117). In 1924, when he defended Unamuno on the occasion of his exile, Ortega declared himself an "extreme enemy of Sr. Unamuno," and gave himself "the authority that always comes from praising one's enemy" (*Obras*, X, 264).

5. We find, among others, Azaña, born in 1880; Castro, 1885; Díez-Canedo, 1879; García Morente, 1886; Madariaga, 1886; Maeztu, 1875; Antonio Machado, 1875; Mesa, 1878; Moreno Villa, 1887; Onís, 1885; Pérez de Ayala, 1881; Salinas, 1891.

6. In May 1918 Castro, along with Ortega and four other professors from the Faculty of Philosophy and Letters in Madrid (García Morente, Menéndez Pidal, Cossío, Besteiro) signed a declaration in favor of the *Junta para la Ampliación de Estudios* (Redondo, I, 201); in November of the same year he signed a document of the *Unión democrática española*, whose content was analogous to Ortegian stands (Redondo, I, 238). He is listed as a contributor to the publishing house Calpe, related to *El Sol*, in 1919 (Redondo, I, 310); in fact he published editions of the *Condenado por desconfiado* and *Fuente Ovejuna* for their Colección universal in that same year. A long gap follows until 1928 when Castro is mentioned as a collaborator in *El Sol*. When the dramatic crisis that forced Ortega and many collaborators not to write for *El Sol* in March 1931, due to this newspaper's having passed over to the control of Monarchists, Castro was among them (Redondo, II, 247). Along with Ortega, Castro became a collaborators of the new newspaper *Crisol* in April of the same year (Redondo, II, 254); and he appeared as a friend of *Crisol* when he was the new ambassador in Berlin, May 1931 (Redondo, II, 274). But as soon as the policy of *El Sol* changed, Castro began sending occasional articles to the famous Madrid newspaper.

7. The only biography contained in *Semblanzas y estudios españoles*(1956). At the beginning of this publication it is stated that Castro collaborated from its founding (1917) in the great Spanish newspaper *El Sol"* (p. xxv), but the first article that appeared in *El Sol* seems to be the one included in vol. 3 (pp. 217-224) of *ENC*, dated January 26, 1923.

8. First published in Spanish in *La Rassegna* (Florence), Año XXVII, no. 4 (August 1919), pp. 187-200; reprinted in *ENC*, II, 91-122.

9. Emilio Cotarelo is considered a "very bad editor" of Lope; Adolfo Bonilla, it is said, has published a great deal, but "I fear that the novelty of the proper appreciation of the facts or thinking in depth does not always equal in quality the abundance of material" (*ENC*, pp. 111-112).

10. *ENC*, p. 113.

11. See Juan Marichal, "Américo Castro y la crítica literaria del siglo XX," in *Estudios*, p. 332.

12. *La enseñanza del español en España*, p. 6.

13. Ibid., p. 72.

14. *Obras*, II, 275–307; *Enseñanza del español*, p. 19. The volume of 'sketches," *LEL*, could tell us more about Castro's pedagogical ideas and their similarities to Ortega's, but I have not been able to locate it in the Biblioteca Nacional, Madrid.

15. *PCer* (1925), p. 11.

16. Ibid., p. 8.

17. Ibid., p. 17.

18. *Cervantès*, p. 56, n. 1.

19. Ortega talked about Menéndez y Pelayo and Valera as critics in these terms: "In these circumstances, how could one hope he would put Cervantes in his place? There was the divine book eruditely mixed in with our mystical little friars, our torrential dramatists, and our lyric poets, deserts without flowers" (*Obras* I, 340). There is a certain snobbishness in this hasty criticism of all of sixteenth- and seventeenth-century Spanish literature.

20. *Obras*, I, 327, 337.

21. Ibid., p. 363.

22. *PCer* (1925), pp. 240, 244.

23. Ibid., p. 241. *Obras*, I, 367.

24. *PCer* (1925), p. 232.

25. *Obras*, II, 121 ff.; p. 124.

26. *Obras*, V, 553–626.

27. *STE*, p. 35.

28. *Obras*, V, 455.

29. *STE*, p. 125.

30. Juan Marichal, *La voluntad del estilo* (Barcelona: Seix y Barral, 1957), p. 282; before that in *Revista Hispánica Moderna*, (July-August 1955), states that "there has not been, contrary appearances aside, and even in spite of what he himself leads us to believe, a hiatus or break between his works before and after 1936." In effect, it is natural that there should be hints of Castro's later ideas in his early work, since those later ideas are often elaborations of Ortega's or Unamuno's ideas from long before the Civil War. We should say that what changes is, more than anything else, his vital style: more European, wary, derivative of Menéndez Pidal, adult in *El pensamiento de Cervantes*; more "Iberian," bold, Unamunian and, paradoxically, youthful in *España en su historia*. Between them are the illusion of 1931–1932, the concern of 1932–1936, and the desperation of 1936–1939. What Marichal does when he asserts the continuity "even in spite of what he himself leads us to believe" is also to affirm the validity of the first Castro (almost forgotten except for a few of his writings) and the complementary nature of the two. Similarly, Julio Rodríguez-Puértolas wonders: "Does Renaissance humanism, combined with Erasmian critical philosophy necessarily exclude Cervantes' being an outsider in Spanish society

due to his impure origin?" and answers: "I sincerely do not think so; both factors necessarily combine and complement each other" ("Américo Castro y Cervantes," in *Estudios*, p. 387).

31. *STE*, p. 204. Rafael Lapesa points out the violent opposition between this "Renaissance" interpretation of *La Celestina* and the second Castro: "even though Menéndez y Pelayo and Ramiro de Maeztu had already noted that Rojas's Jewish origin might have contributed to the bitterness of the work, Castro, in 1929, was not interested in this factor" ("*La Celestina* en la obra de Américo Castro," in *Estudios*, p. 251).

32. *SEE*, pp. 405–411; reprinted in *ENC*, II, 201–210.

33. *SEE*, pp. 405, 407.

34. Ibid., p. 422.

35. See "El problema histórico de *La Celestina*," in *STE*, pp. 211–212.

36. *SEE*, p. 432; *ENC*, II, 237.

37. *SEE*, p. 419; reprinted in *ENC*, II, 211–220.

38. *HCer* (1957), p. xi.

39. *LHE*, Part I, p. 39; Part II, p. 48; Part II, p. 45.

40. Ibid., Part I, p. 5.

41. Ibid., Part I, p. 7. We must classify in the same vein the suppression of the following phrases: "Without documentary evidence of the possible relationship between fourteenth-century Christian eremitism and the Muslim variety . . . "All of this is very distant from what will one day be the mysticism of St. Theresa, and especially, the austere and anti-spectacular attitude of St. John of the Cross" (*LHE*, Part II, p. 13; omitted in *AVH*[1949], p. 75). On the contrary, in the early version, where he said: "The Hieronymites are an outgrowth of a branch of Franciscanism that had grown on the fringes of the official and clearly orthodox part of the order" (*LHE*, Part II, p. 14 n.), in 1949 he added: "and from the anacoretism of the Sufi holy men" (*AVH*, p. 77). In the last edition he added: "one more consequence of the inhabitants of Spain being how they were, a terribly uncomfortable fact for conventional historians" (*AVH* [1970], p. 156, n. 156).

42. Ibid., Part I, p. 9. In Part II, p. 52 we read: "It was easy for European Catholicism of the modern age, in societies characterized by hard work and rational organization, to permit itself all the luxuries related to reconciling opposite viewpoints; in those societies, Catholicism has already meant a subsidiary aspect of living, and not the wholeness of living." Ortega's influence probably accounts for the difference between two Catholicisms—a living faith and an inert one—that he deduces from the "theologians" (see "Historia como sistema" in *Obras*, VI, 17, first published in Spanish in 1941, but in English as early as 1935). The opposition between Spain and Europe appears in "Algunas deducciones de lo anterior," a section added to both versions of *Aspectos*, in the following extreme way: "Which is worth more, Goya or the atomic bomb? Where one was, the other could not have been" (*AVH* [1949], p. 160; Cervantes is added to Goya in *AVH* [1970], p. 136). Enrico Fermi who "directed the first controlled nuclear chain reaction" (*Encyclopedia Britannica*, ad vocem Fermi),

was born in Rome, earned his doctorate in Pisa, and was a professor in Florence and Rome. We all know that in these cities, and in Italy in general, there were no painters of renown. (For a further elaboration on what Castro thought about Ortega, up to 1940, see in this volume Castro's "The Meaning of Spanish Civilization," which undoubtedly Prof. Meregalli was unable to consult. *Editor's note.*)

43. *AVH* (1949), p. 15.

44. *LHE,* Part I, p. 2.

45. *LHE,* Part II, p. 22; *AVH* (1949), p. 89.

46. *AVH* (1970), p. 127 n.

47. Stephen Gilman, "Américo Castro como humanista e historiador," in *Estudios,* p. 127.

48. *ESH,* p. 10.

49. Ibid., pp. 12-13.

50. Ibid., pp. 40-41.

51. Ibid., p. 272.

52. Ibid., p. 272.

53. Ibid., p. 309. Ortega went further: "I call 'judgmental' everything that refers to values and appraisal. With it I renew an excellent tradition started by our Seneca and continued by the sixteenth-century Stoics" ("Para una topografía de la soberbia española," first published in *Revista de Occidente* [1925]; now in *Obras,* IV, 461 n.). Ortega chose arrogance as the characteristically Spanish 'vice,' as opposed to vanity: "Who doubts that this attitude toward life exudes a harsh flavor of grandeur!" (*Obras,* IV, 465). Ortega pointed to the Basques as the purest examples of Spanish pride. I do not know if he was thinking specifically about Unamuno, but the essay is one of the most Unamunian ever written by Ortega. And the most Castronian. Castro collaborated in the *Revista de Occidente* in 1924 and 1925 (Cf. E. Segura Covarsí, *Indice de la Revista de Occidente* [1953], pp. 21-22).

54. *ESH,* pp. 9, 613. In a somewhat crude way José Luis Abellán states: "The historicism that inspired him—and according to which the nation is not a concretion of any intemporal essence, but rather an historical product with an identifiable origin—fell back on the concept of 'lived experience' in a romantic essentialism, since for Castro 'Spanish' comes to mean an absolute essence like the 'national character' or *Volksgeist* which, although it was forged in the circumstances of the tenth century, became something so decisive that only by ceasing to be Spanish could we free ourselves from its destiny" (*Filosofía española en América: 1936-1966* [Madrid: Guadarrama, 1967], p. 274).

55. See the vibrant pages of Vicente Llorens, "Los años de Princeton," in *Estudios,* pp. 287-302.

56. *ESH,* pp. 641, 616.

57. During his German years, Ortega, who had already received a classical education in one of the few places where it was possible in Spain at the end of

the nineteenth century—that is, in a Jesuit school—had studied classical philology and had even thought about dedicating his entire life to it.

58. *RHE* (1954), p. 60. Prior to this time Castro almost gives the impression of not knowing of his existence; "Dilthey may today call Servet a brilliant thinker" (*ESH*, p. 176). (There is at least another mention of Dilthey. See *The Meaning of Spanish Civilization*, p. 11 of this volume. *Editor's note*)

59. *RHE* (1954), pp. 67, 322.

60. Ibid., p. 617.

61. *Obras*, I, 341.

62. See Guillermo Araya Goubet, *La evolución del pensamiento histórico de Américo Castro*, p. 79.

63. Ibn Ḥazm, *El collar de la paloma*, translation and introduction by E. García Gómez, prologue by J. Ortega y Gasset (Madrid: Sociedad de Estudios y Publicaciones, 1952); pp. 50–56; prologue reprinted in *Obras*, VII, 43.

64. *Obras*, VII, 43.

65. Ibn Ḥazm, *El collar*, p. 50.

66. Ibid., p. 55.

67. *RHE* (1954), p. 414.

68. Quoted in Eusebio Rey, S.J., "La polémica suscitada por Américo Castro," *Razón y Fe*, 157-4, no. 723 (April 1958). The article contains a careful overview of the reception first of *España en su historia* and later of *La realidad histórica* in Spanish intellectual circles. Claudio Sánchez-Albornoz's reaction was similar, as is well known.

69. *RHE* (1962), p. 16. Castro cites the work as *Interpretación de la historia universal*; however, it is actually *Una interpretación de la historia universal* (the one by Arnold Toynbee, severely criticized by Ortega), a work published in 1960 and now in *Obras*, IX, 11-242.

70. *RHE* (1962), pp. 41-42.

71. *Obras*, VIII, 355-356. See also Rodríguez Cepeda for an application of this term to the eighteenth century.

72. *RHE* (1966), p. 35.

73. *ECD* (1961), pp. 34, 125.

74. Ibid., p. 110.

75. Ibid., p. 111.

76. *ECD* (1972), p. 173. The provisional or "confidential" nature, like a "private annotation" of *España invertebrada* is extremely clear in Ortega's mind, even in the 1922 prologue (*Obras*, III, 37). He described it in 1934 as "a very modest, unpretentious tome"; to him it seems like "a schematic panorama" constructed "poorly, with very few facts and materials like Robinson" (*Obras*, III, 43, 45). But Ortega added: "I know that one day, I hope very soon, there will be some real books on Spanish history put together by real historians." At

this point Castro's noble ambition comes in. The Castronian link to *this* Ortega is confirmed on reading *España invertebrada*: "The secret of Spain's main problems lies in the Middle Ages" (*Obras*, III, 119). Ortega's statements, limiting the value of *España invertebrada*, could be related to the reservations about it expressed by several commentators: Cf. César Barja, *Libros y autores contemporáneos* (New York [1935], pp. 112 ff.); Claudio Sánchez-Albornoz contradicted Ortega's thesis in the *Revista de Occidente* itself.

77. *ECD* (1972), p. 173.

78. It sometimes seems that Castro's intention is to reveal the subconscious origin of a psychopathic state in the hope of freeing the Spaniards from it. It seems that he proposes "a kind of psychoanalytic treatment in which the cure consists in bringing to the light of consciousness certain irrational stands" (A. van Beysterveldt, "Itinerario hacia Américo Castro," in *Estudios*, p. 75). But Castro himself seems very addicted to the psychosis and very fond of it. Pedro Laín Entralgo wonders in the same volume: "Why has there been, and why does there continue to be among us a confusion between ideological differences and vital hostility?" (p. 10). Was Castro an exception?

79. *CCL*, p. 50; *CCE* (1966), pp. 140, 347. I do not find any allusions to Ortega in one of Castro's last essays, "Cómo ahora veo el *Quijote*."

80. Science "is made up of two distinct operations: one is purely imaginative, creative, what man puts forth out of his own entirely free substance; another which is in confrontation with what man is . . . with man's surroundings, with events and facts" (*Obras*, V, 16).

81. The implications of this singularization were perceived by José Rubia Barcia: "Some considerations that he himself makes and that could be used—*I want to believe erroneously*—to aid and comfort some theoreticians of the current Spanish situation" ("Américo Castro y la realidad histórica de España," *La Torre*, Año IV, no. 14 [April-June 1956], p. 42, italics mine).

Part V
Epilogues

13

THE HISPANIC INHERITANCE
OF IBEROAMERICA

Marcos A. Morínigo

Américo Castro wrote two seminal books on Spanish America
in addition to articles in journals and newspapers during the
fertile period of his renewed interest in Hispanic forms of living
(1938–1972). He finished both books almost simultaneously in
Princeton during his first year of residence in that university
and both appeared in 1941, one in New York and the other in
Buenos Aires. The volume published in Buenos Aires, *La
peculiaridad lingüística rioplatense y su sentido histórico* evolved
over a period of several years (1923–1940). In contrast, *Iberoamérica, su presente y su pasado,* developed rapidly in response
to pressing educational needs.[1] Its purpose was to explain to
North American university students the unique character of
Hispanic life and the reasons for the marked differences in its
forms and objectives as compared to Anglo-Saxon America, in
spite of a certain fundamental unity between the two Americas
based on common problems not shared by Europe, Asia, or
Africa. In this work Castro attempts to explain the existence
of the two Americas not only as a consequence of a geographical
fact, but also, and above all, as a human fact derived from the
history of the groups inhabiting them and the inevitable continuity of that history to the present.

At first glance *La peculiaridad lingüística* is a book with a
very limited goal. At its core, however, there is also a painstaking
inquiry into the reasons for the peculiarity of the Argentinians'
attitudes towards a common language, explicable only in terms
of the particular history of the Argentine community, but at the
same time inscribed beneath the cupola that encompassed the
rigid organization of the Spanish Empire. Strictly speaking, the

linguistic investigation in this work is overshadowed by a general inquiry into the complex network of threads that made up the fabric of the real life the Spaniards were obliged to lead once they were settled on the banks of the River Plate, breaking the dense mesh of laws, ordinances, and institutions with which the mother country wanted to govern them. This book, written in part early but undoubtedly over a long period of time, has *Iberoamérica* as its complement; but in order to appreciate clearly and subtly Castro's interpretation of the peculiarity of Spanish-American life and its meaning, we must read both of these books.

The priority of *La peculiaridad lingüística* derives from the author's profession as a philologist, attuned to the history of the Spanish language, its overseas expansion, and the history of its transformations and discrepancies with regard to its European origin and development. This entire process was the inevitable result of the transplantation of the Spanish language to lands with a history, humanity, and nature different from its native country.

Castro's professional interest led him to accept the chair of philology, which the University of Buenos Aires offered him in 1923 when it incorporated that discipline into the curriculum of its College of Philosophy and Letters. Along with the chair went the directorship of the corresponding Institute whose goal was to train philologists sufficiently prepared in theory and practice to undertake the study of the characteristics and regional peculiarities of American Spanish. Both themes had aroused the interest of Iberoamerica since the latter part of the preceding century. Once settled in Buenos Aires, Castro enthusiastically devoted himself to the task at hand; he had great expectations and was anxious to succeed at his new commitment. He observed with admiration the commercial, industrial, and intellectual activity of the River Plate coast along with its progress in technology and government.

He predicted a promising future for the region both materially and culturally. As a kind of echo of that first strong impression we can still read in *La peculiaridad*:

> The countries bordering on the River Plate are, without a doubt, the most active and cosmopolitan section of Latin America. Her

major cities, Buenos Aires and Montevideo, have attained heights that seemed impossible only a hundred years ago. River Plate thought and art are antennas sensitive to everything associated with worth and effort; it is an intensely receptive attitude that will soon be converted into a creative power. . . . Poetry, the novel, and the essay have all attained more than one complete "goal" there. Science and philosophy number names of great distinction among their cultivators.[2]

The optimistic view of his first encounter does not, however, succeed in disguising a shadow that spread over the picture, diminishing its splendor, and to his keen philologist's and linguist's eyes could not go by unnoticed. Castro observed that the spoken language in Buenos Aires did not coincide with the intensity of the city's cultural life that had so aroused his sympathy: "the language on the shores of the River Plate exhibits traces of disorder and even of instability."[3] How could such an imbalance be explained? In his investigations into this incongruity Castro immediately saw that the problem went beyond purely linguistic or philological considerations and that its roots actually lay in the social and political history of the country in particular, which, in turn, fits into the American history of the Spanish Empire as a whole.

The history of each region in the empire was, of course, different from any other section, in spite of the uniformity of laws and institutions that theoretically governed them all. Castro discovered that the Spaniards, unlike other Europeans, not only settled on the land, but also settled into the lives of the natives with their different cultural traditions as well. By the same token, the natives were persuaded gently or by force to participate in the life plan of their conquerors. Since the indigenous population of each region not only had dissimilar cultures, but were also in varying stages of development—some advanced and others incipient—the forms of life, that is to say, the real history of each region, had to be different as well. Any history of the American sector of the Spanish Empire, therefore, must consider regional characteristics before the advent of the Spaniards because, according to Castro, "Iberoamerica is . . . a result of the intertwining of the outlook on life of the peoples of the Iberian Peninsula with the outlook of the Indians who inhabited the American land before the arrival of the Spaniards and the Portuguese."⁴ A deep and thorough study should be made of the way the modes of Hispanic life and culture were introduced into the different regions of America, particularly during the first centuries of colonial life.

Castro devoted himself wholeheartedly to the study of these themes. But this did not diminish the amount of attention to what he considered the "shocking" linguistic reality in which he found himself immersed, nor did it retard the rhythm of his teaching activity designed to train the investigators that Spanish-American philology needed. At that time he planned to study and take inventory of the characteristics of River Plate speech in the course of a seminar with his Argentine students in order to coordinate his projects. On the one hand, an abundant and reliable amount of data would be obtained on the language as spoken in Buenos Aires, and on the other, by directing his budding disciples in Specific research projects on individual linguistic aspects, Castro would be helping to prepare them for future studies. In 1924 he further contributed to fulfilling his pedagogical commitments by publishing the first *Cuaderno del Instituto de Filología,* which reproduced three articles, all relevant and opportune for his purposes: "La lengua española" by Menéndez Pidal, "La pronunciación correcta" by T. Navarro Tomás, and "El español de América y el latín vulgar" by M.L. Wagner, which had been translated from the German under his supervision and was only vaguely known to philologists in the Hispanic world at that time.

In that same year Castro was obliged to return to Spain because of the imminent publication of his great book *El pensamiento de Cervantes,* in addition to other commitments. This did not, however, cause him to abandon either his project on the language of Buenos Aires or his concern with American life. Years passed without his being able to pursue them in situ. But toward the end of 1936, overflowing with the anguish caused by the tragic Civil War that was to bring about such a profound commotion in his thinking and in the orientation of his studies, Castro once again found himself in Buenos Aires for a short time. Among a series of pressing tasks, he began to prepare the groundwork for the seminar, which had been suspended since 1924. The seminar was, in fact, resumed in 1937, under less than favorable circumstances, only to be discontinued again shortly thereafter.

Castro then left Buenos Aires for the United States where he settled at Princeton in 1940 to teach courses and seminars on aspects of the language and civilization of Spanish America. These studies, representing the mature fruit of his research and reflection, culminated in the publication of the two books in question the following year. But before referring to the key points of each work individually, we must repeat that precisely during those years when Castro was concerned with the definitive editing of both works, his thinking—as a result of the hurricane that was the Spanish Civil War—was eagerly working to explain the causes of that war, or rather, to investigate the reasons for Spain's inability to tolerate the peaceful coexistence of groups with differing viewpoints.

Scholars of Castro's work point to the year 1938 as a turning point in his interpretation of Spanish history. Fired by his passionate investigation in this new direction, he offered the first fruits of this change in *España en su historia* in 1948. This was the work that inaugurated his own personal course of Spanish historiography and which opened, and continues to open, such a deep furrow under new titles and forms. But even before that time, the attentive reader can already discern in these two books on Spanish America the whitish halo announcing the coming light that begins to appear on the horizon. In them appears the early germination of the seeds of some of Castro's key concepts in his interpretation of Hispanic forms of living which he elaborated upon and modified in his later works. Hence the importance of these two works in the evolution of Castro's thought.

I shall now try to document Castro's opinions and explanations about Spanish-American modes of living with excerpts taken at random from both books which, in my opinion, are unambiguous and therefore need no additional comments. These ways of living, even today, continue to be, both essentially and contingently, traditionally and quintessentially Hispanic. Thus Castro affirms the existence of an historical parallel between Spain and America after its independence. He argues that, in spite of the apparent spirit of Enlightenment, liberalism, and the adoption of democratic institutions, at least on paper, Rosas' policies in Argentina—absolutism in the political and social spheres and the predominance of everything vulgar and rustic over anything refined and cultured—were the American counterpart of Spanish rule under Ferdinand VII and Carlism:

> I am progressively more inclined to delve into the meaning of every Hispanic event, great or small, by means of its articulation in the whole complex of Hispanic life.[5]

> What links Iberoamerica to her tradition . . . is . . . the inevitable circumstance that the inner forms of life in Iberoamerica and in the European Peninsula are one and the same. *Both are spontaneously the way they are, and they need to live otherwise*; they both coincide in their arduous search for their own destiny.[6]

Hispanic countries—for better or worse, like everything in this world—find themselves inscribed in an Hispanic tradition and destiny and cling more tenaciously to them the more they endeavor to deny or elude their heritage. What happens or stops happening to them must be seen in reference to that essential way of facing life. Thus, in order to understand their politics, art, or language, we must look at their history in its compressed totality, since only within this totality do the facts and partial views take on meaning.[7]

The present state of the Iberoamerican world is incomprehensible if it is not set in relation to the past of the Iberian Peninsula and to its indigenous antecedents.[8]

The intimate relationship between Iberoamerica and Spain has nothing to do with the imperialist dream of Spanish Fascism. . . . Ideally . . . a very strong Spanish America would yield ever more valuable results, all very different from those of Spain and Portugal, even though they all issued from the same distant origin . . . it is equally unacceptable for certain specialists in Latin America in the United States to try to ignore the inner historical unity between Iberoamerica and the Iberian Peninsula.[9]

The Spanish and Portuguese were driven by their will to dominate, by their religious faith, and by their ambition to accumulate wealth; patient and organized work hardly interested them, nor did inventing machines, or encouraging industry and commerce so as to make their wealth work for them. Their aspiration to achieve aristocracy and the expansionist visions of religious orders were stronger motivations than individuals' desires to become rich by industrially exploiting the natural resources or organizing great mercantile adventures.[10]

The Spaniard was never interested in reasonable dialogue with the world around him, which he does not want to rebuild by means of any conceptual discoveries . . . ultimately the only thing that really interested the Spaniard was his own aureola, the circle of transcendence of one kind or another by which he felt glorified. That is why religion and superstition were important to him, as were regal dignity and all things pertaining to nobility . . . Hence the utopian ideology, the search for gold in order to enlarge the world in a flight of magic and art . . . Hence the Spaniards' aptitude for a kind of art that produced highly charged realities, not adjustable to any individual, as are technical abilities . . . The Spaniard . . . took from life what was necessary to nurture his other world, for example, gold, the magic key that opened the way to temples and palaces.[11]

[The Spaniard] never tried to understand reality; he tried to possess it totally and in one piece. Hence the audacious and heroic dash of the Conquistadors who came to America to marry the land and the Indian women, and to create cities that one day would be the capitals of nations.[12]

The incentives for the Conquest were lust for gold and lust for power; the principles that kept these men of steel together were the glory of God and veneration of the King . . . Spanish life was based on grandiose myths and was unfurled in poetic images: religion, royalty, noble splendor, individual heroism, artistic expression in all its forms . . . the Spaniard needed to feel sustained by faith in something higher than himself. When the monarchy and nobility lost power and prestige, when religious sentiment lessened and there were no more empires to conquer, the Hispanic peoples in America broke up . . . They remained together only so long as they participated in the same illusions and the same acts of respect toward something they considered above them: religion, monarchy, and faith in the greatness of personal heroism.[13]

Spain did not propose to triumph with her commerce and industry; she did in America exactly what she was doing in Spain:encourage religion, art, letters, a sense of human dignity, monumental grandeur, social hierarchy, illusions, in short, everything that contributed to the Spaniards' feeling of being exalted over the earth . . . Spain was incapable of administering her empire in a reasonable and useful way. If we look at it from other points of view, we will simply not understand either the past or the present of Spanish America.[14]

Spanish civilization in its sociopolitical aspect did not work where the royal-noble principle, in harmony with the ecclesiastical idea, could not maintain groups and individuals in a state of tension. When this delicate balance was upset, the consequences were disastrous.[15]

For the Catholic, religion continued to be the search for the supernatural through the Church and its symbolic rites. In this way we can understand why Spanish Catholicism cultivated a religious art that grew in splendor just as the Protestant reformation was taking root in Europe and spreading to America.[16]

As a result of the foregoing, the machine of the Empire did not work opportunely in America except in areas blessed with fabulous wealth, precious metals, the nearest thing to prodigious miracle working . . . In the countries without precious metals, or far away from their routes, or out of their spheres of influence, it was impossible to set up the special system of Hispanic devotions and hierarchies, based on solemn religious fervor, nobility, or monumental art.[17]

With religious faith, lordly and martial incentives, and an exalted sense of personal worth . . . the Spaniard rushed to the conquest of the New World and expressed in works of lasting beauty his religious faith and his sense of human culture. Today in Spanish America there are residences of heads of state, public libraries and universities located in magnificent artistic buildings erected between the sixteenth and eighteenth centuries. The greatest jewels of Spanish American art are, however, the hundreds of churches that adorn the land. France, Holland, and England left not a single trace of real art in America during those centuries. . . . Social organization [in America] was inspired in that of Spain. The great gentlemen were lords of the land, and the peasants (in America, the Indians) worked it.[18]

The Spanish Empire in its final form was like an immense cupola limited only by the maximum transcendence of the divine. Beneath that, concentrically and putting it all into a hierarchy, the royal, noble, artistic, and ceremonial prestige all acted, in a concerted effort to reach higher and attain greater social heights in this world and go beyond it religiously. Under such a splendid structure great undertakings were accomplished in Europe and America, congruent with the system.[19]

The Iberoamerican seeks to rise above the masses through his own personal refinement, money, influence, intelligence, or any other way he can. He lives by studying life and by studying himself, because he keeps on living within the Hispanic way of being.[20]

[The well-educated Iberoamerican] aspires to perform an important role in his city, and to devote himself to liberal tasks, or simply to study life and enjoy the pageant of his own distinction. . . . Ultimately the authentic Iberoamerican cannot conceive of wealth greater than that of property or control over land, and he is as inept in money matters as his Christian ancestor of the Middle Ages.[21]

The Iberoamerican, incited by poetic illusion, became interested in the beyond of the other world and tended to neglect the prose or daily life; he wanted to glimpse some of the divine wonders and for that very reason promoted art in which we always sense echoes of something extraordinary and superior to man.[22]

Castro does not ignore the permanent lack of social discipline apparent in America from the days of Columbus on in the power struggle between government and religion, in the continuous rebellion of subordinates in the violation of precise instructions, in a whole range of disturbances repeated wherever the circumstances are repeated, and persist throughout colonial life. This is demonstrated by Castro's explanation of the peculiarities of Spanish-American life and by his convincing argument that they have robust and traditionally Hispanic roots: "Besides, such fights had old antecedents in Spain as a result of the battle between two rival transcendencies.[23]

He also points out that "the domination of those magnificent lands [of Mexico] is related to certain acts of insubordination, which, properly interpreted, help us to understand the Iberoamerican character then and now.[24] But the same could also be said of Panama, Peru, Chile, the River Plate, and Venezuela. In a world so organized, the Iberoamerican was no different from the most traditional and authentic Peninsular man in terms of his ideals about life.

After illustrating Castro's interpretation of the particular forms of Hispano-American life with the succinct, but clear examples above, we shall now discuss his interpretation of the River Plate's linguistic peculiarity, as well as his book of the same title, which he considered to be only "a part of what one day might be a book about the language of Buenos Aires."[25] He devoted long hours of study and reflection to the subject, which he continued to think about even in his last years.

As we have already pointed out, the study of the causes of the social relaxation of linguistic norms in the River Plate region, in contrast to other equally remote or marginal regions in the empire, had scarcely begun when philological investigation was superseded by sociohistorical inquiry. With this step the problem became inscribed in the domain of specifically Hispanic life styles.

In Amado Alonso's *El problema de la lengua en América,* which was published in 1935 but which reflects his concern with the problem dating from 1927, he attributes the River Plate's linguistic disorder mainly to the surfeit of foreigners and scarcity of directing minorities. In contrast, Castro argues that the "disorder introduced by the foreigners is due less to the force of their numbers or their mechanical action than to the outlook of the country that took them in."[26] 'The essential part of history [or, rather, of its explanation] seems to consist of the Argentine character prior to the arrival of foreigners in great numbers; this peculiar nature was founded on the absence of authentic hierarchies and on the slightly perverse pleasure that there were none."[27] In other words, this condition was rooted in the anarchy and disturbances that characterized River Plate life from the time of its colonial origins. At the same time, this situation was itself caused by political and religious motives as well as social and administrative factors. Foremost among the many causes of that anarchy was the fact that the strict hierarchical system of mutual respect enforced by the empire within its domains never managed to reach the Plate region. Since the River Plate was situated outside the sphere of imperial authority, the individual initiative of the most dedicated and audacious figures or of those groups desirous of assuring the superiority of their interests with a clear disregard for rules and regulations would prosper there.

Toward the end of the eighteenth century the viceroyalty of Buenos Aires was established to contain Portuguese expansion on the left bank of the River Plate. The village, which had been founded in 1580 and which over a period of almost two hundred years had failed to justify the title of "city" bestowed on it by its founder, became the viceregal capital and the seat of correlative institutions. A handful of buildings, barracks, convents, churches and even a few brick dwellings were constructed. Spanish officials, soldiers, and public servants arrived, mostly from Peru. More important was the fact that trade could now be conducted directly with the metropolis and the rest of the colonies, which gave promise of rapid progress. As merchants became more prosperous, they began to set themselves up as a part of the ruling class, affecting aristocratic airs as a result. Both the city and the surrounding countryside began to swell. Political and military events beginning with the British invasions of Buenos Aires and Montevideo in the first ten years for the nineteenth century and ending with the wars for independence (1810–1824) placed the initiative of the region's most vital activities, and even the government itself, in the hands of activist but relatively uneducated groups. They were particularly unruly. Power fell into the hands of the gauchos in the country and their counterparts, the lower classes in the city. The military leaders, who were usually politicians as well, and the politicians, who typically retained some military rank, recruited their armies from among these two groups. But in order to be assured of the dubious loyalty of these lower classes, the leaders were forced to conform to the somewhat barbarous habits and customs of their recruits—among others, their language which was traditional, archaic, rusticized, and impoverished as much by its physical isolation as by its lack of contact with courtly language or literature. Moreover, they had inherited their speech from comrades in Garay who were Paraguayan half-breeds in the majority by eight to one; all of them were bilingual and more fluent in the Guarani of their mother than in the Spanish of their father. Thus, over a period of more than two centuries the language created many expressions rooted in the surroundings and incorporated into its lexicon elements taken from the surrounding Indian languages—Guarani, Quichua, Araucan—as well as from African slaves and numerous Portuguese and Brazilian immigrants who settled in Buenos Aires and became artisans, merchants, and smugglers.

Meanwhile, the cultured urban minority of upward-striving courtiers along with the proselytizers of culture and progressivism tried, with the power that chance had placed in their hands, to bring the country up to date. Political democracy was proclaimed; there were periodicals and cultured lyric poetry and theater, libraries, schools and academies were established. There were attempts to modify and dignify daily conversation. But all of this was very short-lived. "The tenuous reflection of eighteenth-century culture that reached the River Plate influenced isolated individuals, but it left intact—neither more nor less than in Spain—both the rural and urban masses grounded in a rudimentary existence without any inner discipline."[28]

The result of all this anarchic license was that power passed into the hands of Juan Manuel de Rosas (1830–1852), the leader of the gauchos, the urban rabble, and the blacks who had only shortly before been set free. Those who did not fit into these groups lived in defeat, stifled by the vulgarity and vital energy of the winners, who, befitting their authority, socially valued certain kinds of behavior appropriate to their backwardness. Among them, their vernacular, which, on occasions was also used by the better educated people in imitation of the masses. Thanks to this situation, the fate of River Plate Spanish was sealed for some time to come. In his stimulating book Castro takes up its vicissitudes in chapters devoted to those changes. The Spanish of the River Plate region, particularly the colloquial and everyday standard variety, is as it is: disorderly, unruly, incorrect, infested with inappropriate expressions and foreign intrusions, in short, anarchic, because every language reflects the life of the community it expresses. This is particularly true of the deepest, the least conscious, and therefore, the least controllable levels of the spirit. The River Plate community was anarchic, rebellious, capricious, and belligerent from the start, as much because that has also been the Hispanic way since the time of its origins in the Iberian Peninsula as because of the lack of discipline resulting from the absence of restraints that a respect for hierarchical organization always imposes. A respect that in the River Plate rarely worked due to the historical circumstances already enumerated.

The reasons the author puts forth to explain the River Plate's linguistic peculiarity are, in my opinion, clear and convincing. And the entire book is an example of Castro's historiographic method, which starts from life rather than from books or abstractions.

When Castro put his sympathetic curiosity and his exceptional talent into these two books, he did so in the cause of clarifying Spanish-American modes of living. He gave to all of us Hispano-Americans a valuable instrument to help us attain a better awareness of our past, which, in turn, is necessary to attain a better awareness of our future. And for that we must fervently thank him.

NOTES

1. References are to the first and second editions of *La peculiaridad lingüística* and to the fourth edition of *Iberoamérica: Su historia y su culture (IHC)*. A note at the beginning of *La peculiaridad lingüística* states: "The following essay on the language and history of Argentina was read in part at the Congress of Teachers of Iberoamerican Literature held at the University of California, Los Angeles, in August 1940. I attended this meeting as a guest of the Del Amo Foundation (Los Angeles), to whom I express my deepest gratitude at this time." *PLR* (1941), n.p.; (1961), p. 23.

2. *PLR* (1941), p. 9; (1961), p. 27.

3. Ibid., pp. 9-10; p. 27.

4. *IHC*, p. 4.

5. *PLR*, p. 37; p. 44.

6. *IHC*, p. 23.

7. *PLR*, p. 40; p. 46.

8. *IHC*, p. 23.

9. Ibid.

10. Ibid.

11. *PLR*, pp. 38-42; 44-47.

12. *IHC*, p. 7.

13. Ibid., pp. 19-20.

14. *IHC*, p. 92.

15. *PLR*, p. 43; p. 48.

16. *IHC*, p. 7.

17. *PLR*, pp. 42-43; pp. 47-48.

18. *IHC*, p. 6.

19. *PLR*, p. 40; p. 46.

20. *IHC*, p. 105.

21. Ibid., pp. 18-19.

22. Ibid., p. 17.

23. *PLR*, p. 43; p. 48.

24. *IHC*, p. 47.

25. *PLR*, p. 23.

26. *PLR*, p. 25; p. 35.

27. Ibid., p. 27; p. 36.

28. Ibid., p. 62; p. 64.

14

A NEW MODEL FOR HISPANIC HISTORY
José Luis L. Aranguren

Spanish culture—and I use the term here in both its meanings: culture originating in Spain and culture about Spain—was brilliantly represented during the first third of the present century by two entities. One group was made up of the members of the Institución Libre de Enseñanza (Free Institution for Learning) together with the Centro de Estudios Históricos (Center for Historical Studies) whose last director was Ramón Menéndez Pidal. The other one encompassed those gathered around the *Revista de Occidente* (and around the publishing house Espasa-Calpe and *El Sol*), directed by José Ortega y Gasset. Next to, but outside of these groups stood Miguel de Unamuno, also an eminent representative of Spanish culture, who functioned as a fiercely independent outsider. Américo Castro was a very well-respected scholar who belonged wholeheartedly to the first group at the beginning. His new concept of history, however, the subject of this essay, came about because of his relative alienation from his original school and from his subsequent but obvious rapprochement with Unamuno and Ortega, even though his exile was undoubtedly a decisive factor in his change of thought. Let us examine in some detail the scope of this undoubtedly too peremptory, abrupt, and overly simplified affirmation.

Menéndez Pidal's school was philological and literary, and in this sense Américo Castro continued the brilliant tradition of his teachers, from the point of view of having recourse to primary sources and sensitivity for linguistic and literary phenomena. But to this aspect he soon tended to add a cognitive, doctrinal bias, which appeared, for example, in *El pensamiento de Cervantes* (1925). The Centro de Estudios Históricos represented an open, eclectic concept of history. We may be sure that this concept was no longer that of the old history framed in terms of politics and war, nor could it be about history's heroes either, in the fashion of Carlyle. Kings, heroes, and their deeds all pass away. What remain are the accomplishments, the objectification in the form of culture—"the objective spirit"—of that "doing." With the exception of cultural religious objectification, neither the history of religiosity or "spirituality" (Pourrat) nor the history of "religious sentiment" (Brémond), was studied by this school, doubtless because of its "lay" bias. From "culture," the so-called history of culture, what mattered most to this school were institutions and especially juridical institutions, the history of law in the broadest sense of the term. Establishment history never became objectified in pure cultural history but, on the other hand, even when an attempt was made to take social and economic factors into account, it remained quite distant from socioeconomic history with a Marxist influence in a theoretical sense. "Academic" history thus found itself almost halfway between the "cultural" superstructure and its base, history reduced to the interplay of economic relations. What was done was not Culturalism, much less Marxism. Rather, we might call it an eclectic, smoothed-over historical positivism. Even at that, a very relative positivism: the Myth of Castile (Fernán González, the Cid, Spain = Castile) was parallel to and occurred contemporaneously with the poetization and literaturization of Castile by the Generation of 1898.

Here, then, is the historical tradition into which Américo Castro would have had to place himself academically when he transferred his interest from the restrictive bounds of literary history to history in a broad sense. But it did not happen this way. The physical separation, due to exile, from a school that essentially remained rooted in Spain, meant that Castro must live in a new *situation,* one which I tried to describe in an early work, "La evolución espiritual de los intelectuales españoles en la emigración." The philological, literary, and historical investigations of the group went ahead without interruption, as much as was possible, and even the same projects were pursued as the ones the group had been working on before the war.

The one exception was Dámaso Alonso's work, only, however, in its least erudite portions. This phenomenon inevitably led the group into becoming a kind of cultural Establishment (as I have called it on other occasions) parallel, in spite of itself, though politically opposed to, the official Establishment. And like it, the cultural Establishment, aside from obvious differences, became indifferent to its present time and so, also, became anachronistic. And it was that new existential *situation* in which Castro found himself forced to live—a situation much more like a "rupture" than an "evolution," as I called it—which impelled him to seek inspiration outside the bounds of professional or academic history. He found it in those two great teachers, his compatriots and forerunners of existentialism, Unamuno and Ortega.

From Unamuno, Castro learned to direct his historical gaze onto "the man of flesh and blood" (*el hombre de carne y hueso*), onto the Spaniard and his feelings about the meaning of life, usually ignored by academic historians. He particularly focused on the feeling which, in the broadest sense, we must consider as a religious one: "the tragic sense of life" (*el sentimiento trágico de la vida*). This sentiment as it appeared in the first version of the work by that title referred not only to men but also to nations, notably, of course, the Spanish nation. This Spain is very different from the rest of Europe; it is not the Spain of "work' (bourgeois), but that of "labors" or deeds, discoveries, and conquests, the Spain of Arabic, or rather, Moorish origin and holy wars. It is the Spain that must seek its real nature within itself, the one described by Ganivet and Unamuno. The difference is that Castro is concerned with issues of being and identity, whereas Ganivet presents imperatives and value judgments. Américo Castro learned from Unamuno what I will take the liberty of calling an "ontological distinction," that is, the difference between the Spanish (Castilian) and the European essence.

What he learned from Ortega was no less important. If man has no nature but only history, and the former is only a result or condensation of the latter (existence precedes essence, as Sartre was to say later), then there could be no "being" or "essence" assigned a priori to Spain, no "national character" such as the *psychology of nations* attempted to study. Spain's metaphysics—since we are dealing with an authentic metaphysic—is no longer essentialist but rather existential. It is not "given" but, rather, comes to be realized, achieved, or conquered *in its history* (*España en su historia*). In Ortega's *Invertebrate Spain* we find a contradictory concept referring to "Who made history?" simultaneously "natural" (the Visigoths, the Romanized barbarians) and "historical" (the emergence of Castile). Nevertheless, Américo Castro did not care what the Arabs, Christians, and Jews were like before they arrived in the Peninsula. His interest was only what they came to be once they were forced to live there. And if the United States is a "melting pot" of immigrants from the most diverse backgrounds, Spain was unity in diversity with its tension among Christians, Moors, and Jews. Spain was the history of a frontier, like that of the United States, only as much turned in on itself (the holy war, Santiago Matamoros—St. James the Slayer of Moors) as directed outward, the collective feeling and the history of an "insecurity" (Ortega) and a "living by denial of life" (Unamuno). Spanish history passed through two distinct phases: a more or less uneasy coexistence of three peoples simultaneously fighting and influencing one another, followed by the attempt to eliminate "the other Spain" (expulsion of the Jews and later of the Moors, hard times for the New Christians or converted Jews and their descendants, successively metamorphosed into Erasmians, mystics, Biblical scholars, humanists, and later, perhaps as liberals, devotées of Krause, and Republicans).

Thus, within the style of "existential history" and under the direct influence of both Unamuno and Ortega, Castro's concept must be viewed as a brilliant construct. And like most brilliant constructs, one-sided. That Don Américo found "verification" for his theory wherever he looked, is not surprising; it is easy to make history, a malleable substance, respond according to what is asked of it. It is a question of the hermeneutics of the "circle." An initial overall approach intuitively elicits an interpretation or theory. Once this hypothesis shapes the historical matter (that which is historifiable or worthy of being included in that paradigm), the only data "chosen"—we can go even further, the only data "seen"—are what will confirm that original interpretation or theory.

But this is not the real question. It is actually a problem of interrogation, search, and method. As I have already noted, I do not believe that anybody pursuing the existential method or road has ever, anywhere, gone so far as Américo Castro. His is a wholly existential vision of Spanish history, obsessed by the vital experience (*vividura*) and the dwelling place of life (*morada vital*) of the Spaniards, the structure of their mentality and sensibility, their way of fitting into the world, and their sense of life. The tragedy of the "alienated" descendants of converted Jews—all those who Don Américo assumed were in this category and no doubt many more—and the opposing tragedy of those Spaniards whose "alienation" consisted precisely in *not* being the descendants of converted Jews and who felt obliged to insist again and again on their identity as Old Christians, both made up a part of Spain's historical reality. Undoubtedly only a portion. But can this do as an explanation for the entire phenomenon? Is personal, existential experience—opponents would say, psychological—enough to account for everything that occurred? This great discovery was made mainly on the basis of the source Castro was most familiar with, literature as an expression of the intimacy of the living experience or state of mind (the "reading" of a literature that, besides, is not usually that of the twentieth century).

Castro established his literary existential analysis with a very broad perspective on reality, accepting or rejecting other sources only secondarily. For example, according to Castro, Benito Arias Montano was probably of Jewish ancestry, although this has not yet been proved. Nevertheless, not only did he not experience any persecution because of it, but rather he enjoyed the full confidence of the Duke of Alba and even Philip II himself. In Antwerp, due only to the frequency of his dealings with the famous printer, Plantino, and other Flemish friends, he secretly converted to the "Family of Love," as the Dutch scholar Ben Rekers has shown. As a result of his supracon-fessional persuasion, more extreme than either the Catholic or the Protestant orthodoxies, he was led to publish highly sus-picious writings, which, however, did not occasion any serious complications for him thanks to his good reputation and the favor he enjoyed. Nor did these writings stop him from prosely-tizing in the Escorial itself—the monastery in which Philip II has his palace—or later in Seville. He was even allowed to die in complete peace. Here, then, is a curious case: Arias Montano, from a Jewish family (assuming that he really was, as Américo Castro affirms), derived his "converts" concept of religiosity from Flanders and Germany, parallel to the way in which, centuries later, Unamuno was to extract his "Spanish" concept of the tragic sense of life, anguish, and desperation from the Dane Kierkegaard.

As I pointed out earlier, one of the defects of the "lay" Center for Historical Studies consisted in not having paid sufficient attention to the history of religiosity or to religious sentiment, to the history of spirituality, without which Spain's history cannot be understood. In his own rigorously orthodox and exclusionist fashion, Menéndez y Pelayo had already seen this. Later on and much more generously, Marcel Bataillon also recognized the problem, and today, among other perceptive scholars, Pedro Sainz Rodríguez and Eugenio Asensio are coming to grips with this issue. It must be emphasized that all these men were preceded by Américo Castro who began to liberate himself from that bias acquired from his original school very early.

But the history of religion—or, as some call it, with what is, in my judgment, an inadequate phrase, of "religious ideas"— requires a substantive treatment, and if one wants to study history as such, religion should be a complementary study. Likewise, other compartmentalized partial histories should be complementary: social history (in conjunction with sociology), economic history, ecological or geographical history (what was called human geography in my youth), demography and statistics applied to history, etc. The great historian Jaime Vicens Vives saw the exaggeration—"too much Unamunian anguish"—of this purely existential history. Here we definitively touch on the limits of Américo Castro's concept of history, excluding, of course, Marxism (his *bête noire,* for reasons much more hermeneutic than ideological); structuralism ("the Mediterranean" as the impersonal, historical subject in Braudel was another of Castro's "personal issues"); and curiously in the author who insisted that Spanish reality be rooted in plurality—Christians, Moors, and Jews—excluding also the differential pluralism of all "the Spains" (that is, of all the regions in Spain), since Castro's version of Spanish history, like all those grounded in Menéndez Pidal's school, was in reality a history of Castile and her role as the unifier of the other "kingdoms"; and, finally, excluding any examination of the issue referring to the political-religious option of a *Catholic Spain* ("unity of belief" as "choice" and "decision").

Américo Castro's inattention to the political nature of ecclesiastic-religious factors (Spain, a prime example of a Counter-Reformation state) and to the meaning of economic factors (the importation of precious metals from the New World, mercantilist-economic politics, economic consequences for the Peninsula of such a strategy), is comparable only to his lack of interest in everything structural (as opposed to the personal-existential). Ortega's concepts of "historical reason" and "history as system" are conspicuously absent from his work. Historical "rhythms," "inertias," and the *tendances lourdes* of certain structures, as opposed to the "versatility" of others; the cultural lag of some institutions as opposed to others; the alternations between protractions of past time and advances toward the future; the breaks or "lapses" in continuity; evolutions and involutions; progress and stagnation; all of this, in short, every bit that is not susceptible to being lived experientially or existentially, is foreign to Don Américo's historiology and historiography.

His work, supremely of his time, has been forever marked by existentialism, or rather, by existential philosophy in its two differing but, for Castro, complementary versions: Unamuno and Ortega. The ontological-existential *problem of Spain* was the theme of his provocative historical meditation. And I am convinced that the experience of the Civil War and his exile were the liberating factors for this magnificent system of thought. Whether or not one is in agreement with it, no one can justifiably deny it the rank of a new model for Spanish history. And whether or not one is in agreement with it, Américo Castro's work deserves to be considered a work of art, comparable in the field of history to Burckhardt, and comparable, for the skeptic Paul Valéry, to the most rigorously, the most architecturally conceived philosophical constructions.

15

LITERATURE AND
HISTORICAL INSIGHT
Stephen Gilman

Américo Castro, Spain's last great solitary warrior of the intellect, is now at rest. In the combative tradition of Juan de Mena, Nebrija, las Casas, Quevedo, Feijoo, Sanz del Río, Sarmiento, Unamuno, and Ortega, he has, since the publication of *España en su historia* in 1948, aimed a ceaseless bombardment of books, monographs, essays, speeches, and interviews at the defensive minds of his compatriots. But not only with Sarmiento's and Nebrija's time-honored purpose of eradicating their "barbarie." His further hope was, very simply, to induce them to realize how who they were has made them what they are. If that could be achieved, he believed, at first in one or two minds and afterwards in many, there might result another epoch in which pent-up or stunted creative energies could once again be released. Being Spanish could once again become "una alta posibilidad de ser hombre."

Castro has been accused on occasion of attempting to imprison Spaniards in their past, conceived of as a fixed mold of national characterization. Nothing could be further from the truth. He was interested in the past, first, insofar as it was a record of creative freedom (Juan Ruiz, Rojas, Velázquez, Galdós) and, second, insofar as understanding old freedom might result in new freedom. How was it possible for such a phenomenon to occur again? Cervantes and Lope too (in his way) knew who they were and who they had been. But Castro's contemporaries, at once repressed by history and dazzled by ephemeral progress, have been content to rest with foreshortened versions of the past prepackaged either by Marx or by Marquina.

The voice of the prophet is still. And those technicians of history who were made uncomfortable by its assaults on the routine of their thinking will be better able to brush aside its sonorous challenges. Why is Castro so disturbing? His fundamental assertion that history is axiological and that the past must be worthy of history (otherwise its record will be a mere chronicle) has disconcerted many of his most reputable colleagues, not because it reverts to the antique ethical-exemplary view of the historian's task (Juan de Mena was the first name on my list of precursors) but because it gives it a new and far more demanding validity. History—Castro urges—is not the politics, sociology, or economics of preterite societies but rather an arena in which the human condition, beset by political, social, and economic circumstances, scrutinizes itself and from its anguish recreates in ever original expression its sustaining values. Which is to say that for Castro Clio belongs not to the sciences (a female corpse to be dissected in seminars that pretend to be laboratories) but once again, alive and eternally beautiful, to the humanities. It is less important for the historian to tell us how the past worked (the rise and decline of empires, parties, and periods) than it is to lead us to comprehend how a given historical movement could make possible a *Poema del Cid,* a *Celestina,* or a *Don quixote.*

If this be dismissed as "existentialism," let Castro's adversaries make the most of it. That label is notoriously overused and imprecise, but it *is* true that, along with the Hispanic tradition of lonely intellectual combat, Wilhelm Dilthey, Max Scheler, Nicolai Hartmann, and their followers contributed substantially to the earlier phases of Castro's intellectual adventure. At least in part their effort to relive the past and their abiding concern with the realism of value is continued in Castro's work and renders it both irrelevant and irritating to those inimical to freedom. In disheartened moments after his return to Madrid Castro expressed the fear that, after his barrage of disconcerting new facts about how Spain really was would be silenced, he might be pigeon-holed as a last vocal representative of an obsolete mode of thought. This, of course, is nonsense. As Solzhenitsyn has proclaimed and exemplified, even under the most adverse conditions, what matters in history is man.

Be that as it may, what cannot be denied by changing fashions of historical understanding is Castro's elucidation of literary and artistic significance. Facts can be ignored or explained away by those who choose to do so. But the decisive discussions of *Las hilanderas* or of the "Batalla de don Carnal" simply cannot be dismissed by anyone who observes the one or peruses the other. What Castro has shown us is now a part of their meaning as incontrovertibly as if proved mathematically.

Let us consider a single example: the interpretation of quatrain 1,105 of the *Libro de buen amor* in chapter xii of *La realidad histórica de España* (1954). The passage reads as follows:

> De parte de Valencia venian las anguillas,
> salpresas e trechadas, a grandes manadillas:
> davan a Don Carnal por medio de las costillas;
> las truchas de Alverche davanle en las mexillas.

> From Valencia way came the eels, salted and split, in
> big schools; they struck Lord Meatseason right in the
> ribs, the trout from Alberche all struck him on
> the cheeks.[1]

Castro's perception that the warlike eels are at once alive and dead, that, even while salted and dried for the table, they attack Don Carnal as if swimming upriver to spawn is self-evident as soon as explained. The further observation that, in the miniature world created by the image, Don Carnal must be standing chest deep in the water suggests why the trout strike him on the cheeks. They too are on their way to spawn (the blind biological mass movement in both cases suggests a military charge) but, unlike the eels, their characteristic movement is to break water as they go so that they leap upward at his face. Whatever the objections to Castro's theory and practice of history, this explanation (and innumerable others like it) is utterly undeniable. And at the same time cruccial. Even a single image in a poem as great as the *Libro de buen amor* is of importance to mankind. The only outstanding problem is how on earth did we read the quatrain before 1948. Or didn't we read it at all?

All of which leads us toward the specific intention of the present essay: to show how Castro's marvelous and irrefutable *explications de texte* of the *Libro de buen amor* are based not on rhetorical principles but on historical insight. Only knowledge of what the fourteenth century was really like for Spaniards living in it could open the locked door of the poem and reveal the sense of Juan Ruiz's otherwise obscure imagery. I don't mean, of course, that historical evidence (a lost *Arte de trovar* perhaps) might explain how the eels could be at once in the water and on the table. Rather what I hope to make clear is double in nature: how meditation on those peculiar times led Castro to see the metaphorical ambivalence (excluded from Chaucer and Jean de Meung) in the first place and how a sensitive rereading of the poem showed him what to look for in the past and how to think about it. If we conceive of historical explanation and literary appreciation not as opposed methods but as complementary perspectives into an identical moment of creation, we may refute the accusation of circular thinking or the grudging admission that Castro was a superb critic and perceptive philologist who had no business posing as an historian. Instead, the accuracy and the revelation of his textual commentary—the revolution he effected in our reading—will serve to validate Castro's vision of the past. We too may then be enlisted in his magnificent endeavor: erasure of the artificial frontier between values and facts.

Having reread the major works of medieval literature and having been freshly astonished by the poetic anomalies of the *Libro de buen amor* in its nation and time, Castro asked himself the question he had asked or was to ask of every major creation by Spaniards: How was it possible? The answer that Juan Ruiz was a genius (or even as we now think "un ingenio clerical") is at once a truth and an evasion. What Castro wanted to know was far more rigorous and revealing. How could Juan Ruiz have been the sort of genius he was in the times into which he was born? And how could his audience of fourteenth-century Castilians have understood him so well and participated so enthusiastically in his work?

His search for answers led Castro to meditation on what he called the new situations ("las nuevas situaciones," the title of chapter xi) in which men found themselves living during the reigns of Sancho el Bravo and Alfonso XI.[2] The chapter (xi) that resulted tells it all far better than I can. But in brief resumé, principal among Castro's observations is the sudden increase in prestige and self-confidence on the part of the newly dominant Castilians: "The Moors and the Jews, especially the latter, regarded thirteenth-century Castile as a political power that was taking the place of the vanished caliphate of Cordova."[3] Yet at the same time there was a conspicuous loss of "epic tension" and the commencement of the profound political and social disorder (a kind of Arabization of the body politic) that was to last until the accession of Isabella and Ferdinand. Furthermore, in spite of his sense of superiority, the individual Christian found himself coexisting daily—and often intimately— with an immense new population of erstwhile enemies who were demographically and culturally superior: "the Christians did not possess enough reserves of 'Occidentalism' or enough people to replace or transform the volume of Islamico-Judaic culture they had captured."[4]

The human results of this interplay (or overlapping) of historical "situations" were as might have been expected. On the one hand, the grandchildren and great grandchildren of the stern and laconic armies that had been amazed by Seville and Cordova after their conquest were no longer as timid as in the times of Berceo about expressing "the inner reality of a person who himself appears in the prose and speaks for himself"[5] (Here Castro cites extremely interesting examples from Don Juan Manuel.) And, on the other, they were now willing to admit into their poetry, prose and art not just Alfonso the Learned's Muslim learning and morality (the stuff that is called in German *Stoff*) but what Castro describes as the "inner form" ("forma interior") of the Muslim sense of life on earth. The Moors who in earlier epic tradition had been a "they" to be taken seriously only as antagonists or serfs had become "ours," if not in clothes, food, or faith, at least in awareness partially shared. That is to say, Castro is less concerned with acculturation in the anthropological sense than with the amalgamation of two radically opposed varieties of conscious existence.

At this point Castro is ready to return to the text of the *Libro de buen amor,* which he now interprets as life lived within the foregoing *situaciones* and raised to an exalted level of artistic self-expression. Juan Ruiz is above all "a poetic voice expressing personal awareness of an 'I'" ("una voz poética que habla desde la conciencia de una persona").[6] We may not know anything about the biography of Juan Ruiz, but, nevertheless we hear him ("sentimos su presencia") in every line. He watches his own talent or ignorance and exults over both; he caresses his "book" in the very act of turning it over to "an anonymous public"; he remembers and freely reinvents his "experiencia sensible" as if he were still feeling the chill of the "sierra." Affirmation of the author as a personal voice—made possible by history, in history, as history—is the basis of Castro's profoundly new critical vision of the *Libro de buen amor.* Neither literal autobiography (Menéndez y Pelayo) nor accumulation of topics (Lecoy) but creative self-consciousness in the first person singular is the genetic code of this wonderful verbal organism.

This, of course, does not mean (and my readers will hardly be in need of the warning) that Juan Ruiz was a Romantic *avant la lettre* ultimately concerned with *son coeur mis à nu.* Far from it. His life existed in symbiosis with all life; it was a springboard for a fantastic plunge into all the lives (animal and vegetable, urban and rural, poetic and musical) he had met in all their multiplicity. At which point Castro appeals to the Arabic counterculture as the mechanism of historical possibility and goes on to compare the darting, bending, twisting exuberance of the lives and images of the book (all within an external frame of Christian didacticism) to the artistic style called Mudéjar. I would doubt myself (and even Castro in later years was less than certain) that the *Collar de la paloma* (*The Dove's Neck-Ring*) was, in fact, known to Juan Ruiz. But I don't think it really matters. The suggestion of influence implicit in certain of Castro's sentences and comparisons actually tends to obscure Juan Ruiz's far more profound poetic assimilation of the Arabic sense of life or, to use Castro's own neologism, of the Arabic *vividura.* The uniqueness and utter lack of poetic precedent of the *Libro de buen amor* not only has never before been explained satisfactorily; it had not really been observed until Castro made this cultural rapprochement.

Anyone who has taught or studied Spanish medieval literature chronologically will have experienced in person the poetic revolution to which I refer. Less than a century after Berceo, who saw life on earth as at once sinful and fallacious (or at best as a stiff and innocently picturesque *signum* covering spiritual reality or *res*), there suddenly appeared a poem, an endless, deathless poem, in which life itself in all its gaiety, deceit, ambiguity, spontaneity, avidity, timidity, and polarity takes over the solemn liturgical quatrains of the *mester de clerecía* and even invades from within the massive structure of allegory. The tenderly Romanesque miniatures that constituted Berceo's portraiture of life in Castile are swept in a neap tide of vital celebration. For Juan Ruiz, I dare propose, the magnificently carnal (in both senses of the word) Easter Parade was the climax of his creation.

But there is no need to paraphrase any further Castro's luminous perception and brilliant presentation of a liberated poetic awareness in joyous contemplation of the characteristic rhythms: the slow, lumbering pace of an ox ambling through the streets ("vino *su* paso a paso el buey") and behavior: the peddler walks along with her tambourine, ringing its bells ("la buhona con farnero va taniendo cascaveles") that were its living circumstance. What does need still to be stressed is *how* Castro was suddenly able to comprehend the ancient text in all its novelty from within. The freedom of the Muslim mind from excessive categorization, from the Greek notion of the substantial nature of things ("la idea griega del ser"), the sense of existence as an endless skein of creation and commentary, the refusal to divide the urges of life into brackets of sensuality and his fourteenth-century contemporaries. And it was through Castro's historical comprehension of these possibilities (in a sense because he used the *Libro de buen amor* as a poetic time machine) that the poem opened itself to him, and quatrain after quatrain took on new meaning forever after.

In conclusion, let us return for a moment to the phalanx of eels. As Castro himself stated, comparison of their spawning to a military charge would seem as alien to an Arabist as to a student of Christian medieval poetry. It is a crossbred image, in a sense a grafted image (how significantly fond Juan Ruiz is of the verb "enxerir"!), which derives its creative freedom from that very fact. The eels and the trout, observed closely "con buen amor" in their biologically programmed vital urges and their characteristic movement, can be at once alive and ready for allegorical consumption only for a poet freed of habitual categorization. And insofar as alive, spontaneously following the instinct and built-in rhythms of their kind, they are so only for a poet who sees life as a self-justifying continuum. This is only one example out of the many Castro adduces, and in all of them we sense the same explosive poetic freedom. To have demonstrated the influence of Ibn Ḥazm beyond question might have been useful in order to obtain the assent of certain of Castro's colleagues. But we as readers are hardly in need of that sort of superficial proof. In our delighted, deeply refreshed readings of the poem since 1948 we have witnessed how historical knowledge and critical insight acting, not just in unison but in a state of indifferentiation, have given us a treasure.

NOTES

1. *The Book of Good Love,* translated by R.S. Willis (Princeton: Princeton University Press, 1971), p. 302.

2. See *SSH,* chapter xi, "The End of the Thirteenth Century: A New Direction," pp. 369-391.

3. Ibid., p. 370.

4. Ibid., p. 371.

5. Ibid., p. 386.

6. Ibid., p. 392.

INDEX

(Personal names from text and notes, titles of publications from text
only, and some special terms)